BEHIND THE
COUNTER

BEHIND THE COUNTER

SHOP LIVES FROM MARKET STALL TO SUPERMARKET

PAMELA HORN

SUTTON PUBLISHING

First published in 2006 by
Sutton Publishing Limited · Phoenix Mill
Thrupp · Stroud · Gloucestershire · GL5 2BU

British Library Cataloguing in Publication Data
A catalogue record for this book is available from the British Library.

ISBN 0-7509-3930-3

Typeset in 10.15pt Photina MT.
Typesetting and origination by
Sutton Publishing Limited.
Printed and bound in England by
J.H. Haynes & Co. Ltd, Sparkford.

CONTENTS

Serving in a shop is not just a matter of 'shoving' packets of goods over the counter, nor is it just till-ringing. It is a job which, in some trades, needs study and training, and which in all trades calls for ready, good advice and a genuine spirit of helpfulness and politeness. . . . Shop assistants have moved a long way in conditions and public respect since I was employed in a shop, first as errand boy and then as shop assistant. I started at eight in the morning. I finished at half-past nine in the evening, ten on Fridays, and midnight on Saturdays. It was years before we got an early closing day, and then it was five o'clock. I enjoyed the work . . . but it was a dog's life, especially as I was trying to read and study in my spare time.

The Rt Hon. Herbert Morrison MP, later Baron Morrison of Lambeth (1888–1965), in a Preface to P.C. Hoffman, *They Also Serve. The Story of the Shop Worker* (London, 1949), pp. v–vi.

LIST OF ILLUSTRATIONS

1. Interior of a draper's shop, *c.* 1800, with the draper's wife in attendance on two customers.
2. A child customer in a chemist's shop, informing the proprietor that her mother had made a mistake in the medicines she had taken.
3. A street trader selling oysters, *c.* 1900.
4. A street seller vending greengrocery and laying down her cash terms to her young customer.
5. This shopkeeper is taking a stern view of an impolite youngster wanting to buy two halfpenny herrings!
6. Staff at Dalton-in-Furness Co-operative Society shop, Lancashire, *c.* 1900.
7. A small butcher's shop – the business of Andrew Adams at New Headington, Oxford, *c.* 1910.
8. Advertisements for drapery staff.
9. An assistant in a milliner's shop flattering a very plain customer in order to make a sale.
10. William Whiteley (1831–1907), the dynamic London department store pioneer.
11. Department store assistants waiting at a cash desk, *c.* 1900.
12. Two shoe salesmen seeking to please a coy lady customer wanting a 'dainty' pair of shoes.
13. A sale day at Peter Robinson's department store in London, *c.* 1900.
14. Advertising blurb for a small town tailor and outfitter at Abingdon, *c.* 1920. He had clearly not learned the art of tasteful window dressing as every window was crammed with goods.
15. Drapery businesses for sale, with amounts of capital needed by would-be purchasers.

ACKNOWLEDGEMENTS

I should like to thank all who have helped with the preparation of this book, either by providing photographs and documents or in other ways. They include Mr Frank Danning, Mr Leonard Chamberlain and Mr G.S. Mabon, who have provided reminiscences and other material regarding shop life in the twentieth century. I am also grateful to the Co-operative College, Manchester, and its archivist Gillian Lonigan; to the ESRC Qualitative Data Archival Resource Centre, Qualidata, University of Essex; to the Southampton Heritage Centre, and especially Sheila Jemima; and to the Union of Shop, Distributive and Allied Workers, Manchester, for the material and other help they have provided.

I have received much efficient assistance and guidance from staff in the libraries and record offices where I have worked and to them, too, I should like to express my gratitude. They include Bath Record Office; Bath Local History Library; Berkshire Record Office; the Bodleian Library, Oxford; the British Library; the British Library Newspaper Library, Colindale; the British Library of Political and Economic Science, London School of Economics; Cardiff Local History Library; the Centre for Oxfordshire Studies, Oxford; the Corporation of London Record Office; the Family Records Centre, London; the Guildhall Library and Record Office, London; Hampshire Record Office; the Imperial War Museum Sound Archives; London Metropolitan Archives; Manchester Local History Library; the National Archives, Kew; Oxfordshire Record Office; the People's History Museum Library, Manchester; Southampton Archives; the Trades Union Congress Library, London Metropolitan University, and particularly its archivist, Christine Coates; Westminster Archives Centre; the Women's Library, London Metropolitan University; York City Archives; and York City Reference Library.

Finally, as always, I owe a great debt to my husband for his unfailing help and advice, and for his company on some of my research 'expeditions'. Without him this book could not have been written.

Pamela Horn

Shillings and Pence Conversion Table

Old money	Decimal	Old money	Decimal
1*d*	½p	1*s* 8*d*	8½p
2*d* or 3*d*	1p	1*s* 9*d* or 1*s* 10*d*	9p
4*d*	1½p	1*s* 11*d*	9½p
5*d*	2p	2*s*	10p
6*d*	2½p	2*s* 6*d*	12½p
1*s*	5p	3*s*	15p
1*s* 1*d*	5½p	5*s*	25p
1*s* 2*d* or 1*s* 3*d*	6p	10*s*	50p
1*s* 6*d*	7½p	20*s*	100p (£1)

INTRODUCTION

I have emphasised the diversity of the retail trade. . . . There were – and still are – gulfs between the skilled craftsman/retailer and the straightforward unskilled shopkeeper; between the large concern and the small; city, town, suburban and rural dealers; proprietors and managers; high-class, mixed and working-class traders.

Michael J. Winstanley, *The Shopkeeper's World 1830–1914*

During the two and a half centuries that separated the early eighteenth century from the 1960s the nature of shops and the kind of people who worked in and around them underwent a transformation. That applied not merely to the scale of the business conducted and the sort of goods offered for sale, but also to the standing of those who worked in them. At the beginning of the period most retailers had a low reputation, being seen as men or, more rarely, women, who performed little service beyond acting in their own narrow self-interest. In 1680 an anonymous critic referred to those 'home-traders . . . whom we call Shopkeepers' who added to their own wealth by 'buying cheaper and selling dearer' without in any way contributing to the 'National Riches'. In his view, 'one poor Manufacturer' gave 'more in a year to the Wealth of the Nation than all such Retailers and Shop-keepers in England'.[1] Nearly seventy years later another commentator stressed the need for those engaged in the fashion trades to be obsequious and polite at all times: 'A Lace-Man . . . ought to speak fluently, though not elegantly, to entertain the Ladies; and to be Master of a handsome Bow and Cringe; should be able to hand a Lady to and from her Coach politely, without being seized with the Palpitation of the Heart.'[2]

To Daniel Defoe it was essential that retailers spent their time on the premises as: 'customers love to see the master's face in the shop, and to go to a shop where they are sure to find him at home'.[3] He must remember, too, his dependence on the whims of the buyer and that his shop was 'a place to be invited into, not to be commanded into; and therefore we see the best shopkeepers do not think it below them to stand at the door, and with cap in hand . . . to ask their customers to come in, to see if they can please themselves, and find what they have occasion for'.[4]

The reservations with which retailers were regarded continued into the nineteenth century, with the occupation associated with 'notions of greed, pettiness and narrow-mindedness'. As one writer put it in 1843, it was 'next to impossible to apply to a well-dressed man in the street a more offensive appellation than "shopman"'.[5] Even at the end of the century the Cambridge geneticist William Bateson castigated contemporary society in similar terms when he complained of its 'sordid shopkeeper utility'.[6]

However, during the second half of the Victorian era attitudes began to change, at least at the top of the retailing world, as large department stores became familiar sights in city centres, and flourishing multiple chains brought to their owners not only wealth but advancing social status. Many acquired landed estates and were able to move into the upper ranks of society. This was true of Sir J. Blundell Maple, of the famous furniture firm in Tottenham Court Road, London. His business empire extended worldwide by the end of Queen Victoria's reign and its customers included an impressive array of European royal families. In 1883 Sir Blundell acquired an estate at Childwick in Hertfordshire, where he began breeding racehorses. The Childwick Stud Farm became the largest horse-breeding establishment in Britain, and shortly before his death in 1903 Sir Blundell was elected to the prestigious Jockey Club. He also acquired property near Newmarket, where he entertained his friends lavishly during important race meetings. He was an active Conservative MP and an energetic philanthropist.[7] A member of the Prince of Wales's social circle, he was knighted in 1892. In 1897 he became a baronet in Queen Victoria's Diamond Jubilee honours list.

Maple was not alone in combining shop ownership with an active social and political life. Other Victorian and Edwardian proprietors of leading stores followed a similar path. In 1904 T.H.S. Escott noted: 'The interval separating the social life of retail traders from that of the professional classes [has] been largely bridged over by the rural hospitality of [those] who, during business hours, stand behind their Bond Street counters. . . . Latter day Liberalism found a notable supporter in Mr J. Barker, head of a mammoth drapery firm in Kensington, now in Parliament and expecting a baronetcy. Mr C.D. Harrod has a hunting box on Exmoor and is visited by academics and parliamentarians. The daughters of Mr Whiteley of Westbourne Grove provide wives for Indian staff officers.'[8] Prominent figures like these were, of course, in a tiny minority. Most of those connected with retailing were in a small way of business, operating either as independent shopkeepers or as owners of firms with a few branches only. Some set up shop in their own home, with little or no training and with equally limited stock and equipment. Even after the First World War this was the case. One man remembered how his wife 'caught the craze for shop keeping, so I made a counter and shelves and our front room was a shop'.[9]

For those who fell on hard times, retailing offered an alternative to unemployment, despite its precarious nature. In 1921 the Cornishman James Treloar returned home when there was a miners' strike in the South Wales coalfield where he had been working. He decided to set up a greengrocery business: 'I started with a pony and waggon . . . delivering vegetables from door to door.' Later he moved into a shop which he and his wife ran and they combined this with his delivery rounds.[10] A few years earlier Mrs Wolfendale of Bolton had established a small 'parlour' shop to help keep her family. Although her husband was a platelayer on the railway he was a heavy drinker and regularly got into debt, which she then settled. According to her son, Mrs Wolfendale sold 'bits of grocery' during the day and retailed chips from her kitchen at night. She also had a machine to re-foot people's stockings. Yet despite her efforts the business did not pay and it was shut down. The family then had to move home, to smaller and cheaper premises.[11]

The kinds of shops that were set up varied significantly on a regional basis, to meet local consumer preferences and to respond to the per capita income of the population and the size and speed with which that population was growing.[12] The shopping needs of a Victorian industrial town were likely to be very different from those of affluent resorts like Cheltenham, Bath or Southport. Nonetheless, even in the middle of the twentieth century it was the multiplicity of independent traders who continued to take the largest share of the nation's retail business. In 1950 it was estimated that only between 4.5 and 6 per cent of total trade was attributable to department stores, while multiple chains, such as those engaged in selling groceries, footwear, clothing and chemists' goods, took around 18 to 20.5 per cent. The remainder was divided between the co-operative stores, with 10 to 12 per cent of the total, and the 'independents', who took 61.5 to 67.5 per cent. These latter, then, still accounted for around two-thirds of the nation's retail business, although this had dropped from the nearly nine-tenths of total trade they had enjoyed in 1900.[13]

An equally significant change took place in the position of those working in shops over the years. In the eighteenth century most of those engaged in retailing, other than as proprietors, were either family members or those working as apprentices and shopmen (or, more rarely, shopwomen). Most of these employees would hope to set up in business for themselves at some time in the future, once they had secured sufficient capital or credit and had made the necessary business connections. Marmaduke Strother, an apprentice in Mr Robinson's drapery store in Hull in the mid-1780s, recorded in his diary the success of a one-time colleague:

> Mr Somerscales was formerly in the same state that I am in: about 2½ years since he married a young woman who was a servant in the same House and took the Shop and Effects of Mr Wm. Pearson Bankrupt and by his Industry and Perseverance has thriven where Pearson cou'd not. He has now bargain'd with Mr Joseph Chapman for the succession of his Shop and Business and do not doubt he will do well. . . . Mr Chapman commenced the world without 50£ Sterling and has been in Business about 18 or 20 years. It is reported that he is worth 6000£.[14]

At the end of Strother's own apprenticeship lack of capital prevented him from taking a shop as he had planned to do. He returned in some frustration to his native York, where he obtained a post as shopman to Roger Beckett, who had opened a woollen draper's shop in the city in the spring of 1785.[15]

During the nineteenth century it became more and more difficult for youngsters to go into business for themselves. Instead they had to settle for life as a full-time shop assistant. In 1912 a former grocery hand called this the 'evolution of a new industrial order'. As a result of the 'rapid transformation of the private shop into the big limited company, with branches in all the large and small towns . . . the shop-assistant is the poorly paid mercenary with which the big combatants make a dead-set at the private trader and have at each other's throats'.[16] Yet despite the problems, as we have seen, small shopkeepers did survive and in some cases flourished well into the twentieth century. Nonetheless, the transition from apprentice or shopman to proprietor of a business was far more difficult than had once been the case, so that by the early twentieth century there were perhaps 800,000 shop assistants in the country, of whom around a quarter were women.[17]

Lee Holcombe has commented on the way in which from the mid-nineteenth century the application of mass-production techniques to the manufacture of consumer goods and the pre-packaging of many items of grocery had contributed to this broad trend:

The decline of the craft tradition tended to transform shop assistants from skilled into unskilled workers. The old system of apprenticeship broke down, and the use of formal indentures, the payment of premiums, and service for specified, lengthy periods of time gradually disappeared. 'Apprentices' were still taken on in shops at low wages to learn the business . . . but they received no regular instruction and merely picked up knowledge of the trade as best they could. In any case, the duties of most shop workers were fast becoming mainly those of keeping the stock tidy and of showing merchandise across the counters and receiving payment. . . . The upper and middle classes considered shop workers to be about on a level with the servant class, while the working classes sneered at their pretensions to [middle-class] respectability, derisively calling them 'counter jumpers'.[18]

The gibe struck home. W.F. Fish, who reluctantly took a post at a drapery store in Victorian Greenwich, ironically called his reminiscences *The Autobiography of a Counter-Jumper* and lamented the invidious distinctions drawn between a youngster employed in a retail business and 'his superior brother in the wholesale'. 'The "wholesale" youth frankly regarded the poor, lowly, retail fellow as his inferior and openly snubbed or patronised him. The man who sells linen in 40-yard lumps is accepted as a merchant prince, whereas the 12-yard length man is quite outside the pale, he is merely a shopkeeper.'[19]

Some contemporaries, like William Paine and P.C. Hoffman, both former shop assistants, regretted the lack of solidarity among those employed in retailing, as well as the petty snobbery that existed between those working in different kinds of business. 'The draper's assistant affects a certain superiority over the grocer's assistant,' wrote Paine, and 'the grocer's assistant has his own idea about the draper's assistant; the ironmonger's assistant is criticised by both, and in his turn is alive to the merits of his own position; while the chemist's assistant looks down on all.'[20] Such attitudes made trade union membership difficult to establish.

After the Second World War the growth of self-service shopping led to a further deskilling of the rank and file of staff in retail establishments. The process had begun in a small way in co-operative stores in London during the war, as a response to the shortage of labour, and after 1945 it was the co-operative movement which for a time continued to lead the way. In 1947 there were estimated to be only ten self-service shops in the country. Three years later approaching 500 traders described their shops as wholly or mainly self-service. By the mid-1960s that total had reached over 20,000. Trade was still largely concentrated in the grocery sector, but the concept had begun to spread to other areas as well.[21] It was with self-service shops that the future of retailing increasingly lay.

PRECURSORS OF CHANGE

The major developments in 'behind the counter' life so far discussed took more than two and a half centuries to come to fruition. However, it was in the eighteenth century that the process began, as the number of retail outlets proliferated. According to Peter Earle, even at the end of the seventeenth century there were shops not only in every country town but in many villages, while the number of retail establishments in London was already one of the city's main visitor attractions.[22] In 1688 Gregory King estimated there were around 50,000 shopkeepers and during the course of the following century that total climbed, to reach perhaps 150,000 to 170,000 by 1800.[23] The expansion was stimulated by population growth, the effects of industrialisation and urbanisation, and the greater ease of distribution brought about by transport improvements. In 1701 the population of England stood at an estimated 5.5 million. That figure rose to 5.77 million by 1751, and then accelerated to reach 8.66 million in 1801 and 9.88 million a decade later.[24] Furthermore, whereas in 1700 perhaps 19 per cent of the population of England and Wales lived in towns with a population of 2,500 or more, at the end of the century that had climbed to 31.6 per cent of people living in such towns.[25] By 1801 it has been said that England was 'one of the most densely populated countries in the world', with much of the rise occurring in the manufacturing and mining areas of the Midlands and the north, and in the capital city itself.[26]

Accompanying this was the changing structure of employment, with an increase in those in the middling ranks of society who could afford to purchase a greater variety of goods and services. The growth of imports such as tea, sugar, tobacco and fine quality fabrics played a part, too, as did alterations in consumption patterns. The increased popularity of tea drinking, for example, created a demand for teapots, cups and saucers, sugar bowls, tea spoons and the like. Tea, sugar and tobacco were core commodities in many general shops at this time and, as Nancy Cox points out, even small tradesmen offered some of them for sale. Hence when George Bayley of Broseley died in 1717 his personal estate was valued at under £10 but included £1 5s 5d for 'Sope and Tobacco & small things to sell'.[27]

Transport changes, with improved roads, better vehicles, more efficient coastal communications and the construction of the canal system in the second half of the eighteenth century, widened the catchment area for the supply of food and manufactured goods, both from Britain itself and from overseas. Mass-production methods, albeit on a limited scale, were being applied to the production of textiles and pottery and while that adversely affected the fortunes of some producer-retailers, it gave opportunities to many shopkeepers to extend their range of goods for sale. The creation of a national carrier system also helped to promote trade. In the 1760s the small Westmorland town of Kirkby Stephen had a regular carrier service to at least seven other centres, including Newcastle upon Tyne, Lancaster, Kendal and Sedbergh. It was linked to London by way of Kendal.[28] All of this meant that by the mid- to late eighteenth century shopkeepers could obtain their stock from a wide range of suppliers. Abraham Dent of Kirkby Stephen combined running a shop and wine merchant's business with brewing and dealing in knitted stockings. Over the period from 1756 to 1777 he purchased goods from 190 suppliers. In 1763 alone he bought from 47 of them, with almost all his groceries coming from a variety of provincial dealers.[29]

In other cases orders were placed by correspondence, with the goods then dispatched by the manufacturer or wholesaler by land or by water, according to the shopkeeper's geographical location and personal preference. To stimulate trade, manufacturers supplied samples of their products, together with price lists, so that selections could be made. Walthal Fenton, a clothier and draper from Woodhead near Cheadle in Staffordshire, for example, received specimens of metal buttons from a Birmingham firm in February 1776, and cloth samples from various textile producers. Although he was a draper, he sold a small range of other goods, too, perhaps when customers placed special orders. In January 1794 he ordered six barrels of oysters from London suppliers, to be dispatched to him in six separate instalments. Information on the quality and prices of tea, coffee and cocoa was received from the London dealers with whom he traded, and they advised him on the most advantageous time to buy. On 26 March 1791, for instance, they reported: 'Best Bohea is a Halfpenny per Pound lower. . . . We think that the Teas in general are good, and of a safe Price to buy.'[30] A growing range of intermediaries also played their part both inside and outside the central wholesale markets, including agents, factors, cheesemongers and the like. Commercial travellers, or 'riders' as they were known, were sent out by manufacturers, too. When the representative of a Trowbridge woollen clothmaker was unable to reach Walthal Fenton because of lack of time, his employer hastily wrote to explain the cause and to send 'a few Patterns for your Approbation; if any of [them] please, your command will be esteemed'.[31]

Meanwhile, growing numbers of people living in the newly expanding towns and industrial villages were no longer able to grow their own food in the way many had done when they lived in the countryside or in small rural towns. Instead they had to rely on markets, itinerant traders and shops. As we shall see, markets were widely patronised for perishable goods, particularly foodstuffs, while itinerant sellers were popular, especially among poorer migrants to the towns, since they were a source of supply familiar in the villages. But in London, too, street hawkers remained important well into the nineteenth century, at a time when the capital's population was rising rapidly from around 575,000 in 1700 to 900,000 a century later. At that date it was the western world's largest city.[32] Even with the rapid expansion of other towns and cities during the following hundred or so years, the capital continued to account for a major proportion of the population, forming 13.2 per cent of the total number of people in England and Wales in 1851. By 1901 that figure had risen to 16.4 per cent .[33]

London, as well as being a major manufacturing and trading centre, was the focus of the nation's political and social life, too, especially during the Season, when members of high society met together for entertainment, gossip and the settling of marriage partnerships. In the eighteenth century, therefore, alongside the numerous vendors of basic foodstuffs and clothing to cater for the mass of the population, there was a vast array of shopkeepers offering a variety of high-quality and fashionable goods in the West End and the City. Among them were linen drapers, goldsmiths, instrument-makers, music publishers, milliners, tailors, chemists, tea and coffee purveyors, porcelain, china and glass retailers, and many more besides. 'It is almost impossible to express how well everything is organized in London,' declared Sophie von la Roche enthusiastically of the capital's shops in the 1780s, 'every article is made more attractive to the eye than in Paris or in any other town.' She was particularly impressed by the shopmen's skills in displaying their wares:

We especially noticed a cunning device for showing women's materials. Whether they are silks, chintzes or muslins, they hang down in folds behind the fine high windows so that the effect of this or that material, as it would be in the ordinary folds of a woman's dress, can be studied. . . . Behind great glass windows absolutely everything one can think of is neatly, attractively displayed, and in such abundance of choice as almost to make one greedy.[34]

She was struck, too, by the fact that the 'elegant dressing of large shop-windows' was not merely 'to ornament the streets and lure purchasers, but to make known the thousands of inventions and ideas, and spread good taste about, for the excellent pavements made for pedestrians enable crowds of people to stop and inspect the new exhibits'.[35] In this way retailers were performing an educative role as well as a purely commercial one.

London influenced taste and consumer demand throughout the country, especially in regard to the fashion trades. Provincial drapers, milliners and other clothes retailers were anxious to assure customers that they had garments in accordance with the most recent London – or, more rarely, Paris – fashions. Typical of many was the advertisement inserted by Mrs Thackray, a York linen draper, in the *York Courant* of 3 May 1785. In it she begged 'leave to acquaint the LADIES, that Mr Thackray is now in London and has sent down several Elegant SPRING PATTERNS in superfine Chintz, Calicoes, &c. with a Variety of the most fashionable Goods, particularly SPRIGG'D and TURBAN MUSLINS, &c. &c. which will be sold on very reasonable terms'.

Outside the capital, in centres frequented by the well-to-do, such as Bath, Brighton and York, retailers also catered for the 'luxury' trades. In Georgian Bath, writes Trevor Fawcett, shops ranged 'from the humblest booths to fashion boutiques and embryonic high street stores'. As in London, the Bath fabric shops exhibited brightly patterned silks and cottons so as to show them to best advantage. Even so, in 1787 one draper in fashionable Milsom Street lamented that such was the wide variety of his stock that 'a window display could not do it justice'.[36] Then there were high-class milliners, like the two Miss Hoblyns, who appointed milliners to the Duchess of York in 1798. They, declares Fawcett, no doubt traded 'with unsullied reputation', but with others there was some room for conjecture.

Ann Thicknesse considered milliners 'in general . . . very *convenient* sort of people', always willing 'to help customers cheat their husbands with inflated bills. . . . Often employing unmarried young women, milliners faced criticism on that score, too. A [Bath] guide of 1747 warned parents about the "vast Resort of young Beaus and Rakes to Milliners' Shops", of the ribald talk there and the risk to their daughters' morals.' And nearly fifty years later, in 1795, the advice still applied. Elizabeth Mandell's at 41 Milsom Street was, it seems, just such a honeypot: 'Where, *boot'd and spur'd*, the gay macaronies,/Bestride *Mandell's* counter, instead of their ponies' – their excuse probably being the men's ruffles and cravats to be found among an array of feminine satins, lace, coloured crape, ribbons, fans and trimmed straw bonnets.[37]

In 1784 one of the newly published trade directories, which were coming on to the market in increasing numbers in the final decades of the eighteenth century, confirmed the wide range of goods offered in Bath. More than a hundred shopkeepers were listed. They included 18 drapers, mercers, tailors and haberdashers, 10 grocers and tea dealers (one also offering drapery), 14 wine merchants, 7 jewellers and goldsmiths, 7 booksellers, and a number

of hosiers, glovers, milliners, hatters and lacemen alongside more mundane
traders like ironmongers, braziers and cheesemongers. A similar pattern can
be identified in York, where of just under 90 shopkeepers listed in the same
year, there were 25 drapers, mercers and haberdashers, 9 grocers and tea
dealers, 4 confectioners, 4 butter factors, 4 wine merchants, 5 jewellers and
watchmakers, 5 chemists and druggists, 2 booksellers, a music seller and a
variety of hosiers, glovers, leather sellers and saddlers, and upholsterers.[38] It
was customary to omit humbler 'general' shopkeepers from the directories at
this date, catering as they did for less affluent tastes. Yet, according to Daniel
Defoe, those 'little retailing shops [were] the life of all our trade'.[39] Through
them 'the bulk of the business is carried on'.

In some cases London retailers set up branches in Bath to cater for visitors
during the busy winter Season. In April 1800 Riviere, a jeweller who had
been trading in Milsom Street, inserted an advertisement in the *Bath
Chronicle* expressing 'his grateful thanks to the Nobility, Gentry, and the
Publick, for the numerous favours and kind patronage conferred on him
during the present Season, and informs them, that he leaves Bath on the
14th of April for London; where all orders will be most punctually attended
to, addressed to No. 63, NEW BOND-STREET. N.B. Attends *Cheltenham* as
usual during the Season.'[40]

Many shops catering for the wealthy had elaborate furnishings and fittings.
Claire Walsh has drawn attention to high-class London establishments which
even in the eighteenth century boasted an extensive array of mirrors, glass
display cases and the like, and with an arrangement of mouldings and
classical pillars 'at dramatic points in the shop'. The furnishings catering for
the comfort of customers included upholstered chairs and stools, attractive
display tables, silk curtains and pictures on the walls, alongside the shelves,
cupboards and drawers which contained the stock.[41]

Daniel Defoe, however, condemned shopkeepers who spent large sums on
elaborate interiors of this sort instead of on the goods they were selling. 'It is
a modern custom', he wrote in 1726, 'to have tradesmen lay out two-thirds
of their fortune in fitting up their shops . . . in painting and gilding, fine
shelves, shutters, boxes, glass-doors, sashes, and the like. . . . It is true that a
fine show of goods will bring customers . . . but that a fine show of shelves
and glass-windows should bring customers, that was never made a rule till
now.'[42] However, shopkeepers aiming to attract well-to-do customers were
aware that in the new commercial climate attractive premises were
important, and during the eighteenth century their numbers increased.

On the other hand, many provincial shopkeepers, either through lack of
funds or because they faced less severe competition or had a less demanding

clientele, continued to run their businesses on far simpler lines. Some set up a trestle board or stall before the shop or the shop window, with sales conducted through the window itself, without any glazing. In other cases unglazed frames, such as lattices, were adopted for window displays.[43] William Wood, a shopkeeper, innkeeper and agriculturist from Didsbury, Lancashire, as late as the 1780s continued to conduct his cash sales through the window, although he did also make sales within the shop itself. In that event he recorded the issuing of bills, which doubtless meant that he was giving credit.[44]

The adoption of a fixed price and 'ready money' policy for payments was pursued by a minority of retailers in the early eighteenth century, not merely when they adopted an 'open window' method of sale, but within shops, too. Peter and James Ferry, London silk weavers, took a shop in Bath in the early eighteenth century and by the 1740s had adopted a 'fixed price' regime rather than allowing haggling. In 1744 their advertisement for brocaded and patterned silks and velvets included the rider: 'N.B. The Lowest Price will be fix'd on each Piece, without any Abatement.'[45]

But most shopkeepers, reluctantly or otherwise, recognised the need to offer credit to attract and retain customers. This created problems when clients proved slow payers. Thus when the famous Georgian cabinet-maker Thomas Chippendale was short of cash, he appealed to Sir Edward Knatchbull to settle an outstanding debt, but without success. 'As I receive my rents once a year,' declared Sir Edward firmly, 'so I pay my tradesmen's bills once a year which is not reckoned very bad pay as ye world goes.'[46]

Even among more modest retailers, long-running accounts and bad debts caused difficulties. William Stout, a Lancaster shopkeeper, estimated that in his early days he had lost between a third and a half of his profits in bad debts.[47] The account book of Mary Medhurst and Thomas North, shopkeepers at St Mary Bourne, Hampshire, during the period 1762 to 1783 confirms the long credit some customers expected. One persistent debtor at this shop was William Burges. His account began in October 1765 with the purchase of candles, wine, butter, sugar, tobacco, nails, cloth and thread. By September of the following year his debt had grown to £6 11s 6d and early in the following month 10s 6d was paid off. Over the years other small sums were handed over, but fresh debts were incurred. Even in July 1783, when the account book ended, more than 14s was still outstanding.[48]

The anxiety of Thomas Turner, a village shopkeeper from East Hoathly in Sussex, concerning a debt of about £18 owed by 'Master Darby' in 1758, illustrates the problems faced by a small tradesman should a debtor prove recalcitrant and payment could not be secured:

In the morn as soon as I had breakfasted I set out for Lewes in order for to commit the management of the debt due from Master Darby to me into the hands of Mr Rideout, but . . . Mr Rideout was not at home; and, fearing a delay in the affair might prove of a dangerous consequence (I mean as to my getting of the debt), I therefore committed the same into the care of Mr Burtenshaw . . . who proposes to send for a writ this day and to arrest him a-Saturday next. The debt I swore to be due to me is £17 though I am pretty confident it is more than £18. Oh, what a confusion and tumult there is in my breast about this affair! To think what a terrible thing it is to arrest a person, for by this means he may be entirely torn to pieces, who might otherwise recover himself and pay everyone their own. But then on the other hand . . . some of this debt hath been standing above 4 years, and the greatest part of it above three years. I have tried very hard to get it these two years and cannot get one farthing. They have almost quite forsaken my shop, buying nothing of me that amounts to any value, but every time they want anything of value, they go to Lewes. And I have just reason to suspect they must be deep in debt at other places, for undoubtedly no people of £200 a year go gayer than Mrs Darby and her two daughters.[49]

It is clear from this that Turner expected his credit customers to pay off at least part of their account at regular intervals and to continue to patronise his shop. They also needed to be credit worthy, and when these requirements were no longer being met, he put the matter into the hands of an attorney, despite his dislike of going to law.[50]

The cash-flow worries of small businesses were made worse by the general shortage of small coinage to settle debts in the eighteenth century, thereby encouraging the granting of credit. As Dorothy Davis points out, for most of the eighteenth century no new silver coinage was struck, 'and while trade and population were increasing, the existing silver coins, so far from keeping pace with the need, were wearing out and getting lost'. Counterfeit money was also in circulation, as well as foreign coins, while some of the more substantial shopkeepers issued their own trade tokens for giving change. These would only be accepted locally.[51] It was in these circumstances that Thomas Turner spent sleepless nights anxiously considering his financial situation, as on 16 September 1757, when he noted that 'almost all the people in the parish seem to be growing poor and are so long [to] pay that no tradesman I am assured can bear it, for even the best will not pay above once a year'. Often he had to wait to settle up with customers at one of the many local fairs, and he spent fruitless days travelling from one debtor to another, trying to collect what was due to him.[52] Yet, despite his fears, the business prospered and he was eventually able to purchase the shop premises which initially he had only rented.

Others were less fortunate and their difficulties were compounded on occasion by their poor, or non-existent, book-keeping skills. In some cases carelessness was the cause. In 1697, for example, William Stout of Lancaster decided to give up his shop to his apprentice, John Troughton, when the youngster came out of his time, and instead to take up overseas trading. This did not prove very successful and when in 1704 Troughton was arrested for debt, Stout felt obliged to salvage as much of the business as possible for the benefit of the creditors. He purchased most of the former apprentice's stock and resumed his role as shopkeeper. As he noted sourly, when Troughton's goods were sold and the money he had owing to him had been collected,

> the whole amounted to about fower hundred and therty pounds . . . his debts amounted to above twelve hundred pounds, so that the division to each crediter was six shillings eight pence in the pound and no more. And . . . he got his liberty, but made no good use of it to gaine his reputation or his credit, but continued to abuse his best friends and relations. . . . He roved about in the town and country some time, and after went to Liverpool and London.

Eventually Troughton got a position as a ship's writer or steward on a ship upon a 'voiage to America. But neither he nor the ship ever returned, but supposed sunke at sea.'[53]

Problems associated with bad debts and the granting of credit continued to plague retailers – and their suppliers – well into the twentieth century. Only a few of the more confident, or determined, Georgian shopkeepers followed the example of Simon Pretor, a grocer, haberdasher and banker of Sherborne in Dorset, in charging interest on overdue debts.[54]

Food, clothing and textile shops dominated the shopping streets of most towns throughout the eighteenth century. The number of stationery and book shops, ironmongers' stores, china shops and the like was limited by the relatively low demand for their goods outside the more affluent centres of consumption. Some retailers sought to overcome this by diversifying into other trades as a way of boosting profits. In Winchester Thomas Blagden combined bookselling and printing with the retailing of stationery, the running of a circulating library and the sale of hats 'of all sizes, prices and colours'. He kept a medicinal and perfumery warehouse, too.[55] And when in 1784 another bookseller, William Dawkins of Gosport, Hampshire, sold his business, his stock-in-trade comprised, in addition to 'printing Articles, Books,

Stationery', musical instruments and sheet music, 'with many other Articles in the Jewellery and Silver Way. Also Cutlery, and Hardwares.'[56]

Simon Pretor of Sherborne was still more ambitious. He seems to have started his grocery shop, including the sale of tea, by the early 1750s, and he also offered haberdashery, stationery and other goods on both a wholesale and retail basis, as many other substantial shopkeepers did at that time. By the early 1770s he had moved into banking and in the mid-1790s, shortly before he sold his retail business, he seems to have left the running of the shop largely to his two assistants. He apparently only concerned himself with securing supplies from the wholesalers, whose agents visited him. He also sent out one of the assistants to drum up business for the shop, and took a firm line with suppliers whose goods did not match the quality anticipated. One man was told: 'Your Roll Tobacco will not sell – it grows mouldy. I must return it.'[57]

In major cities like London and York, where accommodation was at a premium, many shopkeepers took in lodgers to supplement their income. One estimate suggests that in the capital in 1797 more than two-fifths of retailers let lodgings; in York it was around a third.[58]

The more perceptive or ambitious shopkeepers reacted to the widening commercial opportunities by advertising their wares in the newspapers, and this was especially true of those connected with the fashion trades. The makers of patent medicines and beauty products often advertised on their own account, too, mentioning the shops where their nostrums could be purchased. Thus in October 1762 the makers of Dr James's Powder for Fevers and 'other inflammatory distempers' pointed out that it was sold by the bookseller and publisher J. Newbery at his premises in St Paul's Churchyard, London: 'It is extremely effectual in the Small Pox, Measles, and St Anthony's Fire', the advertisement encouragingly observed.[59]

A more personal kind of advertisement was the trade card, issued to customers or potential customers and again stressing some special service or product on offer. Samuel Denton, a woollen draper, mercer and tailor of Halifax, for example, drew attention to the training he had received in London from 'B. READ, Inventor and Teacher of the Arithmetical System of cutting to fit the human shape'. Denton assured possible clients that they could depend on having their orders 'executed equal to any House in London & as he keeps every Article in the Woollen Drapery Business of the best quality which he will sell at very low prices he hopes to merit the support of the Public'.[60] This he seems to have secured for he ran his business in Halifax from 1822 until at least 1853.

Some shopkeepers opened outlets in more than one town, perhaps responding to the opportunities presented by a weekly market in another locality. Thomas Green, a friend and fellow shopkeeper of William Stout in Lancaster, set up a second shop at Burton in Kendal, which he attended in person every market day, leaving a shopman in charge for the rest of the week.[61] More glamorous secondary outlets were opened in the provinces by London retailers, while large provisional dealers moved in the reverse direction and established outlets in the metropolis. They included the confectioner Keelings of London and Tunbridge Wells and the goldsmith Nodes, seller of trinkets and knick-knacks, who had shops in New Bond Street, London, and in Brighton.[62]

Even the modern device of a 'loss leader' to attract shoppers into their premises was adopted by some retailers. According to R. Campbell, it was common for grocers to sell sugar at a loss and then to recoup this by putting up the price of tea and other commodities.[63] Certain traders claimed to have made 'special' purchases of products which they would sell 'much under the general prices for Ready Money'.[64] Even bogus 'fire-damage' sales were arranged by some unscrupulous dealers. An anonymous 'Old Draper', who worked for a draper in Whitechapel in the early nineteenth century, remembered that when a small fire occurred on the premises, a special sale of 'damaged' stock was arranged:

> They burnt great holes in a few lengths of common prints and calicoes and kept the shutters of the fancy window up. Efforts were made to keep up the illusion by singeing the edges of other articles. . . . The subterfuge was successful and an immense crowd gathered on the sale day. . . . Stockings were bought at full price with singed tops. . . . We found . . . we had . . . cleared off whole piles of goods that would have taken us several weeks to have sold under ordinary circumstances, while nearly all the . . . goods bought for the occasion had been cleared out. This rendered it necessary to scour the City and pick up all the old cheap lots that we thought likely to be useful.[65]

He claimed that this was the start of the 'selling off' system in London.

A final change to be discerned among growing numbers of late Georgian retailers was the emergence of specialist shops in the larger towns and the more affluent resorts, and the increasing attention paid to locating a business in a prestigious position. When Francis Place, a tailor and leather breeches maker, opened his shop in London in April 1801 he was determined it should be in Charing Cross Road, where he and a partner had previously built up a considerable reputation in another property. He refurbished the new premises, boasting later that he had had 'the largest plate glass windows in London' at that time. The goods were also of a superior quality 'and I sold from the windows more goods for about three years than paid journeyman's wages and the expenses of housekeeping. This ready money business made it unnecessary for me to borrow money of any body. . . . It looked well that there should be several people employed about the shop, and it was to me essential that I should be at liberty to attend to the customers.' He had, nonetheless, a low opinion of many of his clients:

> I knew . . . that the most profitable part for me to follow was . . . to make myself acceptable to coxcombs, to please their whims, to have no opinion of my own. . . . I knew well that to enable me to make money I must consent to submit to much indignity, and insolence, to tyranny and injustice . . . I never yet knew a man who did not think he was behaving respectfully towards his tailor when his conduct was of a very offensive description. . . . I can imagine nothing except being a footman or a common soldier as more degrading than being either a barber or a tailor.[66]

But his ability to swallow his pride and accept these unfavourable aspects of business life paid off. By 1816 he estimated his net annual profit was more than £3,000 and in the following year he handed over the management of the shop to his eldest son.[67] He retired at the age of just 46 and was then able to pursue the political interests that he had had to keep concealed during his retailing career in Charing Cross Road.

Chapter 1

OUTSIDE THE SHOP: MARKET TRADERS AND TRAVELLING SALESMEN

As a general rule, in all small provincial towns the markets are going down in consequence of the alteration in the customs of trade . . . there may be a few exceptions in London, Birmingham, Manchester, and so on, where they have a larger area to work on; but the trade is diverted into shops, and from shops again to the travelling shops that are going round the country. . . . There are always plenty of people on the lookout to leave the market and establish themselves in shops, and you must compromise with them, to keep what there is.

Joseph F. Mark, lessee of Helston, St Austell and Penryn markets, Cornwall, to the *Royal Commission on Market Rights and Tolls*, Parliamentary Papers, 1888, vol. LIV, p. 168, Qu. 7588 and 7592.

FAIRS, MARKETS AND MARKET HALLS

Fairs and markets were traditional retail outlets which both underwent major changes over the years. Many succumbed to the competition from shops and other trading ventures, such as municipally owned market halls. These latter, being normally open every day, were able to cater for the needs of a growing urban population, living in overcrowded homes with few storage facilities and with too little cash to make bulk purchases. By contrast, markets usually operated once or twice a week, while fairs were often annual events.

Fairs were the first casualties of the new order, many losing their role as suppliers of consumer goods during the eighteenth century. Where they survived it was often as livestock marts or, in certain parts of the country, as hiring fairs for the recruitment of agricultural labour. Even among the survivors, increasing emphasis was placed on the entertainments offered, with sideshows, carousels, the vending of cheap trinkets and the provision of refreshments, including drinking booths, well to the fore. This led to complaints about rowdiness and accusations that the fairs were attracting 'undesirable' elements like beggars, pickpockets, fraudsters and drunkards. 'Cheap Jack' salesmen also attended, such as the anonymous son of a Portsmouth butcher, who began his selling career at a Birmingham fair in the 1830s, 'buying a few goods and . . . selling from off a pot-crate'. Eventually he purchased a large covered cart and a horse which enabled him to visit a circuit of fairs held in the spring and autumn.[1] Cheap Jacks sold a range of household utensils, as well as tools, watches, bridles, saddles and even guns.[2]

During the same decade Joseph Hepworth, a travelling draper based in York, visited a number of fairs (and markets) in the north of England, accompanied by members of his family to help with the selling. In June 1833, for example, he and two sons went to Borough Bridge Fair. They spent around five days there and sold modest amounts of merino, velveteen and other cloths, amounting to £6 12s. But bed and board for himself and his sons cost £1 2s 2d and the outlay on the goods sold was £4 4s 9d. So with a total expenditure of £5 6s 11d, his profit amounted to about £1 5s. Sometimes he was less successful. A visit to Stamford Bridge Fair towards the end of the same year realised £15 4s 9d. But his expenditure, including board and lodging for himself, a son and daughter, was £15 12s. Overall he computed his net profit for the year at £2. In 1834 it amounted to £1 12s 6½d. Perhaps not surprisingly, in 1835 he went bankrupt.[3]

The pace of change nonetheless varied, and some fairs continued their traditional commercial role into the Victorian era. In the mid-eighteenth century William Owen's *Book of Fairs* mentioned the specialisms of each of those listed, so that in its 1756 edition it noted that at Andover, Hampshire, in May there were vendors of millinery, while the August fair at Carlisle offered linen, and that at Market Harborough in Leicestershire in October dealt in pewter, brass, hats and clothes.[4] In Yorkshire specialities included boots and shoes at Egton and Seamer, and cloth, brass, pewter, tin and millinery goods at Grinton. The October fair at Barnsley proffered 'swine, cheese and goosepies'.[5] Owen's book was reissued on several occasions, the last edition appearing in 1859.[6] It was an indication that fairs were providing a useful commercial service far longer than is sometimes suggested.

Thomas Turner, the East Hoathly shopkeeper, regularly visited fairs in Sussex during the 1750s and 1760s. Although he relished the amusements they offered, he used them to buy supplies like chamois leather, and on occasion to settle debts. In September 1757 at Selmeston Fair he met Thomas

Bean, to whom he paid 4s 'for making out my perry'. He sold rags he had collected around East Hoathly to papermakers at Maidstone Fair, arranging with a dealer for their disposal on commission, and receiving some reams of paper in part exchange, as well as cash.[7]

Stourbridge Fair near Cambridge was one of the most important venues. In 1724 Daniel Defoe claimed it was 'not only the greatest in the whole nation, but in the world'. Its rows of booths were laid out in streets and many of them were occupied by tradesmen from London.[8] Over sixty years later Henry Gunning was similarly impressed by the wide selection of articles sold, ranging from farm produce to manufactured goods. Stourbridge was especially famed for its cheese and, according to Gunning, 'not only did the inhabitants of the neighbouring counties supply themselves with their annual stock of cheese, but great quantities were bought and sent up to London'. Other items on sale included woollen cloth from Yorkshire and the West of England, pottery from Staffordshire, and leather goods, while booths were taken by silk mercers, linen drapers, furriers, stationers, vendors of toys and knick-knacks, and suppliers of musical instruments. The most conspicuous salesman at the fair, wrote Gunning, was a man named Green from Limehouse in London. His booth occupied three times as much space as that of other traders. '[He] dealt in tea, sugar, soap, candles, and every other article in grocery that housekeepers could possibly require. His goods were of the first quality, and he sold them as cheap as they could be bought in London; so that any family in Cambridge, or within thirty miles of it (who could afford the money), laid in their annual stock at that season.'[9]

Yet despite its trading role, Stourbridge, too, was noted for its vulgar entertainments and heavy drinking. Gunning referred to the 'mixture of dwarfs and giants, conjurors and learned pigs' present, as well as 'a great number of drinking-booths'. In 1700 critics commented on the brothels that flourished there and claimed that men went there not to do business but to 'Drink, Smoke and Whore'.[10]

Nevertheless, if the commercial role of fairs was declining, indirectly they continued to promote trade. They offered opportunities for local retailers to meet and to build up contacts. That certainly seems to have applied to Thomas Turner, whose brother Richard was engaged as a shopman by a Lewes draper, the agreement providing for the youngster to be taken at least once to Maudling Hill Fair, presumably so that he could meet other tradesmen gathered there.[11]

Fairs also benefited shopkeepers by attracting visitors to a town, and it is noticeable that William Stout was keen to have his premises well stocked in readiness for Lancaster's summer fair. 'My sister Elin came to the fair to assist me – and on the market days – and was as ready in serving retail customers as a young apprentice could have done,' he wrote on one occasion. Later, when Elin's health deteriorated, he recruited John Marshall to help in her place on market and fair days, and 'for the same gave him only six pence a day, and continued so many years'.[12]

The stimulus to business was particularly apparent during the autumn hiring fairs, when farm workers came to seek a new employer and to expend some of the wages they had received at Michaelmas on clothing, shoes and other goods. Such fairs survived at Canterbury into the 1880s and in parts of the north of England until after 1914. Despite unfavourable comments about the disorderly conduct to which the fairs gave rise, shopkeepers like Mr Wells of Canterbury lent them strong support:

> I have benefited . . . to a great extent, my trade has been a country trade, and I have realised an independency by it for my old age, and the fair is one of the greatest boons to the trade of the city that we have. There is not anything that causes the same amount of money to be spent as that does . . . [I]f we do away with the fair we shall have all the custom go to Ashford and Faversham.[13]

The Mayor of Canterbury did not share Mr Wells's enthusiasm, referring sourly to the 'evil influences' exerted, 'which we should like to avoid even at the sacrifice of a little trade'.[14] In the long run that negative attitude largely prevailed.

One of the fairs' commercial weaknesses in an expanding urban society was that the food and manufactured goods they offered were too irregular in supply to meet everyday needs. To a lesser extent similar problems applied to traditional weekly markets, while the fact that they were usually held out of doors on a market place or in the streets meant they often spilled out on to the highway, obstructing traffic and generally disrupting life in the surrounding area. The noise, disorder and bad smells associated with them, and the dirt and refuse they left behind, outweighed their trading benefits in many eyes. In Southampton the vegetable sellers moved out of the market place into the High Street, while in Plymouth the butchers' shambles invaded a nearby churchyard.[15] In badly organised markets even the allocation of selling space was haphazard. At Portsmouth as late as the 1880s a market for poultry, butter, eggs and farm produce was held in a street about 60ft wide and around ¾ mile in length, with the stalls set up along the edge of the pavement. The sellers stood in the gutter but, according to one observer, the stall spaces were appropriated by the first comer. So those who wished for a particular location were 'obliged either to take up their position by midnight, or to buy a standing of someone who has taken possession. The charge for stallage is 1½d, but a man who has to buy a standing of another may have to pay 3d or 6d for it. Several witnesses spoke . . . of men and women lying in the streets all night to ensure their places; and robberies and free fights are described as common occurrences.'[16]

There were protests, too, about the discomfort of trading in the open air for both vendors and buyers. 'I had to crawl underneath the van to get out of the rain,' a market seller in Brighton complained, while in Scarborough stallholders conducted their business on dirty ground 'exposed to winter storms. "It is rather too much to expect," stated a critic of the unenclosed Bolton market, to come to the market and "stand there with wet clothes on".'[17] Other problems arose when an animal, perhaps a cow or pig, ran amok through the streets, after escaping from a dealer or butcher, while traffic hazards were created by the throng of carriages, traders' carts and wagons on market day. At the beginning of the 1820s this led to the widening of market streets in Manchester 'to keep pedestrians from being crushed'.[18]

But markets were nonetheless welcomed for their flexibility and the fact that their expenses were minimal. If stalls were not provided by the market owner they could easily be constructed by the traders themselves at little cost. The open stalls allowed space for the display of goods and thereby reduced the need to advertise. Townspeople, for their part, appreciated the fresh produce offered for sale, for by concentrating on perishable foods, markets – especially in the earlier years – offered a service complementary to that provided by shops, which specialised in dry goods. 'In the history of market institutions,' declared Roger Scola, 'three groups of traders – butchers, fruit and vegetable dealers and fishmongers – figured most prominently.'[19] Markets also allowed local farmers and market gardeners to sell their poultry, meat, eggs, fruit and vegetables direct to consumers, rather than relying on middlemen. Even if the farmer himself could not spare the time to engage in selling, his wife or another family member would attend in his stead. At Reading in the early nineteenth century Mary Russell Mitford recalled the Butter Market area, 'where the more respectable basket-women, the daughters and wives of farmers, and the better order of the female peasantry, used to bring eggs, butter and poultry for sale on Wednesdays and Saturdays'.[20]

Even in the early twentieth century Maggie Joe Chapman, who grew up in Swaledale, remembered that while some of the neighbours 'let their cheeses go to Gill, the grocer that used to come once a month, in exchange for flour, or ground rice for making puddings, and such', her family preferred to sell for cash in the open market.

Once a fortnight, in summer, my father used to get up at four o'clock in t'morning, pack his cheeses in his trap, and go to Barnard Castle market with them, which was twenty mile. . . . He'd put cheeses out on flags in marketplace, and that's where we used to stand, and pit people from up north came down to buy 'em.[21]

Later, however, they too gave up retailing and instead sold their cheese to a co-operative store in Durham.

In Bath complaints about the crowded confusion in the High Street on market days led to the building of a covered market as early as the 1770s. Regulations were tightened and restrictions imposed on stallholders' trading hours. Hygiene standards were improved and the new market, with its neat rows of stalls and tempting displays of produce, was much admired. Particular traders attracted their regular customers, among them Mrs Piozzi, who years later recalled nostalgically her time in Bath: 'Warren the Cheese Monger, the deaf & dumb Fish Boy, with poor Mrs Cooper who sold Greens – shall I see [them] no more at the Market in *that* City?'[22]

Around 1800, as space in Bath market began to run out, fresh regulations were introduced. Henceforth 'no butcher, poulterer, fishmonger, greengrocer or other trader was to be allowed a double stall. Country butchers were . . . given preference over residents in allotting stalls.' And after 1801 anyone not selling provisions (e.g. dealers in cheap pottery, tolerated until then) was officially banned.[23]

Efforts were also made to ensure that purchasers were given the correct weight, so that in March 1753, for example, officials went into the market to weigh the butter being sold. This they did, and according to the *Bath Journal*, they 'took away a great Quantity (which was given to the Poor) that was under Weight; particularly twenty-five Pounds from one Woman'.[24] Just over thirty years later several measures 'with elastic bottoms' were seized from country gardeners selling their goods on the streets. The measures, on 'being found deficient', were duly burnt.[25] Although such inspections were spasmodic in this and in other markets, they did offer buyers a degree of protection against unscrupulous salesmen.

In Manchester, where the markets were controlled until 1846 by the lord of the manor (a member of a Staffordshire landowning family named Mosley), improvements came slowly. By the 1770s there was pressure on facilities, so during the eighteenth century several smaller, specialised markets had been established in streets around the market place. But as the stalls spread there were complaints that the area was filled with 'perpetual throngs'. The Mosleys jealously guarded their right to restrict meat and fish sales to the market sites and resorted to the courts to enforce this when necessary. Hence in June 1825 when John Walker opened a shop for the sale of fish in the Market Place, he was warned by Mosley's solicitor. This he ignored, so legal action was initiated. The case was heard at Lancaster Assizes in the spring of 1826 and in view of the 'all-embracing nature' of the manorial rights, judgment was given in favour of Mosley. However, only 'nominal damages of 1s and costs were awarded against Walker'.[26] Similar irksome restrictions applied to the butchers, with large numbers selling meat outside the markets, only to be checked by the manorial authorities threatening prosecution.[27] Not until the council acquired the market rights in 1846 were the butchers allowed to set up shops outside the market, providing they paid a licence fee. This led to an immediate drop in the revenue from Bridge Street, the largest of the meat markets, and by 1850 two-fifths of the stalls there were unoccupied.[28]

Meanwhile, one of the effects of transport improvements, in Manchester and elsewhere, was that farmers became less dependent on local markets to dispose of their produce, and instead sold to middlemen. Sometimes these were traders coming out from the nearby large towns or else produce was dispatched by road, water (including canals) or rail to wholesale markets a distance away. Occasionally the arrangements were more informal. In the late 1860s it was said to be not uncommon for a farmer's wife in Cumbria taking 'her cartload of poultry, butter and eggs' to market, to be intercepted on the journey 'by a middleman from Manchester or some other manufacturing town, and the whole contents purchased by the roadside'.[29] Increasingly, therefore, retail markets became dominated by 'professional' salespeople, who purchased their goods from wholesalers, while the number of producer-retailers fell sharply. Foodstuffs were brought in from a wide area, including foreign imports.

Shopkeepers had an ambivalent attitude towards markets and their sellers. On the one hand they welcomed the additional trade normally generated. William Stout's busiest days were those when the market was held and, as an apprentice, he had had to 'make up' goods during the rest of the week in readiness for market day. That included packaging sugar, tobacco, nails and similar items. On market day itself three or four of the youngsters were employed 'in delivering out goods, so that we had a full trade then, and the best of customers'.[30] Later, as we have seen, when he had his own shop he called on his sister and then a paid assistant to help him cope with the extra rush of customers on market days.

Even in the 1880s the importance of the market in stimulating business was recognised in some places. At Hitchin in Hertfordshire proposals to relocate the market away from the centre of the town led to objections from a number of tradespeople. 'I am in favour of things going on as they are at present . . . in the market, because it brings a good many people . . . on Tuesday whom we as tradesmen would not otherwise see,' claimed one man. Another declared: 'If the market were moved . . . towards the station . . . it would ruin the trade of the town, because the traders would not come into the town. They would come to the station, transact their business, and then go away.' Similar views were expressed at Chippenham.[31]

But elsewhere there was criticism of the noise and disorder generated, and the competition which adversely affected the shop trade. At Braintree in Essex, where by the late 1880s the market was very small, complaints were nonetheless made about the 'obstruction to business' caused by the traders' stalls. Mr Pryke, a tailor in the High Street, claimed that the space in front of his shop was occupied by different vendors. 'Sometimes, during the last three months, we have had stack-cloth sellers within a few yards of the shop shouting at the top of their voices, and the noise is so great that frequently in the shop one can hardly be heard to speak. This takes place on Wednesdays.' The manager of the London and County Bank similarly objected to the presence of a fish stall in front of his premises, to say nothing of a butcher's stand during the winter months. The stench of the fish during the summer was particularly unpleasant.[32]

Another point of dispute was that market traders could come to a town and pay as little as 6d for a stand, as was the case at Cockermouth in Cumberland, while local shopkeepers had to pay their full rates and taxes. They 'can sell things paying, you may say, nothing', declared Christopher Mayson, an irate shopkeeper, in 1888. 'They will place their stall right in front of my shop, and customers can hardly get into the place, and they are constantly shouting and making a noise, which is injurious to trade. I think it ought to be stopped.'[33]

Particularly frustrating to retailers, however, were the prescriptive rights of some market owners to prohibit sales in shops on market days. At Chard in Somerset butchers who wished to sell in their own shops rather than go into the market had to pay 3s a week for the privilege. A similar arrangement applied at Penryn in Cornwall, where a market toll of 1s 6d a week was demanded. One shopkeeper, whose business was in a poor part of the town, avoided paying the toll by refusing to sell meat on market days.[34]

Yet if shopkeepers had mixed views about the influence of markets upon their trade, there is little doubt of their benefit for labouring families with small and uncertain incomes. As Janet Blackman has noted, market retailers had the great advantage of lower overheads, 'and built up their reputations on quick cheap sales of fresh foodstuffs. . . . Apart from the advantage of lower prices in the market-place, there was still an element of bargaining between seller and buyer which was virtually unknown on shop premises' by the mid-nineteenth century. They also offered goods within the price range of poorer customers. Shoemakers at Sheffield in 1818 pointed out that their footwear was 'very different' from that sold 'in the shops, being more suitable for the lower orders of Society than the fancy articles sold in the shops'.[35]

Customer loyalty was built up, too. At Denton near Manchester, where there were stalls selling lengths of material, thread, trimmings and knitting wool, it was common for a system of 'putting away' to apply. The customer chose the wool she needed for a garment, paid for and took away part of it, and left the rest, sufficient to complete the work, with the seller. It was put into a bag marked with the purchaser's name, and she would buy it in instalments. 'To sell this on a market meant that the stall holder had to bring all the parcels each week, as well as fresh stock to attract new customers. Notices limiting the length of time for which wool would be "put away" were an attempt to hasten slow knitters and those undertaking mammoth garments.'[36]

Markets were particularly busy on Saturday nights as working people came with their week's pay to purchase food for their Sunday dinner and to enjoy any entertainment on offer. In the late 1880s, in addition to the long-established London markets, such as Covent Garden for fruit and vegetables, Billingsgate for fish, Smithfield for cattle and so on, there were 130 informal retail street markets under the control of the London County Council.[37] One of the council's tasks was to raise hygiene standards, and there were complaints in the late 1890s that growers coming to Covent Garden collected manure from the surrounding area in their carts and then placed empty vegetable containers on top.[38]

Among the smaller street venues was that at Strutton Ground in Westminster, where, according to a report of 1893, there were 47 stalls in this very narrow street, including 12 offering vegetables, 6 for flowers, 2 for fruit, 3 for butchers' meat, 2 for fish, 2 for ice cream, 3 for confectionery, and 1 for eggs. In all 16 of the stalls sold non-perishable items, such as haberdashery, earthenware, footwear, hats and second-hand books, while 9 offered second-hand clothes. A few of the shopkeepers also erected stalls on Saturdays in front of their shops, but most of the vendors were coster-mongers. 'This market is a great convenience to the poor in the immediate neighbourhood who so largely use it,' declared the 1893 report.[39]

Walter Southgate, who was born in Bethnal Green in the 1890s, remembered the importance of the market to his family. He recalled the 'old gels' who sold second-hand clothing, often obtained from the auction sales of pawnbrokers' unredeemed pledges. They stood in the gutter with piles of garments, turning over each one to advertise their wares, 'and making a running commentary on each article as it was held up for inspection'. According to Southgate, his mother never possessed a 'brand new garment or hat. All her clothing she purchased from these women and she thought highly of her "bargains".' On Saturday night, like many poor but thrifty housewives, she came to the market late in the hope that the butchers would be selling off their meat cheaply, so as to dispose of it before Sunday – a practice that was common in the days before refrigeration. 'If unsuccessful, she would trot off on Sunday morning with a few of her neighbours to Bethnal Green Road or London Fields market and buy a few block ornaments, as this cheap meat was called. She and others would buy very cheaply the "left overs" from the Saturday trading as they lay exposed on the stalls to dust and flies.'[40]

Southgate recalled the general liveliness and excitement on Saturday nights, when the East End street markets became

hives of activity, noise and bedlam. The stalls would be lit with naphtha flame lamps. . . . The noise was deafening with each stall holder and shopkeeper bellowing to the crowd as it pushed its way along the narrow pavement. . . . Little sneak thief urchins would slyly move about the stalls 'lifting' anything edible within their grasp. It was . . . midnight before the noise ceased and then the council workmen stepped in to clear away the debris.[41]

Sometimes, as Henry Mayhew had noted in the middle of the century, the London costermongers who hawked their wares around the highways and byways for most of the week would take a stand in the street markets at the weekend. One vendor of cakes travelled to 'all the fairs and races, and is more in the country than town in the summer and autumn', commented Mayhew, but when in town he sold 'large quantities of plum-cake in Smithfield, sometimes having 2£ worth and more on his stall'.[42] Street markets persisted in London into the twentieth century and beyond. But elsewhere attitudes were changing, especially in the industrial districts. As people became better off, the unregulated market place and the confusion of street stalls came to be seen as generally disreputable.[43] It seemed unacceptable that 'respectable housewives' should have to do their marketing in such uncouth surroundings.

In response to this new mood, market halls began to be built. Liverpool was a pioneer, providing a covered municipal market hall in a fine spacious building, equipped with gas lighting and a water supply, in 1822. Sometimes, as with the Shambles and Bazaar constructed in the early 1820s at Leeds, the initiative was taken by private individuals. In this case it was two butchers who were the prime movers. The new Shambles included 60 shops arranged in two rows within the hall, 50 of them rented by butchers. This replaced the town's previous derelict and unsatisfactory premises. A novel aspect was the construction of a large room above the central block of shops, called the Bazaar, and let out in compartments to dealers for the sale of fancy goods, millinery and clothes. Two other market halls were built in Leeds soon after, this time financed by joint stock companies. One, the Central, had a total of 67 shops and 56 stalls, selling meat, fish, fruit, vegetables and dairy produce. There was also a balcony for the sale of fancy goods. The South Market catered for the vending of butter, eggs, and poultry, as well as meat, manufacturers' goods and other commodities.[44]

These Leeds initiatives, taken to meet the needs of a rapidly growing industrial town and to end the inconvenience of the previous open-air markets, were unusual in being financed by private enterprise. In many towns the reform movement was led by the local councils, as in Liverpool, and became a matter of civic pride. Although open markets often continued alongside them, the halls offered a more regular supply of goods, being open normally on every day of the week except Sundays. They provided many of the benefits of shops, as they were under cover, but at lower cost. A number had storage space for the stallholders. In 1888 at Blackburn market hall one man with a fruit and flower business not only had ample space behind his stall to keep his stock, but also a gas cooker and a telephone, for which he paid extra. He could place orders for fresh supplies without leaving the market and was described as the 'biggest florist in Blackburn'. Another man's large drapery stall was fitted up like an ordinary shop.[45]

Market halls offered a multiplicity of products under one roof. They supplied not merely foodstuffs, which were always important aspects of their business, but manufactured goods and refreshments as well. In 1852 Durham's new market accommodated 'butchers, clothiers, hatters, ropers, potters, booksellers, coopers, tinmakers, shoemakers, bacon and cheese factors, glovers, worsted dealers, basket makers, gardeners, quack medicine vendors, confectioners, blacking makers, hardware merchants, sellers of implements of husbandry, and sellers of fish, potatoes and fruit'.[46] Unlike shops, where goods were often out of sight, visual inspection of merchandise was encouraged. By the end of the century new kinds of products, such as sewing machines, bicycles, phonographs and records were on offer in some places, while in Birmingham's market hall the pet stalls were a great attraction. This diversity of wares has led Deborah Hodson to label the market hall a 'municipal stores' or a 'one-stop shop'.[47] It could almost be regarded as the poor man's department store.

But the advent of market halls brought about other changes. Their rules and regulations usually specified what articles could be sold and where, while the process of buying and selling itself became more standardised and less haphazard.[48] Emphasis was placed on hygiene, goods were better displayed, and new standards of behaviour were set for sellers and buyers alike. By-laws laid down the rents and market tolls payable, the authority given to market officials to inspect produce, and what was expected by way of general conduct. At Salisbury, for example, by-laws drawn up in 1858 forbade 'swearing, noise disturbance, offensive language, indecent or vulgar behaviour, and smoking', while at Burnley the selling of coconuts was banned because 'it attracts rough people'. In that town the market inspector could 'eject persons who used "disgusting language", were abusive, violent or drunk, who created an obstruction, or who engaged in quarrelling'. That included the stallholders. At Leeds a firm of fruit sellers were reprimanded by the Market Committee for the 'habit of making a great noise and wearing an objectionable costume in front of their shops, causing annoyance to the other tenants, and unduly attracting customers'.[49]

As a consequence of this emphasis on 'respectability' a new middle-class clientele was attracted to markets in some towns. At Warrington ladies who had 'refused to visit the uncovered market could be found shopping in the town's new market hall. Blackburn's market was popular with . . . ladies because it had many dry goods and drapery stalls.'[50]

Most stallholders welcomed the improved facilities, although some objected to the regulations. At Blackburn Sidney Bury and James Thompson both complained because the by-laws required the market to close at 8 p.m. in winter, although in summer it remained open until 9 p.m. By contrast, at Burnley, Accrington and Chorley the stalls could stay open until 9 p.m. all year round. Bury saw this as a particular problem on Wednesdays:

We depend principally upon the Wednesday afternoon and night for the marketing of the workpeople. They work till half-past 5 in the mills, and sometimes they do not get out till a quarter to 6, or 6 o'clock, and then they have to go and get their tea, and dress themselves up a little to come to the market. The bell rings out at half-past 7, and the lights have to be out half an hour later, and by the time those people get up to perhaps the seventh stall, where there is a certain amount of stuff that they may want, it will take them nearly an hour . . . and the lights have to be out. What I complain of is that we have to put away our things in the dark, we are not allowed to have a light. . . . At Accrington you can have light until half-past 9, and at Ashton, Chorley, and Burnley too.[51]

At Devonport there was friction over the competition provided by hawkers, who were allowed to ply their trade in the streets without paying any market tolls, and also at the way in which country traders, ostensibly selling their own fruit, vegetables and farm produce, competed with specialist providers. James Whitfield, a butcher, declared angrily: 'I do not think it right that they should sell pork and beef in the fruit market. We have to pay a heavy rent. . . . My rent is 4s 9d [a week], and they pay about 1s. I have been here 11 years. I complain that people who are supposed not to sell meat at all, sell at a cheaper rate.' Another man with a confectioner's stall claimed that his sales of sweets had dropped since these were being sold in the fruit market.[52]

But some stallholders, like Michael Marks at Leeds, were able to progress from market trader to shop owner. Marks was a penniless immigrant from Poland when in 1884, with the help of Jewish friends, he began working first as a pedlar and then hired a stall in one of Leeds's open-air markets. He could trade there only twice a week, and to enable him to earn a living he needed outlets in towns where the market fell on different days. He found these in nearby Castleford and Wakefield. Then he obtained a place in the Leeds covered market hall, where not only was his merchandise protected against the weather but there was trading every day. His goods were displayed with the price clearly marked, so that there was none of the bargaining which was still associated with much market trading. The goods were classified by price, and above the penny section he hung a board with the slogan: 'Don't ask the price, it's a penny.' This was a brilliant advertising ploy and as his business grew and spread to other towns, he applied the slogan to those sites as well, selling nothing that cost more than a penny. This included haberdashery and a wide range of household goods, including pots and pans, pegs and mousetraps. By 1894 he had established eight 'penny bazaars', including one at a shop at Cheetham Hill, Manchester. It was in that year he went into partnership with Tom Spencer, who supplied the accounting skills Marks himself lacked.[53]

Michael Marks was a gifted and single-minded entrepreneur, destined to found one of Britain's leading chain stores. But other, less eminent, businessmen combined shop ownership with running a stall in the market hall. At Blackburn in 1888 a quarter of the market hall tenants listed in a trade directory for that year also owned or operated a shop. At Rochdale many of the butchers had stalls in the market as well as private shops. They sold the 'choice portions of the beasts' to better-off customers in their shops and disposed of 'the rough portions . . . for the benefit of the poor people' in the market.[54] Over the years, as market hall traders became well established, they set up tenants' associations in some towns to arrange social events and to offer a united front in their dealings with the town councils which often owned and regulated their premises.[55] Out of 769 owners of markets and market halls in England and Wales in 1886, 313 were held by local authorities; in a further 41 cases the markets were managed by the local authorities but not owned by them.[56] In 274 cases ownership was vested in private individuals. Five years later it was estimated that just over half of the country's markets were under cover.[57]

Ada Carlile's father was one stallholder who was able to set up a shop, selling fruit and fish. Mr Carlile had married at 18 years of age and had then taken a retail and wholesale fruit and vegetable stall in a Nottingham market. According to Ada, the family's link with market trading went back many years, with her grandmother selling in the same market, though then 'they used to throw all the . . . fruit and vegetables on the floor, they didn't have a stall to put them on'. Ada began to help in about 1907, when she was around 8 years old: 'I've worked from six in the morning 'til twelve at night . . . in my father's place. . . . I used to have to go and mind my dad's stall . . . the goods that me dad sold, so nobody took them . . . early in the morning. . . . [And] he'd come later on and set the stall out, and then I used to have to work . . . I'd be selling.' Her mother was there, too, and they stayed until about midnight. It was unpaid labour, although when Ada got a little older her mother made her 'take half a crown out every week', and this she put in a savings bank. When she left school at 14 she worked for a year on the market stall, and then went to serve in her father's fruit and fish shop. But after a few months she left to become an errand girl in a lace firm, although she still had to work in the parental shop on Saturdays.[58]

This use of child labour to help out at busy times was a common aspect of market trading. In London in 1902 it was noted that large numbers of children helped their parents who were costermongers and street traders, especially on Saturdays. One 10-year-old from Chaucer Board School for Boys in Southwark sold watercress with his parents from a coster's barrow from 6 p.m. to 8.30 p.m. on weekdays and from noon to midnight on Saturdays. Another 13-year-old sold flowers with his parents from 5 p.m. to 9 p.m. in the week and all day on Saturday, as well as on part of Sunday.[59] In 1903 the Employment of Children Act forbade the employment of all children between 9 p.m. and 6 a.m. and street selling by any child younger than 11. Unfortunately the Act's vagueness on certain points and the permissive nature of other aspects reduced its effectiveness. Implementation depended on local authorities, and even in 1913 only about two-fifths of them had produced by-laws to cover street trading.[60]

On the eve of the First World War there were signs that market halls, like the open markets and fairs before them, were coming under pressure from the diversity of fixed shops, including multiple chains, department stores and co-operative businesses, as well as independent shopkeepers. The growth of suburbs meant that residents were less inclined to make purchases in central town markets. Instead they patronised local shops, although here transport facilities could play an important role. At Accrington the success of the market hall was partly attributed to the fact that a municipal tramway linked the town to the surrounding countryside. Oldham, too, was connected to towns in the surrounding area by trams and it was to 'keep people in those towns coming to Oldham that the town built a new market hall in 1906'.[61] But to the traders the halls became less attractive locations for their businesses, especially as local authorities lost interest in market improvement, and in some cases they were closed. The market in Maidstone went out of business in 1890, while 'in Glasgow at about the same time the public Bazaar Market was closed to retail trading because the "great extension of Glasgow in every direction . . . and . . . its equally plentiful supply of shops of all kinds . . . seem to supersede the usefulness of the Bazaar as a general retail market".'[62] At Exeter the fact that door-to-door selling had become endemic in the town was put forward as the reason for its two market halls being in decline. In some places the issue of street trading became a topic of heated debate and political dispute, especially in smaller towns or cities like Exeter which were experiencing relative economic decline.[63] It is to the role of the travelling salesman that we must now turn.

ITINERANT TRADERS

For centuries pedlars and hawkers had played an important part in the nation's retail system, supplying foodstuffs and some consumer goods to townspeople, and a range of mostly non-perishable products to country people. They offered a useful service to customers not merely by bringing goods to the door but by breaking down bulk items into small quantities – a few buttons, a length of ribbon, a sheet of pins – and they offered articles to poorer people at prices they could afford. At a time when shops were still relatively thin on the ground, they offered an alternative to the facilities offered by markets and fairs. They were important in London, too, where in the mid-eighteenth century it was said that only the comparatively well-to-do used shops, with the mass of the population buying what they needed from street sellers.[64] Contemporary prints show itinerant vendors displaying anything from oysters, fish, fruit, vegetables and milk to earthenware, cheap ballads, chapbooks and various metalware products. Matthew Boulton, whose firm in Birmingham manufactured steel buttons, buckles, watch-guards and much more besides, stressed to his London agent the importance he attached to this kind of petty trading:

> We think it of far more consequence to supply the People than the Nobility only; and though you speak contemptuously of Hawkers, Pedlars and those who supply *Petty Shops*, yet we must own that we think they will do more towards supporting a great Manufactory, than all the Lords in the Nation, and however lofty your notions may be, We assure you we have no objection against pulling off our Hats and thanking them 4 times a Year.[65]

Selling on the streets, as John Benson has noted, offered working people 'the opportunity of supporting a modest business on their own account. The great attraction of street selling was . . . that it needed neither specialised skill nor large amounts of capital, particularly if undertaken on a part-time basis.' Goods could be sold from a simple tray or basket, sometimes being offered as a disguised form of begging, or, more ambitiously, from barrows and pack horses, which could be hired.[66] Stock could be obtained with a loan or on a sub-contract basis, while in the case of producer-retailers, like gardeners, farmers and some craftsmen, it offered the opportunity to earn cash from goods they themselves supplied. Even in the early twentieth century there were those who, as at Corsley in Wiltshire, combined marketing activities with gardening or running a smallholding. They included women who would walk to Frome with a basket to sell produce from door to door, or more substantial dealers who collected butter, eggs, fruit and vegetables from local farmers and others, to whom they paid 'a little less than market price'. They then sold these to customers in Frome or Warminster.[67]

Street trading was also followed, perhaps on a temporary basis, by those who had lost a regular job or who suffered seasonal unemployment, or who were too old or too young to earn a living in any other way. Early in the eighteenth century Mary Risebrook, a young widow from Shadwell in London, sold butter and eggs in this way before she got employment winding silk for 'throwsters'. She then took up laundry work and child minding. 'She has left off one employment and taken up another in hopes to get a better livelihood', it was reported.[68]

A century and a half later Henry Mayhew met an Irish orange seller near Coldbathfields prison in London. She had turned to street vending when her husband, a labourer, became unemployed. She was trying to earn enough 'to keep a bit of life in us', while he looked after the children. 'We don't live, we starve,' she declared bitterly. 'We git a few 'taties, and sometimes a plaice. To-day I've not taken 3*d* . . . sir, and it's past three . . . I don't know what will become of us, if times don't turn.'[69] However, when Mayhew went to see her the next day, he found that her husband had obtained work some distance away and she had given up her street selling to search for lodgings nearer to the new place of employment.

Often the goods sold by hawkers differed according to the seasons. In the mid-nineteenth century a costermonger in London might begin the year selling fish and then in early summer he would switch to strawberries or raspberries. From those he turned to gooseberries and to cherries. Currants, plums, apples and pears followed. When these had ended, he would sell vegetables, until the fish season began again. Or perhaps he would vend vegetables or crockery in the morning and second-hand goods in the afternoon.[70] Anything was offered for sale which seemed likely to yield a profit.

According to Mayhew, the costermongers purchased their goods at the wholesale 'green' and fish markets and in many cases they would have regular rounds. These might extend from 2 to 10 miles. 'The longest are those which embrace a suburban part; the shortest are through streets thickly peopled by the poor, where to "work" a single street consumes, in some instances, an hour. There are also "chance" rounds. . . . The costermongers, moreover, diversify their labours by occasionally going on a country round, travelling on these excursions, in all directions, from thirty to ninety and even a hundred miles from the metropolis.'[71] It was a precarious way of life, affected by weather conditions, general employment levels and the incidence of epidemic disease. One London costermonger, John Babbington, was forced to take up country hawking by the cholera epidemic of the late 1840s. The fruit trade in London fell off sharply and in June he decided to try his luck outside the capital, selling tin cups, song sheets and a range of similar goods at fairs. In December he returned to London 'a richer man by many pounds than I left it'.[72]

Even at the end of the nineteenth century, when shops had become the mainstay of the retail system, costermongers played an important part in the life of London. It was one which had 'no parallel in any other city' in Britain. It was the task of the hawker in the metropolis 'to save his customers the trouble of going to market by taking the market to them'.[73]

In many of the growing suburbs, too, where shops were still in relatively short supply, itinerant traders made a significant contribution. In Exeter, for example, despite the complaints of shopkeepers and market traders about the competition they offered, the town authorities were reluctant to ban them, even in the 1880s. To do so 'would occasion the greatest possible inconvenience to a very large class of householders, because the city spreads a great way . . . so that a great deal of hawking must be done. . . . [A] certain class of householders, the lower middle class, are entirely supplied by people who come to the door', it was claimed.[74] At Wolverhampton in 1910, when a gardener obtained a cottage and 2 acres of land, he began immediately to deliver eggs and poultry for a friend on a part-time basis. This gave him a chance to sell his own produce, too, and by the end of the year he had built up a round of around thirty customers for his eggs, potatoes, poultry and vegetables. Other people sold milk from door to door.[75]

These trading opportunities were, however, more limited for those who had a country trade as pedlars and packmen, travelling on foot or with a horse and covered van. An inventory of the stock of Joseph Gipson, a Hampshire pedlar who died in February 1702/3, reveals a range of finery and lengths of cloth designed to appeal to female customers. It included lace, ribbons, caps, silk hoods and a 'parcel of Small wares'. The whole pack was valued at £60 12s, including £15 for 'Seven pieces of Lace' and £5 in cash.[76]

During the eighteenth century, however, a new kind of retailer came to the fore, the 'Scotch draper', who specialised in the sale of cheap mass-produced textiles. These itinerant traders 'travelled slowly and laboriously from town to town . . . conveying huge and weighty packs on their backs . . . stored with hosiery, drapery and other necessary articles'. The Scotch drapers were willing to sell on credit, collecting small weekly or monthly sums from regular customers, in addition to cash sales. According to Dorothy Davis, by the end of the century there were thousands of these drapers plying their trade across the country.[77] They purchased their goods from wholesalers or direct from the manufacturers, who used them as agents. Sometimes individual shopkeepers would combine wholesaling with their normal retail activities. Among them, in the early nineteenth century, was an anonymous 'Old Draper', who supplied cheap cotton lace and similar articles to hawkers and pedlars who came to his Bristol shop. But he was ambivalent about the trade, welcoming the business it brought him but concerned that at a time when he was trying to boost his shop's reputation, the appearance of these 'ragged and dirty' customers would suggest that he was carrying on 'the very lowest trade' only. He found a solution by opening up a back room for these humbler clients and requiring them to enter it through a private door.[78]

Even at the end of the nineteenth century the Polish immigrant Michael Marks was able to begin his business career as a pedlar in the countryside around Leeds, carrying on his back a pack of buttons, mending wool, pins, needles, tapes, tablecloths, woollen socks and stockings. His supplies came from the firm of I.J. Dewhirst Ltd of Leeds, wholesalers who regularly sold to pedlars. Dewhirst offered Michael Marks a loan of £5, which he used to purchase goods from the firm's warehouse. As he paid off the debt by instalments, he was allowed to make fresh purchases up to the same amount. In this way his business expanded until he was able to hire a Leeds market stall.[79]

James McGuffog was another hawker who prospered from humble beginnings. Robert Owen was apprenticed to him in 1781, by which time he was carrying on a substantial drapery business in Stamford, Lincolnshire. His customers included 'the nobility and principal families and farmers around Stamford'. According to Owen, his master had commenced life in Scotland with a capital of 2s 6d, which he laid out by purchasing goods to be hawked in a basket. Gradually he progressed from a basket to a pack and then to a horse and covered van to accommodate his stock. By then he had moved to Lincolnshire, selling to customers of 'the first respectability' in that county. It was they who persuaded him to open a draper's shop in Stamford 'for the sale of the best and finest articles of female wear, for which, for some time in his travelling capacity, he had become celebrated'.[80] When Owen began his apprenticeship, Mr McGuffog had already been established there some years and 'was beginning to be so independent that he made all his purchases with ready money and was becoming wealthy'.[81] Those who bought for cash, of course, could expect to get a better deal from the supplier.

Another well-to-do Scotch draper was a man named Aldridge, who travelled around Norfolk. He enjoyed the patronage of the Revd James Woodforde at Weston Longville, calling at the parsonage every ten weeks or so with a cart loaded with lace, linens, muslins, ribbons, kerchiefs and much more besides. On more than one occasion Woodforde not only purchased lengths of cloth for himself and his niece, who lived with him, but dress material for his maids and waistcoat pieces for the menservants. Aldridge called on Parson Woodforde for at least twenty years, and in March 1801 Woodforde noted that he had spent around £4 with him, including some cotton for a 'Morning Gown for myself', dress lengths for the two maids, waistcoat pieces for the three menservants and two 'coloured Handkerchiefs for my two Washerwomen'.[82] Relations between customer and vendor were evidently warm, for Aldridge was given food and drink when he called. Even Jane Austen succumbed to the blandishments of the 'Overton Scotchman' in 1798, commenting drily that he had been 'kind enough to rid me of some of my money, in exchange for six shifts and four pairs of stockings'.[83]

But during the nineteenth century, as shops became more numerous in villages and market towns, and as transport facilities improved, especially after the coming of the railways, so the role of pedlars and hawkers in the countryside diminished, except in the most remote districts or for specialised products. Some hawkers sold fish, for example, for which regular supplies were much restricted in the countryside. Wallace Arter, from Bishopsbourne in Kent, remembered 'an old lady from Canterbury named Olive . . . who used to push an old pram loaded up with fish – not fresh fish, only kippers and bloaters – call at every house, pass on all the scandal, have a cup of tea, possibly sell a couple of bloaters and push on back'.[84]

However, if from the mid-nineteenth century the importance of itinerant traders diminished in the countryside, that did not mean their overall numbers declined during the Victorian and Edwardian eras – quite the contrary. Although precise figures are difficult to compute, because of the part-time and elusive nature of much of the trade, the population censuses suggest that the basic core of full-time street salesmen in England and Wales more than doubled between 1851 and 1911, rising from 25,747 at the earlier date to 69,347 at the later. They also rose in comparison with the rest of the population. As John Benson notes, in 1851 'there was one such trader to 696 other people; in 1911, one to 520'.[85] Furthermore, in 1851 almost half of them were located in three urbanised areas – Lancashire, the West Riding of Yorkshire and London. Lancashire alone, with 5,707 male and female hawkers and pedlars, had 22.2 per cent of the total.[86] London, with 3,723, had 14.4 per cent, but that is almost certainly a gross underestimate. Henry Mayhew at around this same date estimated there were about 40,000 men, women and children selling on the capital's streets, 30,000 of them employed as costermongers, 4,000 as street vendors of 'eatables and drinkables', and 5,000 offering stationery, books, papers, engravings, crockery, textiles and other manufactured goods.[87] There were, in addition, 2,000 street sellers of 'green stuff', such as watercress and groundsel. This trade yielded very poor returns and was generally taken up by the very young or the very old, who could earn a living in no other way.[88]

With the increase in the number of shops, however, the activities of these itinerant traders aroused the hostility of established retailers, who argued that by moving from place to place such men and women avoided paying rates and taxes and were consequently able to undercut settled tradesmen. 'The Shopkeeper has the Milk where the Pedlar has the Cream; the Shopkeeper has the Gleanings where the Pedlar has the Harvest', wrote one disgruntled pamphleteer as early as 1730.[89]

Half a century later retailers in the parish of St Botolph in London complained of the large numbers of 'disorderly Persons' who were 'Hawking, Buying and Selling Old Cloaths' in the area. Among them were 'Theives (sic) and Vagabonds who found a ready Sale for their Stolen Goods'. They did 'great Damage and injury' to reputable tradesmen 'and fair Dealers' who were paying 'large Rents and Taxes for their Houses and Premises'.[90]

In June 1785 shopkeepers in Kent summarised the retailers' general grievances when they told the House of Commons that the itinerant salesmen (and women) in their county were harming legitimate businesses by taking ready cash at a time when coinage was in short supply. In addition, they contributed 'nothing to the numerous Parochial Assessments, while the Petitioners are subject to every change, by Reason of their Residence, are obliged to give long Credit in their Dealings, and are frequently subject to great Losses'. Particularly damaging was Kent's proximity to France, since this allowed the hawkers to sell 'contraband and smuggled Goods'. They likewise imposed on the 'inexperienced Part of the Public damaged *English* Goods, which they pretend be . . . cheap Bargains to the Purchasers'. They pressed for legislation to 'restrain such Description of Persons from vending Goods'.[91]

To meet some of the concerns of the shopkeepers (but also to raise revenue), the government had in the late 1690s imposed a system of licensing on itinerant traders.[92] This required hawkers and pedlars to pay £4 apiece for a licence, plus a similar amount per head for any pack animals they might use in connection with their trade. But there were accusations that the regulations were widely flouted and in any case those selling either fresh food or goods made by themselves were explicitly exempted from the licensing scheme. In 1785, under pressure to raise additional tax revenue, William Pitt, the prime minister and chancellor of the exchequer, introduced a duty on retail shops to be imposed on all shop premises with a rental value of £5 per annum or more. The imposition caused an immediate outcry from retailers and partly to placate them – but also to discourage smuggling – Pitt proposed to end the system of licensing for pedlars and hawkers.[93] This would have abolished their right to trade.

Most retailers welcomed the proposed ban but it caused dismay not only among the pedlars themselves, whose livelihoods were about to be snatched away, but among some of the country's manufacturers. Textile producers protested that such a move would cause them great difficulties. The Manchester manufacturers, for example, argued that they derived 'very great Advantage' from the 'considerable' quantity of goods purchased by these travelling salesmen. They went 'from House to House in country villages and Districts, remote from Towns where Shopkeepers reside', and by that means 'great Quantities of *British* Manufactures are sold, which otherwise would not be disposed of'. If the prohibition were applied, cloth producers would be badly affected and 'great Numbers of industrious Families . . . thrown out of Employ'.[94]

Others joined in the campaign. The manufacturers and wholesale merchants of Kendal, Westmorland, pointed out that not only did the hawkers and pedlars widen the market for manufactured articles, but they sold many goods on credit, and were themselves in debt to the manufacturers and wholesalers. If this form of dealing were outlawed, they would be unable to collect the money due to them and in consequence would be unable to reimburse their own creditors. Both groups would be losers thereby. One petition claimed that the 'itinerants' were owed £40,000 by labouring families around Halifax alone.[95] In a heated debate in the House of Commons, one MP even claimed that 'a more fatal stab could not be given to the internal commerce and trade of the kingdom, than by abolishing so useful a body of men as the hawkers and pedlars'.[96]

Under this pressure, and faced with petitions sent in by the pedlars, hawkers and Scotch drapers themselves, Pitt relented. The itinerants would be allowed to carry on but would have to pay a licence fee double the existing rate. In future a dealer on foot would be charged £8 a year instead of the current £4 and he or she would have to pay £8 per annum for each horse or other animal employed in carrying on the trade. Hawkers could not sell within 2 miles of any city or market town except on market or fair days, under a penalty of £10. Similar fines were imposed on those travelling without a licence or who were unable to produce one when required. However, those selling fresh food or goods of their own manufacture were, as before, exempted from the licence duty.[97]

If this move satisfied the manufacturing interest, it was regarded by many shopkeepers as a 'betrayal' of a promise to remove an unpopular source of competition. As the Kent retailers angrily noted, they had 'hitherto forborne to represent their Uneasiness' in respect of the shop tax because they believed the licensing system for hawkers and pedlars was to be abolished. But now that was no longer the case.[98] In some areas, as in Suffolk, retailers vainly sought to persuade magistrates to prohibit pedlars and hawkers from plying their trade within a county.[99]

After four years of opposition from shopkeepers, particularly in London, the unpopular shop tax was repealed and in that same year the hawkers' and pedlars' legislation was amended too. From 1789 licences reverted to their pre-1785 level of £4 for a man or woman travelling on foot and a further £4 a year for each animal used in the business. As before, the duty had to be paid when the licence was taken out and penalties of £10 continued to be imposed on those who traded without a licence or who were unable to produce one when required to do so. For forging a licence the penalty was £100, and in cases where one was lent, each party to the transaction forfeited £40, with the lender losing his licence as well.[100] The hawker or pedlar was unable to sell within the immediate environs of any city or town, other than one in which he or she was a resident, except on market or fair days. This latter restriction was, however, abolished in 1795 because it had been 'found inconvenient to the Manufacturers in general, and also detrimental to the Revenue'.[101] To ensure that penalties could be recovered from offending sellers it was now possible for magistrates to distrain on a trader's goods in order to secure the relevant sum.

Over the years the licensing arrangements were further modified. By 1871 pedlars carrying goods on their back were required to pay 5s only for a licence, this being issued by the police in the area where they intended to trade. If they moved to another district an additional 6d had to be paid. A decade later this provision for extra police endorsements on the licence was removed.[102] In 1888 the licence fee for dealers who normally travelled with a horse and van or pack animal was reduced to £2 for the vendor and £2 per head for his animals.[103]

Meanwhile, as these amendments to the licensing scheme were being implemented, a growing number of towns promoted their own Improvement Acts, which included in them a clause allowing hawking to be restricted within their borders. Sometimes, as at seaside resorts, where growing numbers of street vendors sought to target holidaymakers, the aim was to protect the resort's reputation. At Weston-super-Mare in the 1880s a desire to eliminate the 'undesirable fairground atmosphere' created by the multiplicity of dealers led to their activities on the foreshore being regulated. The move gave rise to loud protests from the vendors themselves, but the town authorities were unmoved, explaining the action had been taken to protect their recent investment in a seafront promenade: 'the noise and annoyance on the foreshore had become intolerable'.[104] Restrictions were similarly imposed at Torquay, with tolls exacted on hawkers on each day of the week on which they plied their trade. But this failed to satisfy the shopkeepers, who thought that all hawking should be banned. The hawkers themselves naturally resented having to pay any toll.[105]

Elsewhere restraints were imposed as a result of pressure from shopkeepers or market stallholders, angry at the competition the 'itinerants' represented. At Weymouth, for example, stallkeepers who paid 1s 3d for a day's trading in the market complained that hawkers could sell the same goods throughout the town by paying 9d a day toll only.[106] Indeed, in some places, including Bath, hawkers were allowed to ply their trade without having to meet any charge.

The regulatory system was, therefore, extremely patchy in the way it operated and in the early 1890s an official report summed up the dilemma faced by town authorities:

The question whether hawking should be permitted without restriction, or permitted under licence, or absolutely prohibited, is a burning one in a large number of market towns. . . . On the other hand, it has been strongly urged upon us that the hawkers or costermongers supply food to the poorest persons and that they should be encouraged, and that the powers of Local Authorities should be limited so that they may be unable to check free trade in food.[107]

The report's own preferred option was the imposition of a licence fee to regulate the trade but with the down-payment required so small that it would not hamper the food distribution role of the street sellers.

Other, more sophisticated versions of itinerant dealing were also being developed, particularly in the second half of the nineteenth century, with the appearance of increasing numbers of tallymen and their more 'respectable' colleagues, the credit drapers.

Although the tally system of selling on credit was long established, as in the case of the Scotch drapers, during the Victorian and Edwardian years it took the form of traders going from door to door selling goods on an instalment plan from samples they carried with them. On the plus side, this enabled working-class families to acquire new clothes, furniture, ornaments and other goods which they would not otherwise have been able to afford. But critics argued that it encouraged householders to get into debt and to buy articles they did not really need. The womenfolk were thought to be particularly susceptible to the tallymen's blandishments. Subtle flattery and sexual innuendo were part of the successful salesman's routine.[108]

At Middlesbrough Lady Bell complained of the way the tallymen came round to the doors of workmen's houses offering 'all kinds of wares on the hire system . . . a mangle, a thimble, an umbrella, a china dog, a writing-case, a cupboard, a piano, a gramophone – I have known of all these things being bought'. They usually called when husbands were at work and the women would enter into agreements which they could not afford. Sometimes, too, a wife in need of cash would purchase an article on the hire system and then pawn it. That gave her a small lump sum, but if she subsequently missed a week's payment, both the purchase and the weekly deposits paid were forfeited. The position was further complicated if the purchase had been pawned and the woman was unable to redeem it.[109] This could lead to the tallyman seeking to recover his debt through the county court, a move which might, if the court found in his favour, eventually lead to the debtor's imprisonment. Tom Race of Leeds was repeatedly brought before the county court for debts his wife had contracted with a tallyman and he expressed outrage at the way in which such traders were allowed to operate. He considered packmen to be 'the curse of this West Riding District'.[110]

Credit drapers were anxious to distance themselves from the unsavoury reputation of the tallymen, even though their role was very similar. Many of them owned shops, warehouses and factories and employed, as salesmen, a number of assistants and travellers. They claimed that they took great care in assessing the financial resources of customers, so that large debts were not allowed to mount up.[111] Many joined trade associations to press their case for official recognition and to enable them, if necessary, to recover debts without resort to the court system. But most credit drapers were anxious to stress that their trade was not only highly respectable but exerted a democratising influence on market relations. In 1894 a Lancaster tallyman proudly compared 'his trade's extension of credit facilities to the working-class consumer with John Bright's successful campaign to expand the parliamentary franchise from men of property to working men'.[112]

Tallymen and credit drapers were very special kinds of travelling salesmen. They dealt mainly in clothing and consumer durables and made regular weekly or fortnightly visits to customers to collect instalments of cash and perhaps to take new orders. Their relatively discreet role differed markedly from that of more traditional street vendors who patrolled the highways and byways loudly calling out to advertise their wares. At Bolton at the end of the nineteenth century Alice Foley remembered the colourful assortment of regular traders who visited her street. There was the 'fly-catcher man' who wore a tall hat with a broad sticky band, black with captive flies, and an old lady known as 'Owd Sally', who pushed a pram from which she earned a scanty living selling watercress, radishes and lettuce. She wore 'a poke bonnet, long black cloak, and a man's heavy boots. . . . We also had a pale stuttering boy who hawked muffins from door to door, whilst on wintry nights the hot-pea man came along, swinging his bell and inviting custom for his mushy-green peas, giving off a savoury smell on the chilly air.'[113]

In the impoverished districts of the larger towns and cities children worked on the streets selling newspapers, matches, and a range of other low-value goods. At the end of the nineteenth century efforts were made to limit the hours during which they could work and fixing a minimum employment age for those selling on the streets. However, many towns were slow to enforce the provisions, partly for fear of incurring expenditure by employing staff to implement the regulations.[114] Jack Brenner began his street-trading career in early twentieth-century London as a teenager, selling cheap wallets and matchbox cases. He summarised his motives and those of many of these youngsters: 'I didn't care where I went as long as I made a profit.'[115]

In the late Victorian years some shopkeepers themselves became involved in mobile selling, sending out carts of provisions to meet the needs of country people. In Swaledale Maggie Chapman's family took advantage of the delivery service offered by Mr Gill, the Askrigg grocer. Once a month, on a Monday, Mr Gill went round the farms with a pack on his back full of 'vests and knickers and underwear, and he took his orders then for . . . groceries . . . and then his cart came . . . Wednesday, wi' t'stuff on. He used to come for orders with a blooming old push-bike, that wasn't hardly fit to ride.'[116] Another commentator reported that in the south Midlands, Cornwall and Devon butchers' carts went round the villages at least once a week on a Saturday: 'It is surprising', he wrote, 'to find to what distance tradesmen's carts will travel for the sake of the labourers' custom.'[117] Broughs of Newcastle upon Tyne adopted a different approach. They dispatched groceries to families in the nearby mining villages by way of carriers' carts, and relied on the carriers to collect the payments due and to bring in fresh orders. For this they paid the carriers a commission of 1s per cwt on the goods delivered, 1d per order brought in, and 3d in the £ on all cash collected.[118] Later the firm employed its own travellers to handle the trade with more distant customers, before opening branches in some of the larger communities.

Chapter 2

SETTING UP SHOP

In almost all country towns at that time, every one had his own peculiar kind of connexion. . . . Therefore, a man commencing business in the country, unless he had lived in one town a number of years as assistant, and had made a connexion or succeeded to some old-established trade, or became a partner in a house, did not stand a very good chance . . . unless he went to very great lengths to make himself known . . . connected with which attempts there was always thought to be something discreditable.

Reminiscences of an Old Draper (London, 1876), pp. 190–2, on shopkeeping in the first half of the nineteenth century.

TRAINING AND BACKGROUND

Already at the beginning of the eighteenth century shops were established not only in towns but in many villages as well. During the course of the following decades their numbers increased, partly in response to the demand created by a rising population, as well as by greater industrialisation and growing consumer wealth among certain sectors of society. Prosperous county towns like Chester and Worcester offered a range of luxury goods to the well-to-do. Chester, for example, had more wine merchants, drapers, furniture dealers and booksellers than any other Cheshire town, at least up to the 1830s.[1]

But small communities had their shops as well. In the 1780s returns in connection with the 1785 Shop Tax (imposed on premises with an annual rental value of £5 or more) show that out of sixty-four places in Cheshire with shops, about half had just a single retail outlet, and a further dozen or so had merely two. This excludes those selling bread, meal, flour and bran only, and those whose premises were rented at less than £5 per annum, since both categories were exempted from the tax.[2] Similarly in Suffolk, where in addition to the three boroughs of Bury St Edmunds, Ipswich and Sudbury, 137 villages and market towns had shops in 1788–9, or between one in three and one in four of the total, with just sixty-four of them having a single outlet. Some of the parishes were extremely small, like Thwaite, which had 129 residents at the time of the first census of population in 1801, and Elvedon, with 134 residents at that date. In all, 24 Suffolk parishes and townships which had shops in 1788–9 had populations below 300 people in 1801.[3]

It is likely that the businesses set up in the smallest communities were established by people without any special retail training, merely as a way of earning extra cash or of achieving a precarious independence away from the drudgery of life in a factory or workshop. Sometimes such shopkeepers would have more than one occupation, so that in the early eighteenth century Walter Collett, a London saddler, also ran a potter's and chandler's (that is, a small grocer's shop) off Drury Lane.[4] Others, like the Hampshire shopkeeper Samuel Brown, who died in 1742, carried out smallholding as well – something which a number of country tradesmen did.[5] Again, in the late 1820s Robert Sharp, a village schoolmaster at South Cave in Yorkshire, opened a general store to be run by his wife, although he himself lent a hand from time to time, not very successfully. 'Misfortunes attend me,' he wrote ruefully on one occasion: 'last week I made a mistake and mixed Brimstone amongst Starch, from which I did not escape very easily. This day the Oatmeal pot fell down when I was in the Shop, and who was blamed for it but unfortunate me.'[6]

In the final years of the nineteenth century a few retailers took on paid 'official' posts, as at Ermington in Devon, where a local shopkeeper also served as clerk to the school board. However, it was noted he made little effort to enforce attendance by the children in case that alienated some of his customers.[7] Elsewhere the creation of a national postal service required 'permanent bases throughout the country for its efficient operation' and this, too, assisted shopkeepers. Acting as a sub-postmaster or mistress provided a small additional income but the service also attracted the local population and encouraged them to make purchases other than stamps.[8]

Some families opened a shop as an insurance against future illness or unemployment. In the late 1820s William Lovett, a London cabinetmaker, and his wife decided to use their savings to start a business which Mrs Lovett would manage while her husband continued his work as a skilled craftsman. The aim was to provide 'for the old age and infirmities sooner or later almost sure to overtake us', as Lovett noted. They linked up with a pastry-cook and confectioner, who promised to supply them with goods on advantageous terms. Unfortunately the venture did not prosper. Lovett himself became ill and his wife gave birth to their second child. In these circumstances they decided to give it up, 'but not before we had exhausted all our own little means, and had involved ourselves in debt'.[9]

As John Benson has commented, the pressures and desires which 'drove the destitute and casually employed to sell on the streets encouraged their better-off neighbours to open . . . small corner shops'.[10] In Bolton Alice Foley remembered the numerous tiny, cramped general stores 'usually kept by disabled miners and widows. . . . Mother shopped at a higgledy-piggledy place kept by one of her old friends named Kitty. Neither mother nor Kitty could read or write, but they had their own symbols for reckoning up the score which later was chalked up on the door leading into the living-room.'[11]

However, those seeking to run more prestigious or more specialised businesses, or who were producer-retailers, like bakers, tailors, jewellers and watchmakers, would normally serve an apprenticeship. Once they had opened their shop they might rely on untrained family members and even domestic servants to help behind the counter or in other ways, as William Stout did in early eighteenth-century Lancaster. Both Alice Allured and Charlotte Hill, two maids employed by a Ramsey grocer, Joseph Gibbs, in the 1830s, assisted in the shop on occasion. They were especially in demand on market days and on Saturday evenings.[12]

In the 1720s Daniel Defoe stressed the importance of wives playing a part in their husbands' business because if they did not understand the running of it they were likely to be cheated should they be widowed. They would find it 'difficult to recover their husband's debts' or 'to get a good price' for the goodwill of the business, and in consequence were 'often reduced to beggary'.[13] A number of women were clearly aware of this danger, and in their advertisements would even state that they had taken over from a late husband. They included Ann Wood, who inherited a successful sports shop from her husband in Lewes high street during the 1830s. When she advertised herself as a 'Rifle and Pistol Maker', she was careful to mention that she was the widow of the 'Late Joseph Wood'.[14] Presumably she had kept on her husband's workmen and was merely managing the business.

Some wives proved shrewd entrepreneurs. Hannah Morton, born in Derbyshire in 1806, came to Hastings in Sussex with her husband to open a china and glass shop. By 1851 she was running the business as a widow and had three children, aged 2, 5 and 15. Under her direction the enterprise prospered and she moved to larger premises before setting up branches in the area, including one at St Leonards, which was run by her widowed daughter. Mrs Morton retired in 1877 and lived above her shop in the main street in Hastings until her death a decade later.[15]

But for those who needed training and experience – as well as capital – before launching off on their own account, an apprenticeship offered the first step on the ladder. This involved serving a fixed term (usually six or seven years) with a master or, more rarely, a mistress. It meant living in the employer's house or in accommodation provided by him, with board, washing and sometimes a little pocket money supplied. It was customary for the apprentice's family to pay a premium, which could be a considerable sum in the case of the most prestigious trades or of masters with a particularly good reputation. For grocers in London in the mid-eighteenth century premiums could range between £20 and £100, according to the class of business carried on, while for haberdashers it would probably be a more modest £10 to £50, and for mercers, who dealt in fine quality fabrics, it might reach from £50 to £400.[16]

In the provinces the sums involved were lower, with £50 more usual for those seeking to become mercers. The sons of families of more limited means might pay only £8 to £12 for an apprenticeship to a tailor, glover, butcher or baker in the eighteenth century.[17] In April 1754, when Richard Turner, Thomas's young brother, was bound to a Sussex shopkeeper at the age of only 11, the premium involved was £10. In return for this, Richard was to receive pocket money of 10s a year for the first year, rising by instalments to £3 10s a year, paid quarterly, in the seventh and final year. The master had the option, however, of asking for a further £1 4s from the Turner family when the seven years had expired. It was an option he did not exercise.[18]

Nonetheless, some critics voiced their doubts about the value of this kind of preparation. As early as 1747 R. Campbell in *The London Tradesman* condemned lengthy apprenticeships as a waste of money for most parents seeking to fit their offspring for a retail trade. Of grocery, for example, he declared dismissively that retailers merely purchased their goods from wholesalers and made their profit from the difference between the buying and selling price. Although the trade could be profitable, it needed 'no great Genius' to prepare for it. 'They have nothing to learn but the Market Price of Goods, and to be so cunning as not to sell for less than they buy.' Once the apprentice became a journeyman, or shop assistant, he must be able to write a good hand and understand 'common Arithmetic', as well as be 'alert at weighing out, to give his Master the Advantage of the Scales'. But this could be learned in a month or two. In fact, as he would be dealing 'in what are now esteemed the Necessaries of Life, he need only set up in a good Neighbourhood at a Distance from one of the same Trade, to have a tolerable Chance for a Livelihood'.[19]

Campbell made similar comments regarding the drapery and hosiery trades, concluding cynically that it might suit a retailer to take an apprentice for seven years because by so doing he would save himself the expense of a paid employee. But when the youth was out of his time, he had little to show for having spent 'the most precious Part of Life, in learning to weigh and measure out a Pound of Sugar or a Yard of Ribbon', and he had still to find the means to earn his living.[20]

In reality, of course, there were other skills to be learned which Campbell did not mention. These included how to dress a window, the best means of advertising, where and how to contact wholesalers, the merits and disadvantages of selling at a fixed price, and, most importantly, how to serve the customers. Where credit was extended to purchasers, it was important to learn how to assess their trustworthiness. Furthermore, until well into the nineteenth century, and to some extent later on, too, expertise in tea-blending and coffee roasting was central to the reputation of a specialist grocer. As Roger Scola points out, in large grocery shops assistants were trained in particular specialities, 'to the point where the young George Heywood, starting out in his own business in 1815, felt uneasy about having to perform a range of tasks in which he was unskilled: "I find it very strange breaking sugars being unaccustomed to it. I don't know which sorts will do best together".'[21]

But most shopkeepers, especially in the eighteenth and early nineteenth centuries, had few inhibitions about extending their business beyond the core trade. The records of James Bentley, a Manchester flour dealer, reveal that over the period 1799–1802 just 44 per cent of his outlay for stock was on flour and meal, while 18.5 per cent went on butter and cheese, 6.5 per cent on tea, and 11 per cent on sugar. The remaining 20 per cent or so was used to purchase such diverse goods as potatoes, bacon, salt, raisins, coffee, treacle, spices, rice, soap, starch, candles, tobacco and snuff.[22] The tea and sugar were bought from one or two major suppliers and much of his cheese came from a single local dealer, but for flour he traded with a number of sources outside Manchester. Butter, too, was purchased from several different traders.[23] Knowing with whom to trade and when were part of the expertise which a good apprenticeship could provide.

In the drapery and millinery trades apprentices had to learn the importance of keeping up with the latest fashions, with London and Paris the principal sources of information. Once established in their own businesses, they might visit London or even go to France to make their personal contacts. During the 1780s Susannah Towsey ran a little drapery and haberdashery shop in Chester, at first with her sister and then, after marriage, on her own account. The shop stocked goods chosen in London and both sisters made trips to the capital in the 1780s and 1790s. From 1800 the duty passed to a forewoman, a Miss Legge, and from 1806 she was replaced by 'a young lady from one of the first houses in Town'. In

1782 Susannah gave instructions to whoever was embarking on the long trip to the capital, written in very precise terms:

> If Wednesday be a fine day go up as soon as you well can to be out early. In the first place call at Steward Spavold and Smiths, where settle our accounts and look at modes of all sorts, at the white silk, the blue and green. Do not buy any. Ask if they have any black . . . Then go to Harris and Penny, pay their bill, and just look at what kind of fancy gloves they have to sell. Tell them that the gloves they called maid were most of them small girls, that they were too dear, that as their account was a small one it had . . . been almost forgot.[24]

Further detailed directions followed before the list concluded: 'Come home in a coach and write me as much as you will feel yourself inclined to do.'

Sometimes the salesmanship skills learned in one trade might be applied to another. John Maple, born in 1815, the son of a Sussex yeoman farmer, was apprenticed to a Surrey grocer and draper in 1829. His widowed mother agreed to pay a premium of £25, in five annual instalments, for his training. The apprenticeship was completed in 1835, when John was 20, and he then stayed on as a paid assistant for two more years before moving to London. By this time he had become aware of the growing importance of improvements in home furnishing and he decided to apply the lessons he had learned in the drapery trade to selling household goods. He looked around for a cabinetmaker in need of someone to help market his furniture and within a short time was engaged by a Lambeth manufacturer in a substantial way of business. There Maple met and befriended a fellow employee, James Cook, and in 1841 he and Cook went into partnership, opening a shop in Tottenham Court Road as wholesale and retail drapers, but also offering their services as 'Carpet Factors, Cabinet Manufacturers, Upholsterers and General Furnishing Warehousemen'. After a decade the partnership was dissolved and from then on John Maple traded under his own name. His trade card indicated the transition from what had begun as a purely warehousing and retailing venture to manufacturing.[25] On these foundations one of London's most prestigious furniture firms was to be constructed.

When an apprentice started up in business a well-respected master or mistress might be mentioned in promotional advertising as a way of attracting customers. In August 1785 William Horsfall, a young ironmonger, advertised in the *York Courant* 'to inform his Friends in particular, and the Public in general, that he had opened a SHOP in the Shambles Street, Barnsley'. He then listed the products he intended to stock but prefaced this by mentioning that he was 'Late Apprentice with Mr JOHN WILSON'. Wilson was clearly an established shopkeeper.[26]

At the end of the eighteenth century some apprenticeships were reduced to three or four years only, and that trend became more marked in the next hundred years. Hence when Robert Owen obtained a position with Mr James McGuffog, who ran a high-class drapery in Stamford, Lincolnshire, it was for three years only. During the first year he served without pay, in the second he received a salary of £8 and in the third £10, with board, lodging and washing provided throughout.[27] In practice, Owen stayed with the McGuffogs for four years before deciding to widen his experience by going to London. While in Stamford he became 'familiar with the finest fabrics of a great variety of manufactures'. Business was conducted in a leisurely fashion and he had plenty of opportunities to use his master's 'well selected library', since most of their commercial activities took place between 10 a.m. and 4 p.m. each day. He was to find conditions very different in London.

Robert Owen's period as a trainee with Mr McGuffog was a pleasant interlude. For many others it proved a drudgery, involving a good deal of heavy manual labour. The anonymous 'Old Draper', who was apprenticed to a Whitechapel draper at the age of 13½, after his father died, remembered that the apprentices and the young male assistants carried out all the rough work in the shop. When he arrived he found that he and a fellow apprentice were to sleep on truckle beds under the counter at one end of the store.

> We used to go in the young men's room to 'dress' after breakfast, not washing ourselves till various duties were performed. . . . I used to take down the shop shutters and put them up at night, beneath the weight of which I could scarcely stagger along, clean the brasses on which the name was engraved, and the lamp-glasses. I also cleaned the *outside* of the shop windows, the *inside* the young men used to clean.[28]

The shop had a policy of selling at fixed prices and did not allow any bargaining. This made it easier for inexperienced assistants when they were serving. But it was the long hours to be worked which the youngster found particularly testing. 'Ten o'clock at night was our ostensible hour for shutting up five days in the week; but there was often work to do after that time, which would last another hour or two. . . . On Saturday nights we shut up at twelve o'clock, and I have often been in the shop helping to straighten up till two or three o'clock on Sunday mornings.' Later his employer bought another business in Limehouse, and there they opened on Sunday mornings as well, from 8 a.m. until the church services began. During those hours they sold shirts, stockings and a range of other articles.[29]

In order to encourage sales, even the youngest members of staff were offered premiums (or commission) if they disposed of slow-moving stock. 'Young as I was, I soon became one of the recipients of weekly premium money, frequently taking from 12s to 15s per week, while there were many men twice my age who would, perhaps, take only 3s or 4s.' In those days, according to the 'Old Draper', good salesmen were spoken of by fellow members of the trade in terms of great respect. But in such a 'pushing and ticketing' establishment as this, customers 'were often bullied into buying goods they did not want'.[30]

The 'Old Draper' stayed on at this firm after his apprenticeship ended until the long hours began to affect his health, and he was advised by a doctor to rest. After a short break he took a post in a 'City house, where a superior trade was done, and the hours were fewer'.[31]

Herbert G. Wells, apprenticed around half a century later, in 1881, to Hyde's Drapery Emporium in Southsea, found conditions little better than those experienced by the 'Old Draper'. But unlike the latter he hated the routine of the shop and the 'tight-lipped little men with half his brain' who tried to tyrannise him.[32] The day began at 7 a.m., when, like most drapers' apprentices, he and his fellows went down to the shop to clean the windows, unwrap the goods and fixtures, and carry out the dusting. At 8 a.m. 'we raced upstairs to get first go at the wash basins, dressed for the day and at half-past eight partook of a bread and butter breakfast before descending again. Then came window dressing and dressing out the shop. . . . Then I had to see to the replenishing of the pin bowls and the smoothing out and stringing up of paper for small parcels.' He was also sent out on errands – something he welcomed – and so the day continued until at 8.30 p.m. the assistants were allowed to go upstairs for their supper of bread and butter, cheese and small beer. Lights out was at 10.30 p.m.

During his second year Herbert had to don a black morning coat with tails and begin to serve 'small and easy customers'. But he proved to have little aptitude for this and his days were punctuated with cries of 'Get on with it, Wells', 'Wells Forward' and 'Has anyone seen Wells?' His mother had apprenticed him for four years and had already paid £40 of the premium of £50 when during the second year he felt he could endure it no longer. He ran home, much to his mother's distress, for she had 'set her heart on giving [him] the good sound start in life which drapery alone could offer'. Eventually he was allowed to leave, his indentures were cancelled and he became a student assistant teacher at Midhurst Grammar School.[33]

In the late nineteenth century the apprenticeship system began to break down in retailing, especially in the grocery and drapery trades. New mass-production methods meant that, for example, grocers no longer had to learn to blend tea, since much of it was sold ready packaged. Other goods, such as biscuits, cocoa, oatmeal and the like were becoming standardised, and manufacturers and wholesalers showered shopkeepers with promotional posters and placards. 'There is now little apprenticing in London,' declared Mr Cushen, chairman of the Metropolitan Grocers' and Provision Dealers' Association in 1895. 'Both masters and men dislike the system. . . . There is the usual result that men do not know their work so well as they used to; but this is not a matter of such importance as it used to be, as a grocer's business now consists so largely in selling proprietary articles.' However, he claimed that even then 'the most successful men are those who are judges of tea, coffee, sugar, etc.'[34] Mr Panet, a former manager of a tea merchant's shop in the City of London, agreed that apprenticeship was dying out in the capital. 'It is not wanted. . . . Goods used to be delivered in bulk; they now nearly all come in packet form. Few grocers . . . thoroughly understand their business, and the blending . . . is done for them.'[35] Pride in the traditional grocer's skills nonetheless survived, and in the provinces in particular apprenticeship did continue, albeit on a reduced scale.

Similar developments took place in the drapery trade, with one suburban London linen draper claiming that formal apprenticeships were 'out of date'. He recruited his female trainees for three years but drew up no binding agreement:

> Then they can leave if they like & the employer can get rid of them if they do not suit. . . . The knowledge that the engagement is on these terms makes the assistants more careful of the employer's interests and increases their desire to learn quickly.[36]

This hard-headed approach to training was also adopted by the Oxford drapers F. Cape & Co., with apprenticeships for the girls reduced to two years and there being no requirement for them to live on the premises. So when Lizzie Cox was apprenticed on 1 April 1895 to learn 'the whole trade of Retail Drapery', the agreement was for two years with her parents paying a premium of £5. This would be returned at the end of the term if she went on 'satisfactorily'. However, if she lost time through illness or for any other reason that had to be made up at the end of the apprenticeship.[37] During the two years she was to receive no pay and was to serve the firm 'diligently & well'.

Once the training had been completed, whether by apprenticeship or by some less formal arrangement, many young drapers and haberdashers from the provinces were anxious to gain experience in London. Among them was William Whiteley, apprenticed in 1848 at the age of 17 to Harnew and Glover, the largest drapery shop in Wakefield. Whiteley resolved to make his future, and his fortune, in the capital after visiting it in 1851 for the Great Exhibition. When his indentures expired in 1855 he left the following day for the metropolis, where 'he set himself to master, patiently and systematically, every detail of the London drapery trade'. This he did with great success until he had saved enough to open his own haberdashery and fancy goods shop in Westbourne Grove in 1863. It was the beginning of a spectacularly successful retailing career.[38]

More than half a century earlier Robert Owen had obtained a situation with Messrs Flint & Palmer, a large drapery on Old London Bridge. It was conducted on the basis of small profits for cash sales only, and unlike many Georgian shops it had a 'considerable number' of assistants of both sexes. Owen was paid £25 a year and was lodged and boarded on the premises. But he found the daily round very different from the relaxed atmosphere at Stamford, with its fixed routine and aristocratic clientele:

> The customers were of an inferior class – they were treated differently. Not much time was allowed for bargaining, a price being fixed for everything. . . . If any demur was made, or much hesitation, the article asked for was withdrawn, and, as the shop was generally full from morning till late in the evening, another customer was attended to.

The duties of the assistants were onerous. They had to be up, breakfasted and dressed to receive customers in the shop at 8 a.m. and in those days, commented Owen, dressing was 'no slight affair':

> Boy as I was . . . I had to wait my turn for the hairdresser to powder and pomatum and curl my hair, for I had two large curls on each side, and a stiff pigtail, and until all this was very nicely and systematically done, no one could think of appearing before a customer. Between eight and nine the shop began to fill with purchasers, and their numbers increased until it was crowded to excess.

This continued until late in the evening, usually until 10 or 10.30 p.m. during the earlier months of the year. Dinner and tea had to be hastily gulped down. 'The only regular meals at this season were our breakfasts, except on

Sundays, on which days a good dinner was always provided.' When the customers had left, the stock had to be put in order, since there was 'no time or space to put anything right . . . during the day. This was a work to be performed with closed doors after the customers had been shut out . . . and it was often two o'clock in the morning before the goods in the shop had been . . . replaced to be ready for the next day's similar proceedings.'[39]

After the spring season the pressure of business eased, and the assistants were able to get to bed between 11 p.m. and midnight. But Owen found the life exhausting and when, after a few months, he received an offer from a Manchester wholesale and retail draper to work for him, he accepted. It also meant an increase in pay to £40 a year, as well as board, lodging and laundry. The customers were generally upper middle class, and living conditions were far more comfortable than at Flint & Palmer's.[40]

For many young shop assistants, once they had gained experience and perhaps amassed some savings, the next step was to go into business on their own account. For this three things were necessary – capital, access to credit and good local connections. The first two requirements will be discussed later in the chapter, but for good long-term prospects it was essential to have the right contacts, too. As Marmaduke Strother commented gloomily at the end of his apprenticeship to a Hull draper, 'I can never think of Settling here upon a new Foundation, as there are already added to the former number of Drapers 4 young Men of my Acquaintance who are now about Settling, & they have been born here and amongst their Friends & Relations will overstock the Trade so as to leave but little for one that is an Alien. . . . There are now 8 Drapers & the Addition of 4 More will greatly diminish the Trade in the hands of individuals.'[41]

Some youngsters had a family already in trade and could join the business or, as with Thomas Turner at East Hoathly, they could set up near a family enterprise. The two shops could then work together when buying stock or perhaps help out during a staff shortage. Moses Turner, who worked for his widowed mother, would occasionally come to East Hoathly to help his brother if Thomas had to be away from his shop.[42]

Sometimes strong religious links could be an advantage. At Long Crendon in Buckinghamshire, where there were tensions between Anglicans and Nonconformists, it was noted that there were 'Church shops and Chapel shops, and people buying groceries would go out of their way to patronise one from their own religion'.[43] Likewise at Marlborough in Wiltshire the leading London grocery wholesalers James Budgett & Son were optimistic about the prospects of a potential new customer named W. Jeremy, noting that he and his wife possessed 'a little money' and also had strong

Nonconformist convictions. At Marlborough there was 'a good opening' for him since there was 'no dissenter grocer' and the local dissenters had 'promised to rally around' to make the business a success.[44]

On occasion an employee followed his master or mistress when the latter retired from business and thereby enjoyed the goodwill that this continuity of service made possible. Joseph Gibbs had been employed as 'foreman' by Mrs Baines, a Ramsey grocer and draper, for about four or five years when he bought the business in 1832, on her retirement. Gibbs had ended his apprenticeship in 1813 and had served as a journeyman for about nineteen years before taking on the ownership of a shop. Unfortunately his lack of accounting skills and his heavy borrowing led to bankruptcy within little more than two years.[45]

In some corporate towns, especially during the eighteenth century, restrictions on those wishing to trade could be enforced by the local guild or municipal authorities. This applied in York, where by long tradition those wishing to follow a trade or to keep a shop had to be freemen of the city. That status could be gained by patrimony, apprenticeship, official exemption (for example, by having served in the military) or by purchase. A fee of at least £25 was required for this last option. For small retailers such an outlay was out of the question, and even some of the more affluent ignored the restriction, thereby risking prosecution. So blatant did this disregard for the rules become in York that in November 1775 the Corporation appointed a committee to investigate the situation and recommend what action should be taken. The Corporation's House Book showed that of the 239 'offenders' identified, 87 agreed to purchase their freedom. They included substantial retailers like the bookseller and stationer Robert Spence, who in 1797 reportedly had an annual income of £350, and the hosier Mark Anthony Robinson, whose income in 1797 was put at £150 a year. Robinson also let lodgings, like a number of other shopkeepers in the city.[46]

Out of the 239 men and women listed, 164 were in the distributive trades. They included coal dealers, ale sellers and meal vendors as well as shopkeepers. It is clear from some of the evidence that many of these operated on a very small scale. Thus George Thompson, a 'papist', was employed as a 'menial servant' by a Mr Fermer on the outskirts of York. He was charged with running a grocer's shop, 'the Door of which . . . opened into an Entry'. This discreet location did not protect him, and Thompson agreed to give up the business, leaving his wife 'to sell all his goods on Hand'. But he seems to have thought better of the decision, for in 1777 he was admitted a freeman of the city and by 1784 was licensed as a tea dealer. The excise list shows his tea stocks were very modest.[47]

More unfortunate was Thomas Bowen, who had been in business as a grocer. He was prosecuted and suffered a judgment by default. This led to his imprisonment for debt and he only obtained his discharge by surrendering his effects 'under the Act for the Relief of Debtors'. But it meant giving up his shop.[48]

At the bottom of the economic scale were shopkeepers and itinerant traders deemed by the committee to be too poor to pay the admission fee to become freemen. They were divided into two groups. One section was allowed to continue trading by paying £1 to the Corporation. The other, the very poorest, paid only 10s. Both groups were permitted to stay in business from year to year, with the proviso that if their situation improved they might be called upon to become freemen in the normal way. Just 31 tradesmen fell into the very poorest category. They included 10 of the 17 hucksters (or petty shopkeepers) identified as trading illicitly, as well as Thomas Denton, a bookseller, John Carter, a butter seller, and James Woof, a tailor. On a gender basis, 7 of the poorest 31 traders were women, at least two of them widows for whom running a small shop was doubtless one way of earning a living.

These corporate rights continued in York and in some other towns until the mid-1830s but enforcement of the powers was very spasmodically applied.

Some shops were established by manufacturers to sell their goods direct to the public. Among them was the leading pottery firm of Josiah Wedgwood. In his anxiety to promote sales in London, Wedgwood opened a warehouse there in 1765 and then moved to larger, more fashionable, showrooms in Newport Street, St Martin's. There he displayed not only the creamware table services for which he was famous but a new range of 'ornamental wares, including shelves of handsome "antique" vases'.[49] Early in 1772 two reliable Wedgwood employees were dispatched to open a similar shop in Dublin, while his partner, Bentley, hired premises for the same purpose in Bath. Bentley persuaded his sister-in-law Ann Ward and her husband to give up their haberdashery business in Holborn to manage the Bath enterprise. The shop opened in September 1772 but sales proved disappointing, largely because of the out of the way location of the premises. After two years a new site was obtained in fashionable Milsom Street, where Ann Ward was able to report an increase in custom. But fresh stock was needed, too, since existing vases had been 'seen so often & ye best picked and . . . People don't like what is Left!' Affluent customers were always on the look out for novelties.[50]

It was, however, on his London showrooms that Wedgwood lavished most attention. By a 'judicious use of shows and exhibitions' he kept up sales and soon took new premises at Portland House, Soho. These were rapidly thronged by members of high society anxious to see his displays.[51] This success led other manufacturers to follow his example, such as the pottery manufacturers Spode and Minton, who displayed their wares in much the same way.

In the nineteenth century some of the men's mass-tailoring firms also followed a similar path. Isaac Moses took elaborate premises in Aldgate and employed 'inviters' at the entrance to induce people to come into the store.[52] During the 1880s the Leeds tailoring firm of Joseph Hepworth opened its own shops and started selling ready-made men's and boys' clothes direct to customers. By the First World War this firm and Blackburn's, another Leeds tailoring business, were integrating their retailing activities with their manufacturing concerns. In 1914 Hepworth's alone had 150 shops.[53]

Variations on this theme were the truck shops set up by mining and iron-making companies located in remote rural districts, to supply food and clothing to their workers in places where there were few private shops. But when coupled with a policy of 'long pay', they could become instruments for the exploitation of the employees, as well as undermining the business of any independent retailers who might set up. Until 1831 some firms even paid their workers in goods rather than in cash. When this became illegal under the Truck Act of that year, they developed an alternative strategy of paying the men at intervals of a month or longer, and pressurising any who sought advances during that time to lay out the sums allowed in the company shop. Men who failed to spend the money advanced in the shop were known as 'slopers' and the next occasion they wanted an advance they were likely to be refused. The result was that workers actually handled little coinage and because they were unable to obtain cash advances to spend elsewhere they purchased articles in the shop which they subsequently re-sold to settle bills with other tradesmen with whom they dealt. These traders would then sell the goods in their own business but would allow the workers less than they had had to pay at the company shop.[54]

In the early 1870s Mr Williams, a grocer at Ebbw Vale in South Wales, explained how the system operated. Sometimes the men brought flour to him, which he purchased at 2s a bushel below the company's price. 'I take tobacco from the men. For years when they were selling it for 1s 4d a quarter I used to give 1s, but I was so much over flooded with it that I was obliged to reduce the price to 11d. That would not do still, and I had to reduce it to 10d. . . . I invariably sold it for 1s ready money. I bought candles also at about 1½d a pound reduction. I buy the company's sugar at 4d that they used to sell at 6d.'[55] Another Ebbw Vale shopkeeper confirmed the prevalence of the system. 'Men come to my shop with goods and sell me their company's goods, candles, tobacco, bacon, cheese, butter, meat and lots of things. . . . They raise money in that way to pay their clubs and shoemaker's bills. . . . I believe this kind of business is done with every trade in Ebbw Vale, with tailors, shoemakers, greengrocers and everything. It is a great part of the business of the town.' For his part he was happy with the arrangement. 'It pays us very well.'[56]

But not all retailers were so content with a scheme that limited the amount of cash in circulation. In Aberdare the setting up of a truck system at the ironworks at the end of 1850 led to complaints from the existing tradespeople that it had caused a 'large diminution of business' for them.[57] To circumvent the truck legislation, employers with company shops sometimes set up a pay office separate from the truck shop but at the same time gave 'notice' to those who failed to deal in the shop 'that [they had] no further occasion for their services'.[58] Shop managers were encouraged to ensure the system was successful by being given commission on the profits to add to their basic salary.[59] Furthermore, as a former employee at the Blaenavon Company's shop admitted, there was 'not much of civility with regard to giving [the customers] a choice of goods. They would be told, "There it is, you can take it if you like, and if not you can leave it." We had not time to let them pick and choose. If they wanted bacon and there was none they would have to take cheese.'[60] However, in the final decades of the nineteenth century, as mining and other industrial communities became larger and as facilities improved, the truck system and its variants faded away.

For many shopworkers, meanwhile, their dream of owning their own business was destined never to be realised. This became increasingly true in the later Victorian years, as retail establishments grew larger and there was a growth in chain stores and co-operative societies. Many men and women simply lacked the capital and the entrepreneurial skills to set up on their own, or if they did so and the venture failed, they had then to seek employment elsewhere. That was true of Mr Wright, who in the mid-1890s was manager of a draper's shop at Harringay in London. He had been apprenticed in Exeter and had then gone to Bath for two years before moving to London. In the late 1870s he had taken a shop in Hampstead with his wife, who was a first-class dressmaker. Together they had worked the business up but when Mrs Wright died the dressmaking side of the enterprise fell away. Ultimately the shop was closed and Mr Wright had to seek work elsewhere. 'Today small shops are in an infinitely worse position than 20 years ago,' he declared gloomily. 'It is a saying that two fail & the third succeeds.'[61]

FINANCIAL ARRANGEMENTS AND BUSINESS CONTACTS

The amount of capital needed to set up and run a retail business varied according to the size of the enterprise and the quantity and quality of the merchandise to be traded. Some shopkeepers were owners of property and had the use of large capital sums; others had negligible assets. At the end of the nineteenth century Charles Booth described a small London shopkeeper of his acquaintance who rented premises for 3s 6d a week. His fixtures and fittings cost a mere £2 and comprised a 'wooden screen betwixt door and fire, two tables, a counter, small and large scales and weights, a good corner cupboard, and some odds and ends'. The stock cost around £1 16s or £1 17s a week, and the takings averaged about £2 15s per week. Most of the sales were in 'penn'orths and ha'porths' and the goods on offer were mainly purchased from large retail grocers who offered a wholesale service to their small brethren.[62] Nonetheless, despite the limited scale of the business, after a year £25 had been saved and put in the bank.

Already in the mid-eighteenth century it was estimated that at least £100 capital was needed to support almost any sort of retail establishment. Most shopkeepers required a good deal more, probably at least £500, while such genteel trades as that of draper needed at least £1,000. Anyone wishing to deal 'in a big way would have to double or treble these sums'.[63]

Nearly a century later Whittock, in a *Book of Trades* published in 1837, suggested that grocers could begin trading with a capital of £400 to £600, particularly if they sold for cash only. In haberdashery, where stock turnover was often slow, 'business could not be started with less than £400' and £800 was needed to begin 'on a tolerable scale'. An ironmonger, if he limited his stock to items of 'prime necessity', might start up with £400 to £500, but if he wished 'to serve builders and others, who take long credit' much more would be required.[64] In Whittock's view, while it was 'possible to begin business in most trades . . . with a capital of £400 to £600', to purchase 'a really good business as a going concern . . . involved access to £1,000 or more'.[65]

Nonetheless a number of men began with far less. Edward Weaver, a London shopkeeper, started up with £25 and Joseph Collins, a Brighton butcher, had just £50.[66] Even at the end of the nineteenth century Robert Roberts's father purchased a run-down shop in a poverty-stricken part of Salford for £40 – a sum which he borrowed from his sister.[67] Yet those who started with such limited funds were always vulnerable to a downturn in trade or a rash of bad debts, leading to bankruptcy. It was Mrs Roberts's hard work and shrewd common sense that enabled the family's corner shop to survive.

In amassing the cash needed to commence business, shopkeepers could rely on loans from family and friends, as Mr Roberts did, or they might depend upon an inheritance. In 1688 when William Stout set up shop in Lancaster he used funds he had inherited from his father to cover most of the amount needed. They came to £119 10s and he borrowed a further £10 from his sister, 'which I kept many years', and £12 from an acquaintance, which he was able to repay within twelve months. He rented a shop for £5 a year and early in 1688, when his apprenticeship ended, he and some neighbours rode to London to buy stock. He took with him £120, and when he reached the capital he went 'to such tradesmen as I was recommended to, and bought of sundry persons goods to the value of two hundred pounds or upwards and payed [sic] each of them about halfe ready money, as was then usual to do by any young man beginning [to] trade'.[68] The goods were dispatched by sea to Lancaster, while William returned as he had come. He broke the journey in Sheffield where he laid out about £20 in Sheffield and Birmingham metalware, presumably for the ironmongery side of his shop.

When Stout retired from business in 1728 he handed the store over to his nephew, who had been his apprentice. It included stock to the value of £370 and weights, scales, chests, boxes and 'other utensils' worth about £20, as well as the use of the shop, cellars and warehouse rent free. He also gave his nephew £32 in cash so he could go to Sheffield to make additional purchases, and he offered to help run the shop, too. Within months, however, the nephew's casual attitude to business led Stout to withdraw.[69]

Borrowing from friends or commercial contacts was another possibility. When Joseph Gibbs, the Ramsey draper and grocer, started up in 1832 he borrowed £500 from two business acquaintances, his own contribution amounting to a meagre £5. Over the course of the next two years he obtained occasional small loans from a Ramsey chemist, too, though these seem to have been promptly repaid, unlike his major borrowing. This, coupled with his need for trade credit and his lack of book-keeping skills, led to financial disaster within little more than two years. In 1726 Daniel Defoe had warned that a tradesman's books were 'his repeating clock . . . and upon his . . . fully acquainting himself with his books, depends . . . the comfort of his trade, if not the very trade itself'.[70] Gibbs took no such precautions. For example, although sales to credit customers were entered in a day book, he kept no record of cash sales. He also allowed the servants to take money from the till as and when they needed it for housekeeping purposes. According to one of them, this amounted to about £2 a week. 'We paid for everything as we had it at the time and I went to the Till for the money.'[71] No attempt seems to have been made to carry out stock-taking and when Gibbs's business failed his debts amounted to at least £800 or £900 and included money owed to commercial creditors as far apart as woollen manufacturers in Rochdale and Huddersfield, drapers in London and a tobacco merchant in London. In the event the confused state of the business and Gibbs's own pathetic attempts to prevaricate about his personal assets led to bankruptcy proceedings dragging on until the end of 1845, although the original fiat of bankruptcy had been issued on 28 November 1834. Two dividends were finally paid to the creditors in December 1845, amounting to 4s 1d in the £ and 2s 5d in the £, adding up to around a third of the total sum owing.[72]

In a number of cases, as with William Whiteley in 1863, shopkeepers started up only when they had saved enough to provide a firm financial foundation on which to begin trading. Other aspiring retailers took a junior partnership in someone else's enterprise. In July 1882 a high-class London outfitting and underclothing firm even advertised in *The Times* for a possible partner, to take charge of a country branch. 'If £2,000 is invested a partnership will be secured, or if £1,000 a liberal and progressive salary and percentage of profits given.'[73]

Less formal arrangements were made, too. Beverley Lemire has highlighted how in the eighteenth century the mutual support provided within the Anglo-Jewish community led to business premises being shared with newcomers, especially in London where rents were high. Sometimes the enterprises seemed oddly matched. Thus a Jewish dealer in clothes named Hannah Jacobs 'traded out of the house of a Mr Levi, a poulterer'. Elsewhere 'tenants . . . stored stock in the private homes or shops of other salesmen'.[74] At the end of the nineteenth century a variation on the theme was provided by Italian shop owners in South Wales. A number set up with funds provided by relatives and friends in Italy but in other instances retailers who were already established in Britain would open up branches and put compatriots in to manage them. They were run on a profit-sharing basis until the newcomers could begin on their own account.[75]

Once the initial capital had been acquired, however, arrangements had to be made to obtain stock. It was generally agreed that those able to buy for cash secured the best terms from suppliers. Thus one of the reasons why Peter Davenport Finney's grocery and confectionery shop in Manchester prospered in the 1750s, according to his brother, was his custom 'of buying for ready money'.[76]

The shoemaker and bookseller James Lackington, who began his shopkeeping career in 1775 with a small stock of leather and books valued at about £5, similarly attributed his subsequent success to the fact that from 1780 he refused to allow any credit to customers and made his own purchases with ready money.[77] He quickly decided to concentrate on bookselling and attracted new 'cash' customers by advertising. His trade grew rapidly until in 1791 he moved to a large building at the corner of Finsbury Square, London. This he grandly styled the 'Temple of the Muses', with an inscription over the door: 'Cheapest bookshop in the world'. According to his catalogue he stocked half a million volumes at any one time, ranged around the rooms and galleries.[78] On one side of the main showroom, Lackington also opened two rooms 'for such Ladies and Gentlemen as wish to enjoy a literary Lounge'. During his first year at the 'Temple of the Muses' he made a profit of £5,000, a huge sum for the early 1790s. In 1798 he retired with a large fortune to his country house in Devon, where he died in 1815.[79]

But most tradesmen relied on trade credit for their purchases, and those who overstretched themselves in this direction, as Joseph Gibbs and many others did, courted disaster. Daniel Defoe had warned of the dangers in 1726: 'He that takes too much credit is really in as much danger as he that gives too much . . . he must be exceedingly watchful. . . . If the people he trusts fail, or fail but of a punctual compliance with him, he can never support his own credit, unless by the caution I am now giving . . . to be very sure not to give so much credit as he takes.'[80]

To secure credit a shopkeeper had to be able to persuade his suppliers that he was a good commercial prospect. In the late nineteenth century, according to one former London draper, contact would be made with a wholesale house and the retailer would then 'place the particulars of his position before them. If the firm [was] satisfied they [became] his reference or "ref" house and when buying from other firms he would refer to this house.'[81]

The records of James Budgett & Son, a leading London grocery wholesaler first established in 1857, suggest that this cautious policy was followed. Their ledgers include comments from other wholesalers as to the credit-worthiness of potential clients, as well as details provided by commercial travellers, evidence from neighbours and (for a fee) details derived from nascent credit agencies and trade publications.[82] The amount of credit allowed was adjusted if customers proved slow payers and sometimes business was withdrawn altogether, with commercial travellers instructed not to call any more. A good moral character could prove an advantage. Of Joseph Sarjeant of Ramsey it was noted approvingly that he had been 'there 25 years, a Wesleyan Local Preacher . . . a *most* respectable man in appearance'.[83] Then there was E.C. Wright of Sudbury, a 'Quakeress & one of the nicest little customers on our Books, can pay Cash for everything'.[84]

Occasionally the comments were more grudging, as in the case of George E. Reynolds, a substantial grocer in Buckingham. In the early 1880s he employed one resident male assistant and an apprentice, as well as two young maids to look after himself, his wife and five children.[85] However, in 1880 the Budgett commercial traveller reported sourly that although 'the principal man there, he is going on the Buckingham style, drink, billiards & gambling, but at present I admit is a good payer'.[86] That was obviously the decisive factor, for Reynolds continued to be supplied with groceries, even though in August 1888 there was another unfavourable comment from the commercial traveller that Reynolds was attending 'all the races he can conveniently go to & plays nap with commercials at all times of the day'.

A firmer line was taken with Davy Crowe of Woodbridge, another long-term Budgett customer. He was normally allowed two months' credit but in 1904 he wrote to the firm apologising for the delay in settling his account: 'ready money has been very slow for a long time, but we are all hoping for an improvement. . . . I have a lot of good customers, but they keep me waiting, & I don't care to write to them as it would not be taken right.'[87] For a time Budgetts accepted this, but the slow settlement of bills continued and in February 1908 it was decided 'the account must be brought to one month's terms, *no* more two months'.

Crowe had obviously failed to heed Defoe's strictures about ensuring that credit to customers was kept under firm control. This remained a perennial problem for shopkeepers, despite the great advances in ready-money business during the second half of the nineteenth century.[88] As James Medhurst, the son of a shopkeeper and publican, declared, even in the early twentieth century: 'You always had to give credit in a little shop. That's what used to keep the general shop going because if you didn't give credit you never got any trade.'[89]

In the eighteenth and early nineteenth centuries bills could sometimes run on for months and even years, and as we saw in the Introduction, this caused great anxiety to small retailers like Thomas Turner. Typical of Turner's laments was a diary entry for 22 December 1758:

> Sure never was a more melancholy time than now. What the reason is I know not, but I have so little trade and my trust [i.e. credit customers] is so great that I think I must be ruined. And how to extricate myself out of my difficulties I am quite at a loss. I should not care how poor soever my own living was, so I had but a prospect of not losing that little I once had.[90]

Robert Roberts remembered many of the same worries existing at his mother's corner shop in Salford a century and a half later. The survival of the shop depended on Mrs Roberts's judgement about the credit-worthiness of customers. If that were faulty, disaster loomed. 'Across the way from us', recalled Robert, 'stood a similar business which was continually changing hands as one little dealer after another slid into near-bankruptcy and left.' But for many poor customers, credit was an essential part of daily existence, as they struggled to make ends meet. Roberts claimed that for 'some poor folk, to be "taken on at a tick shop" indicated a solid foot at least in the door of establishment. A tick book, honoured each week, became an emblem of integrity and a bulwark against hard times.'[91]

Under Mrs Roberts's careful direction the shop's business built up until around 1900 she had approximately 400 customers a week, and gross weekly takings of about £7.[92] According to her son, before 1914 no fewer than eight commercial travellers came to the shop, 'grappling for a share in a trade which . . . never exceeded fifteen pounds a week. . . . Two "commercials" competed, daggers drawn, to supply our establishment with groceries.'[93] On occasion Mrs Roberts was able to use their rivalry to get stock into the shop at a time when her own funds were running low.[94] She kept them on what she gleefully called the 'hop'.

In the eighteenth century the cash problems had been aggravated by the general shortage of small coinage, which made credit trading almost inevitable. Sometimes, both then and later, a barter system would be used to settle debts. In the late eighteenth century William Wood of Didsbury, who combined running an inn with agricultural work, coal dealing and shopkeeping, had around thirty credit customers. Their monthly purchases of shop goods ranged from 5s to £1 10s. At least seven of the customers also bought coal. William and Ann Bancroft both ran regular accounts, with Ann paying off part of her bill by 'spreading mole hills' for Wood. Another customer, Robert Blomily, seems to have carried out work in the shopkeeper's garden for 1s 6d a day, to help meet his debt.[95]

Elsewhere, as with Thomas Turner, a shopkeeper might pay for some of his own stock through barter arrangements. In July 1755, when Turner bought several hats from John Jenner, he settled about half the bill in the form of 'goods', probably groceries, from the shop.[96]

In country areas this practice continued into the Victorian and Edwardian era. In 1898 one Devon labouring family owed the local shopkeeper £4 16s 10d and then added a further £2 2s 10d over the course of the next weeks. In September a cash payment of 10s was made, but a bucket was then purchased costing 1s, along with a pair of boots for 5s 11d and a pair of shoes for 3s 11d. To help meet the cost 5s in cash was brought in plus four fowls, for which credit of 9s was allowed. In the following year 'there was a cash payment of 9s plus a fowl valued at half a crown. Potatoes were sold to the store but by the end of the year £5 5s 10½d was still owing.' The shopkeeper then took the family to court and they had to meet the costs of that as well. In 1899 the debt was still being paid off in small instalments.[97] In another case a smallholder who owed £11 16s to the shopkeeper in July 1901 sold him fowls, ducks and turkeys, as well as bushels of oats, bundles of straw and the greater part of his potato crop. He also carted coke from the railway station for the shopkeeper. By November 1907 he had, without handing over any cash, reduced his debt to £4 14s.[98] But this use of barter very much depended on the attitude of the retailer and whether he could afford to have a debt settled in kind rather than cash.

Adverse economic conditions, such as strikes or a downturn in trade, or an outbreak of epidemic disease that made it impossible for many people to work, also created bad debt problems for shopkeepers. Christopher Hosgood highlights the difficulties faced by Leicester retailers in 1895 during an industrial dispute which affected the town's shoemaking firms and brought its trade almost to a standstill. As Hosgood notes, if the workers experienced hardships, so also did many of the retailers who depended on their custom. Within days of the strike commencing on 9 March, the newspapers were reporting the financial plight of some of them. 'We have an authentic account of one shopkeeper in a prosperous [working-class] district taking only a half a crown yesterday, after a very depressing Saturday', declared the *Leicester Daily Mercury* on 19 March, 'and his experience is that of many more. The result to these classes will be most serious.' To combat the distress, shopkeepers and trade union leaders met 'to ensure that workers' strike pay could go as far as possible', and private arrangements were made between individual tradesmen and their own customers. The dispute was eventually settled in late April, with the factories reopening on the twenty-fifth of that month.[99] But there were casualties among some of the retailers. A.F. Palmer, who had opened a shop in August 1894 in a relatively affluent working-class district, saw his weekly takings drop during the strike from £20 to £11. The business never recovered.[100]

Even the redoubtable Mrs Roberts in Salford found difficulty in coping with mounting debts during the summer of 1911 when about half her customers were either strike-bound or out of work.[101] Similarly in 1913 the failure of a well-known grocer and wine and spirits merchant from Abercarn in Wales was attributed in part to 'bad debts' and 'strikes'. But lack of capital, the loss of some horses and his wife's illness were also cited as factors in his bankruptcy. It would seem his own business methods were at fault, too. He admitted that during 'the last three years he had never taken stock or prepared a balance sheet'.[102] Like Joseph Gibbs many decades earlier, this lack of attention to the keeping of accurate accounts had proved fatal.

Alongside these problems and uncertainties, throughout the period shopkeepers had to meet tax and rate burdens, including excise duties on tobacco, spirits and a number of other products which they sold in their businesses. Particularly resented was the introduction in 1785 of the retail shop tax. The new tax was based on the rent or rental value of the property in which a shop was conducted, with a minimum value of £5 a year established. This meant that small 'parlour' shops with rents below £5 were exempt, as were bread, meal and flour outlets. However, above the minimum the tax advanced in stages, so that for properties with a rent of between £5 and £10 a year the charge was 6d in the £ per annum; this then increased in instalments until for premises with an annual rental value of £25 or more the sum to be levied was 2s in the £. In areas of high property values, such as parts of London, and in fashionable resorts like Bath or wealthy towns like Chester, the burden of the tax was particularly heavy. Chester, for example, had twice as many shops as Stockport and two and a half times as many as Macclesfield but paid four and a half times as much shop tax as Stockport and nine times as much tax as Macclesfield. The reason was that it not only had more retail outlets than the other towns but they were bigger and more prestigious, and hence more highly rented.[103] Similarly, although Stowmarket in Suffolk had twenty-eight shops while Newmarket had only twenty-two, the fact that all except three of Stowmarket's retail outlets were rented for between £5 and £10 a year, while twelve of Newmarket's were rented at £15 or more per annum, meant that in 1788 the latter market town's shop tax yielded £21 2s 4d compared to £3 12s paid by the retailers of Stowmarket. At the 1801 census Newmarket's population numbered 1,307 and Stowmarket's, 1,761.[104]

The measure caused outrage among retailers, who objected not only to the rental basis of the tax, which took no account of business profitability, but to the fact that they alone had to pay it. Wholesalers and merchants were exempt, even though most of them were likely to be more affluent than the shopkeepers. Interestingly, in 1759 the possibility of a flat-rate duty on shops had been proposed, but was criticised as tending to damage small shopkeepers and so was not pursued.[105] The sliding scale proposed in 1785 was a way of avoiding that particular objection.

The Shop Duty Act received the royal assent in June 1785 and came into force soon after. On the day of its implementation there were demonstrations against it. In Bath retailers draped the windows and doors of their shops with crepe and other symbols of mourning. Hostile placards about the author of the tax, the prime minister and chancellor of the exchequer William Pitt, appeared in the city. In nearby Bristol, also badly affected by the new measure, shops were shut for the day and the signs of mourning shown included the tolling of church bells.[106] But it was in London that the most sustained protest was mounted. A committee of retail shopkeepers was formed, with the backing of leading members of the City Corporation. The aim was to organise protest meetings to bring about the scrapping of the tax.

The day after the Act received the royal assent many shops in the capital were closed, with black flags hung from a number of them. Where retailers decided to remain open, for example in Tottenham Court Road and Oxford Street, crowds gathered and the windows of several businesses were broken.[107]

Meanwhile, the Common Council of the Corporation of London authorised the expenditure of up to £300 for the benefit of the committee of shopkeepers. It was to help finance the campaign against an Act which the Corporation felt could endanger the City's own privileges and powers.[108]

Retailers in smaller towns were less affected by the duty than those in the metropolis. Nevertheless many protested at what the Exeter shopkeepers called an 'oppressive' burden which took no account of the 'Income and Advantages of each Individual', but merely the level of the rent.[109]

To add to the retailers' grievances several other measures affecting some of their businesses were passed at around the same time. Those who sold hats, gloves and patent medicines, for example, were required to be licensed, as were pawnbrokers. In their case the relatively large sum of £10 per annum was required in London and £5 a year in the provinces. These payments supplemented the annual excise licences already required for some commodities. In all cases a notice had to be displayed over the shop door signifying that the proprietor was duly licensed. Failure to do this led to a fine. Against this background the *Gentleman's Magazine* quoted the case of a 'little shopkeeper' on the outskirts of Warminster, whose weekly takings rarely exceeded £2 but who was required to pay a duty 'for a licence to deal in hats, for another in medicines, for another in tea, for another to ride an horse, and for another to keep a cart, and, sixthly, his little hut is now assessed to the shop tax!'[110]

To placate some of the protesters, in April 1786 the government reduced the tax on smaller properties and also exempted retailers who were too impoverished to pay church or poor rates.[111] But for premises with a rent or rental value of £30 a year or more, the levy remained at 2s in the £. This infuriated the London shopkeepers, who in February 1787 described the concessions as 'a mere mockery of justice, and almost . . . an insult upon the inhabitants of the metropolis'.[112] Their dissatisfaction had some validity in that in 1787 the assessment for the whole country for the shop tax was approximately £59,000 and of that amount £42,709, or 72.4 per cent, came from Middlesex. The shopkeepers of Westminster and the City of London alone paid £29,897.[113]

Eventually the campaign of lobbying and protest succeeded and in April 1789 the shop tax was repealed. Pitt himself had clearly decided it was a measure not worth defending. The fact that the levy proved difficult to collect and its annual yield of around £56,000 fell short of what had been originally envisaged doubtless influenced his decision. The only proviso was that all arrears of tax had to be paid.[114] However, other burdens remained, such as the window tax, which was increased in the late eighteenth and early nineteenth centuries, the inhabited house duty, and many others. Hence a survey of householders and others in the Cornhill Ward of London in 1797 revealed that a hairdresser, David Laing, with an estimated annual income of about £50, had to pay £18 rent, a tax on six windows, an inhabited house duty of 9s, and a number of other imposts. The comment was made: 'Very poor & frequently relieved by casual charity.' Similarly, Henry Dawson, mercer, with an annual income put at £150, paid £30 a year rent, a tax on twenty-three windows and an inhabited house duty of £1 2s 6d, in addition to other duties. He, too, was described as 'very much distressed'.[115] Their plight was aggravated by the fact that in many parts of London the shopkeeping trades were overcrowded, 'swollen well beyond the needs of the society'. The ratio of persons per shop in Clerkenwell in 1797 was put at thirty-one, and for the St Luke's district at thirty-five persons per shop. Most were 'petty shops catering for the daily necessities of the inhabitants', and many of their owners only got by through letting lodgings.[116]

With the ending of the French Wars in 1815 the tax burden was eased, although for many shopkeepers rates and taxes continued to cause resentment. This was particularly the case when they compared themselves with itinerant traders who, they argued, contributed little to either national or local revenues. In July 1888 George Eustace, a Reading newsagent, complained in typical vein of the people who brought 'goods into the town, and they escape tolls, and rates and taxes and everything in the shape of burdens, to the detriment of those who bear the town burdens'.[117] The fact that rate demands increased in the last years of the nineteenth century all over the country fuelled these feelings. National rate revenue doubled between 1895 and 1908, and there were places like Exeter where a rate of 2s 4d in the £ in 1887 had jumped to 6s 2d in the £ by 1914.[118]

Nonetheless, despite the financial problems experienced by retailers in the years before the First World War, there is little doubt that corner shops and village stores played an important role in the life of their communities, not only through the credit they might extend to regular customers in time of need but through their wider social impact. Most of their clientele were local and for the very poorest the shop's shelves served as their 'larder', since they could not afford to buy in bulk. According to Robert Roberts, some did not even purchase 'for the day, but for the meal'.[119]

There was much gossip and a nurturing of communal spirit as well, as customers took their time over their orders. Alice Foley recalled as a child running in and out of the shop at the end of the row where she lived 'for odd pennyworths of jam or treacle, whilst rough navvies popped in for a "screw" of tea or a penn'orth of tea dust. We had a jovial neighbour who frequented the shop and, seated on an upturned box by the counter, often called out "It's nobbut me, Mrs Walker; I durn't want owt, I've only cum' eaut o't road o' yon lot." There she sat for a good half-hour chatting and joking with customers, then off she went nourished and refreshed. . . . Mrs Walker was known to remark "Eh, I wouldn't leave this place even if I were loasin money; it's worth it for t'entertainment".'[120]

Mrs Roberts at her shop in Salford not only dispensed advice on the treatment of family ailments or the disciplining of a child, but wrote letters and filled in forms for her less literate customers. She would then read aloud the correspondence they received in reply.[121]

Some shopkeepers, like John Paton's grandmother in Aberdeen, exerted a degree of dominance over the lives of their neighbours by their power to give or withhold 'tick'. John's grandmother was a 'self-appointed censor of morals and licensed critic of manners. Even the boldest of local Viragoes quailed under the lash of her tongue. She had established herself as unchallenged "boss" of the street and held herself free to speak what she called . . . "the god's truth" about anything and anybody.'[122] But most shopkeepers, like Mrs Roberts, were more benign, and their premises served as a clearing-house for gossip, 'a central feature of women's cultural network'.[123]

A minority of retailers organised clubs for regular customers. These were designed to encourage thrift and to provide guaranteed sales for the shopkeeper. In the late nineteenth century it was noted that in York Christmas or 'Goose' clubs were being run by tobacconists, rather than publicans, as had once been the case.[124] Samuel Hayes, who owned a grocer's shop at Ingham in north Lincolnshire, likewise organised a club, with 'poor people' paying 'sixpence or a shilling a week to be credited on the club card'. When club day arrived, they came 'to choose and buy what they wanted . . . and they were entertained to tea and some form of social entertainment . . . and it was all provided by the family and staff'.[125]

This was very different from the kind of service expected by middle- and upper-class customers from their retailers. A suitably servile attitude had to be displayed and they might even have to bribe a household's domestics in order to retain custom. One London grocer claimed that in his trade anyone dealing with households in the West End would have to hand over cash gifts to the cook from time to time. If he failed to do so, his 'tea would stink for a very long while'.[126] He had to display deference to the householder himself too. W. MacQueen Pope, writing in 1948, recalled nostalgically the sycophantic stance displayed by tradesmen in his youth.

> A complaint made them tremble, a threat to take your custom elsewhere brought them figuratively to their knees with abject prayer and apologies. They could not do enough. The housewife was their living, their prosperity, their very existence depended on her favour.[127]

When a middle-class couple moved to a new district, 'there was a state of siege. Tradesmen of all kinds came to the door, begging their custom. They waylaid them and solicited their favour.' It was possible 'to live for a week on the free samples which poured into the house. And civility was the rule. Let a person in a shop be rude – a customer was lost for ever!'[128]

With such diversity among retailers, both in financial terms and in social standing, as Thea Vigne and Alun Howkins have commented, 'it is unrealistic to speak of shopkeepers as a homogenous group'. In the towns there were poor specialist shopkeepers, such as greengrocers, who needed no more capital than general dealers and who were 'low in the social order of shopkeepers'. Other specialists, like chemists, drapers and jewellers, seem 'usually to have been higher class. . . . In rural areas where shops were fewer, specialisation nearly always meant a step up the social ladder, for a sparse population could not support a diversity of specialists of varying size and importance. . . . At the bottom end of the scale family labour was absolutely crucial and economic insecurity very great. . . . At the top end the family was rigidly removed from the shop, and although there may have been some economic insecurity the business still provided a firm base of prosperity for a local political and social career.'[129]

Chapter 3

CO-OPERATIVE STORES AND MULTIPLE RETAILERS BEFORE 1914

While the department stores were making a bid for the retailer's wealthier customers, the multiples and co-operative stores were capturing his more reliable working-class trade. . . . Both concentrated initially on a narrow range of standardised products for which there were steady, consistent levels of demand and accessible sources of supply. . . . Both were initially heavily concentrated in purveying foodstuffs, especially non-perishables, which they emphasised were pure and unadulterated, the co-ops in particular posing as early health food shops. By 1914 both had made inroads into other markets, especially clothing and household goods.

Michael J. Winstanley, *The Shopkeeper's World 1830–1914*
(Manchester, 1983), p. 36.

CO-OPERATIVE STORES

Consumer co-operatives became firmly established during the second half of the nineteenth century but in 1875 their share of total retail trade probably amounted to only 2 or 3 per cent, rising to 7 or 8 per cent by 1910.[1] However, the first attempts to establish them came many decades earlier, and were part of a continuing concern among working people about the price and quality of their food. At a time when adulteration was widespread, the provision of pure foodstuffs was a significant moral imperative for early co-operative societies. It was with the supply of flour, butter, tea, sugar and other basic necessities that the earliest co-operators were concerned. Only later were their activities extended to include clothing, footwear, furnishings, books and a range of other goods.

The bulk buying of flour and similar articles of diet went back to at least the eighteenth century. Groups of like-minded work colleagues or friends would band together to finance a scheme and then divide their purchases among themselves. The weavers of Fenwick in Ayrshire, for example, began co-operative storekeeping in a small way in the late 1760s, while the Oldham Co-operative Supply Company was set up in 1795. Men employed at Woolwich Arsenal engaged in co-operative buying from about 1816, and there are several similar examples.[2] Indeed, as Hamish Fraser points out, it was a co-operative society in the Stirlingshire village of Lennoxtown that, soon after its formation in 1812, introduced the concept of paying a dividend on purchases out of any trading surplus that accrued.[3] The dividend was intended to convince customers that they were 'directly involved in the well-being of the enterprise'. According to the committed Victorian co-operator George Holyoake, retailers were divided into two groups: public traders and private traders. 'Co-operators are public traders, who take their customers into partnership. The private traders are they who conduct their business for their private interest alone.'[4]

Unfortunately the early schemes proved inherently unstable. They lacked both legal status and firm financial backing, being dependent for their survival on the dedication and energy of their promoters. If the latter lost interest or proved incompetent, the enterprise foundered. Meanwhile, the process of weighing and sharing out the goods and selling them was in the hands of volunteers, usually members of a society's management committee. Probably they had little experience of such work or of the intricacies of making wholesale purchases to stock their stores. Well into the nineteenth century the secretary of the Tring Society in Hertfordshire complained that co-operatives in the Home Counties were in difficulties because they did not know how and where to get their supplies.[5]

For many early enthusiasts, however, co-operation had a broader role than mere shopkeeping. They hoped that by making a modest investment in a retail enterprise this might lead to 'mutual ownership of all sectors of trade and production', and to the promotion of a new socio-economic order, based on socialist principles and political reform.[6] Some, indeed, regarded storekeeping with contempt, like the New Moral World of 4 July 1840, which saw the development 'as a diversion . . . which had "converted members into money-seeking, money-loving higgling shopkeepers"'.[7] Ultimately these more ambitious objectives were to prove of minor significance, although many societies did expend cash and time on housing, health care, education and leisure schemes for the benefit of members and, on occasion, for staff, too.[8] Nonetheless it was the provision of food, and later other goods, of reliable quality and at fair prices, plus the payment of a dividend on purchases, that were to be the main attractions of the co-operative movement.

Although a few examples of the bulk buying of food can be identified in the eighteenth century, it was in the late 1820s that the first major upsurge in co-operative storekeeping occurred, at a time of political and labour unrest. The textile workers in Lancashire and the West Riding of Yorkshire, where a strong sense of community already existed, were among those most active. But societies were formed elsewhere, too, perhaps 450 of them being instituted between 1825 and 1835.[9] William Lovett was among those involved in this period. He joined the First London Co-operative Trading Association in the late 1820s. The members subscribed a small weekly sum in order to raise a common fund to enable them to open a general store. The aim was to sell food, clothing, books and any other articles that the society's working-class membership demanded. Lovett's own small shop had closed by this time and he was asked to become keeper of the association's store. That meant a cut in pay compared to what he could earn at his own trade of cabinetmaking but he saw it as a 'first step towards the social independence of the labouring classes', and for that reason decided 'to exert all [his] energies to aid in the work'.[10] He saw it as a means of leading the labouring classes to take the 'trade, manufactures, and commerce of the country into their own hands'. But he soon found that his fellow members were not prepared to make the sacrifices necessary to achieve such lofty ideals. Even the shop itself did not flourish. Lack of experience in purchasing stock and what Lovett called the 'prejudice of the members' wives against their stores' led to its demise. The women did not want to shop in one store only and perhaps, too, they did not wish their husbands to know precisely what they were buying.[11]

Within months Lovett's salary had to be cut and his wife took over the running of the business at half the pay he had originally received. It finally collapsed in 1834, as did many of the other co-operatives established at around the same time. In Manchester in 1832 it was reported that three or four years earlier there had been perhaps sixteen trading societies in the town, 'but owing to their repeated failures in consequence of the bad management of unsuitable shopkeepers . . . all that remains now are the mere fragments of four, and these, with the exception of one of them, will shortly be scattered to the wind'.[12] Only in a few places, where alternative retail facilities were virtually non-existent or where the societies were well-managed and members fully committed, did they manage to carry on. The failures, meanwhile, left a legacy of suspicion among many working people about co-operative enterprises, and that wariness hostile private traders did their best to encourage.

The failures included a society set up at Rochdale by a group of weavers. It was formed in 1833 and survived for two years before succumbing to the effects of granting too much credit.[13] However, it was in this town that a new society was to be established which symbolised a renewed faith in retail co-operation.

The Rochdale Pioneers started up in the summer of 1844. Although the society did not introduce new ideas, it combined in a methodical manner the features which were to lead to successful communal selling. It had an initial membership of twenty-eight. Some were weavers; others were socialists, political reformers and teetotallers. The intention was to raise capital by issuing £1 shares, on which interest would be paid. This would finance the setting up of a store to sell provisions, clothing and general household necessities. As a result of past bitter experience, no credit was to be allowed to purchasers, and trading surpluses were to be used to cover the interest charges on the shares and to distribute as dividend to members. This was to be calculated on the basis of their purchases at the store. A salesman and cashier were appointed on a part-time basis from among the members, each being paid 3d an hour for their labours.[14] At first the store opened only on Monday evenings from 7 p.m. to 9 p.m. and on Saturdays from 6 p.m. to 11 p.m. It was to stock pure, non-adulterated goods and to give 'true weight and measure'. The store was set up on the ground floor of a warehouse but when this had been repaired and simple fittings installed, there was little cash left to purchase the stock. Consequently trading started with just '28 lb of butter, 56 lb of sugar, 6 cwt of flour, a sack of oatmeal and some tallow candles'.[15] William Cooper, a weaver and later a stationer, who worked in the shop on a part-time basis until his death in 1868, claimed this limited funding was an advantage. as it prevented the purchasing of too much stock.[16] Only when the buyers had learned what their customers wanted could operations be successfully expanded.

After three months the opening hours were extended to include every evening except Tuesday. On Saturdays they were open from 1 p.m. to 11 p.m., with an extra assistant recruited to work between 6 p.m. and 11 p.m. to help with the anticipated weekend rush. Membership of the society rose steadily from 28 in 1844 to 600 by 1850 and 3,450 a decade later.[17]

In the following years many other societies were formed, encouraged in part by the passage of the 1852 Industrial and Provident Societies Act which gave legal status to all registered co-operatives. Many were small, single-store organisations and as late as 1881 around four out of every five of the 1,101 societies then in existence had one shop only.[18] Even in 1913 there were societies like Chewton Mendip in Somerset, with a membership of 67, annual sales of £157, a wages bill of £11 and a net profit for the year of just £5. Similarly at Budleigh Salterton in Devon, the membership was 79, sales amounted to just £358 for the year, £7 was spent on wages and salaries, and the annual net profit was £24.[19] These may be compared to the Rochdale Society of Equitable Pioneers, with a membership in 1913 of nearly 21,000, a bill for wages and salaries of £27,823 and net profit for the year of £73,168, or the Leeds Society, with 47,252 members, a wages outlay of £101,846, and net profit for 1913 of nearly £240,000.[20]

The smallest organisations were always vulnerable to economic downturns, such as occurred in the late 1870s and again in the early 1890s. They had problems, too, in learning how best to run a store. In Lancashire, Yorkshire and the north-east of England, where the movement's main strength lay, they could often get advice from neighbouring co-operatives. Hence the Stalybridge Society in Cheshire was guided by the experience of stores in Rochdale, Dukinfield and Mossley, and in turn assisted another fledgling organisation at nearby Openshaw.[21] Societies did best when members gave unwavering support. 'I want nothing on my table but co-op' was the comment of one enthusiast.[22] The movement was less successful in large cities like London, Birmingham and Liverpool, where there was little social cohesion and plenty of competing private retail outlets already existed.

A number of co-operatives had to contend with the hostility of private traders, who resented their ideology and the way they were undermining their own working-class trade. Sometimes they sought to pressurise wholesalers into refusing to supply the co-operative stores by threatening to withdraw their own custom if this were not done. In 1865 the Windsor Society reported that suppliers in Slough had refused their business and there were similar problems in Leek in 1869.[23] The journal, *The Grocer*, even launched an abortive campaign in the 1860s and 1870s for a national boycott of co-operative stores by wholesalers but by then the movement had become sufficiently important for these middlemen to value the orders it offered.[24] In a few places retailers refused to serve those who belonged to the local co-op, hoping to force them to give up buying from a store which could not supply all their needs. In 1862, according to George Holyoake, when the cotton famine caused by the American Civil War created much employment in Lancashire, some shopkeepers on the cotton famine relief committees tried to refuse aid to 'poor co-operators . . . until the late Lord Derby . . . interfered, and prevented the continuance of that refusal'.[25] He admitted many 'good natured grocers have often taught us the art of shop-keeping; but, as a rule, they have injured us wherever they could; they have induced employers to dismiss workmen who bought of our stores; they have refused to sell to us . . . and they are doing it still'. That was in 1879 and, as we shall see, one of the most powerful anti-co-operative campaigns mounted by shopkeepers was to take place around two decades later.

In some communities the advent of a co-operative store led private shops to cut their charges. At Whitfield in Northumberland, where the villagers had paid 'enormous' amounts for goods, the establishment of a co-op shop meant that flour and groceries were being sold 'at prices something more like what they could be obtained at Newcastle or Carlisle', declared a report in 1864.[26]

At first most 'behind the counter' work was undertaken by committee members. The system adopted by the society formed at Crewe in the 1850s was typical of many:

> To be a member of the committee in those days meant really to be a voluntary warehouseman, nothing was too rough or dirty for members of the committee to do. Going out in the evening to buy fat pigs, hoisting up flour and hanging up bacon, were some of their chief duties, not to say anything of taking stock every six months when . . . it used to take us from shop closing time at night until just after about four o'clock next morning, when we just had time to get ready to go into the works.[27]

Even at Lincoln, where a shop was set up in a double-fronted house in 1861, with a capital of £40 and a storekeeper appointed to live rent-free on the premises, the committee members did not escape. At first they were responsible for making deliveries to customers in the evenings and at weekends, although before long a boy with a handcart was recruited.[28] After three years the store transferred to larger premises and, in a move shared by some other co-operatives, arrangements were made for private traders to sell drapery goods and coal to members, with agreed financial rebates. This benefited the independent traders by boosting their business and enabled co-op members to buy goods not stocked by their store on advantageous terms. Eventually in 1873 the Lincoln Society opened a new building with three separate shops – a grocery, a drapery and a boot and shoe business. Above were rooms for the conduct of the society's affairs and a large hall for meetings. To the rear was a bakery. Later on further additions were made so that by the early 1890s there were departments for furniture, crockery and tailoring, as well as storerooms, fitting rooms, 'workshops, a library, a reading room and conversation room'.[29] The society also set up branches throughout Lincoln, with eleven opened between 1876 and 1897. Its first rural branch came in 1878 at Welbourn, where there was a manager, and a horse and cart to make deliveries. By 1900 nine more country branches had opened, with those at Sleaford and Market Rasen large enough to have two separate shops, one for groceries and provisions and the other for drapery and footwear.[30]

Not all societies which made a good start were able to emulate Lincoln's success. Some faltered because of economic downturns or because of suspicions aroused by the collapse of a neighbouring society. That happened on Merseyside, where the Liverpool Provident Association was set up in 1851 by about a dozen enthusiasts. It began in a room at a local temperance hotel, offering soap, candles and a few groceries to members. Any surpluses were stored in a cupboard until the next meeting.[31] From this modest beginning, business rapidly expanded. Shop premises were taken and a manager appointed. In the late 1850s three further branches were opened in Liverpool as well as one in Birkenhead, and by 1860 membership stood at 2,200, with £5,154 distributed as dividend on sales over the previous five years. At that date the dividend had reached an attractive 1s 6d in the pound.[32]

The Provident Association's success led to the formation of two other co-operative societies in Liverpool, and in 1863 the Provident itself opened a new store, offering groceries and provisions on the ground floor, drapery, upholstery and hats on the next level, and footwear on the top storey. There was also a dressmaking department and a waiting room. However, within months of the grand opening one of the other Liverpool co-ops had collapsed through the granting of excessive credit to members. This caused 'a scandal to be cast upon co-operation in Liverpool'.[33] Soon the second society disappeared and although initially the Provident Association seemed able to carry on, the demise of the other two societies, coupled with the effects of the cotton famine, led to its collapse at the end of the 1860s. Around two decades then elapsed before the City of Liverpool Co-operative Equitable Society was registered in 1886, with a membership of thirty-eight and its business conducted from the back parlour of the secretary's house. In the early years, despite fluctuating sales, the committee persisted. 'They spent their evenings in weighing goods . . . [and] one of their number carried parcels to the homes of members reluctant to bear their own burdens.'[34] The secretary's wife dealt with the customers in between attending to her domestic chores. Not until the early 1890s, when a manager was recruited from the society in St Helens, was real progress made.[35]

It was symptomatic of the fragility of many of the societies even in these later years that only about 40 per cent of those set up in the third quarter of the nineteenth century were still trading in 1901. Failures were particularly heavy in Wales, the west Midlands and the south-east of England.[36]

Management committees became preoccupied with securing the profitability that enabled high dividends to be paid, since these were felt to be the key to success. This preoccupation sometimes led to a cavalier attitude being adopted towards employees, especially in the matter of pay, but over security of tenure, too. If sales dropped and it was necessary to cut labour costs to maintain the dividend, then dismissals could follow. Such attitudes caused resentment among staff, who felt they were being sacrificed to the 'divi-god'.[37] In 1889 J. Thompson, secretary of the Ashton-under-Lyne Society, conceded that committees and employees, as buyers and sellers of labour, were inevitably opposed to one another and despite the movement's ideals this could mean that the workers were 'treated . . . as divi-making machines'.[38]

As the societies became more firmly established, reliance for the day-to-day conduct of business was placed on paid managers and assistants. In the early years virtually all of them had begun their working lives in the employ of private retailers. Many had little interest or knowledge of co-operative principles. Occasionally, as at Bishop Auckland in 1867, co-operators were able to appoint a paid manager from their own ranks, but usually they came from a private background. They included men like Joe Haigh, who in 1893 applied for a managerial post with Reading Co-operative Society. According to a testimonial, he had begun his career in a private firm and had also been a commercial traveller for a short time. He then became manager of Meltham Co-operative Society. This was a 'country place', where business was done in groceries, drapery and butchery. From there he moved to another country society and then became manager of Ravensthorpe Co-op in the West Riding of Yorkshire. This, too, was a country place 'but a much larger store . . . with several shops'. The testimonial noted that Haigh was not only a 'very good businessman' but a 'total abstainer'. However, he did not get the position. It went to a candidate who was described as having been 'almost . . . brought up' in the co-operative movement and to have its work 'thoroughly at heart'.[39]

The early links of many co-operative employees with private retailing meant that even after the formation of the Co-operative Wholesale Society (CWS) in 1863, and its promotion of manufacturing concerns to pro-duce goods for sale in the stores a decade later, staff were often lukewarm about boosting the sales of co-op products. In 1889 J. Thompson, of the Ashton-under-Lyne Society, suggested that management committees should set up classes to teach co-operative principles to their workers.[40] However, even in 1911 similar complaints were being heard. One contributor to the *Co-operative News* maintained that assistants were doing little to promote co-operative manufactured goods:

> Unless we wish our movement to become merely the agents of capitalistic manufacturers, we must see that this is altered. . . . The real test of loyalty is not the percentage of purchases from the CWS, but the percentage of goods co-operatively produced. And how can production be organised on a

satisfactory basis if committees neglect to instruct the men behind the counter as to their real wishes in this wholly vital matter?[41]

Ironically, however, whatever the faults of salesmanship among the growing number of paid employees, they were firmly under the direction of the management committee of their society. As a result, as Martin Purvis points out, the purchasing of stock was 'subject to greater bureaucratic scrutiny than in most private businesses'. He quotes the case of the Sherburn Hill Society which in 1874 resolved 'that the Manager buy nothing but yeast without the consent of the committee'.[42] Similarly, when the Reading Co-operative Society began selling drapery they told the joint managers of the department to spend no more than £50 on stock, with a proviso that the Co-operative Wholesale Society's London branch should be the supplier as far as possible. Six months later the allowance was raised to £250, plus a further £100 allocated for the supply of footwear.[43] In November 1887 the manager of the butchery department was likewise 'authorised to go to London to select and buy . . . meat (foreign if he thinks it advisable). Cash to be supplied to him by the Secretary . . . up to, but not beyond £25.'[44]

At St Helens the aim was to buy in the most competitive market and that did not necessarily mean patronising the CWS. On 28 July 1884 the manager was authorised to go to Liverpool to enquire into prices there, while in July 1887 he was 'instructed to make inquiries regarding Warrington market with a view to attending same for cheese and potatoes'.[45] The St Helens Society was very successful and in 1899 almost half the town's population shopped at its large central store or at one of its ten branches. Staff discipline was firm and any laxity of conduct was swiftly dealt with. On 3 November 1884, for example, the secretary noted: 'The Chairman was authorised to see John Price, the assistant, and caution him against mistakes and promise him an advance in his wages in one month if he showed amendment and greater readiness to assist the manager in the correct dispatching of goods.'[46]

Strict economy was observed, too. In October 1885 it was decided that 'the shopmen shall be provided with tea Friday and Saturday and that the necessary crockery be got for the purpose'. But less than two months later it was resolved that as 'expenses were going up and owing to the increased staff in the shop', the 'tea provided for shopmen be dispensed with for the present'.[47]

The progress made by the co-operative movement in St Helens aroused the hostility of private shopkeepers. In 1902 their Traders' Defence Association began a campaign to 'educate the public . . . in respect of the injurious effects of co-operative stores on the private trade of the country'.[48] Efforts were made to put an embargo 'on supplies of manufactured goods to the co-op', and anti-co-op candidates were supported in local elections. There was even a boycott 'on the employment in their own shops of any one who shopped at the co-op or was related, however distantly, to someone who did'.[49] A guidebook was issued on *How to fight the Co-op: A guide and commentary based on the St Helens Experience.* For a time these actions encouraged resistance in other co-operative strongholds, with Traders' Defence Associations set up in Hull, Wigan, Leeds, Barrow, Plymouth and Newcastle among others. Trade publications like *The Grocer* cautiously welcomed the movement but within four years interest was waning. Shopkeepers found that their campaigns were losing them custom and were giving publicity to the co-ops.[50]

Sometimes management committees specified that particular goods were to be purchased from a certain supplier, but often the placing of orders was left to the discretion of the storekeeper or manager to buy where he thought it was 'cheapest and best'. On occasion this gave rise to allegations that managers were abusing this freedom for their personal benefit, with suspicions that co-operative custom was 'secured by tips from private suppliers'.[51] James Duckworth, a Rochdale grocer who owned a chain of cheap grocery shops in Lancashire from 1868, claimed that when he took up wholesaling it was necessary to give bribes in order to secure orders from co-ops.[52]

Within the shops themselves there was a division of labour where the size of the staff allowed this. At Denton near Stalybridge in the early twentieth century the manager of the grocery department

> did not normally serve customers though he would do so if they were of sufficient importance or the shop was very busy. One of the senior assistants had the special task of operating the bacon slicer. . . . Several juniors, mainly boys, were employed and spent most of their time 'in the back' weighing sugar into home-made bags of thick blue paper, cutting slabs of salt and performing other menial tasks. It was an obvious promotion to be allowed to appear in the shop and to wear a white coat and long apron to protect, or hide, one's own clothes.[53]

When the CWS opened a drapery section in Manchester in 1874, customers from Denton went to its warehouse to make their selections. The goods were then sent to the local store and there payment was made, either in cash or, increasingly, through the twenty-week club under which an initial shilling in the pound payment and 'nineteen subsequent instalments of one shilling in the pound enabled the customer to buy goods without credit charge'. The aim was to complete the transaction within twenty weeks.[54]

The varying amount of trading surplus secured by individual societies and the preoccupation with maintaining dividend levels led to great pay differences for staff between one co-operative and another. In the 1890s some branch managers, doing a mixed trade valued at £60 a week, were only paid £1 a week.[55] Certainly when Reading Co-operative Society opened a branch at Guildford in July 1886 they paid the manager £1 a week only, plus free accommodation. By contrast, the manager of the tailoring department at the society's central store was appointed in December 1885 at £2 2s a week, plus a bonus based on the society's dividend rate.[56]

Elsewhere, particularly in Yorkshire, societies operated a sub-contract system whereby branch managers were paid a commission ranging from 4d to 6d in the £, with which to run their shop. They were then left to hire and fire staff as they thought best.[57] Often a manager would carry on with the help of his wife and a son or daughter, so as to retain the cash in the family. Or perhaps a boy assistant would be recruited as the only helper. 'I visited one shop', commented one critic, 'where a trade of just over £100 a week is being done by a man and a small boy. It seems very hard work for both of them; but to replace the boy with an adult assistant would take more of the manager's allowance than he cares to lose, so the customer must put up with the inconveniences attendant upon understaffing.' In such shops as the youths grew up, they would be dismissed and replaced by other youngsters who would receive lower pay. One manager's wife complained that it was an unsatisfactory system, and the womenfolk 'didn't ought to have to be in the shop altogether with their husbands'.[58]

The availability of pre-packed goods sent out by the wholesalers and the stocking of proprietary brands, like marmalade from Keiller's of Dundee or biscuits from Carr's of Carlisle, made it easier for managers to run their shops with inexperienced staff, since their duties involved little more than finding the goods on the shelves and handing them to the customer over the counter.[59]

Sometimes a downturn in trade led to staff wage cuts, so as to reduce the outgoings. This happened at Blaydon in County Durham in 1878, when a spell of poor trading during the summer months led to the wages of counter staff and warehousemen being reduced by 5 per cent, and those of most of the society's departmental managers by 10 per cent.[60] An alternative strategy was to require staff to accept short-time working, as happened at Burnley, Padiham and Nelson during the summer of 1908. This meant that employees had to take a week's unpaid leave in turn. In the case of Burnley that amounted to one week's lay-off every six weeks.[61] Staff at Nelson were particularly angry because there had been a small falling off only in trade, and this was attributed not to fewer orders but to lower outlays by members whose spending power had been reduced. They were also buying cheaper quality goods. Hence the amount of work the sales staff had to carry out had not diminished.[62] Similar short-time working was adopted in many other places, including at Hartlepool in December 1908. There the employees were to be suspended for one week in every six, 'this to continue for eighteen weeks – i.e. three weeks' suspension each'.[63] It was an application to retailing of a system of short-time working common in industry during periods of trade recession and familiar to members of the management committees of the co-operative societies concerned.

On occasion economy measures meant staff dismissals, as at Reading in the autumn of 1909, when a salesman was told that his services were being dispensed with because of the need to cut departmental expenses.[64] At Reading, too, where staff bonuses were paid from the 1880s, instead of commission on sales, employees were not allowed to withdraw the cash without permission from the management committee.[65]

Insensitivity in dealing with staff was shown clearly at Stafford in February 1909, when the employees were baldly told that the committee had decided to cut their week's holiday entitlement and to abolish all sick pay. Under the new scheme a branch manager's holidays would amount to five days only, with Saturday excluded, and those of the rest of the staff would be reduced to three days, one of which must include Wednesday, which was the weekly half-day closure. In addition, six employees were to be dismissed.[66] The society also ignored a claim for higher pay which had been submitted a year earlier, even though its grocery managers were being paid at a minimum rate of only £1 8s a week, and a branch draper manageress received just 14s a week. Pay for juniors ranged from 6s per week for those aged 15 up to 15s for lads aged 20. According to *The Co-operative Employé* journal, the proportion of juniors to adults employed by the Stafford Society was particularly large.[67] The dispute dragged on until November 1909, when the committee agreed to introduce a minimum pay rate for male staff members aged 21 and above of £1 4s a week, and for managers of the grocery and drapery departments of £1 10s a week. A similar sum was to be paid to the head butcher. But it refused to make any concessions regarding sick pay and holiday entitlement, or to introduce increases in pay for junior and female staff.[68]

Against these unsatisfactory examples of labour relations there were many societies where employment conditions were far better than those enjoyed by 'behind the counter' staff elsewhere. Opening hours in co-op shops were normally shorter than in private retailing and the 'living-in' system for workers, with all its restraints, scarcely applied.[69] Many societies also helped finance staff outings, while there were cases, as at Haslingden, where the staff wrote to the *Co-operative Employé* in 1908 to express gratitude to the committee and members of their society 'for closing their grocery departments at 6 . . . p.m. on Saturdays, instead of 7 o'clock . . . as formerly'.[70]

Frank Benson, who was born in 1895, joined the co-operative society at Bolton when he was almost 15, as a milk delivery boy. According to him that was 'the first stage of co-operative employment' and for this he was paid 5s a week, with a shilling rise on his birthday. He also had a week's holiday with pay. In his view Bolton Co-operative Society was a 'model' employer. 'It was a great thing to get on the Co-op. It was considered quite a good safe respectable job once you got on the Co-op.' After two years delivering milk, he moved into the gentleman's outfitting department as an errand boy. From there he went into the grocery department, as a kind of apprentice. That involved attending evening classes: 'I joined what we called institute classes and became a qualified grocer', after passing the relevant examinations.[71] Later he took a managerial course and after the First World War he left Bolton to become a branch manager in Southport.

Staff qualifications were offered as early as 1887–88 by the Co-operative Union, when examinations in 'Co-operation' were organised. Book-keeping examinations followed two years later. In the early twentieth century the movement's Central Education Committee set up managers' and salesmen's training courses, along with special training centres, correspondence courses and annual examinations.[72]

Mr J. Wolfendale was also a satisfied employee of Bolton Co-operative Society. He spent almost all his working life as a sales assistant and recalled that working-class families in the town sometimes used their co-op connections to set up a small corner shop. They bought 'a lot of stuff from Co-op which [was] giving three shilling in the pound divi, see. So . . . they get this three shilling in the pound divi off what they buy and feed their big family and what they've left . . . they sell to the people . . . [a] copper [or] two above th' odds. And make the divi on it as well. . . . And there's . . . many a one . . . got a little shop . . . through getting the divi off this stuff as they sold to other people.'[73]

A major concern of management committees was to check petty theft among shop staff and to this end great emphasis was placed on the need for managers to avoid 'leakages' in their stores. Often, as at Reading, this meant they had to provide a cash bond when they entered on their post and, should a shortfall in cash or stock occur, the bond would be surrendered. Very probably they would lose their position as well. At Reading in 1885 the bond amounted to £20, with interest of 5 per cent per annum allowed upon it by the society. The following year it was raised to £25. For some newly appointed managers this could represent a serious burden. In March 1891 the manager of the Guildford branch wrote to enquire whether any concessions could be made on this. He was informed that was impossible and that unless he accepted the terms he would be given a week's notice. However, both sides clearly thought better of this for on 19 March he was confirmed in his post and was allowed to pay for the £25 bond in quarterly instalments of £1 10s[74] His anxiety may have arisen because his predecessor at Guildford had had a deficit in his accounts at the end of 1890 and had been dismissed early in 1891. He had also had to surrender his bond at the same time.[75]

For female staff recruited at Reading arrangements were sometimes even more unsatisfactory. Thus in May 1886 Miss Whitehorn was engaged for the drapery department on the understanding that she would give the first six months of service without pay. Not until 25 November 1886 was she confirmed in her post, at a weekly wage of 5s, 'to be retrospective from date of end of six months' free service'.[76] That small sum was increased to 6s a week in April 1887. Three months later a second girl was engaged for the drapery department. This time she was required to give unpaid service for three months. At the end of that period there was some dispute as to whether her pay should be 5s a week or something less. Initially 2s 6d was proposed but that was overturned a week later in favour of 5s.[77]

The poor pay of female staff at Reading was symptomatic of the situation elsewhere. In 1895 a survey of 762 women over 18 employed in various capacities in co-operative stores in different parts of the country showed that 1 per cent earned less than 5s a week, while a further 21 per cent earned 5s only. Just 13 per cent secured 20s and upwards a week.[78] Nor had the situation improved very much by the early twentieth century. Research undertaken by the Co-operative Women's Guild showed that over a third of women employed in co-ops in the north of England and more than half of those working for societies in the south of England, the south-west and Yorkshire received under 13s a week. In one northern society no assistant in the drapery department was paid more than 10s a week, while a small midland society paid 5s a week to a woman of 19 and 12s to one of 20.[79]

The low wages of women workers was one reason why male colleagues had reservations about their recruitment, seeing them as 'cheap labour' designed to undermine the position of the men. As in most retail establishments at this time, there was particular hostility to the employment of women in grocery departments. Percy Snowden, who became a co-op grocery manager in Yorkshire, remembered that when he joined as an apprentice in 1906 there were 'no women working in groceries in them days. They . . . came in during the First World War.'[80] Even in the 1930s when

Linda McCullough Thew became the first female assistant at Ashington co-op grocery in Northumberland, she recalled the ill-feeling the appointment aroused. Male staff protested at the arrival of the 14-year-old trainee, even though they were assured 'that no female would be in line for promotion'. One of the senior staff made his opposition very clear, declaring: 'It's a great mistake. It won't work. Grocering is a man's job. It's a skilled job. Takes years of training. No girl, or woman either for that matter, is up to it . . . they'll learn their mistake in time.'[81] Linda's young male predecessor had 'milked the till' and had been dismissed in consequence. The committee had then decided to advertise for a girl, probably, as Linda wryly noted, 'to keep costs down'. Despite her unhappy introduction to the job she persisted because, as she later wrote, there was a widespread view in Ashington that to get employment at the stores meant you were 'made for life'.[82]

Most co-operative retailing was aimed at working-class customers. However, in the 1860s a small number of societies were set up, principally in London, to appeal to the middle classes. The process began in the winter of 1864 when a few clerks employed in the General Post Office clubbed together to buy a quantity of tea. They divided this among themselves at a considerable saving in cash, and that initial success led them to extend their purchases to include coffee, sugar and other groceries. In January 1865 they set up the Post Office Supply Association. Originally there were forty members, but business was increased by allowing members' 'friends' to become association customers provided they bought special 6d tickets. In the mid-1860s membership was thrown open to all civil servants, and the name of the association was changed to the Civil Service Supply Association, or CSSA. It derived its initial capital largely from the issue of non-interest-bearing shares, which only civil service officers could buy.[83]

Two similar societies were set up soon after – the Civil Service Co-operative Society, which was registered as a limited company in April 1866 and opened a shop in the Haymarket, and the Army and Navy Co-operative Society, which began trading in 1872, also in London. This was initially for the benefit of army and naval officers but its customer base was soon widened by allowing any shareholder to introduce a friend as an annual subscriber. By 1879 the Army and Navy Society had 13,000 shareholders who had paid £1 each for their shares, plus 5,000 life ticket-holders who had paid a guinea each. There were also 18,000 annual subscribers who paid 2s 6d yearly, plus an entrance fee of 5s. The annual subscribers did not have to be members of either the civil service or the armed forces.[84]

These stores did not trade with the general public but only with members of their respective associations. Transactions were on a strictly cash basis and the prices of goods stocked were published in quarterly lists. The role of sales assistants was limited, although care was taken to hire well-qualified staff and pay rates were rather above those generally available. In 1879 the Army and Navy Stores employed almost 2,000 people, including around 100 women making shirts. Staff honesty was a high priority and a £5 reward was offered to any assistant who informed the management of thefts committed by colleagues.[85]

Customers wishing to make a purchase consulted the price list and filled in an invoice detailing their requirements and the price of each item. This was taken to the cashier's office for payment and to have the invoice receipted. That was then presented at the counter where the orders were collected together. The customers took the goods away with them, unless they wished to pay extra to have them delivered. Mail orders were accepted, too, and deliveries of these were arranged.[86]

Although the associations were co-operatives in the sense that they were jointly owned, they did not have the community spirit of the original societies. George Holyoake referred to them dismissively as 'spurious' co-operatives.[87] They also aroused deep hostility among private retailers catering for the middle-class market, not least because of their price-cutting methods and their mail order business. William Pink, a large grocer in Portsmouth and a former mayor of the town, claimed that the competition from the Army and Navy Stores was adversely affecting trade in his area: 'We have a large number of army and navy gentlemen residing about Portsmouth, and they receive their goods from the London stores. . . . I find the practice of the Civil Service Stores is, that they take proprietary articles, such as pickles . . . and sell them at cost price; but I have found on comparison with other goods, such as tea, that I can undersell them considerably, both in quality and price.'[88] But that was small consolation when 'parties living at Southsea' were dealing with the Army and Navy Stores or its Civil Service rival rather than with him.[89]

However, by the 1880s the three principal London middle-class co-operatives were facing competition from the expanding department stores and from other retailers who were adopting some of their business methods, including their fixed price policy and narrow profit margins. These rivals benefited from the fact that 'anyone could come into their shops without payment of a subscription' and the service they offered was often superior to that given by the societies. At the turn of the century the latter responded by abandoning 'the austere trading methods' which had been so successful in their early years and assuming some of the attributes of ordinary department stores. Nonetheless up to 1914 the customer base remained limited to shareholders and privileged ticket holders.[90]

MULTIPLE RETAILERS

The multiple chain stores and the traditional co-operative retail societies had many points of similarity. Both came to prominence in the second half of the nineteenth century and both concentrated initially on providing foodstuffs to working-class consumers. To this end both took advantage of the growing imports of cheap food and of mass-produced consumer goods to stock their shelves. Both also depended for the day-to-day running of their shops upon paid managers and sales staff, rather than upon the personal attention of a proprietor. And, except in the case of some of the managers, it was rare for staff to be required to live on the premises or in hostel accommodation owned by the business. But there the resemblance ends. The multiplicity of co-op stores were under the control of a large number of separate societies and their respective management committees. By 1913 there were around 1,500 separate retail societies, each priding itself on its independence. They ranged in size from small, single-store enterprises to major businesses like the Leeds Society, which in 1900 had eighty stores under its jurisdiction.[91] The networks of multiple shops, by contrast, were under the control of a board of directors or of individual proprietors, who formulated their general strategy and laid down the staff's working conditions. They were also purely profit-making organisations, without any of the social, moral and educational ideals which, at least in theory, were still espoused by most co-operative societies.[92]

The development of the multiple chains and their long-term success depended initially on the entrepreneurial flair of their founders and upon their ability to identify a market which they could exploit. W.H. Smith & Son obtained a major role in the newspaper distribution business after 1848 through its railway bookstalls, much as John Menzies was to do in Scotland after 1857. In 1848 Smith won the contract to run bookstalls for the London & North-Western Railway and contracts with other railway companies followed, so that outlets increased from 35 in 1851 to 1,242 by 1902.[93] The stalls sold books, magazines and newspapers for the benefit of the travelling public, and from 1860 library facilities were offered, with borrowers able to obtain a book at one station and return it at another. Later the firm expanded into the high streets of many towns.[94]

The Singer Sewing Machine Company also developed a chain of shops for the sale of its sewing machines and accessories, with the first of them opening in 1856. By 1900 there were nearly 400 branches, offering a good after-sales service. The company took the step in the first place because it found difficulty in identifying retailers prepared to carry enough of the comparatively expensive stock.[95] Singer staff needed some specialist skills and even in the 1930s Violet Black recalled the samples or small garments displayed in the shop windows 'to illustrate the type of stitching that the machines could do. And for that . . . we had to cut the things to be made in the workroom. So there was a cutting room, and a machine room.'[96]

Many of the firms, like W.H. Smith, began as small independent businesses which were then built up into large corporate enterprises, financed by share capital and with hundreds of stores and thousands of employees. To ensure success they required four favourable conditions. First and foremost they needed large numbers of consumers prepared and able to buy their goods, and it is significant that most of the firms developed from the early 1870s, at a time when the standard of living of working people was rising. This enabled the new businesses to follow a policy of small profits and quick returns, to boost turnover. Second, a good transport system was required to move goods around the country or to import produce from overseas. That included refrigerated ships to bring meat from Australasia, the United States and South America. Third, success sprang in many cases from the availability of new products or products made in new ways, as in the case of factory-made footwear and men's clothing, or pre-packaged foodstuffs, such as tea, biscuits, jars of pickles, tinned goods and new-style powders which could be transformed speedily into custards, puddings and sauces.[97] Salmon & Gluckstein marketed packaged tobacco products in their range of shops, and Maynard's sold confectionery.[98] Finally, a reliable staff was needed to run the shops and carry out management policy. They were expected to obey orders rather than display initiative and innovation.

It was these characteristics of the 'company shops' that led *The Times* to comment dismissively in 1902 that

a large proportion of the grocer's work of the present-day could be accomplished almost equally well by an automatic machine delivering a packet of goods in exchange for a coin. . . . These shops are nearly all conducted upon the same iron routine system with automatic managers and still more automatic assistants, the brains being supplied from headquarters with the consignments of goods, every shop belonging to a particular company being a duplicate of every other shop.[99]

The multiples were accused of deskilling sales staff by their use of mechanical aids, such as bacon slicers, and by the widespread vending of packaged products. In this they were aided by manufacturers like Rowntree's, who from 1897 stimulated demand for their Elect cocoa by increased advertising and the distribution of samples and leaflets direct to consumers.[100] However, it is important to remember that the deskilling process varied from trade to trade. The technical expertise of butchers, even those employed by firms selling refrigerated meat on a large scale (such as Eastmans Ltd with around 1,800 branches by 1910 and Nelson & Sons with 1,600 branches at that date), did not decline to the same extent as that of the assistant in a tobacconist's shop selling ready-prepared pipe tobacco and packets of cigarettes and cigars, or of workers in most of the multiple grocers' shops.[101]

The deskilling aspect was perhaps seen most clearly in the variety stores set up from the 1890s, such as Marks & Spencer, and from 1909 the American firm of Frank W. Woolworth. In these, cheap consumer goods were openly displayed, with clearly marked prices (3*d* or 6*d* in the case of Woolworth's). Service was kept to a minimum, with the customer almost serving himself. Hence unskilled, poorly paid, mainly female workers could be recruited. By 1900 Marks & Spencer had thirty-six branches, twelve of them in shops and the rest in market halls. The managerial staff was provided by women already in the company's employ. A large store would employ ten or twelve girls under a manageress, assisted by a manageress in training.[102] The Woolworth chain in 1914 had forty-four outlets in Britain, and although male managers were hired, the sales staff was entirely female, with part-timers drawn in to help on Saturdays. In the 1920s a Bradford millworker remembered spending her Saturday afternoons serving in the local Woolworth's store: 'I'd . . . run home . . . have my dinner, get washed and changed and be right up at Woolworth's for one o'clock. I worked there from one o'clock till nine and it was five shillings. If you were on short time you could ask to go in all day Saturday. It was ten shillings for all day.' She took the job because she wanted extra cash to go to dances.[103]

Initially most of the multiple chains were established with the proprietor's own capital or the financial help of his family. Expansion was achieved by increasing turnover massively and where possible cutting costs by eliminating the middleman. To achieve the first objective there was a widespread use of advertising, while the merchandising process was simplified by concentrating on a limited range of standardised products. Sometimes, as in the case of footwear firms like Stead & Simpson and Freeman, Hardy & Willis, retail outlets were set up to sell factory-made products at a time when independent retailers were reluctant to stock the sometimes clumsy, cheap boots and shoes manufactured by the first machines.[104]

One of the early entrepreneurs to follow this policy of having a limited product range and making extensive use of advertising was the Scots-born Thomas Lipton. His parents owned a small provision store in a working-class district of Glasgow, and from an early age he helped in the business. However, in his teens he went to America for four years, finishing up by working in a New York grocery store. It was this spell in the United States that convinced him of the importance of advertising as a way of promoting sales. In his autobiography he attributed much of his success to hard work and the 'Power of Advertisement'.[105]

Lipton returned to Scotland in 1869, aged 19, and again began working in the family shop, doing most of the buying and the window dressing, as well as serving. But his father was not prepared to accept his ideas for expanding the business and so in 1871 the youngster opened a shop of his own in Stobcross Street, Glasgow. He specialised in the sale of ham, bacon and dairy produce, mostly imported from Ireland. His business principles were simple – low prices, no home deliveries and cash payments. As he later wrote, his motto was 'cash down; no credit!' and that applied not merely to the customers but to his own purchases.[106]

Lipton worked long hours, sometimes sleeping on the premises, but he offered the working-class housewives who patronised his shop a clean and attractive environment, while he himself appeared smartly dressed in a white coat and apron. As Peter Mathias has commented, the 'air of smartness and cleanliness [was] calculated to win over the most demanding housewife. . . . No shopkeeper ever set out to court the working-class housewife in quite the same way before.'[107]

After about six weeks the business had prospered sufficiently for a boy to be hired to assist in running messages and doing odd jobs. The lad was shabbily dressed and Lipton, believing this detracted from the appearance of the shop, gave him money to buy a new suit. This the youngster promptly wore to get a better-paid job elsewhere. Despite that disappointing start, Lipton soon found a number of reliable assistants, one of them subsequently becoming a director of Lipton's.[108]

To boost sales the young shopkeeper adopted various advertising stunts, such as parading two large fat pigs through the streets bearing a banner with the words 'Lipton's Orphans'.[109] Cartoons were displayed in his shop window and a monster cheese was imported from America at Christmas and paraded through the streets before being taken to his shop. Extra assistants were hired so that he could go to Ireland to buy from the producers much of the food sold in the shop. This direct purchasing cut out the wholesaler's profit and was later adopted for other products, as Lipton's stock widened. In 1890 he acquired tea plantations in Ceylon to provide tea for his business, while a bakery was set up to supply cakes and biscuits. He also established facilities for ham and bacon curing and a factory for jam making, as well as much more besides.[110]

Three years after setting up in Stobcross Street, Lipton had sufficient capital to open a second shop in Glasgow High Street and a few months later he took over a third business. Soon plans were afoot for further expansion, not only in Glasgow but in Dundee in 1878 and Paisley in 1879. An account of the opening of the Dundee shop mentioned the rows of hams and the large assortment of bacon, butter and cheese on offer. 'A substantial horse-shoe counter gives a large space for salesmen, and it is evident that Mr Lipton intends to carry on an extensive business, for we understand that he has a staff of from twelve to fifteen salesmen, besides three cash boys.'[111] In 1881 he opened his first branch in England, at Leeds, with stores in Liverpool, Birmingham, Sunderland, Manchester, Bristol, Cardiff, London, Swansea and Belfast following in the next eight years.[112] He later claimed that property owners 'all over the Kingdom wrote to me whenever they had a shop to let. If the town was of any size at all I paid it a visit.'[113] Unlike the many smaller, regional multiples, Lipton did not increase his stores incrementally from an established base but sought to place them in large centres of population and in a good location. Before opening in a fresh town he engaged in a campaign of press publicity. In these early years he made it a rule to be behind the counter on the opening day of every new store and claimed to have celebrated his 26th birthday by working fourteen hours at the opening of a shop in Greenock. 'More than that, I made it a practice to serve the first customer myself. . . . With white jacket and apron, I watched the entrance of the first housewife.'[114] By the mid-1880s, with his branch network expanding, he had gathered around him a competent group of 'managers, buyers, cashiers and accountants, to say nothing of the rank and file' to enable him to maintain the momentum of the business.[115]

From the late 1880s Lipton became involved in the tea trade and although there had been packaged tea before his advent, the offering of competitively priced, clearly marked packets in weights of a pound, half-pound and quarter-pound, with the quality prominently displayed, soon achieved popularity not only in Britain but overseas.[116] Within a short time he was handling over 10 per cent of the nation's sales of tea.[117]

But Lipton's was only one example of a multiple enterprise with nationwide outlets. Other major grocery chains followed similar lines, including Home and Colonial Stores, Maypole Dairies, Meadow Dairies, and a number of others. Except for Home and Colonial, which originated in London, most began operations in the industrial areas of the north or of Scotland, only expanding southwards as their capital increased, perhaps through incorporation, or as opportunities for buying up smaller rivals offered themselves. At first these firms concentrated on stocking a standardised range of products designed to appeal to working-class customers. James Jefferys has described the typical multiple provision store in the late nineteenth century as: 'Not so much a shop as a simple structure for distributing a limited number of articles to the public in a limited time and space.'[118] Units were small, with a single counter as almost the only fitting, and the main display of the goods was in the open shop fronts and hanging from rails outside the shop. Most of the trade was undertaken in the evenings, the shops being open until 10 or 11 p.m. and often to midnight on Saturdays, 'and the hissing fish-tail gas jets or oil lamps lit up the heaped piles of eggs, the mountains of butter and margarine, the bacon, sugar and tea that customers were invited to purchase. The staff numbered two or three and the "outside man" in his white serving coat would be shouting the price, value and quality of the goods, enticing and attending to customers and handing or throwing purchases or money back to the counter for weighing, wrapping or putting in the till.'[119]

Inducements to patronise the shop included offers of 'bonus' tea or sugar, while 'in the industrial North dividends on purchases in the form of cash, stamps or free gifts' were available in order 'to compete with the dividend paid by Co-operative Societies'.[120] Some firms used their assistants as part of their marketing strategy. For example, Massey's, a Scottish multiple concentrating on ham, bacon and dairy produce (with tea added after 1880), arranged to have a ham window and a 'butter' window in their shops. The latter displayed butter, cheese, lard and later margarine, and assistants could be seen through the window knocking up butter into saleable packs.[121] Maypole Dairies followed a similar policy, while Home and Colonial Stores had their windows so arranged that assistants could be seen weighing up tea, decked out in chefs' hats.[122] The intention was to show the public that everything was 'fair, square and above board', as regards the weight and quality of the goods on offer.

John James Sainsbury and his wife, Mary Ann, who set up their first dairy shop in 1869, adopted a rather different strategy. Mary Ann's father already owned a small chain of half a dozen dairy shops and the young couple were determined that the milk and butter they sold should be of the highest quality. According to one of the firm's first employees, Sarah Pullen, Mrs Sainsbury made the store famous for the quality of its butter and 'took great pride in the cleanliness of the shop'.[123] By the early 1880s the couple owned around seven small shops. Then in 1882 they opened a 'model' branch in Croydon, with high-quality fittings and a 'cool, pleasant atmosphere', aimed at a middle-class clientele to whom they offered superior foods and greater variety than did the existing multiples. Other branches followed and by 1900 they numbered forty-eight – modest by comparison with firms like Lipton's and Home and Colonial – but sticking to their high-quality strategy, Sainsbury fitted out his stores with marble counters, tiled walls and mosaic floors, with the tiles and floors being produced specially for the firm. He also insisted that every shop should be well lit.[124]

By the beginning of the twentieth century the various grocery multiples had established hundreds of branches and were entering into fierce competition with one another. In 1898, at the time of his firm's incorporation, Lipton had 242 branches open in Britain and 12 more in preparation; in the same year Maypole Dairies had 185 branches, although that total had more than doubled by 1903, and in 1915 there were 958 outlets. Home and Colonial Stores had about 500 shops in 1903.[125] In all, the multiple firms – that is, those having ten or more branches – were taking perhaps 3.5 to 4.5 per cent of the total food and household goods retail market in 1900, a figure that had risen to 6.5 to 9 per cent of the market a decade later.[126]

Centralised policies were needed to run these large enterprises, with bulk buying to keep down costs and a strict hierarchical structure adopted for the management of the staff. The important grades were the buyers, the inspectors and the shop managers. The inspectors were responsible for seeing that the company's general strategy was applied at branch level, with the activities of store personnel closely supervised. Lipton was said to select many of his managers and inspectors from fellow Scots. He also demanded that senior staff adopt (or at least persuade him that they had adopted) 'the strict temperance rule he set himself'.[127]

The inspectors had to ensure that the stores opened and closed at set times, these being fixed according to the custom of the district in which a shop was located. That could mean very late closing in some places. Hence although Thomas Lipton supported compulsory early closing on one day a week, he was determined 'to maintain the competitive position of his shops where no local agreement between everyone in the trade' could be achieved. So in Birmingham in the 1880s the firm's stores stayed open most nights until 9 p.m. but it was 10 p.m. on Fridays and sometimes midnight on Saturdays, the 'great shopping night for the poor'.[128]

Likewise Mrs Elsie Webster, whose father was a shop manager for James Pegram, a Liverpool-based multiple grocery firm, recalled that he sometimes arrived home after midnight on Saturdays. He left each morning at about 7 a.m., eating his breakfast when he reached the shop. He had to remain on the premises all day when he became manager, so 'the shop boy used to come up and get his dinner [in a basket] . . . me mother cooked . . . perhaps two little chops and . . . he had . . . a little bottle of beer and she used to put that in the bottom of the basket'.[129]

It was also the responsibility of the inspectors to check that the correct weight and quality of goods were being sold. To this end they might use surrogates to go into the store to make a purchase, but this kind of 'surreptitious snooping' was much resented by staff.[130] To guard against petty theft it was common to require managers and senior assistants to take out fidelity bonds, much as happened in the co-operative stores. These were designed to cover possible shortfalls in cash or stock. Radius agreements were frequently insisted upon, too, with staff undertaking not to take a post for a fixed period of time in a similar business within a specified distance of their current employment. The agreements could run for between one and ten years, and in some districts might preclude an employee following his trade altogether if he lost his job. Occasionally, companies would take assistants to court for breaches of radius agreements and might win damages from them. In others, 'the courts held that such restrictive covenants were not necessary for the protection of the companies' business', and the cases were dismissed.[131] The rationale behind the policy was that if a worker moved to a rival firm in the neighbourhood, or set up in business for himself, he might take customers with him or pass on confidential information about how his former store was run.

These were issues with which the National Union of Shop Assistants (later the National Amalgamated Union of Shop Assistants, Warehousemen and Clerks (NAUSAW&C)) became involved after its formation in 1891. In the early twentieth century its annual reports detailed some of the cases taken up. One such occurred in 1913, when the manager of a branch in a small country town was threatened with an injunction under a radius agreement. According to the union, he had been dismissed without prior warning one Monday morning, with wages paid up to that date. The union, on his behalf, sued the multiple grocery company for the wages due for the current week, which had begun on the Monday morning, and for a further week in lieu of notice. After some demur, the wages were paid but in the interim the man had secured a post with a local pork butcher who also sold bacon and ham, like his previous employer:

When the firm heard of this, he received a letter from their solicitors threatening to apply for an injunction. After carefully going into the matter, our solicitors advised that we contest the case, and when the . . . injunction was applied for, it was successfully resisted. The firm then tried to induce the Union to come to a compromise, and wanted to know if their costs could be paid, and would the member sign an agreement not to advertise the fact that he had been manager at their establishment in the town. This was refused, and eventually they abandoned the main action, evidently fearing they might lose the case if it went to trial.[132]

To the union's satisfaction not only had its stance been vindicated and the member protected, but its costs were also met. It recommended members not to sign such agreements but recognised this might be difficult if a signature were a condition of employment. It also condemned the fidelity and guarantee societies which accepted premiums from the multiple chains, or their employees, guaranteeing the firms against losses. It pointed out these were not necessarily the fault of the branch staff but could arise from mistakes and inefficiency on the part of the head office.[133] Perhaps not surprisingly a number of the multiples, including Lipton's, were hostile to the NAUSAW&C and dismissed staff if it became known they were members.[134]

The branding of employees as potential thieves was further underlined by a clause in the agreement drawn up for workers hired by Home and Colonial Stores. This laid down that they must be willing 'to be searched at any time by an authorised official of the company'.[135] Home and Colonial also laid down that managers must not leave cash in the shop after closing. They had to take it home with them – something which caused worry not only to them but to their family. Furthermore, although managers might receive commission, it was classed as a 'gift' from the firm and from it they were required to pay for 'all breakages of utensils in use' in their shop.[136] And if an employee should be so bold as to buy any of the company's shares without the board's permission, this was regarded as 'an offence the only adequate punishment of which [was] instant dismissal'.[137]

Mr C.C., an anonymous former assistant employed by Lipton's in the 1890s, claimed that workers were expected to find their own white working aprons, at a cost of about 1s each. They needed at least six of these a year, and were expected to wear white shirts and to dress well and smartly. C.C. thought it was better 'to be in a small shop where the Master superintends than in a branch shop of a big firm under a Manager. Managers', he declared sourly, 'are very jealous, and do all they can to keep back assistants who show ability for fear they should supplant them.'[138]

So while employment in a branch of a large multiple chain could offer prospects of promotion from assistant to manager at a relatively early age and also the chance to move on to manage a large branch and perhaps even to become an inspector, staff were expected to work in a strictly regulated environment. Failure, misfortune or even ill-health could lead to speedy dismissal. According to Mr A., who had managed a shop for one of the multiples, in that firm at least, one week's sickness was regarded as a week's notice, and there was a note to that effect hung up in the warehouse and in the store itself.[139] He also claimed that a man who failed to gain promotion but began to want higher wages as an assistant as he became older, was likely to be dismissed, to keep down labour costs.

Throughout these years the independent traders watched the increased role of the multiples with growing alarm. The bitterness felt by some was expressed in a comment on the eve of the First World War that aspiring to become the branch manager of a multiple shop was not a legitimate ambition: 'these individuals were "not grocers at all, but mere bloodsuckers making profit out of a gullible public"'.[140] Some of the independents sought to meet the competition by forming trade associations and seeking to persuade manufacturers not to supply their larger rivals, much as they had attempted to do in respect of the co-operative societies. But in most cases they had little success. Even in 1906 the Federation of Grocers' Associations only accounted for around one-fifth of all grocers, making it impossible to present a united front to fight the price-cutting policies of the multiples at a national level.[141] More effective were local negotiations to establish a minimum price for certain commodities, such as sugar. In Leicester the town's Grocers' Association contacted the managers of multiple outlets there and gradually developed a tentative working agreement. Also useful were the bulk buying schemes introduced by some associations to improve the purchasing power of members. The Leicester Grocers' Association created a bulk buying combine for selected goods in October 1906 and within three months it was so successful that it was extended to other products.[142] Many associations sought to promote trade skills, too, by encouraging the setting up of training schemes. In 1909 the Institute of Certificated Grocers was inaugurated. Assistants who passed the Institute's examinations would be certified and could later become associates. The aim was to restore the grocery and provision trades 'to their ancient dignity and usefulness'.[143]

Some middle-class grocers reacted by forming branch networks of their own, without sacrificing what they regarded as the high-quality service they offered. Among them were T.D. Smith, a Lancaster family grocer with ten shops by 1914, and the Croydon firm of W.E. Coatman and Sons, which also had ten shops. One of them was in Tonbridge in Kent and the rest were in Surrey, including four in Croydon itself. A delivery service was offered, and according to the son of Coatman's Tonbridge shop manager, the staff, with the exception of the cashier-cum-bookkeeper, were all skilled men. In this case the manager occupied spacious accommodation above the shop and enjoyed 'many perks of the job, manufacturers' free samples and seasonal gifts being gratefully received'. Some important customers were connected with Tonbridge School and the manager himself 'always went for the best orders in the pony and trap and he used to wear top hat and morning coat. He'd go round to the big houses and districts surrounding and sometimes he was in some of these places more or less all day.' He had a good deal of independence in running his shop, and was responsible for paying the wages of the counter assistants and the head provisions man. He received commission on the profits he made, so that his pay of £2 a week and free accommodation was boosted by the quarterly bonus he obtained.[144] Some of these genteel, small-scale 'multiples' prospered, providing they had access to a good middle-class market. Of T.D. Smith's business in Lancaster it has been said that the 'huge increase in turnover' which followed the expansion of the branch network was 'an indication of its general success'.[145]

One area where trade association resistance to the trading policies of the multiple firms had a measure of success was in pharmacy. From the 1870s the activities of Jesse Boot in particular demonstrated that multiple shop methods could be applied even to the skilled and individual trade of the chemist. In the early 1870s Boot added a range of household goods to the herbal remedies on which his father had based his small business. But the working classes were transferring their allegiance from herbalism to the new, heavily advertised, patent medicines. In 1874 Boot decided to enter that trade himself and to undercut the prices that were being charged by the traditional chemists.[146] After a slow start the business flourished, boosted by a major advertising campaign in 1877. By August of that year Boot claimed to be the biggest patent-medicine dealer not only in his native Nottingham but in the surrounding area. Among the cut-price items offered in the early 1880s were Epsom Salts, sold at a penny a pound, when the usual price was a half-penny an ounce, and soft soap, the ordinary price of which was about 4d a pound, but which Boot offered at 4½d for two pounds. In anticipation of the Saturday rush of customers, all his counter men occupied their spare time during the week weighing up quantities of the popular lines.[147]

In the late 1870s he began to meet opposition from the chemists in Nottingham and his unqualified status prevented him from providing a dispensary service, as his rivals lost no opportunity in pointing out. Then in 1880 a decision in the House of Lords, laying down that a limited company could employ a qualified pharmacist to dispense medicines, opened the way. In 1883 Boot converted his business to a limited liability company and set about recruiting a pharmacist to run the dispensary he intended to open.[148] The man selected, Edwin Waring, joined the staff in 1884 and soon caught the cut-price spirit of the Boots enterprise. Whereas prescriptions usually cost 2s 6d each, Waring asked only half that amount, or even less. Before the end of the year Jesse Boot was leasing his first branch shops in Lincoln and Sheffield, and was hiring qualified chemists to manage them, once they had completed an initiation period in the Nottingham shop. Henceforward all Boots shops were controlled by qualified pharmacists. The number of outlets grew rapidly from 33 in 1893 to 126 four years later. By 1914 they had reached 560, boosted by takeovers of smaller rivals as well as by the firm's own branch expansion programme.[149]

So hostile was the pharmacy trade to the Boots enterprise that any qualified men who joined as branch managers were likely to be ostracised by their fellow chemists and refused admission to the local branch of the Pharmaceutical Society. Hence James Mavor, appointed manager of the firm's Hanley branch in 1895 when it opened, was refused membership of the Stoke-on-Trent Chemists' Association a decade later.[150] But because the success of Boot's business depended on these qualified men he had to pay them higher salaries and provide benefits significantly superior to those offered by private chemists. By contrast, the assistants employed were normally unqualified, although by the early twentieth century an apprentice recruitment scheme was being set up to assist promising lads to serve a statutory apprenticeship and study to pass the Pharmaceutical Society's examinations.[151]

In 1885 Boot also established a manufacturing division and assistants who sold the firm's own products were paid commission on the sales, although no such bonus was offered on the products of other manufacturers – a clear incentive to staff to sell the Boots brand.

Boots was not the only multiple firm in the business. Rivals included Taylor's Drug Co. Ltd of Leeds and the Portsmouth firm of Timothy White. Day's Southern Drug Company, of Southampton, expanded its branches rapidly in the 1890s, before its sixty-five stores were bought by Boot in 1901, when he sought to break into the London market. However, it was Boots that aroused the hostility of the private chemists. Efforts were made to persuade manufacturers of proprietary brands to boycott the firm because of its price-cutting tactics. These were not very fruitful but the efforts of the Proprietary Articles Trade Association to maintain the price of certain products did meet with some success, Boot agreeing to observe the price of goods classified under the Association's heading.[152] This may have been partly because with the successful expansion of the business, and its diversification to include libraries, stationery, fancy goods and photographic equipment alongside its core drug sales, Boots appetite for price cutting was moderated. 'As a result,' comments Hamish Fraser, 'there was a great deal less conflict in the trade between the Pharmaceutical Society, representing the small traders, and the multiples in the years immediately before 1914 than there had been earlier.'[153]

Chapter 4

FROM DRAPER'S SHOP TO DEPARTMENT STORE, 1820–1914

. . . if we carry our minds back twenty-five years we can remember the smallness and inferiority of English shops as compared with those of Paris or Vienna, or even some of the smaller capitals of Europe. . . . Each shop had its own speciality, and the more expensive and costly its goods, the more unremittingly conservative was it in its way of carrying on its business. . . . There are two very important changes which have contributed to the temptation of spending money nowadays. One is gathering together under one roof . . . all the necessaries of life. . . . And the other is the employment of women as shop assistants in the place of men.

M. Jeune [Lady Jeune], 'The Ethics of Shopping', in *The Fortnightly Review*, vol. 63 (January 1895), pp. 123 and 125.

DRAPERS' SHOPS

Most drapery businesses during the early nineteenth century consisted of three main departments. These were the piece goods section, which stocked textiles; the haberdashery department, with articles ranging from pins, needles and threads to ribbons and trimmings; and the fancy goods sector, where such miscellaneous products as handkerchiefs, lace, gloves, hosiery and women's caps were to be found. Some ready-made wearing apparel was available in shops 'not aspiring to sell to the higher ranks of society', including hats, cloaks, breeches, waistcoats and ready-made dresses. As early as the 1730s Mary and Ann Hogarth, for example, announced on their trade card that they sold 'Ready Made Frocks, sutes of Fustian, Ticken and Holland . . . blue and Canvas Frocks . . . at reasonable rates'. Later in the century Ham's Muslin and Linen Warehouse on the Strand advertised 'cheap ready-made fashionable dresses, ladies' great coats, petticoats', with the prices carefully listed.[1] Female underclothing was also sold and there were some retailers, like the Banbury tailor and outfitter

William Baker, who offered their own ready-made specialities. In his case these were apparently waterproof leggings and smock frocks, for sale to agricultural customers.[2] A number of shopkeepers provided additional services, too, such as undertaking funerals or, like Elizabeth Brown in Bradford, combining the sale of underwear and clothing with running a circulating library.[3]

As David Alexander points out, these broader aspects were particularly likely in small country towns or in villages, where the 'complete range of cloth and clothing trades might be subsumed in one shop'. He quotes the example of Thomas Gibbon of Wrotham in Kent, who in the 1820s was 'a tailor, milliner, draper, haberdasher, hatter, hosier and shoeseller'.[4] Even in the early twentieth century village shops would sell cheap articles of drapery alongside grocery and household goods.[5]

Advertisements in the trade press indicated the size of a business and the quality of goods sold, as well as the amount of capital needed to set up. In May 1880, for example, *The Drapers' Journal* advertised two shops for sale. One was a 'very desirable little business requiring small capital' in a rural setting, where 'a beginner with about £200 would do well'. In the second case, a drapery and outfitting business was offered in a town in the West of England: 'Returns about £4,000. Good profits. Capital required about £1,200.'[6]

In his survey of London life in the 1890s Charles Booth mentioned further distinctions. He categorised drapers' shops as low, medium or high class according to the clientele for whom they catered or the neighbourhood in which they traded. 'Walworth', he declared, 'is as much above Bermondsey New Road as Lewisham or Holloway would consider themselves above Walworth; and a widening gulf separates these from shops in Kensington, in Oxford Street and in Regent Street', the latter being at the top of his scale. This classification was also linked to the system of payment they adopted, whether they sold for ready money or on credit, with fashionable, high-class shops as those most likely to have 'running accounts'.[7] As in the eighteenth century, these debts might continue for years. A surviving bill issued by John Sinclair, a Bath linen and woollen draper, tailor and hatter, on 20 February 1872, for the modest sum of £3 3s 8d, was only settled finally in December 1875, although small payments on account had been made in the interim.[8]

Thomas Oakman, who held a senior post with Handley & Johnston's, linen drapers of Southwark Park Road, London, in the 1890s, largely concurred with Booth's classification, although he divided shops according to the quality of the merchandise in which they dealt. He considered the shop where he worked to have 'a low class trade', although he thought it superior to similar businesses in the Bermondsey New Road.[9] Its customers were mainly the families of clerks and skilled workers.

These distinctions affected the employment opportunities of shop assistants. According to Oakman, a man or woman who had worked 'in a good house would not go into a low class house, whilst one from such a house would not be taken in a first class house unless under exceptional circumstances'. As an illustration of this he quoted the case of a young man who had completed his apprenticeship in a humble establishment but was then employed by the superior West End drapers Swan and Edgar, through the intervention of the Young Men's Christian Association. He took the post but 'nothing was said about salary', and when he enquired about this he was told loftily that, 'they should not think of paying any salary; he should think himself lucky in getting into such a house at all'. In Oakman's view this approach favoured applicants from the provinces, since they could come armed with apprenticeship papers and perhaps a letter from a local clergyman attesting to their respectability. Such a youngster might have learned his trade 'in a small village shop but the London firm know nothing of the country shop & take him on whereas a lad coming from a larger London shop, might not stand a chance; the employer knowing the shop might think, "We don't want anything of that class".'[10] Oakman nonetheless thought it best for a trainee to start in a small business, since there he would gain a wider range of experience. He should begin in the haberdashery department and then move on to hosiery, household linen and finally dress materials. 'A good haberdasher will be a good draper,' he declared.[11]

As well as the continuities in the drapery trade over the period there were significant changes, too, both in organisation and in employment, to say nothing of the goods stocked. In the 1870s a contemporary considered that one of the most striking developments in goods offered for sale was the wide range of ready-made articles compared with the situation when he began in the trade half a century earlier. At the later date there were 'departments exclusively for women's petticoats, mantles, &c., while there are wholesale houses which keep nothing else but gentlemen's made-up neck ties'.[12] The first boost to the ready-made clothing market in his view had been given when drapers began offering ready to wear women's cloaks with circular capes.[13] 'Off-the-peg' men's clothes, too, appeared. Already by the 1840s E. Moses & Son, tailors, wholesale woollen drapers and outfitters, with shops in more than one London location, advertised their wares showing a 'two column price list, one for ready-made articles, the other for made to measure'. Also included was an assurance that 'Any article purchased, or ordered, if not approved of, exchanged, or the money returned.'[14] It was a surprisingly modern sales ploy.

The widening range of goods sold led to an increasing departmentalisation within the larger stores. By 1870 the high-class London firm of Debenham & Freebody had twenty-seven different departments, including silks, furs, shawls, hosiery, gloves, parasols, household drapery, millinery, ribbons, lace and embroideries.[15] It also had an important wholesale business and in the early twentieth century 'top-hatted representatives from other big stores' bought from the firm's wholesaling division. Its millinery department was so successful that a factory to supply its needs was opened at Luton.[16]

A minority of these large drapery shops, including Debenham's, evolved into department stores, with staffs running into hundreds and even thousands, and with an array of goods and services on offer which went well beyond the draper's traditional trade. However, most businesses continued to operate on a modest scale, much as they had always done, although with an increasing likelihood that more aggressive marketing methods would be adopted to promote sales. These included the use of attractive window displays, large-scale advertising and the holding of seasonal sales. As an advisory handbook of 1912 declared, 'the retail shopkeeper fails in his plans of salesmanship if he does not advertise or take some steps to secure for his own personal aggrandisement the benefits . . . outside advertising is bringing to his door'.[17]

Usually advertisers would emphasise the good quality, low price and fashionable nature of the goods on offer, with special mention made of any purchases from Paris or from France generally. In 1847 Messrs Bland and Halley of York announced to the 'Nobility and Public' that their stock was now 'replete, with the most GORGEOUS DISPLAY OF NOVELTIES ever witnessed in York . . . their recent visit to PARIS, LYONS, LONDON, GLASGOW, PAISLEY, MANCHESTER and other Markets . . . has enabled them to select a STUPENDOUS & MAGNIFICENT STOCK, which will be offered at prices that cannot fail to prove highly satisfactory to Purchasers'.[18]

More restrained was Emerson Bainbridge, who had set up a draper's shop in Newcastle in 1838 with a partner, and who decided to establish a 'French Room' to meet the demand for goods from Paris. This opened in 1846 and according to an advertisement it offered a selection of silks and shawls 'of the most elegant styles', as well as parasols, bonnet and cap ribbons 'in indescribable Variety', cartons of French flowers, gloves from Grenoble and Paris, and 'a few boxes of French Cambric Handkerchiefs . . . of the finest Textures . . . sold at one-third of their Value'. Bainbridge's continued to expand and by 1850 the store was divided into departments, with records showing '23 separate sets of takings at this date'.[19] Soon it moved outside the sphere of purely female fashion, which was the traditional preoccupation of specialist drapers, to offer 'Men's Mercery and Ready-made clothing'. Some articles were made on the premises. As the firm grew into a department store it continued to cater both for the working people of Newcastle and for the substantial middle classes. As late as 1892 it had a department selling pit clothes.

As regards employment in the drapery trades, the biggest change was the feminisation of the work-force during the second half of the nineteenth century. In the late 1850s the *English Woman's Journal* advised its readers that 'ladies could exercise a great influence in promoting the employment of saleswomen in shops simply by insisting that they be served by women'. An address to that effect, signed by about 200 'influential women', was sent to London tradesmen and to the press.[20] Although sceptics cast doubts on female suitability for such a career, in the drapery sector at least the message was apparently heeded. According to the 1851 population census there were 42,189 drapers and silk mercers in England and Wales, of whom 14.5 per cent were women and girls. By 1871 that total had increased to 74,337, with 25.7 per cent of the labour force now female, and by 1911 the figure had reached 150,968, of whom 56 per cent were women and girls.[21] Overwhelmingly they were employees. Of the 84,606 females recorded as occupied in selling drapery and silk mercery in 1911, just over 3,500 were employers or were working on their own account. Among the 66,362 men so engaged, by contrast, about 17,500 (or over a quarter) were employers or were working for themselves.[22] Already, therefore, in the early twentieth century women outnumbered men as employees in the drapery trade, with their overall total rising by more than 340 per cent between 1871 and 1911, compared with an increase of 103 per cent for employment in the trade as a whole. Many worked in London, with around one in five of the men being employed in the capital and around one in eleven of the females in 1911. Most high-class traders also stressed the impeccable middle-class origins of their women sales staff. At Lewis & Allenby, prestigious Regent Street silk mercers and furriers, Mr Lewis claimed that many of his female assistants were 'accomplished girls & all . . . from middle class families. Some are clergymen's daughters.'[23] At that date, in the mid-1890s, the firm had 78 male and 45 female members of staff, including apprentices.

Women were cheaper to employ, easier to discipline, and usually more congenial to the female customers, who made up a major part of any draper's clientele, than were their male colleagues. Lady Jeune made this clear in a light-hearted article published in 1895. In it she welcomed the female invasion, praising the intuitive understanding that was shown concerning the wants of customers: 'they can fathom the agony of despair as to the arrangement of colours, the alternative trimmings, the duration of a fashion, the depths of a woman's purse, and, more important than all, the question as to the becomingness of a dress, or a combination of material to the would-be wearer'.[24] She compared this to the gloomy atmosphere in which the social elite had purchased clothes in the 1870s. Then most of the exclusive shops had little by way of window display and purchasers tended to buy from long-established specialists. Goods were obtained on credit, with bills rendered at the end of the year, 'for no well-thought-of firm ever demanded or expected more than a yearly payment of their debts'. An afternoon's shopping was a dreary affair, with the client received at the shop door by the proprietor or a black-clad shopwalker, who combined the role of buyer with that of 'host to the customer and NCO of the sales staff', as Bill Lancaster has put it.[25] He 'delivered one over to another solemn gentleman, and perhaps again to a third, who found one a chair, and in a sepulchral tone of voice uttered some magic words, such as "Silk, Mr Smith", or "Velvet, Mr A" and then departed to seek another victim'.[26] It was the assistant's task to make sure that the customer's wants were satisfied and woe betide him, or her, if a sale were not made. In many shops a sharp reprimand and even dismissal would follow if an assistant allowed the customer to depart unserved, without calling upon a buyer or shopwalker for help.[27] For Lady Jeune the whole business 'left an impression of responsibility and sadness in one's mind . . . and with a great sense of relief the large doors closed behind one'.[28]

Lower down the social scale the atmosphere was less formal. Drapers had already discovered the benefits of offering goods at fixed prices and for ready money. They were also prepared, when necessary, to increase turnover by bogus promotions, designed to exploit customers' wish for a bargain. Hence damaged or bankrupt stock was proffered at an apparently reduced price. As Richard Lambert drily comments, some tradesmen, 'more inventive' than their fellows, 'would improve upon . . . pretended disasters. A small but real fire might be made the occasion of a vast "sale" of goods imported and specially singed for the purpose.'[29]

The assistants were expected to play their part in securing these sales, and those who succeeded best were regarded as 'smart' and were paid the highest salaries. As a former shopworker wrote bitterly, in such cases 'obsequiousness, fawning, lying are held up . . . as "tact". . . . To palm off spurious articles upon an unwary purchaser, or persuade a reluctant one to an unprofitable bargain, figures as "ability".'[30] Commission on sales was offered as an incentive. On occasion, as with the Glasgow firm of Fraser Brothers in 1897, a bonus system for staff would be introduced in order to boost turnover and thus profits.[31]

Some of the flavour of this hard-headed approach can be gained from advertisements for sales staff that appeared in the trade press. In *The Drapers'*

Journal during the early summer of 1880 a Bournemouth draper sought 'a YOUNG LADY for the fancy and window-dressing, with a knowledge of millinery. Must be pushing. Age, height and salary.' A similar appeal was inserted by a Colchester shopkeeper, looking for a 'Good JUNIOR YOUNG MAN' for 'a pushing trade'. In this case a photograph had to be supplied, together with details of the applicant's age.[32] A good appearance was an important asset for a would-be shop assistant, and that included height. According to the anonymous 'Old Draper' one of the reasons for his success as a shawls salesman was that he was about 6ft: 'tall men were considered the best as shawl-men', presumably because they could display the large expanse of material with an appropriate flourish. Even at the end of the nineteenth century Margaret Bondfield, who became a trade union activist and the first woman cabinet minister, recalled that her short stature was a handicap when she looked for employment as an assistant in Oxford Street. She had served her apprenticeship in Brighton and Hove, ending up at the firm of Hetherington's, where she learned the art of window-dressing, stock-keeping and sales technique from a very able buyer. As her biographer comments, she also learned the harsher side of shop life, and above all the penalties of the 'living in' system.

> Living-in meant a total want of freedom, out of business hours as well as in them. It meant that the assistants had no privacy of any kind. They slept in dormitories (which they were fined for entering out of hours), dingy, ill-ventilated, sparsely furnished, cold in winter, intolerably hot in summer, unbearably stuffy at all times. They were not alone even to wash. They had to keep their clothes in boxes under their beds: for reading and writing there was no sort of provision, nor any other possibility of rest or refreshment of mind or body during the brief hours of freedom from the shop.[33]

Happily not all 'live-in' staff had such miserable memories. A number welcomed the protected environment of the better retail establishments and the companionship offered, especially if they were working in a strange town, away from family and friends. In 1914 Kaye Snow wrote to the press from Margate to say she had applied to live in at the business house where she worked even though her home was in the town. The assistants were 'well provided for and looked after in every way' and it was 'a convenience to be close at hand for business . . . I have lived in London and had to find my own board and lodging, and I would not now care to take a post on those conditions.'[34]

In 1894 Margaret Bondfield left Brighton to seek work in the capital. She had excellent references but they were of little avail in her first few months of looking for employment in an overstocked labour market:

> I would go to the City warehouses early in the morning and get any information I could from the City [commercial] travellers as to possible vacancies. I then had to go off on the old horse buses, sometimes to the other end of London, only to discover when I got there that I was one of perhaps 150 to 200 applicants, that before we had stood in the queue for long a notice would be sent out: 'No good waiting any longer – places filled.'
>
> I have taken the whole of Oxford Street, going into every shop . . . on the chance that there might be a vacancy, and then when I happened upon a vacancy, I was not tall enough. I remember one man saying to me: 'We never engage anyone under five feet eight inches.' Fortunately they were less particular about inches in the outer ring of business establishments.[35]

She eventually got taken on by a small shop off the North End Road before moving to a larger firm in Westbourne Grove, Bayswater, where she was 'fortunate in having an employer whose daily visits to the shop were actually looked forward to by his assistants'.[36] But that did not mean that life was easy. The hours were long, around 76 a week, for a salary of about £25 a year. Even that was reduced by various fines and deductions.[37] The fierce competition for customers waged by shopkeepers meant that drapers kept open for as long as their fellow tradesmen were prepared to do business. In poorer districts and in industrial towns even in the 1890s that could mean until 9 p.m. on Fridays and any time between 10 p.m. and midnight on Saturdays. At a shop in Kilburn where Margaret worked, her employer counted up the amount of his takings after 8 p.m. and declared it had not paid for the gas, 'but he dared not shut up earlier than his competitors for fear he should lose a customer to them. At a small shop in Commercial Road my employer would send me out to scout around and see if the shops over the way showed any signs of closing; if they did we, too, would hastily and gladly put up the shutters.'[38]

However, even when the shop was shut, the staff often had to stay behind to tidy the stock. P.C. Hoffman, who worked at Samuel Lewis's Holborn Silk Market in the late nineteenth century, recalled that when business closed at 7 p.m. the assistants went upstairs to have their supper of bread, cheese and beer. After that they returned to the shop to clear up: 'folding . . . the silks, and hooking up the wrappers over the shelves and display tables. No department was allowed to go until all had been cleared. The "silks" was always the last because of its enormous display. We were lucky to be out by 8 p.m.; often it was 9.'[39]

Meal breaks were brief and in a small shop could be interrupted by the need to serve a customer. At the Holborn Silk Market staff had 20 minutes for dinner and 15 minutes for tea, both meals being consumed on the premises, but those breaks could be curtailed if they were called down to serve: 'The speaking-tube would whistle, and a voice say: "Two wanted for the dresses"; and down two dress men would have to go.'[40]

It was against these long working hours that the Early Closing Association and the shop workers' trade unions struggled in the Victorian and Edwardian years. Their efforts will be considered in the next chapter.

To add to the discomfort of the long hours was the fact that assistants had to remain on their feet, even when they were not serving customers or dealing with stock. For, as Lee Holcombe comments, 'shopkeepers . . . disliked to see their workers sitting about idle, fearing that it would give their establishments the reputation of doing little business and that customers would consider it lacking in respect to themselves'.[41] In 1886 the manager of Finsbury Park Boot Stores complained to a Select Committee on shop hours that his two daughters, who worked as assistants in two large drapery firms, had told him that very few retailers provided seats. Even if they did so, 'the young ladies had better not use them if they wish to retain their situations'.[42] That remained the case when in 1899 a Seats for Shop Assistants Act laid down that where females were employed there should be at least one seat for every three of them, either behind the counter or in some other suitable location.[43] In 1930 Dr Ethel Bentham, a medical practitioner and Labour Member of Parliament, spoke of the 'uterine' problems from which saleswomen suffered, brought on by the long hours of standing. 'I can say it has been told to me over and over again that if any girl does sit down the shopkeeper will find some other job for her to do . . . very quickly, and quite likely she will not have a job next week.'[44]

In firms where commission on sales was offered, the extra sums secured might exceed the assistant's basic salary. That applied to staff employed by the Oxford drapers F. Cape & Co. early in the twentieth century. Thus Alfred Cosford, who had joined the firm in 1897 and was eventually to become one of its buyers, in 1912 received commission amounting to £95 14s 5d at a time when his basic pay was about £79 a year. Cosford had been born at Moreton Pinkney in Northamptonshire and was the grandson of an agricultural labourer. He was to remain with Cape's until February 1935, by which time the shop had become a department store, catering mainly for working-class and lower-middle-class customers.[45]

Such long service was, however, exceptional in a trade where, especially among the men, frequent changes of post were common. According to Richard Lane, himself a draper's assistant working in Lambeth Walk, London, during the mid-1890s, about six to twelve months was 'the usual thing'.[46] Some wanted to widen their experience, others were looking for higher pay or a more comfortable situation. Even high-class firms like Liberty's, the Regent Street specialists in silks and oriental ware, had a surprisingly high staff turnover. A register of employees for the period 1883 to 1894 shows that in five departments of the store alone, of 190 workers recruited 125 had left within that eleven-year period and others had moved to different departments within the business. Furthermore, 62 of those appointed left within twelve months.[47] The vast majority of those moving on went of their own volition. Some of the women left to be married, while 12 employees went away on account of illness, 13 were considered unsuitable and 18 left because of changes within the department where they worked. In 1889 there were 255 members of staff working for Liberty's in Regent Street, including 5 commissionaires, 19 porters and 16 in the packing room, as well as those serving behind the counter or dealing with customers. Long-serving employee, William Judd, who had joined the firm when it opened in May 1875, recalled that they had 'a lot of bazaar work at different places and I was very often at work after 10 o'clock, fixing up and draping stalls; also we used to do a lot of theatre work'.[48]

Proprietors kept a close eye on their staff. Not only was living in, with all that that implied, the norm in many drapers' shops, but in larger firms formal contracts made clear what was expected. At Bainbridge's in Newcastle upon Tyne in the mid-nineteenth century an assistant had to promise to obey the 'lawful commands' of Emerson Bainbridge and his partner, and 'to conform in all things to the rules, fines and regulations . . . of their establishment; and . . . to find for himself all necessary medicine and surgical and other advice'. In return the firm would provide board, lodging and a monthly salary. But the agreement could be ended 'at any time' and 'without any previous notice whatever, and without being obliged to assign any reason for so doing'.[49]

Elsewhere, and particularly in London, end of season sacking was said to be 'common'. The 'flood of unemployment' that resulted, together with 'the terror involved', in one critic's view kept 'shop workers in that state of servility considered necessary to discipline them'.[50] Loss of employment was particularly serious for older workers in an occupation where men were spoken of as being 'too old at forty' to work behind the counter. According to a contemporary, 'under the merciless lash of economic necessity such men would dye their hair, wear elastic-sided boots and even corsets, in a desperate attempt to preserve an illusion of vigour and youthfulness'.[51] Among showroom girls appearance was always important. 'They are engaged entirely for their figures, and they have to endure agonies in the way of tight-lacing and "figure moulding" in order to satisfy the exacting demands of their employers,' declared *Modern Society* in 1910. One firm in Regent Street even specified a maximum waist measurement 'and a girl who [exceeded] it, even to the fraction of an inch, for more than a few days at a time, [was] discharged with little more than a moment's notice'.[52]

In many cases rules were drawn up which affected assistants' leisure hours as well as their work routine. At a draper's shop in East Anglia in 1854 a notice listed what was required:

Store must open promptly at 6 a.m. until 9 p.m. all the year round.

Store must be swept, counter, base shelves and showcases dusted.

Lamps trimmed, filled and chimney cleaned, pens made, doors and windows opened.

A pail of water and scuttle of coal must be brought in by each clerk [sic] before breakfast, if there is time to do so, and attend customers who call.

Any employee who is in the habit of smoking spanish cigars, getting shaved at a barber's shop, going to dances, and other such places of amusement will surely give his employer reason to be suspicious of his integrity and . . . honesty.

Each employee must pay not less than one guinea per year to the church, and attend Sunday School every Sunday.

Men are given one evening a week for courting purposes and two if they go to prayer meetings regularly.

After 14 hours work spare time should be devoted to reading good literature.[53]

The way in which assistants carried out their duties was regulated, too. David Morgan, who opened a drapery store at Cardiff in 1879, considered scissors to be 'the tools of a draper's trade' and sharply reproved a young assistant who had mislaid his: 'No scissors – no draper.' He stressed to staff that his business had been built up by the practice of frugality and saw to it that they practised what he preached. 'Every piece of paper, every bit of string, every pin that came into the shop had to be saved for further use. Any unnecessary use of artificial light had to be avoided.'[54] Yet, despite his idiosyncrasies, he was generally regarded as a good employer. When he died he made bequests to nine members of staff who had given long service to what had by then become one of Cardiff's leading department stores.[55]

In some cases, as with the Crouch End linen draper James H. Wilson, employees were reminded to make themselves agreeable to customers so as to promote sales. In the mid-1890s Wilson had twenty workers living in. Fourteen were women and girls, including a lady buyer. In addition three lads, aged about 14, acted as porters and errand boys and were non-resident. Among the rules Wilson drew up for his sales staff were such strictures as:

> Be industrious; exert yourself actively to show the best variety you have of the goods asked for and to find what will suit, giving your whole attention to your customers, letting them see that serving is a pleasure and not a trouble to you.
> Be patient; preserve perfect equanimity, especially if your customer appears exacting, fastidious or trifling.
> Be polite. . . . Your politeness to customers is money to the firm, and one of the considerations for which you are paid a salary.[56]

Not all assistants were prepared to observe such counsels of perfection. One discontented 21-year-old saleswoman, E.M.P., wrote to the journal *Today* in the mid-1890s to say she had been a shop girl for six years. During that time she had worked at least twelve hours a day and had clearly found her customers less than congenial: 'I sometimes hate women. When I read of a woman being good and sympathetic, I want the writer of that article to come and serve her with a bonnet. I wonder if it ever strikes a customer that we, too, are alive?'[57]

Margaret Bondfield commented on the difference in attitude adopted by upper-class women in high-class shops compared with customers in the poorer districts of London.

> There was a great contrast between the 'West End' trade – a term referring to the class of trade done – and the 'East End' trade. In the latter, although the hours were long, the relationship of server and customer was much more human. Many times I was appealed to, 'Say, miss, which would you 'ave if you was me?' and I realized the self-denial which must precede the purchase of a new article of clothing. . . . We would hear all about the joys and sorrows of the family, and get glimpses of brave hearts under the most sordid exterior. But in the West End, very rarely were we regarded as other than . . . lackeys to wait upon the customers as did their domestic servants. Sometimes they were charming, as only cultured people can be charming; at other times they could be as rude as only cultured people can be rude.[58]

In the mid-1870s another writer suggested that one of the pleasures of shopping for well-to-do women was the experience of being served. While making her selections, 'the dethroned mistress . . . trodden under foot in her own house', exercised the authority of 'an Oriental potentate'. Being patiently served by an 'assiduous' assistant afforded 'mothers and daughters' the chance to 'luxuriate' in a pleasing 'sense of power'.[59]

At F. Cape & Co. in Oxford the firm was run in the 1890s by Henry Lewis and his sons, Lewis having purchased the business in 1893 with cash mainly borrowed from his previous employers, the well-established credit drapers Affleck & Brown of Manchester. At Cape's the management had desks in the shop so they could keep staff under surveillance. The assistants did their best to circumvent this by adopting code words to warn one another when a member of the family approached. For example, when Mr Tom Lewis appeared, they would start 'talking loudly about a pale blue article, "pale blue" being the appropriate words to warn of the approach of Mr Tom'.[60]

All the firms had strict sartorial rules. The women wore black dresses, shoes and stockings and the men dark suits with black jackets and pin-striped trousers. Some of the more senior members of staff wore morning coats, while lady buyers had black silk or satin dresses, perhaps with a train.[61] In some cases male drapery staff were expected to wear a white cravat. This they resented as 'a badge of slavery', although the general public interpreted their elegant attire as 'evidence of prosperity and gentility'. But as Will Anderson, himself a former assistant, wrote bitterly, there was probably 'more well-dressed poverty' hidden in shop life 'than any other trade'.[62]

In small family businesses the situation was less formal. It was common for the shopkeeper's family to work at least part-time behind the counter, and it was rare to pay them regular wages. This was true of Thomas Broad, a Penzance draper, who had been in business for thirty years when he went bankrupt in 1827. Over the period 1816 to 1823 he had made a gift of £150 to one son 'in lieu of Annual Salary' for his services as a shopman, and a second son was given £140 for similar services between 1821 and 1825. A third son, who was working in the shop at the time of the bankruptcy, was not mentioned in the accounts. During the bankruptcy proceedings the latter youngster stated that when his father's creditors called at the shop to demand payment he would tell them the father was otherwise engaged and ask them to come again. Interestingly, at least part of Mr Broad's financial difficulties had resulted from his investment in shipping and in tin and copper mining. These losses amounted to around £2,000, out of a total debt of nearly £5,600 calculated when bankruptcy proceedings began in 1827.[63]

The shop run by Norman Hancock's father in a small Somerset town from the 1890s was on a more ambitious scale. The business stocked a wide range of goods, with dress materials, household goods and underwear for the female customers and caps, ties, socks and suits for the men. Mr Hancock employed four female assistants and two males, all of whom lived in. There were warm relations with many of the customers and on market day refreshments were offered to the 'regulars', with a glass of sherry and a biscuit at 11 a.m. and, for the more important, a 'sit-down midday meal of roast beef, vegetables, Yorkshire pudding, and apple tart', presumably to reward past purchases and encourage new ones. The meal was served on a trestle table in the 'Manchester room', where household goods, bed linen, oilcloth and linoleum were stored.[64] 'It was no unusual thing for twenty people to sit round the table', wrote Norman. The clientele was drawn from farming families and working people, and business was on a strictly cash basis.

When customers came into the shop they seated themselves on chairs while the assistants bustled around, taking down boxes, opening packets, and displaying the goods to best advantage, as well as making polite conversation. Bells summoned assistants from one part of the shop to another: 'If they were short-handed in the show-room they rang for someone to come up, and alternatively if the shop downstairs was crowded a button was pressed to obtain assistants from the show-room.'[65]

Shops like this were the backbone of the provincial drapery trade in the nineteenth and early twentieth centuries. Only a few of the high-fliers were able to expand sufficiently to transform themselves into department stores.

PRECURSORS OF THE DEPARTMENT STORE?
SHOPPING GALLERIES AND BAZAARS

Markets and market halls had long sold a wide variety of merchandise on a single site – one of the characteristics of the Victorian department store. However, the latter had a wider role, too, serving as a focus for fashionable display and for spending leisure hours, as well as supplying a range of customer services such as reading rooms, restaurants, ladies' rest rooms, house agencies, servant registry offices and much more besides. Few of those wider aspects were present in even the most sophisticated market halls and they were still less likely to appear in open-air markets.

Nonetheless the perception of shopping as a leisure pursuit was present in retail establishments well before the advent of the department store. One of the earliest manifestations of this was the shopping gallery, or exchange. At the close of the seventeenth century there were five galleries in London, each managed by owner-entrepreneurs offering a covered shopping area within impressive, normally purpose-built premises. A variety of shops lined either side of the walkways. They were intended to appeal to the social elite and for that reason shopkeepers were charged high rentals for the small, simple, wooden-framed stalls where sales staff displayed their wares. Gallery managers laid down rules concerning retailers' conduct, the control of waste and noise, and the kind of merchandise to be offered for sale. According to Claire Walsh, this took the form of luxury goods such as high-value textiles, expensive apparel and haberdashery, perfume, jewellery, china and books. The aim was to create 'an atmosphere of politeness and refinement' where social leaders could stroll while they inspected the goods on offer and gossiped with friends.[66] Regulations also covered opening hours, questions of hygiene and the prevention of shoplifting. A system of fines and punishments was imposed on those who breached the rules.[67]

The stallholders were normally female and it is possible that some were related to established shopkeepers in the capital for whom this served as a useful additional outlet and perhaps an advertisement for their main business.[68] Concern to ensure that the women and girls working in such a public arena would not be accused of prostitution led to a strict code of conduct being applied. Beadles were installed at the entrances to the building to keep out any of the lower orders or other undesirables who might seek to come in.

A major problem for the galleries was their reliance on the patronage of a small group of wealthy people. If they failed to attract sufficient customers they ceased to be financially viable. In these circumstances most of them had gone out of business by the early eighteenth century. One survivor, the Exeter Exchange, underwent major changes. From around 1773 its upper floor was occupied by a menagerie, although shopping stalls were still rented below. In 1807 Robert Southey described it as 'a sort of street under cover, or large long room, with a row of shops on either hand, and a thoroughfare between them'.[69]

In the early nineteenth century the concept of the shopping gallery was revived, although now under the title of bazaar. These new retail outlets largely followed the pattern of the earlier exchanges. One of the best known, the Soho Bazaar, was set up in 1816. It differed from its predecessors, however, in two main respects. First, its proprietor, John Trotter, promoted it as a philanthropic enterprise 'to encourage Female and Domestic Industry'.[70] Secondly the shop space could be rented by 'persons of respectability' for as short a period as a day, while the amount of space occupied might be adjusted to meet the shopkeeper's requirements. The landlord paid the taxes, supplied the heating and lighting, and provided security arrangements. By offering retailers space on this very short-term basis, Trotter argued he was helping people of limited means to start up in business.[71] All the merchandise must be of British manufacture, unless special permission to the contrary was granted. Every item had to be marked with its cash price, from which there could be no abatement. The reason for this seems partly to have been a desire to avoid haggling between customer and vendor, thereby minimising noise, and partly perhaps a means of discouraging flirtations between the saleswomen and male customers.[72] However, this did not prevent critics from complaining to Parliament that among 'the numerous evils' associated with bazaars was the way they encouraged 'public promenade [and] intrigue', an oblique reference to prostitution.[73]

The rooms were laid out with mahogany-topped counters and there were about 200 female traders. To ensure that business was conducted to high moral standards, all had to provide testimonials as to their good character. Decorum in dress and behaviour was insisted upon, and to guard against illness or unavoidable absence leading to vacant counters, every seller had to provide a substitute. She, like the shopkeeper herself, should be 'in her dress clean, plain, and neat, without feathers or flowers'.[74] Saleswomen must arrive before 10 a.m. each day and the doors were shut at 6 p.m., to allow them time to clear their counters and get away before they encountered any of the 'dangers to which later hours would infallibly expose them'.[75]

The Soho Bazaar proved highly popular and spawned a number of imitations. By 1851 Charles Knight described it as 'uniformly a well-managed concern' with the articles on offer being primarily for the dress and personal adornment of women and children. According to Knight at the height of the Season the 'long array of carriages' drawn up near the building attested to the number of wealthy customers it attracted.[76] It also had a ladies' dressing room for the convenience of customers.

Other bazaars to open in the capital included the Royal London in Liverpool Street. In 1830 it offered visitors the opportunity to spend 'an agreeable hour either in the promenades or in the exhibitions that are wholly without parallel in the known world', commented one enthusiast.[77] The Pantheon began business as a bazaar and picture gallery in 1834, displaying female accessories, children's clothes, books, sheet music and fancy goods. In the gallery pictures were sold on commission and in an upper gallery there was a toy bazaar and an aviary for the sale of cage birds. The Pantheon had a refreshment room, too, and was one of the first West End retail establishments to provide water closets for its clientele.[78]

The bazaar phenomenon was not confined to London. In the seaside resort of Margate, James Jolly, a Norfolk-born draper, set up a bazaar in the 1820s selling china, jewellery, perfumery, stationery, toys and 'novelties'. The business flourished and he decided to seek a new venue to conduct a higher class of seasonal trade. In about 1823 Jolly and his son took premises in Bath on a short-term basis. Later they opened a permanent shop and from 1830 the Paris Depot, as it was known, remained open for the whole year. Subsequently it traded under the grand title of the Bath Emporium and offered both drapery and bazaar goods, all of which were sold for cash. As the store expanded it stocked silks, shawls and ribbons from France and by 1851 had a staff of sixteen male and forty-two female assistants living on the premises. It was on its way towards achieving the department store status which it acquired by the early twentieth century.[79]

Perhaps the best known of the provincial bazaars was opened in Manchester in 1821 by John Watts, a Cheshire farmer-turned-draper. A decade later this bazaar, now a prosperous concern, was rebuilt and in 1831 a prospectus of the new premises was published. Clearly it followed along lines similar to those adopted by John Trotter for the Soho Bazaar. The Manchester venture, too, as well as acting as a retail outlet offered exhibitions of works of art, including 'diorama, physiorama, etc.'.[80] As with the Trotter enterprise, it aimed to give 'employment to industrious Females' and to offer to the public 'the choicest and most fashionable' articles in every branch 'of Art and Manufacture, at a reasonable rate'. The counters were let weekly, monthly or quarterly, with business hours running from 9.30 a.m. to 8 p.m. every day except Saturday, when the closing hour was 9 p.m. Unlike at the Soho Bazaar, retailers of both sexes could rent accommodation, with the counters on the first floor let to males and those on the second floor to females. The 'strictest regard shall be paid to propriety of demeanour and of dress; each person must appear perfectly attired for business, clean, and becoming his or her station, and females will not be allowed to have their hair in papers, or to wear bonnets'.[81]

Goods had to be displayed, with prices marked, by the time the bazaar opened to the public at 9.30 a.m. Those who failed to do this could be fined 1s. Should a substitute be needed because of the illness or absence of the stallholder, prior approval had to be obtained from the bazaar manager. No substitute was allowed under 14 years of age. As at the Soho Bazaar, the proprietor paid all the taxes, provided heating and cleaning and also arranged for a porter to be at each entrance to prevent 'the intrusion of improper persons'. If the rules were broken the manager could give the offending party two days' notice to quit, and if the counter were not given up voluntarily after that time, he had the power to seize any goods left behind and deposit them in a room within the bazaar to await collection. He could also re-let the counter.[82]

Merchants hired counters to sell their wares, employing sales staff to dispose of them, and with the sub-tenants doing all the work, and a management structure in place for the running of the bazaar, the Watts family withdrew from active participation in retailing, leaving the business to be run by several young male assistants and commercial managers.[83] In the mid-1830s three of these were Thomas Kendal, James Milne and Adam Faulkner. The two former, although trained drapers, came from a farming background while the third, Adam Faulkner, was from the Manchester area and was probably already experienced in business. These three became friendly with their employers, Samuel and James Watts, who had now taken over from their father. The Watts brothers sold them the bazaar on 26 December 1835, and about a week later Kendal, Milne and Faulkner reopened the shop, trading under their surnames. They marketed the bazaar aggressively, advertising widely and 'making a speciality of sales of both regular goods and the discounted stocks of bankrupts'.[84] After Adam Faulkner's death in 1862, the firm traded as Kendal Milne & Co. and by 1870 had extended the goods and services offered beyond the initial preoccupation with drapery to include cabinet-making, the sale of sewing machines and funeral undertaking. It issued catalogues and developed a mail-order business. By 1890 it was employing several hundred staff and was described as having 'the largest showrooms out of London'. It became one of the country's earliest department stores.[85]

Meanwhile, as department stores began to appear, particularly from the 1870s, the bazaar phenomenon faded away. Now bazaars were associated with displays of low-priced 'fancy' goods, like Michael Marks's Penny Bazaars, or with charitable events to collect funds for churches and philanthropic organisations. Symbolically, as Kathryn Morrison points out, the last bazaar to be built in London, the Corinthian Bazaar (1867–8) off Oxford Circus failed to prosper and in 1871 was converted into a circus.[86] The term bazaar no longer suggested a retail establishment with social pretensions.

THE DEPARTMENT STORE

By the late nineteenth century department stores had come to dominate the central shopping areas of most major towns and a number of smaller ones as well, including seaside resorts like Southport and Bournemouth. The emergence of a new urban environment, with its mass of consumers and improved transport facilities, made these large shops viable. Equally, they, with their ambitious window displays and widening range of services, served as attractions to draw people to a town.[87] Despite their high profile, however, their precise number before the First World War is difficult to establish, since they were not listed as such in the trade directories of the day. They also varied greatly in size and status. James Jefferys estimated there were perhaps 150 to 200 of them in the country as a whole in 1910, while more recently Jon Stobart put the figure at around 300 in 1900.[88] On a narrow regional basis Gareth Shaw has calculated that in the Birmingham area the five department stores which existed in about 1870 (two of them in Birmingham itself) had increased to twenty-five in 1910, with eight of them in Birmingham alone.[89] Nonetheless, while it is generally agreed that their numbers were growing in the half-century before 1914, their share in the nation's retail trade remained modest, at perhaps 1.5 to 3 per cent in 1910. Only in the sale of clothing and footwear were they significant, contributing around 5.5 to 7 per cent of total trade in these goods in 1900 and 8 to 9 per cent a decade later.[90]

Most department stores began as drapers' shops and expanded by gradually acquiring nearby properties and introducing fresh lines of merchandise. However, a few started in other trades. Harrods commenced life as a grocery shop in Knightsbridge in 1849 and it was not until the 1870s that it began to stock additional products, such as china and flowers. Two decades later millinery, haberdashery, underwear and silks were being sold, although it was only in the twentieth century that the firm became fully involved in ladies' fashions.[91] By 1903 it was also offering 'an impressive array of men's articles' and in 1911 a promotional brochure described 'the attractions of "Harrods as a Man's Store"'.[92]

In other cases, Slopers of Devizes started as a furniture removal firm and Footmans of Ipswich enjoyed a good reputation for furnishings as well as for paper hanging and the sale of perambulators. It, too, had a flourishing removal business before it expanded to become a department store.[93] David Lewis in Liverpool and John Walsh in Sheffield both began as outfitters, for men and women respectively, though Walsh also specialised in bed linen.

Jefferys suggested that for a department store to be so designated it should have at least four separate trading areas under one roof, with women's and children's clothes of particular importance; they should adopt a policy of fixed and open pricing; and they should make great use of advertising.[94] In practice, however, they had a far wider role than this, offering a range of services as well as large displays of fashion goods and novelties designed to attract and entertain customers.

Interestingly, the term department store was not used by contemporaries to describe these retail establishments. They were known as emporia, *grands magasins* or 'giants' in the trade press of the day. The use of French terminology is significant, for while such English stores as Bainbridge's in Newcastle and Kendal Milne's in Manchester had some of the characteristics of a department store by the 1850s, including multiple departments, clear pricing and a large staff, they lacked many of the broader amenities associated with such businesses in their Edwardian heyday. The inspiration for these came from certain major American and French department stores, and particularly from one of the earliest of them all, the Bon Marché, developed in Paris from the late 1860s. This *grand magasin* not only offered a wide selection of merchandise but also put on exhibitions and entertainments.[95] Its fame led a number of English firms to use the title Bon Marché for their own shop signs. The Merseyside men's outfitter David Lewis was so impressed by what he saw on a visit to Paris in the 1870s that he called his new Liverpool store Bon Marché. He also painted its delivery vans in the same striped colours that he had seen in Paris.[96]

Department stores needed access to substantial amounts of capital if they were to succeed and it is significant that in the 1890s a number of them became limited companies. They also needed a wide and varied stock of goods, and this the new mass-production manufacturing processes could supply. Often, as with John Barker in Kensington, the stores bought direct from the makers, cutting out the middleman or, as with Debenham & Freebody, they began manufacturing products on their own account. According to the firm's historian, at a time when Debenham's had 600 members of staff in the main retail store, there were a further 3,000 employed in the workroom and order departments.[97] Likewise at Cockaynes, a Sheffield department store, which had a permanent labour force of 519 in 1912, plus 20 temporary workers, only a little over a fifth of them were directly involved in selling goods in the store. The rest were part of the production processes, engaged in hand tailoring and cabinet-making, or of the delivery service, as porters, carters and the like. There were also several domestic servants.[98] Among the twenty-eight departments at Cockaynes in 1913 there were, for example, a manageress, two assistants and twelve workroom staff engaged in the making and selling of millinery, while the manufacture and sale of ladies' mantles, furs and the like required a manageress, four shop assistants and five workroom hands.[99]

Good transport facilities were needed to bring the custom required to make these enterprises profitable. They were supplied not only by the railways but by horse-drawn (and later motor) buses, by trams and, in London, by the underground railway. In 1912 Bainbridge's boasted that about 2,500 trams passed their doors daily, and William Whiteley, when starting his haberdashery shop in 1863, took account of the proximity of the recently opened

Metropolitan Underground Railway, the first of its kind in the capital. The stores also adopted some of the latest technical innovations, such as plate-glass windows, customer lifts and cash registers. They offered special amenities, too, ranging from restaurants, tea rooms, reading rooms and ladies' rest rooms to various agencies. By the mid-1890s Harrods had a banking department, an insurance department, removal and warehousing facilities and a household service agency, where domestic staff could be obtained.[100]

William Whiteley was to pioneer the large store in England. When he opened his first shop in March 1863 it was to sell fancy goods, especially ribbons, and his small staff comprised two young girls to serve behind the counter and a boy to run errands. Whiteley was determined to build up his store into a large enterprise from the start. He had visited the Great Exhibition in 1851 and had been inspired by the impressive array of merchandise on display. At Bayswater his expansion was rapid. Within a year or two he had departments for the sale of silks, linens, mantles, drapery and dresses, millinery, haberdashery, furs, jewellery, umbrellas and artificial flowers. By 1867 there were seventeen departments in operation and in that year he married Harriet Sarah Hill, one of the two girls whom he had first engaged when he opened the shop. The increasing size of the business meant long hours for them and for the rest of the staff. Mrs Whiteley recalled working from 7 a.m. until 11 p.m. or later. 'We lived at the top of the house – and . . . I can remember times without number sitting on the bottom stair holding a candle while he put up the shutters at night. Sometimes I could hardly keep my eyes open, I was so tired.'[101]

For around ten years Whiteley concentrated on extending and improving his drapery business, but from 1872 he entered upon a second stage of development, launching into new products and services beyond those usually associated with drapers. His first experiments were to provide an estate agency and a refreshment room, both opened in 1872, and a cleaning and dyeing service in 1874. By the mid-1870s he was turning his attention to household goods and the supply of food, to the anger of smaller tradesmen in the area. One of the 'victims' of Whiteley's expanding business wrote to the local press complaining of the 'startling succession of feats in the art of shutting up your neighbour's shop and driving him elsewhere'. In the autumn of 1876 Whiteley transferred his meat department to new premises and this led on 5 November to a noisy, hostile demonstration, in which the local butchers, in blue smocks, took a prominent part. The procession was headed by a vehicle containing a gigantic guy dressed to resemble Whiteley. After dark it was duly burnt. As a result of his single-minded expansionist programme there was no man 'more hated in Bayswater'. Between 1882 and

1887 his store was plagued by repeated fires, which he himself blamed on jealous local tradesmen, although others thought disgruntled ex-employees were responsible. Despite the offering of a reward the arsonists were never found.[102]

Meanwhile, Whiteley had begun to style himself 'The Universal Provider', boasting he could supply everything 'from a pin to an elephant'. Only gradually did the local tradespeople recognise that despite the bruising competition he offered, his store attracted large numbers of people to Westbourne Grove, and some of them at least shopped at rival establishments.

In the 1880s Whiteley's was the largest London store, with nearly 2,000 employees, but others were growing rapidly. For example, the firms of Shoolbred's, John Barker, and Spencer, Turner and Boldero had between 500 and 1,000 workers, while Debenham & Freebody and Marshall & Snelgrove had around 500 employees apiece.[103] In Manchester Kendal Milne had a work-force of 550 at the beginning of the 1890s and at Bainbridge's in Newcastle there were over 600 workers when E.M. Bainbridge died in 1892.[104]

By 1900 it is estimated there were at least a dozen firms in the country with staffs of 1,000 or more. To manage these large enterprises a new management style was needed, with authority devolved to departmental managers and shopwalkers, rather than resting with the proprietor alone. As Michael Miller has commented in his study of Bon Marché in Paris, although middle-class careers were increasing in retailing they were more and more taking the form of 'permanently salaried positions' in an organisation, within 'an impersonal and hierarchical work environment'.[105] At a lower level there were numerous sales assistants, maintenance staff, workroom employees, accounts clerks and transport staff to make deliveries. By the end of the period there were narrower specialisms, too, such as posts as window dressers and store detectives to combat shoplifting. Division of labour and firm discipline were two characteristics of the work environment, within what was a rule-based enterprise.[106]

When hiring sales personnel, department store proprietors gave preference to the young and unmarried. At first they were predominantly male, but over the period there was an increasing recruitment of women and girls. Young workers were cheaper to employ and perhaps 'easier to mould to the store's image'.[107] For young people from working-class backgrounds employment in a prestigious department store could represent upward social mobility. In practice, however, most of the sales staff in the larger stores appear to have come from lower middle-class families.[108] The cost of suitable clothes precluded poorer parents from sending their offspring to such establishments, while, as a Birmingham assistant declared, 'in a shop . . . the girls have to talk properly'. A few firms, like Eaden Lilley's in Cambridge, recruited only 'grammar school girls'.[109]

However, individual preferences could affect recruitment patterns, too. Owen Owen, who opened a drapery shop in Liverpool in 1868 and had within five years expanded to a staff of more than 120 employees, hired a high proportion of them from his native Wales. He regarded his staff as 'an extended family' and years later, when he had purchased an estate in Wales, he invited many of them to spend weekends there.[110] At Bainbridge's in Newcastle, workers came mainly from the north-east of England and the firm followed 'the Newcastle practice of favouring Methodists in their recruitment policy'.[111] So rigorously was this applied that Roman Catholics in the city complained of the unwillingness of the department stores to employ members of their congregation.

Because the posts were often seen as more attractive than ordinary shop work, they were much sought after and the stores could follow a careful selection process. Indeed, when Gordon Selfridge's impressive purpose-built store opened in the West End of London in March 1909, there were said to be 10,000 applications for the 1,200 vacancies.[112] Applicants were influenced by the publicity surrounding this large new enterprise and by the superior conditions offered within its 100 or so departments. A recruitment and training scheme was launched before the store opened and for the youngest staff members there was a two-year course of instruction which included lectures not only on the store's policy and systems but on business ethics and administration, accountancy, buying and selling and the retail trade in general. Two travelling scholarships were awarded annually to one boy and one girl so that they could go abroad in the company of one of the firm's buyers to study foreign stores, markets and methods.[113] Harrods and Debenham & Freebody also had training schemes, with the latter firm having an education department from 1898 which offered evening classes to young assistants, as well as routine staff training.[114] Most provincial stores lacked the finance and the expertise to offer such facilities.

Selfridges was the first store in Britain to make an art of window dressing, with a special display department set up under a manager from Gordon Selfridge's native USA. The *Drapers' Record* praised the initiative and also the 'Undeviating Courtesy' of the assistants. They were 'obeying the rule of cheerfulness set before them by the management when they were engaged'.[115]

Meanwhile, it became the task of department store managers everywhere to instil a 'sense of the ambitions of bourgeois life' into their sales staff, while at the same time discouraging 'any thoughts on the part of the assistants that they were the equals of their customers'.[116] One way of achieving the latter was to segregate them from the customers by way of a counter and by expecting them to stand while the customers sat when they were being served. There were other requirements, too. John Searby, who went to work at a superior Nottingham department store in about 1909, recalled that it was considered 'really a crime to ask a lady her address . . . I knew them all you see. . . . We were expected to know all [of them] . . . they were mostly account customers.'[117]

These distinctions were reinforced by frameworks of 'discipline and bureaucracy'. That included exacting penalties for breaches of a firm's rules. Howard Williams of the large London drapers Hitchcock, Williams & Co. in October 1896 defended this practice in a letter to Margaret Gladstone (the future Mrs Ramsay MacDonald):

> It is no easy matter to carry on a large concern successfully, & to control a number of servants, for the employer cannot get into direct personal touch with or exert his individual influence over each one where . . . he has to rule by deputy. It is necessary to compile rules for the conduct of his business, to avoid confusion, to protect the firm against the public, dishonest servants, careless service, & also to protect his servants against the public, against dishonest fellow servants, & to promote the happiness & comfort of all. And these rules must be obeyed. . . . The alternative to punishment is dismissal. . . . A proper system of fines may be considered a humane method of dealing with offences that can be easily guarded against with reasonable care.[118]

As major employers, department store owners came to adopt some of the principles of labour management which had been applied earlier in factories. This meant much emphasis was placed on good timekeeping as part of the regulatory regime.

In the mid-1890s at John Barker's department store in Kensington, there was a labour force of between 1,400 and 1,500 including shop assistants of both sexes. According to one of the firm's executives, about five-sixths of the females came from other London shops, although nearly all the men were from the provinces. 'A large proportion . . . come from Wales, a few Irish, a fair number of Scotchmen and of course of Englishmen, but the noticeable feature of this immigration is the Welsh.'[119] Sales staff were recruited each March and September to meet the expected demands of the spring and winter seasons, and that policy was adopted in a number of other stores. It created a sense of unease among the assistants as to whether they would be dismissed at the onset of one of the 'slack' periods of the year. At Whiteley's it was the buyers at the head of each department who decided on seasonal dismissals. Twice a year, during January and July, there were the sales and these were followed by a period of weak trading. On the last day of the sale, dismissal notices were sent to the individuals concerned, but not until within about half an hour of closing time. The sales ended on a Saturday and that meant the dismissed employee had to leave that same evening. It was small wonder that the 'Universal Provider' was involved in litigation with his staff, some of whom sought to get their own back by petty pilfering or who instituted proceedings to recover wages in lieu of notice when they faced instant dismissal.[120]

Harrods of Knightsbridge was another large-scale store which expanded rapidly during the 1890s. When Richard Burbidge, who had previously worked at Whiteley's, became general manager in 1891, the staff numbered about 200. Under his leadership the firm expanded until its labour force had reached around 2,500 at the end of the century and 6,000 at the time of the First World War. Burbidge was keen to foster good staff relations and he reduced the previously long hours of work, so that the shop closed at 7 p.m. each evening instead of the 9 p.m. which had applied in the days of Charles Harrod himself. On Fridays it was 8 p.m. and on Saturdays 9 p.m., instead of the 11 p.m. required by Harrod. He introduced an early closing day and ended Charles Harrod's fines for late arrival. Under his direction a Provident Society and a Benevolent Fund were set up and there was access to a medical officer and a dentist. He also 'conducted Sunday Bible classes for the staff at his house', although how many attended is not clear.[121]

Even smaller department stores like Peter Jones in Chelsea employed several hundred staff in the mid-1890s – 300–400 in their case. Similar recruitment levels applied to the suburban firm of Messrs Jones and Higgins of Peckham, while Jones Brothers of Holloway Road, Islington, had 132 male assistants and 90 females, excluding buyers and shopwalkers, in 1895. All were provided with board and lodging, some of them above the shop itself.[122]

The practice of living in came under growing criticism during the period. It was nonetheless something that showed great regional variation. While it was common in London department stores (although not at Harrods), as well as in the south of England and in South Wales, it was virtually unknown in Scotland. In northern cities like Liverpool, Bradford, Manchester and Newcastle upon Tyne, it was either rarely adopted or was in sharp decline at the end of the Victorian era. At Bainbridge's in Newcastle, for example, apparently only male staff lived in, while at Kendal Milne in Manchester in 1891 only around 26 male workers were housed, out of the store's work-force of about 550.[123]

Where living in did exist, it put pressure upon the assistants in that they were 'always within the glance of their master's eye', or that of his surrogates.[124] In addition, if they lost their position they also lost their home, which could be very serious for young workers in a large city without relatives or friends close at hand. But the system had its defenders, including a number of the assistants themselves. Some felt it was an advantage to youngsters coming to London or a major town for the first time because it provided 'the certainty of . . . meals and lodging accommodation' and only clothing and 'extras' had to be found. Such youngsters also had to conform to the firm's rules and regulations and that rendered them 'less liable to temptation' than if they were left to their own devices in ordinary lodgings.[125]

Even the store owners were divided. Owen Owen, whose department store in Liverpool grew rapidly from its establishment in 1868, saw living in as an essential part of his paternalistic concern for the welfare of the staff. In the mid-1880s he erected two hostels, for male and female staff respectively, with a Welsh housekeeper in charge of each of them.[126]

By contrast Ernest Debenham, whose firm had virtually ended living in by 1905, believed that it 'tended . . . to diminish the independence of the staff, and that so far as he could say . . . , the results had fully justified his opinion. The business was . . . better conducted, the assistants were physically superior, brighter and more energetic' than they had been before the change was made. In 1907 out of a staff of 676 only 44 lived in, comprising 15 boys who were indentured apprentices and 29 girl clerks, whose work commenced very early in the morning and whose family did not live near the firm's premises.[127] Derry & Toms in Kensington had abolished living in for male staff, too, since according to Mr Derry the change created 'a sense of personal responsibility' among them. He was willing to abolish the system for the females, but in this case it was the firm's financial position which was the deciding factor rather than the assistants' welfare. 'The premises which the women occupy would become a source of loss,' he declared, 'as they could not at present be applied to other purposes.'[128] When employees lived in, the cost of food and accommodation was taken into account in their pay, with their cash earnings consequently reduced, to the advantage of the firm.

The fact that food prices were rising in the early twentieth century, thereby adding to the costs of store owners, combined with the adverse publicity arising from shop fires in which there were fatalities among resident staff, probably helped to undermine the living-in system in the early twentieth century. In November 1912, when five domestic workers at John Barker's died in a store fire, there was considerable criticism of such arrangements at the subsequent inquest.[129]

On the moral front, as Michael Miller comments, there was always a 'prurient interest in the lives of *petit bourgeois* girls living away from home, making their own living, and concentrated in large stores, where they were in constant contact with young men and exposed to high-pressured dealings with all levels of the public'.[130] Some critics saw the department store as a place of potential depravity, without the 'protection' afforded by living in and its associated rules and restrictions.

That view was expressed forcibly by William Alexander Sergeant, manager of Peter Robinson's in Oxford Street, in July 1907. The firm had 316 male assistants and 408 females living in, most of them sleeping in houses close to the store. Each of the houses was under the charge of a man and his wife, who acted as caretakers. He considered it essential for employees up to the age of 25 to be resident: 'If you let boys and girls go about the London streets at all times of the night, what will they be fit for next day? Half of them will go wrong, especially the girls.'[131] He strongly rebutted criticisms that it was impossible for a man to marry if he wished to remain on the staff of a store where living in was obligatory. He was quite happy, he said, for male staff to marry and live out, provided their income was adequate. But 'we ought not to have people in our employ who are married on about £50 a year; it tends to make them – well, certainly not honest'. According to Sergeant, nobody working in his firm at that time had married on less than £100 a year.[132]

But within this broad structure of department store life, there were variations in the way each enterprise was run and in the regulations imposed. Queries were raised, too, about the legality of the fines that were deducted from pay for breaches of the rules, and whether these breached the provisions of the Truck Acts. That situation was only resolved in 1896 when a fresh Truck Act explicitly included retail shops in its provisions. It became an offence to pay wages other than in cash and assistants were also protected against unfair fines. Employers could still impose penalties but they had to detail them beforehand, in writing, and the sums could only be levied after wages had been paid, rather than by a prior deduction.[133]

Firms were surprisingly anxious to keep their rules confidential. Sensitivity over the issue was made clear in a warning printed at the end of the rulebook of Howell & Co., the largest department store in Cardiff, in the mid-1890s: 'This Copy of Rules is the property of Howell & Co. and must be returned in good condition when the Assistant leaves, otherwise it will be considered an act of dishonesty.'[134] In all, Howell's imposed sixty different restrictions on the staff, as well as some general provisos, with details of the penalties to be exacted if they were not observed. Significantly, when Mr A. Parry, a Cardiff shop workers' trade union official, clandestinely supplied a copy of the regulations to Margaret Gladstone in 1896, he was insistent that she keep the name of the firm 'strictly private'. He asked for the rulebook to be returned speedily 'as I have to give it back to the party I had it from'.[135]

This Cardiff firm's regulations seem almost insignificant, however, when compared to the detailed list issued by William Whiteley. In 1886 there were 176 different conditions included in the new rulebook and even the trade press, often an admirer of Whiteley's dynamic success, found this excessive. At the head of the list of rules drawn up by the 'Universal Provider' was the bleak statement: 'Every Employé is liable to be discharged without previous Notice, and has the same privilege of leaving.'[136]

The 176 rules were divided into fifteen sections, covering working hours and meals, dress, dealings with customers, the drawing up of bills and check sheets, the handling of cash, the packing of parcels, the dispatch of mail orders, and much more besides. For breaches of the regulations, fines ranged from 6d per offence (which applied in a majority of cases) to 2s 6d, this latter being imposed for 'serious' faults like losing or mislaying duplicates of bills and parcel dockets. In March 1889 an assistant in the gentlemen's outfitting department had to pay 2s 6d for 'not putting the amount on corner of Bill'.[137]

Firm instructions were also given on customer relations at Whiteley's: 'No assistant to allow a customer to leave the Shop unserved, without speaking to the Shopwalker, under pain of dismissal.'[138] A shopwalker must always be called 'to conduct a Customer from one part of the Shop to another', with a 6d fine levied on any assistant failing to ensure this. A similar penalty attached to a breach of the rule reminding staff that theirs was a 'Ready Money business. . . . Never ask Customers if they will pay on "Delivery", or have Goods entered, but present the Bill for payment.' At Kendal Milne in Manchester the penalty for this fault was more severe. According to rules issued in 1883, a fine of 2s 6d was imposed for not observing the regulation that assistants 'must in every instance endeavour to get paid for goods sold at time of purchase; never ask a customer if they wish it entered, but present the bill; this is very important'. At that firm 'Gossiping, loitering on the premises or making an unnecessary noise' were strictly prohibited and they, too, attracted a 2s 6d fine for any breaches.[139]

With so many rules to observe it is not surprising that the Royal Commission on Labour should conclude in the early 1890s that for many women assistants:

The constant supervision of the shopwalker, the patience and politeness to be shown to the most trying customers, the difficulty of telling the truth about the goods without incurring the displeasure of the managers, the long standing, the close atmosphere even in well ventilated shops when crowded with customers, the short time for meals, the care required to keep things in their right places and to make out accounts correctly, the long evenings with gaslight and the liability to dismissal without warning or explained reason all tend to render the occupation . . . most trying to the nerves and injurious to health.[140]

Perhaps as a result of the provisions of the 1896 Truck Act and of criticisms levelled at his firm, William Whiteley abandoned the system of fining during the final decade of the nineteenth century. But he did not relax his stringent discipline. Each day a 'late list' was exhibited in a glass case, with the name of the unpunctual offender, his department, his excuse and Whiteley's own caustic comments in red ink.[141]

In Cardiff, Howell & Co. prefaced their list of 'dos and don'ts' with strictures on the way customers were to be treated. Firmly prohibited, under threat of dismissal, was the making of statements designed to mislead or deceive purchasers in order to effect a sale. Nor was the word 'Warranted' to be used in any sale. Although the firm procured 'the best makes of their respective kinds', they could not 'warrant them'. Most importantly, 'Every Assistant must be very attentive and obliging, speaking softly, plainly and correctly to every Customer, especially to the poorer classes, as nothing displays the true character of young people more than the respectful or disrespectful tone or manner in which they address those supposed to be their inferiors.'[142] Under rule 6 the substantial fine of 2s 6d was incurred for selling goods 'at more or less than the price marked'. Any loss incurred by the firm had to be made up as well. Two offences led to immediate dismissal, namely allowing customers to leave without being served and the unauthorised taking for personal use of any article, even such minor items as paper or twine.[143]

In the main 'shop offences' fell into four broad categories. First, there was unpunctuality; secondly there were 'business errors', such as mistakes on bills or wrongly addressed parcels; thirdly, there were breaches of manners, including gossiping among staff when on duty or sitting down in the shop when not permitted to do so; and finally, there were penalties for breaking and damaging goods.[144] In these circumstances it is hard to accept Bill Lancaster's complacent conclusion that department store employment included 'arguably, the most successful example of labour management in modern industry'.[145]

'House' rules relating to the staff who lived in were also common. David Morgan's in Cardiff in the mid-1890s had fifty-six 'business' rules and sixteen 'house' ones. The latter included a prohibition on the use of matches and candles in sleeping quarters, on all 'unnecessary talking and noise', and on putting 'nails in walls', to hang up pictures or photographs. Breaches of any of these attracted a fine of 6*d*, as did the cleaning of footwear in the bedrooms. For smoking in the rooms the fine was 1*s*, with the same penalty exacted for failing to turn off the gas in bedrooms at night. 'Remaining out after 11 p.m., fine 1*s* for first offence'. A second failure to meet the deadline led to dismissal.[146]

At the time of the 1901 census returns David Morgan's had 111 shop staff (50 females and 61 males) living over the store, as well as 9 female domestics. Most of the assistants were young, 63 per cent of them being under the age of 25. Indeed, 20.7 per cent (11 females and 12 males) were under 20. That figure included apprentices.[147] Eventually, after industrial action was threatened by male workers employed by both David Morgan and James Howell in November 1913, it was agreed that they should be allowed to live out if they so desired. This concession did not apply to juniors under 21, however, or to female employees. For those who elected to live out, David Morgan allowed an additional payment of 7*s* 6*d* a week.[148]

The desire to ensure that female staff at David Morgan's enjoyed 'moral protection' meant they must still live in. Miss E. Harnaman, who joined the firm in April 1914, remembered the regimented routine. The juniors slept in a long room called The Barracks, and strict discipline was applied. 'A bell rang in the morning at 7.30; breakfast was at 8.00 and we were expected to be in at night at 9 p.m. . . . The most miserable day of the week was Sunday. Cold dinner winter or summer, and in those days the only place to go was to Chapel. We also had a sitting room with a piano and we had many good times when someone would play and sing.'[149] She continued to live in even after the First World War.

By the early twentieth century, as Gareth Shaw comments, the 'department store had come of age'.[150] As their numbers grew during the Edwardian era a few firms, like David Lewis in Liverpool and Bobby's in the south of England, began to set up branch stores. There were also some mergers or acquisitions before 1914, so that John Barker bought Ponting Brothers in 1907 and Harrods purchased another London rival, Dickins and Jones, in 1914.[151] From the point of view of the staff, there was an increase in welfare provisions in many stores, with some retaining the services of a doctor or dentist for their benefit. At least one week's paid holiday became the industry's norm and in some cases discounts on purchases began to replace commission on sales. This initiative, as Bill Lancaster notes, 'overcame the problem of disruptive rivalry between staff and departments that was endemic to the commission system' and allowed staff to purchase goods which otherwise might have been prohibitively expensive.[152] Sports clubs and drama groups were also set up by many of the firms. Such developments illustrated the 'community' aspect of department store employment at the end of the nineteenth century and helped to set their staff apart from shop assistants working in more modest establishments.

As for the stores themselves, the quality of the goods and services they offered reflected the varying needs and increasing complexity of British society. On the one hand there were the large central London emporia, catering primarily for the requirements of the well-to-do, and on the other, there were suburban and provincial stores serving the less affluent, or the more specialised, wants of their own locality. That applied to those in the growing seaside resorts, like Bournemouth, Torquay, Southsea and many more. In these cases, as Bill Lancaster comments, 'the quality of the store reflected the image of the resort' and was both a product of its expansion and a major force contributing to its development through the attractions it offered.[153]

Chapter 5

LAWBREAKING AND LABOUR RELATIONS

As an employer the Universal Provider . . . was not a pioneer in early closing, or in any other movement for the reform of the welfare of shop assistants. . . . On the other hand, as the bigger London establishments shortened their working day and introduced other improvements Whiteley followed suit. . . . His network of sporting and recreational facilities did not prevent . . . petty thieving for which Whiteley felt himself called upon to put his employees in the dock.

Richard S. Lambert, *The Universal Provider. A Study of William Whiteley and the Rise of the London Department Store* (London, 1938), pp. 148, 155 and 156.

BREAKING THE LAW

Shops, as Beverley Lemire has pointed out, were 'repositories of marketable commodities' and as such were particularly vulnerable to 'depredations by burglars, shoplifters, and unscrupulous employees'.[1] That applied especially to those selling clothing, fancy goods and textiles, since these were easy to dispose of to second-hand dealers or pawnbrokers.

Shoplifting was frequently a female crime, with the women often working in pairs. One would distract the attention of the shopkeeper or his assistant while the other pocketed the goods. The voluminous clothing worn by females during the eighteenth and nineteenth centuries made concealment relatively easy. So widespread had the offence become, indeed, by the end of the seventeenth century that in 1699 a new Act made the shoplifting of goods valued at over 5s an offence punishable by death. In addition, anyone found guilty of theft was to be branded on the face rather than on the hand, as had previously been the case.[2] The 1699 legislation was apparently enacted in response to a petition from shopkeepers in the City of London. They declared that the crime was now so prevalent that it exceeded in value 'all other Robberies within this Kingdom'. They blamed this partly on the failure of many victims to prosecute; they preferred rather to 'compound for the return of their goods' than to bring charges. But still more unsatisfactory was the fact that those who were caught and convicted only received light sentences.[3] The capital provisions of the 1699 statute were a response to that situation, but they also gave the authorities another weapon in that those who revealed the identity of their accomplices, and thereby secured their conviction, were entitled to a royal pardon.[4]

Shoplifting remained a capital offence, at least in theory, until 1826, though the punishment was rarely exacted and in 1706 amendments were introduced allowing for sentences of six months to two years in a house of correction to be imposed on those found guilty of a first offence. There was also a return to branding on the thumb rather than the face. Only the most recalcitrant offenders, therefore, faced the death penalty.[5]

In these circumstances the number of people hanged for shoplifting remained small, so that between 1690 and 1713 just five of the thirteen women hanged at Tyburn were guilty of the offence. Two of those executed in December 1704 were described at the Old Bailey as persistent thieves. Another of the hanged was Janas Walton of Lancashire, who had worked as a servant in the capital for fifteen years before being executed for stealing 16yd of silk from a shop.[6]

More common was the fate of Mary Isles, who in 1750 took a length of cotton cloth valued at 20s from John Chamberlain's drapery in London. She had gone to the shop ostensibly to buy a small piece of material to make sleeves for a shift, but while she was inspecting this in daylight by the door, the shopkeeper's wife noticed a suspicious bulge under her clothing. When the woman left the shop the wife sent her maid to follow, but by the time the girl caught up with her she had thrown the stolen material into a garden, from where it was later recovered. Mary was found guilty at the Old Bailey and was fined 4s 10d.[7]

In another case in 1750 a washerwoman employed by a London grocer was discovered to have concealed over a pound of tea and more than a pound of sugar about her person. She had packed them into two handkerchiefs and suspended a package from each leg. Although found guilty, her fine amounted to only 10d.[8]

Shoplifting remained a problem throughout the period, although it seems to have been one that retailers were often anxious to conceal, either because they did not want the trouble of prosecuting offenders or because they feared unwelcome publicity. In the mid-nineteenth century, however, it took a new twist in that it ceased to involve mainly poor or marginal characters and instead was taken up by the well-to-do and the well-connected. The advent of department stores, with their open displays of merchandise and the 'buzz and excitement' they engendered were blamed for encouraging the offence among middle-class women. However, as Richard Lambert points out, even in 1867 the ballad *Ladies, Don't Go Thieving* was being sold on the streets of London, thereby suggesting that the crime was prevalent before department stores became important, and indicating the public's surprise at finding it carried out by those who were comfortably off:

> Oh, don't we live in curious times,
> You scarce could be believing,
> When Frenchmen fight and emperors die
> And ladies go a-thieving.
> A beauty of the West End went,
> Around a shop she lingers,
> And there upon some handkerchiefs
> She clapped her pretty fingers.
> Into the shop she gently popped;
> The world is quite deceiving
> When ladies have a notion got
> To ramble out a-thieving. . . .[9]

William Whiteley was one victim. He claimed that for every male shoplifter he caught, 300 females were detected. As in earlier times, they frequently hunted in twos, with one engaging the assistant's attention while her accomplice shoved the stolen goods into a capacious pocket or bag. Nevertheless, as Lambert comments wryly, it must have required considerable strength for Sarah Bennett in 1890 to stow away 20yd of silk, or Mrs Olive Magestie to conceal 14yd of black silk in 1894. Small items were taken, too, ranging from tins of potted meat and jars of Bovril to toys and lengths of ribbon.[10]

In the early twentieth century Selfridges, with its lavish displays, was another major sufferer and in the spring of 1909, shortly after it had opened, the Marlborough Street magistrate blamed it for setting out goods 'in such a manner as to be a temptation to theft'. He referred sourly to the fact that he had already had to deal with several shoplifters from the store. One was Lizzie Bright from Clapham Common who walked boldly in, picked up an umbrella, hung it on her arm, and walked away. She was presumably intercepted by a store detective, for in April 1909 she was charged with the theft and sentenced to three months' imprisonment with hard labour.[11]

Nor was it only London that was affected. In June 1909 two girls, aged 21 and 18, who had stolen two rolls of ribbon and a pair of gloves from a draper's shop in central Birmingham, were each sentenced to three months' imprisonment with hard labour at the city's police court.[12]

Shopkeepers, for their part, resented the way magistrates lectured them for putting temptation in the way of customers by not keeping goods locked up in show cases.[13] In some places, including Bolton and Motherwell, restrictions were imposed on retailers who displayed goods outside the shop door, since the police considered this encouraged theft. In 1908 some Bolton shopkeepers were fined for ignoring the prohibition, while in Motherwell in the following year the eight tradesmen charged with a similar offence had their cases dismissed only when they undertook to discontinue the practice.[14]

Elsewhere proprietors who displayed goods outside their premises might employ boys to keep an eye on them. When John Birch Thomas worked in a north London hardware shop selling paints and ironmongery during the 1870s that was one of his duties. 'There were dozens of pails, zinc baths, brooms and brushes, kettles and heaps of other iron and tin things' for him to look after. 'A boy was standing outside the grocer's shop next door looking after and selling eggs which were in long boxes laid out on the pavement.'[15]

One of the complaints of retailers was that middle-class women caught shoplifting often escaped lightly, either because individual stores wished to avoid attracting adverse comment, or, if a court case did result, because the defence usually cited 'biological' factors to explain away the woman's actions.[16] This then resulted in a binding-over or a fine, whereas working-class offenders, like Lizzie Bright and the two Birmingham girls, might well be sent to prison. One such example occurred in January 1909, when Elizabeth Roe, a married woman with genteel connections, was charged with stealing two pieces of silk valued at 8s from the Plummer Roddis store in Folkestone. She had apparently bought some articles in the normal way but while the bill was being made out was seen to take the silk. She admitted the theft but a medical man was then called in by the defence to say that she suffered from mild epilepsy and was at times not responsible for her actions. The magistrates were sceptical, observing that someone who had purchased goods at one moment could 'not be irresponsible for an act of larceny the next'. Nonetheless, as imprisonment might have seriously affected Mrs Roe's health, they imposed a fine of £10, with the alternative of a month's imprisonment.[17]

This 'class dimension' to the punishment of shoplifters continued well into the twentieth century. Bill Lancaster quotes two cases reported in *The Drapers' Record* in 1932:

The first involved a well-off woman from Harrogate who was caught stealing goods worth £4 4s from a large store. Her defence called . . . a specialist in shoplifting, who told the court that the defendant was suffering from 'Psychical Asphenia' which was caused by 'biological changes'. The court appeared to have been convinced by . . . [the] theory, the defendant being bound over for two years with no fine imposed. Two weeks earlier two working-class women were arrested in Bainbridge's Newcastle store in the act of stealing 'various items'. These two women put up little defence and called no experts to speak on their behalf in court, which sentenced them both to 15 months' hard labour.[18]

Shopkeepers were also robbed by their own employees from time to time, despite the precautions most took to guard against this. Indicative of their caution was the note made by Lewis Tomalin shortly before he opened his Jaeger shop in London in 1884: 'Photographs of employés. Make a rule of obtaining, in case somebody bolts with the Till.'[19]

Occasionally staff embarked on a large-scale campaign to defraud their employers, like two male assistants working for Debenham's in 1909. Over a six-month period they stole lengths of cloth from the firm, using female accomplices to get the material away from the premises. They supplied several dressmakers with the material and then spent the proceeds on 'horse-racing, billiards and expensive company'. One was sentenced to three months' imprisonment with hard labour and the second to two months.[20]

Sometimes the thefts were attributed to the assistants' low pay or to a desire to get their own back on a harsh and capricious employer. In other cases they were purely opportunistic. In June 1880 *The Drapers' Journal* concluded gloomily that hardly a month went by without reports of assistants employed by large firms committing robberies. The *Journal* attributed this partly to poor pay but also to the fact that a high proportion were young men coming to London or another big city for the first time. They were 'fresh from the restraints of home and home associations'. Desire to be in fashion meant that many lived beyond their annual earnings of £20 or £30. They might borrow from colleagues to make good a sudden shortfall but in the end 'overwhelmed with difficulties' they would take something from the shop to cover the deficit. These thefts were particularly likely early in the morning when a youngster was sent into the shop to do the dusting and make general preparations for opening up. At that time few people were about to see what was going on. On other occasions cash was stolen from the till and bills falsified to conceal this.[21] Occasionally, as in the case of Martha Trewey, a 19-year-old assistant from Forest Gate in London in 1909, a more elaborate deception was practised. She purchased goods elsewhere, presumably of a cheap quality, and then exchanged them with articles from her employer's store. On confessing tearfully to the offence in court, and with evidence of her previous good character, she escaped with a reprimand and a binding over for six months under the Probation Act.[22]

As with shoplifting, store owners were sometimes reluctant to prosecute offenders, preferring instead to dismiss them and to demand the repayment of stolen cash. William Whiteley, however, had no such inhibitions and the large number of prosecutions he brought against staff members was a sign either of his own unrelenting character or of the demoralising atmosphere in which they worked. In 1886 a large-scale fraud was discovered whereby a group of assistants were found to have extracted various sums of money by manipulating the firm's documents and altering duplicate bills. The following year a youngster was imprisoned for seeking to recover the fines imposed on him by stealing equivalent sums. In 1889 an employee of seven years' standing was sentenced for pawning £30 worth of silk goods and forging entries in his books to conceal the loss. In the same year 'a ledger clerk was found to have concerted with his wife a scheme whereby the latter bought provisions at Whiteley's and resold them elsewhere, while he intercepted the vouchers for the sales and destroyed them'.[23]

There were numerous cases of petty pilfering, too, as when an assistant employed as a meat carver in the provisions department pocketed a shilling which he had picked off the counter. Whiteley pressed charges against him and he was sentenced to six weeks' imprisonment. In another case, in 1896, the Universal Provider prosecuted a married clerk who had worked for him for twelve years and who was helping to support his mother, brother and sisters, because 'on a sudden impulse' he had stolen 2s. When accused, he immediately offered to return the cash but that did not satisfy Whiteley.[24]

Many businesses, however, preferred a more discreet approach. In 1933, when F. Cape & Co. Ltd, the Oxford department store, found that four young employees had taken small sums of money, they demanded repayment and, in three cases also asked the offenders to leave. One of them, a female assistant in her mid-20s, had already given in her notice when the theft was discovered. She was requested to return a blanket she had been given, presumably as a farewell present, and was ordered to 'get the money out of the Co-op bank' to make good the sum she had taken. In another instance an 18-year-old girl agreed to pay back the cash she had stolen at the rate of 2s 6d a week. She was also advised to tell her father of her predicament. She was the only one of the four who did not have to leave immediately.[25] The matter was seemingly hushed up to avoid embarrassing the firm and to prevent the youngsters concerned having a criminal record. It was presumably thought they had learned their lesson.

Similarly low-key methods were adopted by Reading Co-operative Society at the end of the 1930s, when cash went missing from the till. In one case, involving the 'misappropriation of money' by a butchery department employee, he was dismissed immediately and a deduction was made from his bonus account to make good the shortfall. Two other instances involving the taking of cash from the till when the shop was closed at midday led to the managers concerned being reprimanded because they had failed to secure the money in a safe, as they were supposed to do. They were not asked to make good the deficits, however, even though these amounted to the relatively substantial sums of £20 and £40 respectively. However, the manager of the branch which suffered the larger loss was demoted.[26] In one case the reaction was more vigorous, with Reading Borough Police CID called in to discover who was carrying out thefts in the drapery department. As a result of this, two assistants were charged and each was fined £2 10s or a month's imprisonment.[27] Perhaps inevitably when young and badly paid workers were handling cash on a daily basis there was a temptation to steal some, even though the number who succumbed to that was always small.

Shopkeepers were victims of more sophisticated 'thefts', too, carried out by swindlers posing as well-to-do customers. To guard against their activities trade protection societies were formed, the first being the Guardians, or the Society for the Protection of Trade against Swindlers and Sharpers. It was established in London in 1776 and for an annual subscription of £1 1s members received 'the support, advice, and assistance of the Society'. Not until the 1820s did the movement spread to the provinces, but by 1866, when a National Association of Trade Protection Societies was set up, there were seventy-six constituent organisations. At the end of the century the Association claimed a membership of 40,000 tradespeople.[28]

One of the prime purposes of these societies was to collect information on swindlers who sought to obtain, or had succeeded in obtaining, goods on credit. In 1798, for example, the London Guardians alerted subscribers to a 'Young Woman . . . having the Appearance of a Lady's Maid' who had 'lately obtained Goods from Two Members, by representing herself as coming from Two Ladies of distinction to whom she was, in consequence, supposed to be a Servant; but on Enquiry of these Ladies the Transactions turn out to be Impositions'. In another case the Liverpool Guardian Society warned of a man posing as a farmer who had secured a good deal of shirting material from a trusting shopkeeper.[29] Those posing as clergymen were particularly likely to be successful swindlers. As Margaret Finn comments, 'Education, verbal facility, genteel manners and the odour of sanctity all combined to lend men of the cloth the character of credit, as many an unwary tradesman found to his financial cost.'[30] But humbler people could prove persuasive, too. In April 1909 Elizabeth Langsdale, a general servant employed by a Mrs Hunt of Leytonstone, was dismissed. Three weeks later she went into a local draper's to ask for underwear on approval for Mrs Hunt. The draper's assistant supplied goods to the value of £4 16s, and only when they were not returned were enquiries made and the deception discovered. In this case the woman was arrested and brought to court.[31]

Shopkeepers, however, were not merely the victims of crime. They were its initiators as well. Sometimes, as with pawnbrokers, second-hand clothes dealers and owners of chandlers' shops, they were blamed for encouraging thefts. The London magistrate and novelist Henry Fielding did not mince his words when in the mid-eighteenth century he called pawnbrokers 'the receivers of stolen goods' and their shops the 'fountains of theft'.[32] He and those who thought like him claimed that thieves were recruited by such dealers. In 1816 one London policeman declared there was scarcely a chandler's shop in the metropolis which did not buy anything 'that a servant girl . . . can take with her . . . and many girls lose their reputation by the encouragement women keeping these shops give them'.[33]

Pawnbrokers were only too conscious of the accusations levelled against them and during the nineteenth century the *Pawnbrokers' Gazette* informed its readers about important court cases. However, press coverage of incidents where stolen (or hired) goods had been pledged, tended to exaggerate the scale of the problem. In 1870, notes Melanie Tebbutt, the pawnbrokers claimed that the stolen goods 'represented only one in 10,000 pledges'. That estimate was 'revised in 1881 to one in 14,000 after a larger survey'. Such figures, suggests Tebbutt, indicated it was the occasional thief rather than the professional criminal who used their services. Furthermore, pawnbrokers sometimes initiated court actions through their vigilance, or that of their assistants, in spotting property that might have been stolen.[34] The pawnbrokers and their friends asked plaintively why, if they were in the habit of receiving stolen goods, and thereby encouraging theft, more of them were not convicted in court. Only in large cities like London, where pawnshops were numerous, did some of them perhaps serve as a conduit for the easy disposal of stolen property.[35]

More widespread than the misdoings of a few pawnbrokers and second-hand clothes dealers, however, was the adulteration of many articles of food and drink by wholesalers and retailers. The ranged from using harmless but cheap additives to bulk up supplies of more expensive goods, such as tea, coffee and pepper, to utilising dangerous substances like red lead, which was found in items of confectionery, among other things. The aim was to boost profits and the extent to which it was carried on varied from commodity to commodity. Milk and beer were particularly likely to be watered down, while coffee was adulterated by the addition of chicory. In the case of tea, not only were exhausted tea leaves dried and added to fresh supplies but they were supplemented by the mixing in of leaves from English hedgerows, such as ash, sloe and elder. They were 'curled and coloured on copper plates', and between March and July 1818 alone there were eleven convictions for this offence.[36] One involved a grocer named Palmer. He employed agents to collect the leaves of black and white thorn from hedges around London, and paid them at the rate of 2d a pound for those they gathered. He subsequently disposed of the 'tea' he produced for 3s or 4s a pound, this being mixed with the genuine article.[37]

The scale of the problem was highlighted by an inquiry conducted by *The Lancet* in 1851. This revealed that coffee was adulterated not only with chicory but with roasted corn, beans, potato and burnt sugar. Pepper and mustard were frequently so impure that, in the case of the latter, it could 'scarcely ever be obtained' in a genuine form, no matter what price was paid for it. Milk often consisted of between 10 and 50 per cent of water.[38] This survey was followed in 1855 by the appointment of a parliamentary select committee to investigate the issue and take evidence from expert witnesses. Its findings confirmed those of *The Lancet*. One medical man, Dr Hassall, asserted that 'as many as eight or ten poisonous substances might be seen in almost every sweet-stuff shop entering into the colouring of the sugar confectionery'.[39] Nor was the practice confined to retailers in the poorest districts. Dr Hassall had found similar adulteration in 'sweet-stuff shops' in Oxford Street and Tottenham Court Road to that in the East End of London. The aim was to improve the colour of the confectionery, thereby making it more attractive to the purchaser.

Another physician and chemist, Dr Normandy, was concerned at the widespread use of alum in bread. The intention was to make cheap flour look whiter than it otherwise would and to increase the weight of the loaf by causing it to retain water.[40] According to Normandy, there was not 'a single baker' in the capital who made bread without including alum. Boiled rice was added to the mixture by some unscrupulous bakers, again to encourage water retention and thus boost the loaf's weight. Red lead was sometimes mixed with cayenne pepper, although usually the adulteration took the form of ground rice and brickdust.[41] He quoted a case reported in *The Times* on 10 May 1852 in which a Chelmsford grocer named Tibbald was fined £50 for selling pepper so badly adulterated that out of a cask weighing 100lb only 2lb was genuine pepper. The rest was allegedly made up of husks of mustard, chillis and rice.[42]

In such circumstances it is significant that when the co-operative retail societies began to increase during the 1850s and 1860s they made one of their selling points the fact that they only stocked products that were free from adulteration.[43]

In 1860 the first Adulteration of Foods Act was passed. It allowed local authorities to appoint public analysts to examine samples of food and drink, on a complaint being made by private citizens. There was no provision for the analyst to take the initiative by sampling, and even if a vendor were found guilty, a small fine was the usual penalty.[44] Such a half-hearted measure had little effect. Twelve years later, however, a new Adulteration of Food, Drink and Drugs Act explicitly made it an offence to sell 'a mixture containing ingredients for the purpose of adding weight or bulk . . . unless its composition was declared to the purchaser'. The power to appoint public analysts was also widened, although the appointment still remained largely optional. Nonetheless, the new Act was wider in scope and led to more vigorous enforcement than its predecessor. Within three years 150 of the 225 districts authorised to appoint analysts had done so.[45]

During the last thirty years of the century, with food prices falling as a result of growing imports and with the number of analysts increasing, grocers abandoned many of their former malpractices. The fact that those who broke the law were likely to be prosecuted and to have their case reported in the press was a further deterrent. In 1874, a Sheffield grocer and tea dealer, convicted of selling tea containing 33 per cent of exhausted tea leaves, complained of the way the matter had been 'placarded about the town on the posters of the papers, also a large report of the trial was given in the papers; it did us a deal of harm'.[46] He claimed that in the first week after the conviction his takings had fallen by about a fifth. He denied having committed the offence but admitted that a number of retailers in Sheffield had been convicted of selling mustard adulterated with flour and milk mixed with water. He had sold a considerable quantity of 'very good tea dust' to the poor at 1d an ounce: 'In fact I would drink it myself.'[47]

The Merchandise Marks Acts of 1887 and 1891 also provided for shopkeepers to be prosecuted for applying a false description to any product, such as passing off foreign meat as English or selling tea at a weight that included the wrapping paper without stating this specifically. Similarly, the Margarine Act of 1887 sought to stamp out the practice of selling this as butter 'to an unsuspecting public'. These were issues with which the National Federation of Grocers' Associations concerned itself. It warned its members that as regards tea sales, they should include on the wrapper the additional statement: 'This packet is sold as gross weight, including the wrapper.'[48]

However, by the mid-1870s the most noxious and dangerous substances were no longer present in food. As an official report concluded drily in 1874, it might be 'some consolation to the public to know that in the matter of adulteration they are *cheated* rather than *poisoned*'.[49]

One of these less harmful examples of cheating was recalled by a youngster who worked in a back street grocery in the London area shortly before the First World War. As one of his first jobs he was told to fill the tea jars, which were then empty. As there were several of them he asked where the relevant tea chests were, since he could find only two of them. The grocer told him to fill alternate jars from one tea chest and the remaining jars from the second chest. The theory was that if a customer decided to go 'up-market' he or she would move up just one price level. Equally to buy a 'cheaper' tea customers would drop just one price. By filling alternate jars with a different brand the purchaser got a different flavoured tea and was happy.[50] On a similar basis, water was patted into slabs of butter to boost the weight and excessive amounts of soil were left on root vegetables.

There were more serious cases involving the giving of short weight, though, and here the tricks of the trade varied from adding a piece of bacon to the underside of the pan (to make it drop down before the correct weight had been reached), to using faulty scales. Some shopkeepers had a cavalier approach to weighing out goods anyway. According to Robert Roberts, his mother was always meticulous about making sure she gave the exact weight, but his father was less precise. His quarter of a pound varied between 3½oz and 5oz, 'according to the customer's face, reputation and antecedents'.[51] Sometimes the fraud was more deliberate. When Mrs Layton began to help in a small shop in Bethnal Green at the age of 10, during the mid-1860s, she was taught how to weigh bread.

> I was told when I put a piece of bread on the loaf as a makeweight I was to be sure to press it down, so that the scale went down. I was getting quite expert in the art of cheating in weight, and thought I was very clever, when one day my aunt . . . saw me serving in the shop. . . . She soon discovered that I had been taught to weigh bread to the disadvantage of the customer, and when I went home to dinner, she told me she had watched me . . . cheat a poor woman. . . . I felt so thoroughly ashamed of myself . . . I never gave short weight again.[52]

There were other dubious practices carried on at this small store as well. Articles of clothing and household goods were brought in and left, rather like in a pawnshop, in return for food. The practice was illegal, so all the articles had to be brought in clandestinely. As Mrs Layton was then only a child and thus less likely to arouse suspicion than an adult, she was trained 'to help to smuggle things in'.[53]

One of the commonest methods of giving short weight was to use faulty scales and at the end of the Victorian era it became a major task of the Weights and Measures Inspectors to eliminate this. Thus in London, where the responsibility lay with the Public Control Department of the County Council, inspectors discovered that during the period 1893–4 out of around half a million weights and measures examined, about one in every eleven on hawkers' stalls was faulty and about one in twenty-two of those tested in shops. In most cases the owner was warned and the appliances taken for rectification. But occasionally, as at Wandsworth in 1896, an offender was brought to court. In this case the shopkeeper had fixed a piece of bacon to the underside of the goods plate of his weighing machine, to make the weight appear greater than it was. In November 1894 he had been convicted of a similar offence and this repeated dishonesty led the magistrates to impose a fine of £10 and to direct that details of the conviction be published.[54]

In the spring of 1898 seven shopkeepers in New Charlton, London, complained that the costermongers who traded near their premises were damaging custom 'by their sharp practices of False Weights and Measures'. But the local inspector was unimpressed. He pointed out to his superiors that the shopkeepers themselves were 'only one degree removed in class from the hawker' and that four of the complainants had themselves been warned for owning faulty scales. Furthermore, when he visited the location he had found that only one of the hawkers was selling goods by weight. In this case the 2lb and 1lb weights were very slightly defective. 'I gave the owner . . . a verbal caution', wrote the inspector, 'and he promised to have the weights put right.'[55]

During the 1890s the vigilance and persistence of the inspectorate brought about an improvement, and although faulty equipment was still found, its incidence was much reduced. Over the period 1900–1, for example, only one out of every twenty-five of the measuring devices on hawkers' stalls and barrows in London was found to be incorrect, compared to one in eleven seven years before. Among shopkeepers the proportion had dropped to one in every forty-five of those tested, compared to one in twenty-two found defective in 1893–4.[56] The visit of the inspector was, however, always a matter of some concern to small shopkeepers. Robert Roberts remembered that when he or another family member saw 'a heavy, cold-eyed man in the neighbourhood we sped home on the instant – "Weights 'n' Measures!"[57] The daughter of a widowed shopkeeper who kept a small general store in Southampton recalled that they had four sets of scales, to weigh tobacco, sweets, vegetables and provisions, and they had a private firm to check them over every six months. Nevertheless, the arrival of the inspector was always a nerve-racking experience. He would 'come in and take a loaf of bread off the shelf and weigh it to see that it was the proper weight'.[58] She remembered that her mother would not sell fresh milk because 'they were pretty strict with the milk'.

Rarer but more serious offences committed by shopkeepers included setting fire to their premises to claim the insurance, particularly when business was bad. In February 1909 the *Drapery Times* reported on an Edinburgh tradesman who had naively increased his insurance cover even though the stock in his shop was insufficient to meet his original insurance. He then set fire to the premises, despite the fact that there were people living above the shop who might have been injured or killed by the fire. The judge described the crime as 'a most dangerous one to society and to life' and sentenced him to three years' penal servitude.[59]

Finally, when restrictions on shop opening hours were imposed, some retailers sought to evade local authority closure orders. The struggle to achieve early closing will be examined below, but the problem of enforcing the limits laid down was exemplified in the case of Messrs Richards, drapers and outfitters of Barnstaple, Devon, in February 1909. They were prosecuted by the town clerk for serving customers after the 7 p.m. deadline laid down in the order. As this was their second offence he pressed for a stiffer penalty than the 10s fine previously levied. The drapers, for their part, admitted the offence on technical grounds but claimed that strict instructions had been given to the assistants after the first case that they were not to sell clothes after 7 p.m. One of them had ignored this, however, thereby acting contrary to his employers' orders. The bench accepted the excuse and this time the fine was fixed at a derisory 2s 6d, plus costs. These included the sum of £1 1s to be paid to the prosecution to cover the fee of an advocate. The paltry fine was symptomatic of the way in which even when regulations to control late shopping were drawn up they were often treated lightly by those responsible for upholding them.[60] It was one of the reasons why the early closing movement had such a protracted and difficult history.

LABOUR RELATIONS

Although in the eighteenth and nineteenth centuries many of those working in shops hoped to become retailers themselves, during the time they were employees they were expected to behave with decorum and to be well disciplined. In the case of the larger shops, as we have seen, that could include observing a long list of rules and regulations and of being penalised by fines or even dismissal for infringements of them. But even in small businesses, owners often maintained a strict regime, with much emphasis placed on politeness to customers and deference to superiors. One man who worked in a high-class grocery in Southampton around the time of the First World War remembered his employer as a rather miserable old man, who particularly objected to the staff whistling when they went down to the cellar. 'He would go and shout. . . . It didn't matter what, he always had a complaint.'[61]

In the case of larger shops, senior personnel such as buyers or shopwalkers exercised control over younger assistants. Mrs Adela Hill, who went to work at Selfridges in 1909 as a junior when she was 15, recalled this as 'the lowest form of animal life. . . . [It] could be a dog's life, and very often was. My wages were 2s 6d per week with dinner and tea thrown in, and if by any wonderful chance I made a sale of the goods the department stocked – corsets – which I never did, commission was 3d in the pound.' Nonetheless she remained at Selfridges until 1917, although her basic wage was never more than £1 a week. Latterly this was boosted by commission.[62]

A girl who joined the staff of a large millinery shop in Brighton in the 1920s likewise remembered the 'rigid rules and harsh discipline'. This included having the shop door open all day from 9 a.m., even in winter. The girls suffered from chilblains but they were not allowed to warm their icy fingers on the single tiny radiator which was all that the shop possessed by way of heating. There were no official breaks for tea or coffee, 'no matter how we longed for a hot drink to warm us up. We took it in turns to rush to the kitchen and grab a cup of tea, but as often as not had to leave it and dash down to the shop to serve. There was a small gas stove in the kitchen where we could heat our midday meal and – hygiene or no hygiene – we often used to put our feet in the oven to unfreeze them.' The shop's owner sometimes visited in her large chauffeur-driven car and sat at the cash desk watching every assistant. 'If Madam [was] in a bad mood, we assistants [quaked] in our shoes for to displease Madam [could] mean instant dismissal. Dismissal would mean that the girl had to leave without a reference and without one there was little hope of getting another job.'[63]

Marriage bars applied to employment in many of the larger shops, especially those where staff were required to live in, or, at the very least, permission had to be sought for marriage. According to a correspondent to the *Oxford Chronicle* in February 1908 that was 'the rule of *every* business house in the City of Oxford where the system of "living in" is in practice'.

A contributor to the *Western Mail* claimed that in South Wales 'a married man in the drapery trade' was 'in a sorry plight'. Only with difficulty could he obtain a situation. Many in the principality, he declared, 'turn colliers'.[64] However, in view of the relatively frail physique of most male shopworkers, this latter outcome seems very unlikely.

But these general difficulties and tensions between retailers and their staff apart, of the various grievances expressed by shop assistants from the eighteenth to the twentieth centuries, one of the most enduring related to their long working hours and consequent lack of leisure. A trade union activist claimed that 'the question of closing the shops earlier' was the 'paramount question' for workers even after the Second World War. 'It was so in 1825, and likewise in 1891; it is so now in 1949. . . . Shop assistants are moved more by this than by any other issue, including wages.'[65]

Nor was it only the workers who suffered. Shopkeepers, too, were affected, especially when they ran their own small family business. Robert Roberts remembered that even in the early twentieth century his mother, like her competitors, opened at 7 a.m. and closed 'an hour before midnight'. She was 'aching for the hour when the door could be shut and the light turned out; but custom demanded that this, in our shop, and in any other of its kind, be not done one minute before the appointed time'.[66] It was feared that a customer, once rebuffed by a too early closure, would transfer his or her purchases elsewhere. For the same reason some shops opened on Sunday mornings. A Southampton woman whose widowed mother kept a small general store from the First World War until the early 1930s, recalled the mother closing only twice on Sundays. Once was when a nephew was married in Portsmouth and the second time was when she herself remarried. Even then 'people came in on Monday and said "you weren't open yesterday"'.[67]

Not all retail outlets stayed open for such long periods. More prestigious establishments, catering for the well-to-do, would shut at 7 p.m. or 8 p.m. even in Victorian times because their customers were unlikely to shop late at night or to send their servants out to do so. For a similar reason they might delay opening in the morning, whereas those catering for manual workers who had to go to their own work at an early hour would, like Mrs Roberts, be ready for business at 7 a.m. Opening times were also influenced by a shop's location, as well as by its clientele and the kind of trade done. Hence businesses in small towns were likely to have shorter hours than similar firms in large cities, and those in the centre of a town were usually more limited than those in the suburbs. A survey of Sheffield in 1886 revealed that shops in the city centre closed at 7 p.m. on weekdays and 9 p.m. or 9.30 p.m. on Saturdays, while those in the suburbs shut at 8 p.m. on weekdays and

10 p.m. or 11 p.m. on Saturdays. Within the same district, small shops run by their proprietors or those in side streets would stay open very late to catch any passing trade. In the West End of London in 1887 the 'great firms' closed at 6 p.m. or 7 p.m. on weekdays and 2 p.m. on Saturdays, but there were innumerable small outlets in neighbouring streets where 'trade rivalry and competition' meant that work continued, with brief intervals for meals, from 7 a.m. or 8 a.m. until 9.30 p.m. or 10 p.m. on the first four days of the week, to 10.30 p.m. or 11 p.m. on Fridays, and until midnight or later on Saturdays. Some opened on Sunday mornings. For example, fishmongers' and game sellers' assistants had to come in on Sundays to supply fish and game to wealthy households in Mayfair and to nearby gentlemen's clubs.[68] Indeed, retailers of perishable goods, such as butchers, greengrocers and provision dealers normally kept open longer than did drapers and stationers.[69]

It was against this background that the manager of a Stratford, London, drapery could remark loftily in 1909: 'We do what may be termed a "West-end" trade, and all our business is done by seven o'clock in the winter and eight o'clock in the summer. . . . Ours is entirely a high-class trade, and there is no occasion for us to remain open later. We do not cater for the lower-class trade at all.'[70] The lower orders were those most likely to shop late, either because they made their purchases after they had returned from work or because they waited until they had been to the public house or the music hall late at night.

These differences were to play a part when efforts were made to limit opening hours either by voluntary means or by statute. In general the owners of the larger stores favoured early closure, because it would have little effect on their normal business hours, while smaller men claimed that if there were compulsory early closing, this 'would tend to throw all the trade into the larger shops and co-operative stores, and would ruin hundreds of small traders'.[71]

The first attempts at reform came in the second quarter of the nineteenth century, at a time of agitation for a widening of the political franchise and for limits to be placed on factory working hours, at least for women, children and young people under 18. In the early debates on the need for regulation of shop hours reference was often made to the factory reform movement. Yet, despite an appreciation of the importance of legislation in securing improved conditions for millworkers, it was widely believed that to curtail retail opening hours by Act of Parliament was out of the question. It was seen as inimical to English ideas of liberty and of the shopkeeper's right to trade for as long as he chose.[72] Only if proprietors agreed voluntarily that it was in their interest to close their businesses at an earlier time could progress be made. Also ideologically unacceptable to many Victorians was any attempt to put a legal limit on the working hours of adult male assistants. Restrictions might be placed on female hours but even that was regarded as undesirable because it would limit the employment opportunities of women and girls and make it more likely they would be replaced by men. With a male staff, shop owners would be able to stay open later. Furthermore, where businesses were run by a husband and wife, or by a father and daughter, a restriction on female labour would cause disruption and discontent among the families affected. Such arguments were still being advanced by opponents of legislation well into the 1880s.[73]

However, many did accept that working hours in retailing needed to be cut to give staff more leisure. In particular, advocates of early closing argued that 'the Saturday half-holiday' was 'the key to the Sabbath'. Saturday afternoon was 'the time for recreation; that is the time for steamboat trips and cheap railway trains, and for opening Crystal Palaces and British Museums.'[74] Sundays could then be observed in an appropriately religious manner by attendance at church or chapel and by other suitably moral pursuits.

As early as 1825 meetings were held in both London and Sheffield by shopkeepers and their assistants to consider limiting opening hours. In London about 100 drapers, silk merchants, haberdashers and hosiers made some tentative suggestions in that direction but nothing seems to have come of the initiative.[75] Thirteen years later the Metropolitan Drapers' Association was formed with similar objectives of shorter working hours and an improvement in the physical, moral and intellectual development of assistants. In 1842 it changed its name to the Metropolitan Early Closing Association, and by the beginning of the 1850s had become the Early Closing Association (ECA). But whatever its intentions, it failed to propose any specific limits to opening hours, merely demanding a general reduction. To achieve this, as Wilfred Whitaker notes,

> meetings and lectures were to be arranged, sermons to be preached, an appeal was to be made to the public . . . 'to abstain from shopping in the evening'. . . . Finally, efforts were to be made to impress on the assistants the importance of using their free time to improve their mental faculties through literary institutes, attendance at lectures and the use of libraries.[76]

These principles, endlessly reiterated, were to form the basis of the association's campaigns to secure early closing for decades to come. Persuasion and propaganda were the means to be adopted, with tracts distributed and posters displayed appealing to the public to shop early. For as a supporter declared in 1853: 'It is almost in vain to expect that the tradesmen will have the moral courage and the self-denial to close their establishments, and turn away their customers', if those customers continued to shop at a late hour.[77] Efforts should also be made to encourage employers to pay their workers on Friday nights instead of on Saturdays, since this would remove the need for families to do their shopping late on Saturday.

Assistants were called upon by the association to support the cause, too, although as a report of 1848 delicately put it, 'in their efforts for emancipation' they should have 'recourse to only those measures which are of a conciliatory and persuasive description, ever avoiding most studiously all violent proceedings, as unworthy of the object in view'.[78]

With such a cautious appeal for support it is not surprising that most shopworkers displayed little enthusiasm for the association, and they were repeatedly castigated by the movement's leaders for their 'apathy'. In any case they were doubtless aware that the initiative for shop closure lay with the retailers themselves rather than their employees.

Some assistants did join the association because they were forced to do so by proprietors who were supporters and who deducted subscriptions to it from their pay. Others were afraid to become members because their employers opposed all early closing initiatives, and others again felt, and with good reason as the years passed, that the ECA was achieving little. It was all too easy when a voluntary early closing agreement was reached in a particular locality for it to collapse because one or more of the participants broke ranks. This was exemplified by an ECA report on London in 1883 when, at the behest of one pro-closure firm, the association spent much time 'in canvassing the Clothiers and Outfitters of Holborn, for a closing at 7 o'clock instead of 8. An arrangement was at one time completed, but subsequently fell through on account of one house failing to carry it out.'[79] The frustration felt by some shopworkers was expressed in 1859 by a London assistant who wrote angrily of the whole voluntary movement: 'Are we to have early closing, or not? . . . We want no more talk, no more writing; we wish acting, and at once. . . . The law says how many hours the factory hands shall work – why not have the same law for drapery hands?'[80]

In 1881 a new body called the Shop Assistants' Twelve Hours' Labour League (soon known as the Shop Hours' Labour League) was formed to press for legislation to limit the working day in retailing. It highlighted the ill-health of many assistants as a result of their long hours and was headed by Thomas Sutherst, a barrister. He not only organised mass demonstrations in favour of legislation for a twelve-hour working day, but collected evidence on employment conditions in shops. This was published in 1884. According to

1. Interior of a draper's shop, with the draper's wife in attendance on two customers. (*From:* John the Shopkeeper, *a moral tract, c. 1800*)

AN ALARMING MESSAGE.

"IF YOU PLEASE, SIR, MOTHER'S TOOK THE LOTION, AND RUBBED HER LEG WITH THE MIXTURE!"

2. A child customer in a chemist's shop, informing the proprietor that her mother had made a mistake in the medicines she had taken. (Punch, *1842*)

STATE O' TRADE.

Small Girl. "PLEASE, MRS. GREENSTOUGH, MOTHER SAYS WILL YOU GIVE HER A LETTUCE?"

Mrs. G. "GIVE?! TELL THEE MOTHER GIV'UM'S DEAD, AND LENDUM'S VERY BAD. NOTHINK FOR NOTHINK 'ERE, AND PRECIOUS LITTLE FOR SIXPENCE!!!"

3. *Opposite:* A street seller vending greengrocery and laying down her cash terms to her young customer. (Punch, *1869*)

4. A street trader selling oysters, *c.* 1900. *(From: George R. Sims (ed.),* Living London, *vol. 3, 1903)*

SHARP, RATHER!

Boy. "TWO 'A'P'NY 'ERRINS."   Shopkeeper (severely). "IF WHAT, SIR? IF YOU—WHAT, SIR?"
Boy. "WELL, IF Y'A' GOT 'EM!"

5. This shopkeeper is taking a stern view of an impolite youngster wanting to buy two halfpenny herrings! (Punch, *1867*)

6. Staff at Dalton-in-Furness Co-operative Society shop, Lancashire, *c.* 1900. The manager is standing in the shadows at the rear of the shop and the female assistant may have been his wife. This society began in 1868 and became part of Barrow Co-operative Society in 1970. (*The Co-operative College, Manchester*)

7. A small butcher's shop – the business of Andrew Adams at New Headington, Oxford, *c.* 1910. Such a simple business would require little initial capital to establish. (*Centre for Oxfordshire Studies: Oxfordshire County Council Photographic Archive*)

SITUATIONS WANTED.

MILLINERY.—SITUATION required, permanent, as FIRST HAND. Good experience; can serve or keep stock.—Address, E.C., care of Mr. H. Baker, Cheap-street, Sherborne.

MILLINERY.—A Re-engagement in the above as SECOND HAND or Assistant.—Address, Miss A. Whitley, Hoddesdon, Herts.

DRAPERY. — RE - ENGAGEMENT by Young Man. Good-class trade. Linens or Manchester preferred. Tall. Seven years' experience. Excellent references.—A. Williams, at C. Badcock's, Queen-street, Oxford.

DRAPERY.—Young Man (22) requires RE-ENGAGEMENT in heavy department. Height, 5 ft. 11 in. Seven years' experience. London preferred. Best references.—Address, J. B., Office of this Paper.

MILLINERY.—WANTED, RE-ENGAGEMENT by widow Lady, aged 26. Experience in good town and country houses previous to her marriage. Will give time for a fresh start. Satisfactory reference from last employers. Country preferred.—Apply E. H., care of Mr. Dingley, Belton, Grantham.

DRESS and MANTLE MAKING. — Experienced FIRST HAND desires Engagement in good class trade. Can take entire charge.—Dressmaker, London House, Tavistock, Devon.

DRAPERY.—Young Lady, aged 18, just out of her apprenticeship (serves through), seeks RE-ENGAGEMENT. Accustomed to pushing medium-class trade.—Address, A. B., 66, London-street, Reading.

MILLINERY.—WANTED, at once, Situation as JUNIOR ASSISTANT. 2½ years' experience. Good reference.—A. S., 18, Albert-street, Nottingham.

MILLINERY.—SITUATION WANTED for a Young Lady. Can be recommended by Court milliner for good assistant or second hand in a small business. First-class references.—Address, Mater, 68, Crofton-road, Camberwell.

SITUATIONS VACANT.

DRAPERY. — WANTED, an experienced YOUNG LADY (slight knowledge of millinery preferred), for a small business. Comfortable home. As one of the family.—State full particulars and salary, Haddon, 308, Stretford-road, Manchester.

DRAPERY. — WANTED, good pushing JUNIOR for dress department, good salesman and stockkeeper.—State age, salary, and experience to S. Sacret, High-street, Hounslow.

DRAPERY.—WANTED, a JUNIOR for the general trade. A good window dresser.—Send full particulars to W. J. Biggs, St. Clement's, Oxford.

DRAPERS and MILLINERS.—WANTED, good COUNTER HAND, understanding fancy and millinery departments, fulfilling orders. Young Man for drapery; good window dresser; some knowledge of boots and clothing.—Charles J. Smith, Broadway House, Finchley, N.

DRAPERS CLERK and COUNTER HANDS.—WANTED, a LADY thoroughly accustomed to the routine of a draper's counting-house; also Junior Lady Assistants for various departments.—T. H. Ponting and Co., 121, 123, 125, Westbourne-grove.

DRAPER'S and MILLINERS.—Two Male and two Female Apprentices to the general drapery; one Female Apprentice to millinery and dressmaking.—Brown and Sons, Torquay.

MANTLES.—WANTED, in a good medium class trade, Young Lady, as SECOND HAND. Must have had good experience in the department, and be competent to give estimates, &c.—Apply, stating religious denomination, age, height, salary, references, experience, and enclose carte, to C. Badcock, 13 and 14, Queen-street, Oxford.

MANTLE MAKERS.— A Young Lady WANTED, as MANTLE CUTTER and FITTER, and to superintend workroom Will be occasionally required to assist in show-room.—Apply, personally or by letter, stating salary and full particulars of experience, J. H. Gosling and Sons, Richmond, Surrey.

8. *Above:* Advertisements for drapery staff. *(From:* The Drapers' Record, *1 October 1887)*

SOFT SAWDER.

"BUT I DON'T CALL THIS A FASHIONABLE 'AT."
"IT WILL SOON BECOME SO, MADAM, IF YOU WEAR IT."

9. *Right:* An assistant in a milliner's shop flattering a very plain customer in order to make a sale. (Punch, *1890*)

10. *Left:* William Whiteley (1831–1907), the dynamic London department store pioneer. *(From:* Fortunes Made in Business*)*

11. *Below:* Department store assistants waiting at a cash desk, *c.* 1900. *(From: George R. Sims (ed.),* Living London, *vol. 2, 1902)*

A CASH DESK.

12. *Opposite above:* Two shoe salesmen seeking to please a coy lady customer wanting a 'dainty' pair of shoes. *(Punch, 1880)*

13. *Opposite below:* A sale day at Peter Robinson's department store in London, *c.* 1900. *(From: George R. Sims (ed.),* Living London, *vol. 2, 1902)*

A POSER.

"IT'S NOT SO MUCH A *DURABLE* ARTICLE THAT I REQUIRE, MR. CRISPIN. I WANT SOMETHING *DAINTY*, YOU KNOW—SOMETHING *COY*, AND AT THE SAME TIME JUST A WEE BIT *SAUCY!*"

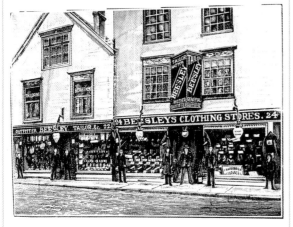

E. H. BEESLEY,
Tailor, Clothier and Complete Outfitter,
- 22 & 24, High Street, ABINGDON. -

DEPARTMENTS.

Ready-made Clothing.	Hosiery, all kinds of Underwear, &c.
Hats, Caps, Best Makes.	
Woollen Warehouse.	Waterproof Coats, Capes, etc., etc. Umbrellas.
Rainproof Coats.	
Shirts, Collars, Ties and Gloves.	Tailoring, Ladies' and Gent.'s
Gent.'s Boots, Shoes and Leggings.	Tailors' and Dressmakers' Trimmings.
Working Men's Clothing of every description.	Travelling Bags and Trunks.

FANCY DRAPERY and Millinery Business, in the outskirts of Leeds. Takings over £1,800; rent £60. Good house; stock and fixtures at valuation; capital required about £350.

LINCOLNSHIRE.—General and Fancy Drapery Business. Best position in the town; owner retiring through ill-health; returns, £1,800; rent £83. Stock and fixtures at valuation; capital about £600.

YORKSHIRE.—Drapery and Millinery Business, in North Yorkshire health resort; very good position; returns £2,800; rent £120. Owner wishes to go South; capital about £1,200.

OLD-ESTABLISHED Drapery Business, in West Yorkshire Colliery town. Vendor who owns the property wishes to retire; returns £5,000; rent £75; lease can be arranged; double-fronted shop. Stock and fixtures at valuation; capital about £1,400.

GENERAL Drapery, Millinery, Costumes, and Dressmaking Business, in fashionable inland health resort; very old-established business; best position, and the principal business in the town; returns £3,000; rent £175. Stock and fixtures at valuation; capital about £1,400.

DRAPERY and Millinery Business, in West Yorkshire town. Good position; returns nearly £2,200; rent £80; capital about £600.

FOR DISPOSAL, the Old-established Drapery Business of Messrs. G. Harrison & Son, Ashton-under-Lyne. Large and commodious premises at a moderate rental; stock optional.
Further particulars respecting the above will be sent on application to JAS. POWELL & SONS, Valuers, 27/45, Osborne Street, Hull.

14. *Left:* Advertising blurb for a small town tailor and outfitter in Abingdon, *c.* 1920. Mr Beesley had clearly not learned the art of tasteful window dressing as every window was crammed with goods. *(Author's collection)*

15. *Below:* Drapery businesses for sale, with amounts of capital needed by would-be purchasers. *(From:* The Drapery Times, *1 May 1909)*

16. *Opposite above: Punch* poking fun at a naive young shop assistant in a small music shop. *(Punch, 1855)*

17. *Opposite below:* A late Victorian ironmonger's shop. *(Punch, 1888)*

TASTE.

Shop-girl (who has been expected to possess Tennyson's "Miller's Daughter"). "NO, MISS! WE'VE NOT GOT THE MILLER'S—BUT HERE'S THE RATCATCHER'S DAUGHTER, JUST PUBLISHED!!"

REPRISALS!

Tradesman (to Old Gentleman, who has purchased Lawn-Mower). "YES, SIR, I'LL OIL IT, AND SEND IT OVER IMM——"
Customer (imperatively). "NO, NO, NO!—IT MUSTN'T BE OILED! I WON'T HAVE IT OILED! MIND THAT! I WANT NOISE! AND, LOOK HERE—PICK ME OUT A NICE RUSTY ONE. MY NEIGHBOUR'S CHILDREN HOOT AND YELL TILL TEN O'CLOCK EVERY NIGHT, SO"—*(viciously)*—"I MEAN TO CUT MY GRASS FROM FOUR TILL SIX EVERY MORNING!!"

18. A demonstration by staff from William Whiteley's store in June 1901, advertising a meeting to oppose the 'living-in' system. P.C. Hoffman is third from the left. He later became a Labour MP. *(Union of Shop, Distributive and Allied Workers)*

19. An outing to Weymouth by staff employed by Frederick Baker & Son, house-furnishers, upholsterers and bedding manufacturers of Southampton, in 1927. This was one of their regular annual outings. *(Southampton Archives)*

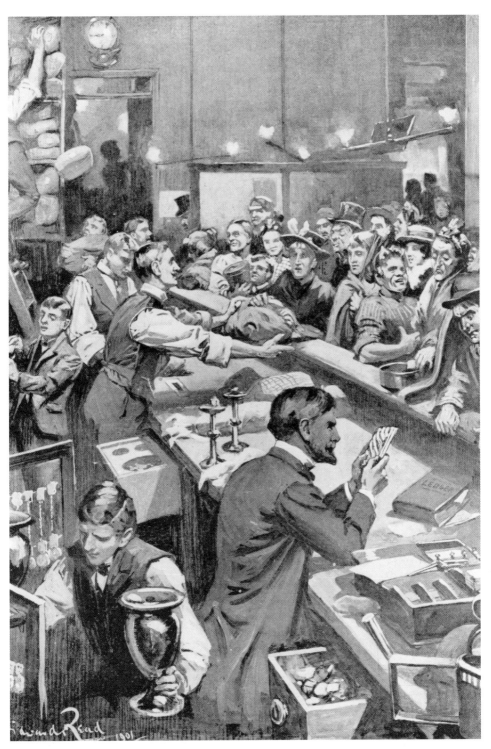

20. Many families relied on pawnbrokers to provide cash in time of need. They also often pawned their 'Sunday best' clothes on Mondays and then collected them on Saturdays, ready to wear on the Sabbath. *(From: George R. Sims (ed.),* Living London, *vol. 2, 1902)*

A SHOP-LIFTER.

21. A shoplifter concealing a pair of shoes while the attention of the shopkeeper is elsewhere. *(From: George R. Sims (ed.),* Living London, *vol. 3, 1903)*

22. After 1918 some tradesmen began to use motor transport rather than horse and cart for making deliveries. Reginald Dollimore was a baker at Ivinghoe, Buckinghamshire, in the early 1920s. He took over the bakery from his father following service in the First World War. *(C.A. Horn)*

23. A customer seated at the counter receiving assiduous attention from a salesman at Charles Badcock & Co. Ltd, drapers, in Queen Street, Oxford, in 1938. *(Centre for Oxfordshire Studies: Oxfordshire County Council Photographic Archive)*

24. A shopkeeper at
Headington, Oxford,
combining selling with
repairs as a way of making
a living, *c.* 1936. *(Centre for
Oxfordshire Studies:
Oxfordshire County Council
Photographic Archive)*

25. A miscellaneous
display at a trades fair
stand in the 1930s. *(Centre
for Oxfordshire Studies:
Oxfordshire County Council
Photographic Archive)*

26. An assistant in a traditional grocery and provisions shop, *c.* 1950. *(From:* The Modern Grocer and Provision Dealer*)*

27. The beginning of the self-service revolution. Sainsbury's new self-service store in Croydon, Surrey, *c.* 1950. *(From:* The Modern Grocer and Provision Dealer*)*

28. A self-service Co-op shop in Worcester, 1961. (*The Co-operative College, Manchester*)

29. The wireless room, evidently with facilities for repairing sets, at the shop of Smallbone Ltd, Oxford, October 1947. (*Centre for Oxfordshire Studies: Oxfordshire County Council Photographic Archive*)

Wilfred Whitaker, these efforts not only stimulated the ECA itself to greater efforts but roused the public to the need for legislation as it 'had not been roused before'.[81]

Both the Labour League and the ECA continued to press for reform in their different ways, with the association pointing to its successes in achieving voluntary agreements in London and in the provinces, where local associations had been formed. In 1883 it claimed that a weekly 'half-day', usually commencing at 5 p.m., had been secured in 329 towns in Great Britain; a decade later that had increased to 800 towns.[82] When the half-holiday was achieved it was certainly welcomed by assistants. A 14-year-old apprentice to a jeweller in Sturminster Newton, Dorset, remembered that when the first 5 p.m. closing was introduced there in 1881 he celebrated the unaccustomed break by riding on his bicycle to Blandford station and then taking a train to Bournemouth.[83]

On rare occasions employees themselves acted to enforce early closing when shopkeepers were trying to renege on an agreement. In February 1891 about forty assistants marched up and down outside the premises of a tradesman in Westminster Bridge Road, London, when the firm refused to join the early closing movement. Two were summonsed for obstruction and bound over, but the protest seems to have had an effect because almost immediately the firm concerned agreed to adopt a 2 p.m. closure on Thursday afternoons.[84]

By the 1880s, however, the limitations of the voluntary movement were apparent, although as yet neither Parliament nor the public seemed prepared to accept legislative regulation of opening hours. In 1888 Sir John Lubbock, a Liberal MP committed to statutory reform, proposed an Early Closing Bill to provide for a general limit to the working day of 8 p.m., but it was rejected decisively in the Commons by 278 votes to 95.[85] One opponent, the MP for Bermondsey, declared that many 'small shopkeepers had told him that practically all their business was done between 7 and 10 o'clock, and . . . if this Bill was passed it meant ruin to them'. Another critic, the Northampton MP Charles Bradlaugh, argued that such an interference in private trading arrangements would be a damaging blow to 'the self-reliance of the individual'.[86] The outcome convinced Lubbock that it was impossible to fix one time for shop closures throughout the country. Instead each locality must be left to set its own limits, much as the Early Closing Association's campaigns had advocated.[87] Any future legislation would have to be framed to take account of these differences.

Meanwhile, in 1886 the Shop Hours Regulation Act was passed as a result of Lubbock's efforts. This restricted the hours of youngsters under 18 working in shops to seventy-four a week, inclusive of meals. A notice to that effect had to be displayed in every shop where such young people were employed, and a fine could be imposed on shopkeepers who failed to observe the Act. It did not include, however, assistants working in their family's own shop, nor did it make provision for the appointment of inspectors to ensure its enforcement.[88] Not surprisingly, it soon became virtually a dead letter and although renewed annually after its initial two-year trial period, it achieved little. In 1892 it was re-enacted on a permanent basis and with local authorities empowered, but still not compelled, to appoint inspectors. Even then its effect was minimal. By 1896 55 county councils and 218 town councils had failed to appoint an inspector, and of the 223 inspectors who were in post (154 of them in boroughs) only 5 worked full time in connection with the Shop Hours Act. The rest performed other duties, such as those of policeman, inspector of weights and measures, sanitary inspector and medical officer of health.[89] Furthermore, the fines imposed on those found guilty of infringing the legislation were paltry, amounting to £1 per case or less. Thus in London during the period 1897–8, when 3,652 inspections of shop premises took place, 982 infringements were discovered. Most were minor, such as a failure to display a copy of the Act in the shop, but in 383 cases written cautions were issued, and in 62 cases, legal proceedings were taken. In all, 59 of these led to convictions, and resulted in penalties and costs for the traders concerned amounting to a total of just £63 16s.[90] To the inspectors it must have seemed a meagre outcome for their labours.

By this time even the ECA itself had lost faith in the voluntary approach. In 1891 it admitted gloomily that after around half a century of 'preaching and teaching', the 'destruction of health and happiness' caused by long opening hours was 'almost as great as ever. . . . It is not public convenience which prevents the further emancipation of . . . victims, but the cheapness of human life – principally that of the shop girl.'[91] A year later it complained of the 'inherent weakness of the voluntary system of early closing', noting that much of its time was spent on seeking to prop up existing agreements or repair broken ones.[92]

The change of policy by the ECA led to a rift in its ranks, with a minority of retailers, based on the South London Early Closing Association, remaining committed to the voluntary cause. By the end of 1892 they had formed the Voluntary ECA, with the active support of John Blundell Maple. In general, it was still the medium and larger shopkeepers who favoured compulsion, whereas the small men did not. Yet if larger firms did close voluntarily, they lost business to nearby competitors who refused to do so.[93] Small shopkeepers, like John Sanders, a Manchester confectioner, responded sharply that the large retailers were 'envious of the bit of trade that the small shops do, feeling that they could show if they were closed, larger profits and dividends'. Many were particularly opposed to the possibility of compulsory closing on Sundays. As Geoffrey Crossick notes, this 'seems to have agitated the very smallest of independent retailers, the least substantial of trades: tobacconists, newsagents, confectioners, greengrocers and fishmongers, as well as the smallest shops in the other trades'.[94] Some of these banded together not only to oppose possible restrictions on Sunday trading but also to agitate against local early closing orders for the rest of the week, too. The most prominent of the organisations, the Shopkeepers' and Small Traders' Protection Association, set up in July 1905, had by 1906 around 8,000 members, with confectioners, tobacconists and newsagents prominent among them.[95]

It was against this background that in 1904 Sir John Lubbock finally achieved his aim of national legislation. A new Act allowed local authorities to make orders compelling the closure of shops, either generally or for a particular trade, so long as two-thirds of the relevant shopkeepers within the local authority's area agreed. But it was soon clear that this mixture of 'voluntaryism' and compulsion was as ineffective as the voluntary movement had been. In 1907 the Home Secretary, Herbert Gladstone, conceded that in 'districts where the Act was most seriously needed' it had been 'practically inoperative':

> For instance, a Salford Order had to be revoked, because Manchester would not fall into line. Under the Act of 1904 only 112 local authorities have made Orders. Nothing has been done by 364 local authorities. . . . [P]ermissive Bills based only upon hopes, wishes and aspirations do not, as a rule, prove to be strong Acts in working.[96]

In all, the 112 Orders issued affected a mere 9,000 shops, covering perhaps 15,000 persons 'out of a possible total of some 800,000 assistants besides shopkeepers'. Gladstone admitted there was a need for fresh legislation, especially as 92 of the 112 Orders related to a single trade only; a mere 20 covered more than one trade in a given locality. Significantly, in these negotiations the shop assistants themselves had no say. Only their employers could decide whether or not to embrace early closing.

In 1911, after much agitation by the workers and their supporters, the government introduced a new Shops Bill. Initially it provided for a 60-hour working week for assistants, exclusive of meal breaks, and with the timing and duration of these also to be clearly specified. During the Bill's troubled passage through Parliament, however, the 60-hour limit was dropped and in its place a compulsory half-day closure was introduced. This applied from

1 p.m. once a week, with no worker to be employed on the premises after 1.30 p.m. Even that limited concession was undermined by other provisions, including the suspension of the half-day closure in the week before any public or bank holiday. It could also be suspended in holiday resorts for up to four months in the year, providing the local authority agreed. To compensate assistants for working this extra time they were to be granted two weeks' paid holiday.[97] That created difficulties, however, if a worker lost his or her job before the end of the four-month period and wished to claim compensation for the additional hours already worked.[98]

In 1912 a fresh Shop Hours Act consolidated the earlier legislation. This meant that any limitation on closing hours in the evening still required the agreement of two-thirds of the traders in a given area before it could take place. As under the 1904 legislation, that proved difficult to achieve, and it was only in the First World War that the issue of the compulsory closing of shops at night was finally tackled. From November 1916 the government required local authorities to enforce an 8 p.m. deadline in order to conserve scarce fuel supplies. Initially this was to apply for the following winter months only, but the restrictions were regularly renewed for the rest of the war and into the 1920s. Significantly the National Federation of Small Traders' Protection Associations, which in 1916 had argued that the change would mean ruination for small shopkeepers, by the end of hostilities was urging the government to continue the system. The ECA, too, noted that for small traders the 'early closing' was an 'emancipation from the "shop slavery" which had previously been their lot'.[99]

In the meantime some shop assistants, dissatisfied with the lack of progress of the Early Closing Association, decided to turn to trade unionism as a means of improving their situation. The first move in that direction came in 1889, the year of the famous London Dock Strike and of a general upsurge of unionism among unskilled workers. When the United Shop Assistants' Union was formed in London in 1889, its leaders called on their fellow workers, in a manifesto, 'to cast aside false and ridiculous class prejudices and take your stand with the ever increasing army of organised labour'. Among the objectives put forward were reduced working hours, the abolition of 'all unjust and tyrannical Fines', the securing of longer, clearly defined, meal breaks, and a general bettering of working conditions, including improved ventilation within the shops.[100] Yet six years later the union president John Turner had to admit it had achieved little. Membership was a mere 200 (of whom just 20 were women). 'Not only do the assistants change their situations & then drop out,' he lamented, 'but very few of them understand the principles of organisation. . . . One of the branches has got almost a new set of members during the past three months. . . . There is a considerable feeling amongst the assistants that it is beneath their dignity to join the Union. They look forward to starting [a business] on their own account altho' the chances are remote & becoming more so.'[101] Family pressure might play a part, too. Turner quoted the case of a female assistant who had paid her subscription to the union but had then withdrawn. On enquiry he discovered that 'she had been home and her people did not like her joining', so she had severed her connections. As Charles Booth later commented, 'the idea that it is beneath their dignity to belong to a trade society is general among shop assistants'.[102]

In 1891 what became the National Amalgamated Union of Shop Assistants, Warehousemen and Clerks (NAUSAW&C) was formed at a meeting in Birmingham of delegates from eleven local shop assistant associations. Most were linked to early closing or half-holiday groups and were dissatisfied with their lack of progress. Only two of the societies called themselves trade unions.[103]

Like its London predecessor, it sought to reduce working hours, abolish fines and secure proper meal times. It offered additional inducements, too, such as legal aid for members in dispute with their employers, and, in the longer term, various provident benefits, including payments during unemployment sickness and disability. Female members could receive a 'dowry', under certain conditions, when they left to be married.[104]

Although the new organisation operated nationally, unlike its metropolitan forerunner (which merged with it in 1898), it still encountered recruitment problems. Partly, as John Turner had already discovered, it was a question of status, with shop workers anxious to preserve what they regarded as their middle-class standing. As a member later observed bitterly: 'The fact of the matter is, shop assistants, as a class, are too aristocratic to join a straightforward, manly trade union. If they would only call it "The Royal Antediluvian Amalgamation of Gentlemen Haberdashers", and the subscription was nothing a week, every mother's son of them would be a member.'[105]

But there were other issues as well, including the lack of any sense of solidarity in an occupation which included many different trades and grades, each insisting upon recognition of its own special position. There was much secrecy, too, surrounding the wage rates received by individuals, even in the same firm. According to P.C. Hoffman, that was something employers encouraged. '"Don't you tell any of the others, mister," was insisted upon when a rise was given or when the salary was first fixed. It encouraged the idea that each in his turn was being paid more than the other. They would like others to think they were better off than they really were.'[106] The large numbers of young people and women employed added to the difficulty, since neither group showed much interest in spending limited cash and leisure time in attending union meetings and paying membership dues. Most of the women hoped to leave the occupation in a short time to be married and so were unconcerned about its long-term prospects. Even among those wishing to participate, the late hours worked made attendance at meetings difficult. As Hoffman recalled, branch meetings often commenced 'at ten o'clock at night and were over in time before the pubs closed at midnight'.[107] In fact the executive committees of both the United Shop Assistants' Union and the National Union met on Sundays during the 1890s. Some members of the latter body travelled long distances on night trains in order to attend, arriving early on Sunday morning and then returning the same evening so as to be 'in time for business at 7.30 or 8 a.m. on Mondays'.[108]

Many workers were anxious not to antagonise employers by attempting to combine. The Lancaster grocer T.D. Smith, for example, refused to recognise trade unions, which one member of the family contemptuously said were for 'those who did not do their job properly'.[109] Margaret Bondfield experienced the fury of one grocer who tore up her union poster while sending her away 'with an exclamation that unequivocally reflected his attitude on her proper place, both as a woman and union member: "Union indeed! Go home and mend your stockings." Put bluntly, employers were determined to maintain a paternalism that treated employees as children.'[110] Hence there were branches where, according to the National Union's journal, *The Shop Assistant*, of August 1897, 'the one great desire of the members [was] to keep their membership a secret. . . . A slavish fear of our employers has been the curse of our lives, and the iron barrier which has blocked all progress.' By 1893, therefore, membership of the NAUSAW&C stood at only 1,294. Even at the end of the century it had reached just 7,551, at a time when there were around 750,000 shop assistants in the country.[111] Not until it became an approved society under the 1911 National Insurance Act did the union's position change. Under the Act all workers earning under £160 a year had to join an 'approved society' for the payment of state insurance benefits, and in these circumstances membership of the union moved sharply upwards, to reach 85,945 in 1913.[112]

In addition to the National Union, a second organisation was formed in 1891 to cater for shopworkers. This time it was for those employed by the various co-operative societies. It was set up in Manchester under the title of the Manchester District Co-operative Association and its aim was to promote the social and intellectual welfare of its members, including the establishment of a jobs registry for those who were unemployed. Working hours in co-operative shops were generally much shorter than those in private business but conditions did vary considerably. So from the early 1890s it became an aim of the association to persuade retail societies to cut hours still further. In 1893 it reported that around ninety of them had made reductions of between one and eight hours a week. 'Of these, ten at least reduced their working week to 48 hours.'[113]

The association was anxious to encourage thrift and self-help among its members by providing unemployment, sickness and death benefits, and it collected data on wages, too, with the aim of drawing up a minimum pay policy. In 1895 the Manchester Association merged with a similar body set up by Bolton co-operative employees, to form the Amalgamated Union of Co-operative Employees (AUCE). On formation it claimed a membership of 2,151 and net assets of £98 2s 2d. Two years later it put forward a demand for a minimum wage of 24s a week for all male employees aged 21 or over, with 'each district and branch . . . empowered to adopt a higher scale if practicable'.[114] Not until 1909 were scales for female workers and juniors put forward, with a recommended minimum of 5s a week at age 14 for girls, compared to 6s a week for boys of the same age. These sums rose progressively until at age 20, the females' upper limit of 17s a week was reached. In 1906 a minimum of 30s a week for branch managers was also added to the proposed national scale.[115]

Not all co-operative societies greeted these initiatives favourably. In July 1913 The Co-operative Employé reported that of 1,262 societies in the Co-operative Union, only 272 had replied to a request for information by stating they paid the minimum wage to both men and women employees. A further 69 paid the minimum to males alone, while 281 replied in the negative, and a further 640 did not answer at all. Some female employees also resented the gender discrimination they encountered. One wrote indignantly to The Co-operative Employé to complain that women were 'not invited to join any educational classes for their advancement' that were arranged for staff. They did not want 'to oust men from positions: our aim is to attain a higher standard of efficiency'.[116]

The National Union recruited among co-operative staff, too, and this led to ill-feeling between the two organisations, with the AUCE accusing its rival of 'poaching' members. Despite sporadic attempts to work together, relations between the two organisations remained difficult until after the Second World War.[117]

The National Union, meanwhile, had developed its own minimum wage strategy, and this was finalised in 1910, with different rates not only for men and women but between London and the provinces, and with variations according to the trade carried on. Thus for drapers, the provincial scale was 26s a week for men and 20s a week for women at age 21, rising to 32s and 26s respectively, at age 28. In London the relevant levels were 31s and 23s, rising to 37s and 29s. In the case of grocery and provisions no female minimum rate was proposed. For the men it was 24s at age 21 in the provinces, rising to 30s at the age of 28; in the capital the rates were 29s, rising to 35s.[118] For shopwalkers, the minimum demanded was 35s a week, and for managers pay was related to turnover.[119]

From 1911 negotiations were started for the adoption of the union wage scale, and although there was limited success, sometimes only after strike action, much remained to be done, especially in regard to the bigger firms and the multiple stores, when the First World War broke out. Negotiations were started, for example, with the Home and Colonial Stores in 1914, with the firm granting some concessions, including higher pay for assistants and increased bonus and commission for the managers. But union recognition was refused.[120]

In the early twentieth century the National Union became involved in other campaigns, too, including efforts to end the living in system, at least for male staff. Apart from the restrictions the system itself imposed on their lives, objections were raised that it deprived them of the franchise at both national and local elections. The residential accommodation provided did not qualify the occupants to vote under the existing property franchises.[121]

In 1901 a well-publicised demonstration against living in was arranged in London and caused something of a sensation. Thirteen male assistants from William Whiteley's department store (including P.C. Hoffman) paraded with sandwich boards along Oxford Street to the West End. They wore top hats and frock coats and their board advertised a mass meeting to be addressed by the well-known preacher Dr Clifford.[122] It proved very successful and a wave of actions against living in then followed. Some secured an immediate end to the system for male workers, with the payment of a compensatory addition to wages in lieu of board and lodging. In other cases, as with J.D. Llewellyn & Son, grocers and confectioners in Neath, South Wales, success was only achieved in 1907 after a strike.[123]

The union's annual report for 1913 recorded victories elsewhere, with the larger Manchester firm of Affleck & Brown and the Exeter store of Messrs Colsons both granting living out to the men: 'A settlement has also been come to with Messrs Pinders, of Nottingham . . . granting "living-out" for the men.'[124] Yet although the system was in retreat, it lingered on, especially for female workers, until after the First World War in some firms. In 1933 the Southampton department store of Edwin Jones proudly claimed that its new hostel, catering for about 100 females, had a large lounge, a lofty dining room and a well-equipped kitchen, as well as a ballroom, writing room, library and games room. Outside were a garden and orchard, two tennis courts and plots of land for those wishing to cultivate their own small garden. 'The bedrooms and cubicles are spotless and the amenities as free from restrictions as in family home life.'[125] That included the holding of dances to which friends could be invited.

Female membership of both the AUCE and the National Union was always in a minority, even though both bodies recruited male and female members on equal terms. In 1914, as Lee Holcombe points out, females comprised only around 27 per cent of the National Union's membership of 81,250.[126] In the case of the AUCE, there were in 1912 some 3,014 women in a total membership of 32,741.[127] Not until the First World War, when women replaced men who had joined the armed forces or entered some other area of war service, did the position change. By 1918, out of a total AUCE membership of 87,134, 36,422 were females, equal to 41.8 per cent. Of these, 32,539 were employed in the co-operative movement and 3,883 in private firms, since by that date the AUCE was recruiting outside the co-operatives, thereby impinging on the membership drives of its National counterpart.[128] Before the war, however, despite the official policy of equal male and female recruitment, some co-operative branches had simply refused to allow women to join, fearing that with their lower pay they would oust the men.[129]

Chapter 6

LEISURE PURSUITS AND COMMUNAL ACTIVITIES

The shopmen didn't have a guaranteed holiday but I think Dad gave them several days off. Tonbridge cricket week was the festival of the year round here and he'd always let them have a day doing the cricket or perhaps let them go after dinner. . . . Part of Dad's agreement was a week's holiday every year and right up to the First [World] War we went away every year. . . . My father was always a Conservative. . . . Trade in those days demanded a lot of tact and nearly all the moneyed people in the area were Conservative, so therefore, it paid you to run with them. . . . Other than bell-ringing practices I don't think father went out much unless it was anything to do with the shop. . . . Mother . . . used to have one or two friends to Sunday tea.

Reminiscences of Harry Headey, whose father managed a superior Tonbridge grocery shop, quoted in Michael J. Winstanley, *The Shopkeeper's World 1830–1914* (Manchester, 1983), pp. 136–8.

LEISURE PURSUITS

For most of the eighteenth and nineteenth centuries the long working hours of shopkeepers and their assistants meant that they had scant time for leisure. Only for the better-off retailers was this less true, since they were able to leave their staff to look after the business while they engaged in political and social activities. In Chester, for example, wealthy tradesmen played a major role in the government of the city. Between 1730 and 1815, 109 of the 176 people holding the position of sheriff were retailers, of whom 19 were mercers and drapers, 18 were grocers, 17 were druggists or apothecaries and 10 were wine merchants.[1]

For those lower down the scale, the situation was very different. Frank Benson, an assistant in a co-operative shop in Bolton before the First World War, remembered as his 'biggest regret' the fact that he had 'to work

Saturday afternoons and couldn't join the Sunday School cricket club or football club'.[2] Sunday school activities nevertheless formed an important part of his life. For the rest, in his late teens there was home-grown entertainment when his parents rented a piano and there were family sing-songs. He went to night school on three evenings a week, and 'other nights I had a bit of homework to do and for the other spare hour I used to go into the reading room at the local library'. However, those who worked in private trade usually finished too late to be able to attend formal classes and instead, like the future Labour cabinet minister Herbert Morrison, they studied on their own. Morrison did not live in, and this gave him some freedom of action outside working hours. Often he got up at 6 a.m., 'reading in a cold bedroom, and taking my books to a coffee shop at night (a halfpenny cup of cocoa was the order) after the shop shut, to economize in light and heating'.[3]

Many retailers and their staff lived over the shop or in adjoining accommodation, and this restricted their opportunity to broaden their circle of friends. For small corner shopkeepers, indeed, gossip with their customers provided one of their principal amusements. They rarely mixed with their neighbours out of the shop since, as one retailer's daughter pointed out, these formed the bulk of their clientele and too great an intimacy with a few of them might have created ill-feeling among the rest and a loss of business.[4] Where friendships were made they were usually with fellow tradesmen or those of a similar social standing. According to Leonard Coombs, whose father ran a village shop at Ickham near Canterbury,

> The people we looked upon as those we could easily mix with and invite into the house or go into their houses, would have been the schoolmaster and his wife, a local butcher . . . and a local baker. Then . . . we had friends in the other villages, such as the manager of Margate Water Works at Wingham, the local builder there, the schoolmaster at Wickhambreaux and the people who kept the mills round here. That was our circle. But we had very little time for socials. Chiefly it was in the form of whist drives. You met them there or at a concert, but to have people into the house was not very convenient because people had got big families. In our case there were six of us in quite a small space.[5]

For many retailers, too, the business itself was a continuing preoccupation, and this often interfered with family life and with leisure activities, at least until the later nineteenth century. Around that time the formation of trade associations encouraged shopkeepers to meet to discuss common business worries as well as to hold social gatherings. But as the son of a substantial draper recalled, his father's thoughts seemed always to be on the firm, and that included meal times. 'Even when he sat down he was still, as it were, attached by some invisible thread to the activities of the shop.'[6] In the case of George Beale, who built up the Meadow Dairy Company into a successful grocery chain in the early twentieth century, it meant that when he took his family for an airing on Saturday afternoons in the car he would combine business with pleasure. While he was driving around he would keep an eye open for suitable premises where he could locate a new branch of his store. This often meant acquiring property in the colliery districts of Northumberland and Durham, where much of his trade was concentrated.[7]

It was to give time for the development of wider interests, especially among the assistants, that in 1856 the Earl of Shaftesbury pressed for the granting of a weekly half-holiday. Where this had been given, he argued, there were 'hundreds and thousands of . . . young men who [were] . . . devoting their leisure hours to the best and most wholesome pursuits'. He admitted that 'some idle lads' would spend their time in less desirable ways, such as going to the theatre and casinos, or similar places, but critics who concentrated on them forgot the 'many steady young men and women . . . who have domestic engagements which they cannot fulfil under the present system'.[8]

Like most reformers concerned with securing free time for those who worked in shops, Shaftesbury and his allies in the Early Closing Association were keen to stress the religious, moral and educational pursuits they hoped would be taken up, rather than the time spent in mere pleasure-seeking. These moralising aspects also featured in many apprenticeship indentures, especially in the eighteenth century. However, as late as 1898 Edward Carn, when bound apprentice to John Banks, a general draper in Arundel, Sussex, had to promise not to contract 'Matrimony within the said Term' of four years, or 'play at Cards or Dice Tables or any other unlawful Games'. He was forbidden to 'haunt Taverns or Playhouses' and to 'absent himself from his said Master's service day or night unlawfully'.[9] Although rarely expressed in this kind of archaic language at such a late date, throughout the period to the First World War and beyond, decorous conduct and general respectability were the qualities most encouraged in young shopworkers. Nonetheless the strictures and restraints did not always have the desired effect. Philip Hoffman, who worked at the Holborn Silk Market in the 1890s, remembered that he and his fellow apprentices were not supposed to leave the premises at all at night, 'except on Saturdays, when they had to be in at 9 p.m. This so-called moral safeguard was to be one of the defences put up by employers of the "living-in" system. . . . But, of course, you could not keep young people immured like that. We got out in various ways. Some of the older apprentices who had the money would seek adventure with prostitutes, and would come back and tell the rest all about it. Some caught disease in that way, and we would hear all about that, too.'[10]

For those shop workers anxious to maintain their reputation and their moral standards, membership of a church or chapel and participation in the institutions and events associated with it provided an important leisure pursuit. Thomas D. Smith, the leading Lancaster grocer, was an 'ardent' Wesleyan Methodist and became a Sunday school teacher at the chapel he attended when he was only 21. Later he was elected superintendent, a position he held for eight years. Subsequently he became auditor of the school finances, a circuit steward and trustee of a number of Wesleyan chapels, including his own. His brother William, a draper, was also a circuit steward and choir master, and many other prominent retailers in the town attended the same chapel, thereby forming part of a close-knit middle-class community.[11]

A similar situation existed in the small Oxfordshire town of Woodstock, where Mr B., who ran a genteel men's outfitting business, and his family were keen Methodists. According to his daughter, all the tradespeople in the town were friendly with one another and there was a strong link with Nonconformity as well. On Sunday evenings informal religious gatherings took place in Mr B.'s home, and he would play the American organ while his wife made coffee for the visitors.[12]

Nonconformity and retailing often went hand in hand even among many department store proprietors. As Bill Lancaster notes, the Newcastle store owner Emerson Bainbridge came to the town in the 1830s 'steeped in the Methodist tradition of the lead-mining districts of the Durham dales. He was a lay preacher at the Brunswick Chapel, a benefactor of the local Methodist building programme and a leading member of the Newcastle temperance movement.'[13] His son continued the tradition and became chairman of the Federation of Free Churches as well as secretary of the Moody and Sankey organisation in Britain. J.J. Fenwick, another Newcastle store owner, was equally active, being superintendent of the Brunswick Chapel Sunday school. He and Bainbridge financed the construction of a new Methodist church in the suburb of Jesmond. 'In nearby Sunderland, the Binns family were devout Quakers and the Welsh department store owners Owen Owen, James Howell and D.H. Evans and the Cornishman Edward Dingle were all Nonconformist.'[14] In Owen Owen's case this involved a change from Wesleyan Methodism to Unitarianism when he moved his home in the 1890s from Liverpool to London.[15]

For humbler retailers, especially those living in the poorer districts of large cities, religious observance might be more haphazard. In the early 1830s 'lady visitors' went from at least one Southampton parish to discuss spiritual matters with some of the local families, including shopkeepers, who lived in an impoverished part of the town. In 1830 Samuel and Jane Ingram, who ran a pork butcher's shop but also stocked other goods, were called upon by Miss Ridding, a solicitor's daughter. She went equipped with improving moral tracts to give to them but noted critically that they were 'either so frequently from home or engaged with customers that there is rarely opportunity for any religious conversation'. On two occasions she enquired after Mrs Ingram, only to be told that 'she was absent, gone to a *Fair*. I shall give her a Tract with 8 reasons for not going.' This was evidently done but the woman was able to assure her visitor that she was already following the suggestions laid down. Furthermore, to Miss Ridding's relief, it was found that she was attending the fairs only to sell goods. 'I had feared it was for Amusement.' However, she concluded gloomily that although Mrs Ingram always spoke civilly to her and was 'willing to read Tracts', she did not behave 'as if she was deeply affected with the Importance of eternal things'.[16]

Sometimes Miss Ridding's reception was much cooler. One small shopkeeper, Jane Polstone, whose husband was away at sea a good deal, was described as not reading 'one small Tract through in a week'. She assured her visitor that she read 'whenever she [had] opportunity' but Miss Ridding was clearly doubtful. As she wryly admitted, the only time she was treated as a welcome guest was when she enquired if the family needed bread: 'I have reason to apprehend that they have neither of them been to Church since I first knew her but she says she will go when she can.'[17] Even efforts to ensure that the three oldest children attended Sunday school had mixed results, in that the eldest girl was kept away to look after the youngest child.

For assistants who lived in, the prolonged working day and, in particular, the late closure of shops on Saturday nights meant that where possible they would stay in bed late on Sunday mornings. The rest of the day would then be spent in getting 'such exercise as the season [permitted] – skating, walking, boating, bathing, or reading', rather than in attending church services or Sunday school. According to one of their number, he had known 'houses of business in which, out of forty or fifty young men, not more than five or six have attended a place of worship during the Sunday'. As Wilfred Whitaker comments: 'No wonder the wiser clergy saw the need to support the claims for time for recreation in the week so that there might be the inclination to worship on Sunday.'[18]

Other youngsters, like John Birch Thomas, attended church and chapel spasmodically when they had nothing better to do on a Sunday. Thomas seems to have regarded the services more as performances than as expressions of religious belief. On one occasion, for example, he attended a service in

Kennington where the preacher told us 'of the awful things that were going to happen in a year or two before the world came to an end, which would be quite soon. I did hear that he had just renewed the lease of his house, but perhaps that was only a tale. Anyhow he seemed sincere. . . . Then I left off going anywhere, but bought a Bible off a stall. . . . I meant to read right through from the beginning, but I soon found that I had to skip many dry pages and pick out chapters here and there that told of wonderful and magical things, like there are in the *Arabian Nights* and just as hard to believe in.'[19]

In the more leisurely atmosphere of the eighteenth century, the village shopkeeper Thomas Turner not only attended church on the Sabbath with his wife, the maid and sometimes his apprentices, but he was friendly with other tradespeople in the village and with some of the farmers. There were invitations to meals and the arranging of indoor games, dances and card-playing, especially during the winter months. In one of his more self-critical moods, Turner described the party games as 'behaving more like mad people', while he considered playing cards, especially on the occasion when he had lost 3*s*, as 'quite inconsistent with that which is right'.[20] But he nevertheless continued to join in. There were visits from friends, like the shoemaker Thomas Davy, with whom he played cribbage in the evening. During the summer he took part in cricket matches or went along as a spectator. Betting was involved, and wagers applied not merely to cricket and horse-racing but to cock-fights and even such trivial matters as the possible date of a friend's wedding or the precise length of a path. There were visits to public houses and to fairs and festivities. Sometimes he drank too much, as on 22 August 1757, when he went to watch two men race for a wager. 'I got never a bet, but very drunk,' he noted in his diary. 'I lay at my uncle Hill's all night.'[21] This came just over three months after he had 'taken up a resolution GOD being my helper, to live a sober, virtuous and pious life'. Outbreaks of drunkenness of this kind were always followed by feelings of remorse and a determination to reform. Hence after his lapse on 22 August he commented: 'I must and will, I am determined, leave off drinking anything strong . . . I was so much in liquor I forgot what I spent.'

Alongside these more dubious pursuits, there were innocent pleasures as well, as in January 1758 when Turner went to the house of James Marchant, the tailor, to hear 'a concert of three violins and a German flute', or when he spent time in his garden.[22] He was a keen reader, too, and owned a small library. He regularly read aloud to his wife and friends in the evening. He also took newspapers, including the *London Gazette* and the *Sussex Weekly Advertiser*.[23]

Similarly sober leisure activities were recorded in the journal of the young Yorkshire drapery assistant Marmaduke Strother. While completing a six-year apprenticeship to a Hull draper named Robinson in 1784–5, Strother not only attended church twice on many Sundays but made notes of the content of the sermons in his diary as well as his own opinion on them. He joined a local debating society and with some friends even set up a small self-help group 'to improve ourselves in the Art of Speaking and Reasoning for the better enabling us to hold a Conversation with Propriety'.[24] Among its long list of rules was a requirement that if while speaking anyone lapsed into 'bad English or runs from his Strain any Person may reprimand him'. Each member was to be 'bound by the Rules of Good Decorum'. It is perhaps not surprising that such a solemn enterprise did not flourish. Indeed, Strother was subsequently shocked to discover that one of the members, a fellow shop assistant named Swaby, had made what he called a 'Bagnio' (that is, a brothel) 'of his Master's house. . . . To frequent the Common Bagnios is bad; if that cou'd content him, something might be said in his favor . . . but to use his Master's house as a Bagnio is using his Master ill & also those who live with him.' It is not clear who the young man's female companion was but she may have been one of the 'Ladies of Pleasure' who frequented Hull and about whom both youngsters had previously been highly critical. On the day after he discovered Swaby's feet of clay, however, Marmaduke decided to keep his disapproval to himself, for as he commented:

> the fewer enemies we have the Better, there is no occasion to add him to the Number. . . . I shall conduct myself in the same manner as I did before my knowledge of this affair, but beware of making an intimate Acquaintance of him for fear he shou'd gain too great a command & attempt to make me a dupe to some of his follies.[25]

In the middle of these rather priggish diary entries it is pleasing to note that Strother decided to take dancing lessons from a master, paying an entrance fee of 5s plus a further charge of 10s 6d a quarter. He clearly enjoyed the experience and some months later described the 'Dance call'd Roger de Coverly [sic]' as his particular favourite.[26]

For those who lived in during the nineteenth century, leisure activities and opportunities depended very much on their employers' attitudes. Many insisted not only that staff return to their quarters by a certain time but that lights were extinguished, under penalty of a fine for non-compliance. In the mid-1890s, when Margaret Bondfield was a London shop worker and a trade union activist, she often contributed short articles to the union newspaper, *The Shop Assistant*.

It was quite impossible for me to write in the presence of any who might
know what I was doing, and as I had not one inch of space I could call my
own, I would wait till one or two of my room-mates were asleep, and then
stealthily, with the feeling of a conspirator, and knowing that I was
committing an offence for which I could be heavily fined, I would light my
halfpenny dip, hiding its glare by means of a towel thrown over the back of
a chair, and set to work on my monthly article . . . [A]lthough this
surreptitious writing was kept up for about two years, I do not think any
breach of rules was ever reported to the firm.[27]

At his first position as an apprentice to a small London draper, W. Fish
recalled that after a 13-hour stint in the shop, the kitchen had to serve as the
sitting room for himself and his fellow assistants, whom he described as a
'poor, down-trodden, down-at-heel company'.[28] Later, when he moved to a
large store with many fellow workers, there were more opportunities for
enjoyment. Years later he described this as the happiest period of his life:

We had house concerts which the various heads would occasionally grace
with their presence. . . . Then there were the almost nightly *unofficial*
concerts in our bedrooms which were flagrant breaches of the regulations
and frequently resulted in each of us being fined. . . . Boxing contests were
a popular form of recreation during the winter evenings; in fact, after
business, our 'Living In' quarters resembled . . . a huge boarding school.[29]

A staff billiard room was provided on the premises by the employers and also
a library. From time to time Fish visited the theatre with friends. According to
him, there were two distinct groups among those working in the store. One
comprised those who preferred 'the more joyous side of life', and the others
were the 'religiously inclined'.

Somehow or other I seemed to fluctuate between the two . . . I think my
attraction to what . . . I will call the 'religious party'. . . . was largely
governed by the fact that at the time I was in love . . . with one of the
cashiers, pretty little Marie Holmes. To catch her smile I would attend church
at St Mary's on Sunday night and morning. I escorted her to religious revival
meetings, missionary meetings, temperance meetings, and at length she
prevailed upon me to join a Bible Class of which she was a member.[30]

But Marie could not understand how, after an evening spent with her at
the Bible Class, Fish could join in a noisy bedroom concert. She accepted

his repeated protestations of remorse, but when he left the firm the relationship ended.

For female staff members leisure opportunities were more limited if they wished to maintain their reputation. At a time when 'respectable' lower-middle-class females spent much of their time in a domestic setting, shop girls were sometimes looked upon askance. 'It is a fact well known to every London shop assistant who keeps his eyes and his ears open,' declared one critic, 'that many of the swell loungers of Piccadilly make it a practice to watch, vulture-like, the large West End houses that employ young women for the purpose of deluding them from the path of virtue.'[31] This was especially true of those anxious to be fashionably dressed and yet unable to afford to buy good quality clothes from their meagre salaries. There were allegations, too, that girls who asked for a pay rise were refused but were instead offered a latchkey. The implication was that they could earn extra cash by prostituting themselves and then sneak back into their hostel after the official closing time.[32]

These claims were indignantly refuted in the trade press, notably when they were repeated by the Revd R.J. Campbell early in 1909. *The Drapery Times* referred angrily to the 'accusations . . . made against respectable, innocent young women'.[33] Meanwhile, James A. Stacey of the Early Closing Association declared that the board of that organisation 'indignantly repudiated' such allegations and that 'in the entire community no class is to be found with greater virtue than that possessed by . . . girls engaged in shops – those of the West End and throughout the metropolis and Kingdom'.[34] But it is perhaps an indication of the pervasiveness of such views that even in the late 1970s a former customer of Jay's store in Regent Street, looking back to the early years of the twentieth century, recalled that the assistants there 'were notorious for their regrettably light behaviour'.[35]

As for the department store proprietors themselves, at the beginning of the twentieth century many shared the opinion of John Lawrie, general manager of Whiteley's, that on 'the ground of morality' alone the living-in system was the best for female staff. 'I have no hesitation in saying that if the parents thought for one moment that their daughters, when coming up to London to enter these large trading establishments, would be compelled to find lodgings outside, they would not let them come.'[36] But Margaret Bondfield's response to this, based on her own experiences of shop life in London, was that the girls received little supervision when they entered 'those barrack shops' in the capital. 'If for no other purpose than to keep these girls in their country homes until they are old enough to act for themselves', it was desirable to abolish living in.[37]

The issue of living in apart, many retailers continued to display a strong spirit of paternalism towards their staff. This was reflected not only in the rules and regulations which laid down what was and was not permitted, but in more positive aspects as well. These included the awarding of paid annual holidays, usually of a week. William Whiteley, however, was more generous in that regard. Any members of staff engaged before 1 March each year were entitled to two weeks' holiday during the summer. Most drapers only gave a holiday after twelve months' service. He also refused to allow employees to work on Sundays, and for that reason would not sell milk since this would have involved Sunday trading.[38]

In other cases outings and excursions were arranged. These might include visits to the seaside or to a well-known beauty spot, with refreshments and free transport provided, or they might involve invitations to spend the day on the employer's estate if he possessed landed property. When Sir Thomas Lipton bought Osidge, a 60-acre estate on the outskirts of London, he arranged an annual entertainment there for members of his London staff. They were met by brakes at Palmers Green and an elaborate programme of sports and diversions was organised. This included 'picnic' games, such as wheelbarrow, sack and three-legged races, and there was music from a band. Lunch, tea and supper were supplied, with ample food but no alcohol served, in accordance with Lipton's own strict pro-temperance views.[39]

Similarly when James Marshall of Marshall & Snelgrove purchased Goldbeater Farm, together with a stretch of land nearly 1,000 acres in extent at Mill Hill, he held a staff garden party and cricket match there each year. The property had its own cricket pitch for the benefit of Marshall's youngest son, who was an All-England cricketer.[40]

Co-operative societies shared in the general approach. In late July 1883 Reading Co-operative Society agreed to close its shops so that the employees could go on their annual outing. The society presented them with their rail tickets, too.[41] Early in the following year the staff were allowed 'the use of the large room at the Central Stores' so that they could hold their yearly tea. Trade union branches, too, arranged excursions, as in August 1908 when members of the Workington branch of the Amalgamated Union of Co-operative Employees, 'to the number of sixty-two, journeyed by rail and cycle to Bassenthwaite Lake . . . for the annual trip. A pleasant time was spent in boating and fishing on the lake, bowling, and other sports.'[42]

One of the clearest manifestations of employers' paternalism and of their desire to promote good feeling among the staff was, however, the way they established sporting and other clubs for their workers. This was especially the case among larger firms in the final quarter of the nineteenth century.

Behind the interest perhaps lay a belief, widely held at the time, in the virtues of 'muscular Christianity' and its associated moral benefits. These included the inculcation of a sense of fair play, the development of self-control and an 'unenvious approbation of another's success'.[43] William Whiteley, despite his generally harsh disciplinary approach, encouraged his young male employees to take part in games and in 1870 he founded the Kildare Athletic Club for their benefit. Each year he presided over its annual gathering, with races run and substantial prizes presented to the winners. Later the Kildare Choral Society, the Kildare Musical Union and the Kildare Rowing Club were formed, while there was also a Dramatic Society, which performed some of the popular plays of the day. In 1888 these various recreational activities were given a building of their own, called the Hatherley Institute, of which Whiteley was President. By that date membership of all the clubs amounted to about 600, or approximately one in four of the total employees.[44]

At Bainbridge's in Newcastle there were cricket and football teams which played matches early in the morning, before the start of the working day. Elsewhere, as Frank Danning of Wadebridge in Cornwall recalled, there were special Wednesday afternoon matches, so that shopworkers could play on their half-day.[45] In London competitions were sometimes arranged between members of the clubs of the leading metropolitan department stores. In February 1909, for example, a large gathering of members and supporters of the affiliated clubs of the West End Athletic Association met at Wembley Hill for the annual cross-country race. Six teams entered, from William Whiteley's; Spencer, Turner and Boldero; Harrods; Shoolbred's; Marshall & Snelgrove; and Liberty's. Proceedings ended, somewhat inappropriately to modern eyes, with a smoking concert held in the evening at the Green Man, Wembley Hill.[46] Owen Owen, too, was extremely proud of the staff cricket and tennis teams, seeing sport as a means of drawing the workers into an even closer community. He hired a sports ground in Liverpool, where his store was based, to enable them to play.[47]

For those not interested in physical activities and particularly for female members of staff, there were choral societies and drama groups, while lectures were organised from time to time, and in some cases dances were put on. At Liberty's these were held from the early 1880s. 'We had three every year, plain and fancy dress,' remembered a female member of staff who worked there at that time.[48] There was also a library for the assistants which Arthur Liberty had founded soon after he opened the business in the mid-1870s.

But paternalism had its darker side, not merely through the imposition of fines and penalties for breaches of the rules but in the way it treated staff almost as children. This was made clear in comments by Mr Cushen,

chairman of the Metropolitan Grocers and Provision Dealers' Association in
the mid-1890s in an interview with one of Charles Booth's researchers.
During the thirty years he had been in business, which was up to about three
years before the interview, he had always had his men living in and had done
'all he could to make their lives happy and comfortable'. They had taken their
meals with the family but there were restrictions, too:

> he forbade them to frequent public houses but allowed each man to get beer
> from the housekeeper at any time as long as they did not abuse the privilege.
> He built them a small stage and got up theatricals, concerts, and social
> evenings. They certainly had to work hard, but not so hard as he did.[49]

In the 1920s Mrs W., employed by a Lancaster grocer, also experienced this
kind of interference, although less directly since she did not live in. Her
employer was a member of the church which her family attended, so this
common background may have partly accounted for his close 'supervision of
her life, not only inside the shop, but outside as well. He had a puritanical
dislike of dances.' Once, when she was invited to a Christmas party, she took
her dress to the shop so that she could change into it without going home.
After tea, however, her employer announced they would start packing
currants. He kept her at this for most of the evening. 'I tried not to let him
see me, but I was actually crying. The dance finished at ten o'clock, and I
arrived at a quarter to ten. The shop officially closed at seven but he didn't
think I should go.' He also insisted on her wearing black stockings, at a time
when few other young women were doing so.[50]

Patriotic motives led to some employer initiatives at the larger stores,
especially in London, as in 1859 when fear of a French invasion led to the
formation of the Volunteer Corps. The aim was to augment the regular army
and to instil feelings of loyalty to queen and country. Some store owners even
introduced a Saturday half-day closing so that their workers could attend
training sessions. Among the earliest of them was Shoolbred's. In 1864 the
Inspector-General of Volunteers described its company as one of the most
efficient in London.[51] Its officers were members of the firm and it was supported
wholly at Shoolbred's expense. At its fiftieth anniversary celebration in May
1909 it was reported that more than thirty members of staff had taken part in
the South African war at the end of the nineteenth century, and the firm had
kept their situations open for them until their return.[52]

A similar initiative was taken at Marshall & Snelgrove, with the firm
defraying the cost of the equipment and James Marshall's second son Thomas
made captain of the company of Volunteers.[53]

Early in the twentieth century new military threats emerged in Europe and in response the Territorial Army was formed in 1908. Again the proprietors of the department stores became involved. Indeed, Sir John Barker, head of the large Kensington store, was one of the most enthusiastic supporters of the scheme and he used his influence to persuade other shop owners to allow twenty-one days' holiday on full pay every year to salesmen, warehousemen and clerks who, with the employer's agreement, joined the Territorials and spent at least fourteen days thereof in camp.[54] Within weeks a number of firms had agreed to this, including Debenham & Co., Derry & Toms, Dickins & Jones, D.H. Evans, Selfridge & Co., Liberty & Co., Marshall & Snelgrove and John Barker & Co. itself. *The Drapery Times* praised the effort as 'peculiarly gratifying to all who value the birthright of the liberty-loving British'.[55] North of the border speakers at the Glasgow and West of Scotland Retail Drapers' Association also lent it their support, although for some of them at least it was largely because the Territorials were a volunteer movement designed to avoid the need for conscription. That was regarded as far more disruptive for employers.[56]

Among the workers the move had a more mixed response. Mr G. Francis, an organiser for the National Amalgamated Union of Shop Assistants, told a branch meeting in Manchester that they were being 'confronted with a new danger'. Although employers refused 'to compel the assistants to join the Union there was in certain quarters a tendency to press the staffs to become members of the Territorial Army'. The masters were not forcing assistants into military service but there was '"preferential treatment" when it was found necessary to curtail the staff'.[57] To underline his concerns, at least one speaker at a meeting convened by Sir John Barker in London to press the need for 'Trade Territorials', suggested that it was 'wise and just and patriotic, where everything else is equal' to give those who volunteered 'preference in engagements and promotions' and to make sure that young assistants who preferred to watch football in their spare time 'should be compelled to work harder or later to admit of their Territorial colleagues having the necessary time for parades or drills, or firing practice at the range'. His remarks were loudly applauded by the audience, who represented the large employers of labour in London.[58]

Meanwhile, the wealthiest retailers, including those who owned the most prestigious department stores or were founders of the new multiple chains, were often anxious to be assimilated into 'high society'. Even in the late eighteenth century critics accused certain members of the London 'shopocracy' of extravagance:

Do not . . . a considerable portion of them live in a style of opulence and even of splendour? Do they not keep their horses, their whiskies, and their phaetons? Have they not their country lodgings, and their country villas? Have they not their clubs where they regale at ease and leisure? Their private entertainments and their public dinners; where luxury if not riot predominates? Do they not, in general, enjoy a much greater share of the conveniences and superfluities of life, than landholders of far superior property?[59]

Provincial shopkeepers may not have reached this standard of Georgian affluence, but here, too, some of them sought to enter landed society. Several Chester retailers, for example, owned properties in Wales, while in 1812, when John Swanwick retired from his Macclesfield linen draper's business, he moved to Brereton in south Cheshire to lead the life of a country gentleman.[60] Some drapers and mercers in Cheshire also left considerable estates when they died. In 1811 John Brown of the renowned Chester drapery business, left property valued at £12,500 at his death.[61]

In the mid- and late Victorian era this trend became more apparent. In 1867 Emerson Bainbridge took a lease on Dissington Hall, an attractive late Georgian property, where the younger members of his family took up field sports with enthusiasm.[62] Owen Owen acquired property in his native Wales, which he visited for rest and relaxation and to play golf. When he lived in London he took an active part in the capital's Welsh circles, and was a close friend and backer of David Lloyd George, later to be prime minister.[63] He was a major property developer as well, and by 1908 was constructing a large housing estate at Dollis Hill in West London.[64]

Sir Thomas Lipton's entrance to high society was secured by philanthropy and his yachting exploits, which led to friendship with the Prince of Wales, later King Edward VII. Once he had been accepted in this way, it was difficult to exclude other members of 'the rich shopocracy'. For 'what could possibly be said against people like Mr Harrod, whose shooting box on Exmoor was visited by "academicians and parliamentarians, . . . [and] Colonel F. Dickins (of Dickins & Jones), a dashing officer of the Victoria Rifle Volunteers . . . ?'[65]

In the case of Blundell Maple, in 1883 he 'made good his aspirations to be a country squire and join the ranks of the landed gentry' by acquiring an estate at Childwick in Hertfordshire, where he bred and raced horses, won cups for his farm produce and had good coverts for shooting. Alongside his sporting pursuits he could be seen as 'part of the glittering audience in the boxes at the Covent Garden Opera House'.[66] Sir John Barker's land purchases were more modest. He owned a 300-acre estate at Bishop's Stortford, which he farmed using the most modern methods. He was also famed for his polo ponies, while his enthusiastic support for the Liberal Party led to his becoming one of the first aldermen to be elected to the new London County Council in 1889. He was president of Hammersmith Liberal Association and founder president of Bishop's Stortford District Liberal Association.[67] As we shall see, his interest in politics was shared by a number of other retailers during the nineteenth and early twentieth centuries.

COMMUNITY ACTIVITIES

The contribution of shopkeepers to community life ranged from the carrying out of parish and municipal duties to participation in national politics, in trade associations and, in the case of the wealthiest members of the shopocracy, in dispensing charity on a grand scale.

The literacy and numeracy skills of retailers varied widely, but in many cases their ability to read, write and add up, as well as their experience in ordering and checking stock and in dealing with commercial travellers, gave them skills which few in their community could match.[68] This was especially true in rural areas during the Georgian and early Victorian periods and led to their being asked to take on such public offices as those of overseer of the poor, churchwarden, tax collector and highway surveyor. That applied to Thomas Turner of East Hoathly. Over the decade 1756–66 he served as churchwarden on three occasions, as overseer of the poor for four years, and as surveyor of the highways for one year. He was collector of the window and land taxes in his parish from 1760 to 1766 and, as David Vaisey notes, in 'almost every year he was called upon to write up the accounts of the other parish officers . . . his skills in both writing and casting accounts were constantly in demand by those who needed to have bonds drafted, wills written, inventories drawn up, or charity moneys distributed'.[69] He was even asked to read wills to the mourners after funerals, presumably because no one else could do so: 'went to the funeral of Master Goldsmith . . . where I read the deceased's will to the relations', is one such entry in June 1757.[70]

The literacy and the organisational abilities of shopkeepers were also called upon following the extension of the franchise after the passage of the first Reform Act in 1832. Among other things, this gave the vote to male householders with properties of an annual value of £10 or more.[71] The middle-class men who benefited from this included many shopkeepers. Indeed, until the vote was extended again in 1867 to cover all male householders living in urban areas, they constituted perhaps a quarter to a third of the entire electorate in some towns.[72] After enfranchisement many of them worked hard on committees registering voters and preparing canvass books. Later they were to become some of the strongest supporters of the Liberal Party under William Gladstone. They were attracted by its policies of free trade, economical government and the emphasis on individualism.[73] The Gladstonian message aroused feelings of power and personal commitment among people who had hitherto been regarded as being on the fringes of middle-class society. As Nossiter points out, to participate in this way the larger and more successful retailers could leave their shop in the hands of staff, while their clientele 'was often sufficiently varied to offer protection against severe [political] pressure from any one landowner, magnate or party' that took a different view from theirs.[74] Nonetheless, there were examples of undue influence being exerted by powerful opponents when tradesmen supported the 'wrong' party. In 1843 in Durham there was 'Lord Londonderry's list of tradesmen to be "excommunicated" in the event of disobedience to his lordship's wishes in a local election'. In another case a loyal supporter of the Northern Reform Union in the corrupt borough of Berwick-on-Tweed, 'was forced into taking a mean shop "not one-fourth large enough" for his needs' and then watching his enemies 'drive off his customers' by the use of personal pressure.[75] In Nottingham ironmonger Jabez Jacks, who was an 'ardent' supporter of the Liberal Party, at one election in the 1860s had his shop attacked by Conservative supporters angered at his invective against their candidate.[76] In fact politics proved Jabez's undoing in the long run, in that he spent more and more time discussing parliamentary matters in the local tavern, leaving the running of his business to subordinates. One of them swindled him and eventually his neglect of the shop led to bankruptcy.[77]

Nonetheless, in Newcastle, Gateshead and Sunderland more than half of the shopocracy in each town voted Radical in the mid-1830s, and tradesmen and artisans of moderate means were 'overwhelmingly Radical' at Bath in 1841.[78] Even in strong Tory boroughs like Cambridge many tradesmen voted for Liberal candidates around the middle of the nineteenth century.[79]

Influence could, of course, be exerted by a shopkeeper's working-class customers, both before and after they obtained the vote. This could be achieved by policies of 'exclusive dealing', whereby they refused to buy from retailers who failed to support their favoured political party. 'Religion, politics and membership of voluntary societies could substantially affect a trader's business', writes Barrie Trinder in his study of Victorian Banbury. As a local critic stated in 1874, 'the shopkeeper, willingly or unwillingly, [was] compelled to sacrifice every vestige of manly independence, especially he whose lot is cast in a country town. . . . He votes at an election, not to serve his country, or to save her from ruin, but to please his customers.'[80] Evidence from elsewhere, however, suggests this was an exaggeration. In his first pastorate Mark Rutherford discovered that although Mr Lane, the grocer, was denounced by the parson on account of his Nonconformity he was still able to attract Anglican customers. They 'preferred tea with some taste in it from a Unitarian to the insipid wood-flavoured stuff which was sold by the grocer who believed in the Trinity.'[81]

Similarly in Woodstock Mr B., with his high-class gentlemen's outfitting business in what was virtually a Tory pocket borough, nonetheless played an active part in Liberal politics in the town, as well as voting for the party. When his daughter was asked if he had felt under pressure from his wealthier customers to take a different position, her reply was emphatic: 'No, no. . . . Nobody would have dared to question my father. . . . My father had one line and it was straight, and he never deviated a scrap.'[82] But smaller shopkeepers or those whose business lacked status might be more cautious. The Bicester retailer Mr C., who ran a small mixed shop in a working-class neighbourhood, was reticent about his political opinions. As his daughter noted drily, 'he had to get his living out of all people . . . and discretion is the better part of valour sometimes'.[83]

Retailers of an independent and Radical frame of mind would, on occasion, use their administrative skills to help in the running of local societies, including, in particular, the agricultural trade union movement of the 1870s. During that decade English farm workers for the first time established a national organisation to advance their claims for improved wages and working conditions as well as better housing. Among those assisting at this time was the Norfolk grocer and general dealer George Rix, who was a Primitive Methodist local preacher, an active Radical, and secretary of the local branch of the National Agricultural Labourers' Union.[84] In Oxfordshire the prosperous Woodstock draper, Gabriel George Banbury, who was a strong Liberal supporter and Methodist local preacher, backed the agricultural union movement in the county from its inception in 1872. He became the first district treasurer and his son John served as auditor. Another Woodstock retailer, William Brotherton, also lent support.[85] There were similar examples elsewhere.

Not all retailers, of course, were Liberal or Radical voters. Besides the effect of personal preference or outside influence, John Vincent in his survey of mid-Victorian pollbooks has identified butchers as being particularly likely to support the Conservatives. Grocers, by contrast, were mainly Liberal voters. The Conservative stance taken by those in the meat trade may have owed something to their links with farming, a sector which traditionally supported the Tories, or it may be that they, like wine merchants and jewellers, 'looked for reward in higher quarters than from mere townspeople'.[86] As such they often appeared 'as a sort of upper servants' to the Tory landed classes. In the case of wine merchants and jewellers, the influence of their Conservative clientele may have been reinforced by their personal stake in the community as substantial tradesmen.[87]

Only in the final years of the nineteenth century did the allegiance of large numbers of retailers to the Liberal Party begin to waver, as the reformist policies of 'new' Liberalism, with its commitment to increased welfare provisions, improved education and better housing, led to higher rates and taxes. Shopkeepers who had embraced the *laissez-faire*, tax-cutting, 'cheap government' philosophy of mid-Victorian Gladstonian liberalism baulked at the prospect of higher rate demands. As Michael Winstanley comments, by failing to recognise the depth of this discontent the Liberals lost support at both national and local level. The Conservative Party, meanwhile, began to adopt the former Radical belief in economy and low taxation. Growing numbers of erstwhile loyal members of the Liberal-voting shopocracy drifted into the Conservative ranks during the early twentieth century.[88]

The political preoccupations of the more substantial retailers from the 1830s onwards were not confined to events on the national scene. Particularly after the passage of the 1835 Municipal Corporations Act, which enfranchised householders who had paid poor rates for at least three years, and excluded from the council chamber all save those with over £1,000 capital or who paid £30 per year in rates, shopkeepers became prominent in the affairs of the reformed corporate boroughs. At the same time they served as members and electors of other local government institutions which grew up from the 1830s, such as boards of poor law guardians, improvement and police commissions, and local boards of health.[89] According to Richard Cobden, it was the shopocracy which 'carried the day' in the campaign for the incorporation of Manchester in 1837 and 1838, and of the 64 members of the town's first council, 10 were shopkeepers, compared to 34 who were merchants and manufacturers.[90] In the succeeding decades, as the more prestigious members of the community withdrew from council membership, the number of retailers greatly increased. In 1899, when Beatrice Webb visited Manchester, she found they had become dominant, and she was scathing in her condemnation of their narrow vision and cheese-paring policies. 'The abler administrators', she concluded, 'have no pretension to ideas, hardly any grammar – they are merely . . . hard-headed shopkeepers divided in their mind between their desire to keep the rates down and their ambition to magnify the importance of Manchester as against other cities.'[91]

The trend was reflected elsewhere. In Middlesbrough as late as 1872 there were 10 ironmasters and 7 shopkeepers on the council, but by 1912 the shopkeepers had increased to 15 and the ironmasters had shrunk to a single representative. Already in 1880 there were complaints in the local newspaper at this withdrawal of leading citizens from the council in favour of what the newspaper called 'sectional representation': 'Now the butchers are to the fore with some unsavoury grievance; then the publicans bumptiously demand to be heard. . . . Unless some great political principle is involved, the one consideration should be to elect men who by their intelligence, respectability and knowledge of the town's requirements, are fitted for a seat in the local Parliament.'[92] This was not mere snobbery, for the preoccupations of Middlesbrough's shopocrat councillors remained narrow and devoid of major social initiatives, including the provision of leisure facilities for the mass of the population.[93]

In smaller towns, where shopkeepers were in close personal contact with the electorate through their daily business, they were able to gauge the local mood and plan their political strategy accordingly. At Denbigh in Wales, for example, by the early 1880s eleven of the council members came from the shopkeeping classes, including an ironmonger, a printer and a chemist.[94] A similar trend has been noted in Pontypool, where position and power increasingly rested with the 'shopocracy'. For their part, the ratepayers who elected them expected them to restrict their 'individual and collective civic ambitions to a scale commensurate with that of the town'. Among those selected was Peter Eckersley, a Pontypool marine stores dealer with little formal education, but who was nonetheless able to 'instil an image of himself in the public mind as a suitable leader'.[95] First chosen in 1873, he served almost continuously for around thirty years, and was acknowledged to have devoted himself to civic life.

Part of the reason for shopkeepers' concern with 'economy' was an awareness that they, as small businessmen, had to pay out a considerable share of their sometimes precarious income in rates and taxes. But partly it was because they appreciated that high taxation reduced overall consumer spending, to their disadvantage.[96]

In the early twentieth century shopkeepers increased their hold over local government in many towns. 'In Blackpool', comments Michael Winstanley, 'throughout the 1900s shopkeepers never held less than 45 per cent of the seats, twice the level of the previous decade. In Macclesfield they comprised 33 per cent of the councillors in 1890, 50 per cent in 1898 and over 50 per cent every subsequent year up to 1914 by which time they were filling the mayoral office too. A similar situation obtained in Oldham, Blackburn and

Accrington. . . . Symbolically, the leader of Cardiff's [victorious] "Economy" party after 1903 was a draper; shopkeepers everywhere continued to champion their traditional "Radical" policy of retrenchment.'[97]

Many retailers became part of the local 'establishment' through their participation in municipal politics. Henry Lewis, who had purchased F. Cape & Co., the Oxford drapery store, in the 1890s, was elected to the city council in 1907 and served on it until his death in 1921 – the year when one of his sons became Mayor of Oxford.[98] In Chester the Brown family, owners of the prestigious department store, played an important role in developing the town's amenities. During the last quarter of the nineteenth century they dominated local Liberal politics, with both William and Charles Brown serving as town councillors. Charles was elected mayor six times, and under the brothers' influence considerable improvements were carried out, including to the River Dee, where riverside promenades were created.[99] Similarly, James Beale, founder of an up-market department store in Bournemouth, was elected a councillor in 1900 and served as mayor in 1902. He became an active campaigner for civic improvements, including the rebuilding of the seafronts, and played a leading role in establishing Bournemouth as a high-class shopping centre and resort.[100]

Still more ambitious was J. Herbert Marshall, proprietor of the Midland Musical Depot in Leicester. He amassed an estate valued at nearly £50,000 and was a Freemason, the founder of 'the Leicester Philharmonic Society, a noted philanthropist and Chairman of the local Conservative Association'. He was elected to the town council in 1888, and became a magistrate in 1892. Four years later he served as mayor and for his services to the city received a knighthood in 1905.[101]

In Lancaster the leading grocer T.D. Smith did not take any public office but both his son and his grandson did. Edward G. Smith became a borough magistrate in 1913 and a county magistrate seventeen years later. He was a committed supporter of the Liberal Party and was co-opted on to the town council in 1916. He continued to sit on it until he was elevated to alderman in 1929. In 1928–9 he served as the mayor. Other interests included presidency of local horticultural societies, membership of the board of governors of two grammar schools and chairmanship of the cricket club. He also founded the Lancaster Lads' Club, the League of Help and the local branch of the YMCA.[102]

However, like many retailers in the late nineteenth and early twentieth centuries, the Smiths' involvement in municipal matters did not preclude activity in connection with their trade. The increasing competition of multiple chains, co-operative shops and department stores, combined with a desire to protect traditional skills, contributed to the rise of trade associations in the late Victorian years. A growing number of retailers began to draw a sense of their commercial identity from their association with fellow tradesmen.[103] In Lancaster Thomas D. Smith and his son Edward were instrumental in setting up the Lancaster Grocers' and Provision Merchants' Association in 1897 and served as president on several occasions. Edward also became involved with the National Federation of Grocers' Associations, which was formed in 1891 'to protect trade interests by linking together local associations throughout the country'.[104] He was elected president in 1932–3, while his son Francis also became a prominent member of the National Federation.

Concern at the decline of independent retailing in the face of competition from 'big business' lay behind the formation of many of these trade associations, although particular bitterness was reserved for the co-operative stores. In March 1909 the chairman of the Scottish Retail Drapers' Association referred to the 'menace of co-operation' and suggested they should boycott 'any house which is supposed to supply the co-operative stores'.[105]

But the trade associations had more positive aspects as well, both in the commercial sphere and in social matters. The former included a desire to supply quality goods to customers at a fair price by the establishment of buying combines.[106] In other cases contracts were arranged for the inspection of scales and weighing machines on preferential terms to members of grocers' associations. During the First World War there was an upsurge of support for these latter associations as they carried out negotiations with the government's Food Control Committees and similar official bodies on behalf of members.[107]

As well as the associations established in connection with individual trades, there were wider organisations covering a broad spectrum of retailers. One such inter-trade grouping was set up in Blackpool, with the resort's storekeepers joining to obtain free legal advice, mutual plate glass insurance, a benevolent society, a campaign against dubious trade practices such as mock auctions, and protests over rates. Regular social gatherings and annual dinners were also arranged.[108] These social aspects were to prove important in promoting camaraderie among the tradesmen in a town. Leicester Grocers' Association, for instance, held whist drives as part of their regular social programme, and in the summer picnics were arranged to places of interest, with games for the children and a cricket match for the menfolk.[109]

Wives joined in some of the events. In Manchester in March 1909 the Manchester, Salford and District Traders' Defence Association and its 'ladies' section' arranged a whist drive and dance, while a month or so earlier over 200 people attended the annual dinner of the Chorley and District Tradesmen's Association and Chamber of Trades.[110]

On the national political stage, meanwhile, some of the country's leading retailers became Members of Parliament. They included Sir John Barker, whose first efforts to enter the Commons ended in disappointment when he contested Maidstone in 1888, 1898 and 1900 in the Liberal interest. Although he was elected on the third occasion he was subsequently unseated on petition by the Conservatives. In 1906 he was finally successful in Penryn and Falmouth and held the seat until 1910.[111]

Blundell Maple was another political activist, although in his case in the Conservative cause. He, too, was unsuccessful in his first bid to enter Parliament, when he contested the South St Pancras constituency in 1885. Two years later he won at Dulwich and held that seat until his death in 1903.[112]

Although it was more difficult for shop staff to take an active part in politics, other than through their trade unions, than it was for their employers, a few former assistants did enter the Commons in the early twentieth century. They were supporters of the newly formed Labour Party and included James Seddon, an ex-grocery shop worker who became a union organiser and was elected as Labour member for the Newton division of Lancashire from 1906 until his defeat in December 1910.[113] Margaret Bondfield, who served for ten years as assistant secretary of the National Amalgamated Union of Shop Assistants (between 1898 and 1908), before leaving to work in other areas of the labour movement, unsuccessfully contested the Northampton seat in 1920 and 1922. She succeeded in December 1923, only to lose in the October 1924 general election. She became MP for Wallsend in July 1926, again in the Labour interest, and remained as the Member for that constituency until her defeat in the political turmoil of the 1931 general election. In 1929 she became Minister of Labour in the new Labour government, and was the first woman cabinet minister.[114]

Philip Hoffman, a regional organiser for the Shop Assistants' Union, also became an MP, being elected for Essex South East in December 1923. He, too, lost in October 1924 but was successful at Sheffield Central in May 1929. He held the seat until 1931.[115] In all of these cases, however, it was through their involvement with the Labour Party and with trade unionism that they achieved parliamentary seats rather than through their employment as shop assistants.

One final area of community activity remains to be mentioned, namely the philanthropic initiatives of some of the leading shopocrats. Blundell Maple, for example, provided excursions and entertainments for some of the poor children of London and also helped raise funds for University College Hospital, which was near his Tottenham Court Road store.[116]

William Whiteley's contribution was still more impressive. In a bizarre twist to an eventful life, Whiteley was murdered in January 1907 by Horace

Rayner, who came to ask for financial help on the grounds of being the 'Universal Provider's' illegitimate son. Whiteley refused and was about to call the police when the young man shot him. At his death his estate was valued at almost £1.5 million and his bequests included around £1 million for the construction and maintenance of homes for the 'aged poor' on a 225-acre estate at Burhill in Surrey. It became known as Whiteley Village, a title which would surely have pleased the egotistical and dynamic department store pioneer. Other legacies included £5,000 for 'Whiteley Christmas Gifts' to be distributed among the poor of Paddington, and £5,000 to the Whiteley Sports Trustees to finance prizes for the encouragement of cricket, football, rowing and swimming among people living within a radius of 5 miles from Westbourne Grove.[117]

Chapter 7

THE FIRST WORLD WAR AND ITS AFTERMATH

Salesmanship isn't the science of selling people goods they do not require – it is more the art of teaching them to require and buy the goods you have for sale. Every assistant should be made to realize the importance of the impression he makes on the customer he serves.
'Practical Teaching in the Grocery Trade', in *Grocery*, July 1924.

THE IMPACT OF THE FIRST WORLD WAR

The outbreak of the First World War in August 1914 profoundly affected not only the country at large but, more narrowly, retailing, too. In the long run it helped to alter the gender balance of shop workers in favour of women, it led to the compulsory regulation of opening hours, it encouraged a sharp decline in living in in many of the businesses where it still survived, and it gave an impetus to amalgamations, especially among the department stores. In the short term retailers had to cope with staffing shortages and with greater government control, including, from the end of 1917, the introduction of rationing for a range of foodstuffs.

As soon as hostilities broke out people tried to stock up on food, thereby putting pressure on shops selling groceries. At Robert Roberts's small parental store in Salford:

A rush of customers to the shop gave us the first alarm – sugar, flour, bread, butter, margarine, cheese, people began frantically to buy all the food they could find the money for. 'Serve no strangers!' my mother ordered after the first hour. 'Only "regulars" from now on.'[1]

At the same time she sent her children in relays to join queues that had formed outside Lipton's, Maypole Dairy and the other multiple shops on the high road. 'One day of our foraging, I remember, brought in 28lbs of margarine and 20lbs of sugar, which my mother promptly sold off in small lots at a penny a pound profit.' Better-off families from the suburbs came into town with horses and traps and carts to buy up sugar and flour by half-sacks. Roberts claimed this sometimes led to 'near riots', with shop windows broken and the police called in.

Sugar was scarce throughout the war, despite the actions of the special Sugar Commission in overseeing the allocation of supplies. Prior to 1914 around two-thirds of the nation's sugar had come from central Europe, with which Britain was now at war. But the price of all foodstuffs rose in response to the pressure of demand and the difficulty of securing adequate supplies either from overseas or from Britain's own resources. Not until January 1917 was the Ministry of Food set up to coordinate policy. In the meantime average retail food prices rose by 50 per cent between 1914 and 1916, with a further sharp increase in 1917, until price controls began to be introduced by the newly appointed Food Controller.[2] Some goods were more affected than others, so that between July 1914 and the spring of 1916, the price of sugar rose by 128 per cent, of flour by 60 per cent and of bread by 52 per cent, whereas for butter and margarine the respective increases were put at 34 per cent and 16 per cent.[3]

By the end of 1918 the average retail price of foodstuffs had risen by more than 100 per cent over the war years, and there were allegations that retailers were profiteering. To some extent these suspicions were confirmed by the trickle of prosecutions of shopkeepers accused of overcharging after price controls were imposed in 1917. These led to fines and even imprisonment, although much depended on the attitude of individual magistrates. In January 1918 the trade journal *Grocery* reported that Hailsham JPs had fined an Eastbourne grocer £104 for selling jam at above the maximum price, while at Lambeth the magistrate declared that in future 'all these profiteering cases are going to prison, there will be no fines. . . . Everybody – butchers, grocers and butter sellers – will go to prison after this week.' On that occasion he fined two tradesmen, from Brixton and West Norwood respectively, £35 apiece, plus costs, for selling margarine at above the maximum permitted level. On the other hand, at a North London police court David Keer, a grocer and provisions merchant from Tollington Park, was only fined 5s for charging an excessive price for butter, with a further 5s costs; he also faced similar penalties for failing to exhibit a notice in his shop showing the price of butter. But the total sum of £1 was scarcely a serious deterrent.[4] There were instances, too, such as that involving a Staffordshire grocer who was fined for selling bacon at above the controlled price, where those overcharged were apparently 'reluctant to give evidence because of being afterwards unable to obtain supplies'.[5] Indicative of the changed relationship between shopkeeper and customer was the wry comment in the *Liverpool Courier* that whereas before the war,

> The grocer, with a supple back, addressed the customer respectfully, 'And what may your next order be?' To-day it is the customer who asks apologetically, 'Could you possibly let me have a quarter of margarine?' When the grocer realised his power he began to use it. . . . Perhaps the most signal example of his emancipation was the institution of a staff dinner hour.[6]

There were, inevitably, allegations of favouritism, too. In *Akenfield*, Ronald Blythe recorded the bitterness of a Suffolk wheelwright and blacksmith at the unfair distribution of food in his area. 'The farmers' houses were full of food, dairy butter, sweet cakes, meats – everything. They got it off the shopkeepers. They had some kind of mutual arrangement.'[7] Even *Grocery* admitted that retailers sometimes told customers deliberate untruths as to the quantity of certain goods they had in stock, especially 'such things as tea, jam and matches'. One man, on being asked why he had told a woman he had no marmalade when he had sold a jar to another client shortly after, replied that the first person had not been a 'regular': 'I cannot let my regular people go short for her.' Gossip caused problems too. If one customer were sold something in short supply, and she told her neighbours, they, too, would come to the shop 'and when met with a refusal' would respond sharply that Mrs B. had just had some and they must have it too. According to one grocer, having to decide whom to supply was 'one of the most awkward problems in trade' during the war.[8]

In certain cases, conditions might be imposed on the sale of scarce commodities, by requiring customers to buy other products as well. Already in the spring of 1916 it was reported that grocers were refusing to sell sugar unless tea was also purchased, and a similar policy was applied even by the major multiples. Many refused to sell sugar unless 'other goods' were purchased, 'the other goods being as a rule margarine'.[9] These 'conditional' sales were outlawed in March 1917 but it is clear from subsequent prosecutions that this did not end the practice. As late as October 1918 a branch of Lipton's in Portsmouth was fined £10, plus costs, for applying restrictions to the sale of jam. According to the Portsmouth deputy town clerk, the firm had been convicted on four previous occasions of a similar offence.[10]

Food adulteration increased, too, with a Walsall Wood grocer being fined £2 for selling coffee adulterated with over 50 per cent of chicory, while a Norwich man who sold a lard substitute containing 14 per cent excess water was fined the derisory sum of 3*d*.[11] Bacon, too, had water added to it, while another deceit practised by the unscrupulous was to mix together butter and margarine and charge a butter price for it. On occasion, as with a Hastings grocer and alderman, margarine was sold as butter. In this instance the man was fined £20, as well as experiencing the disgrace of being found out committing such a mean trick.[12]

Consumers sometimes took matters into their own hands by demanding to be sold scarce goods they knew to be in stock. This could lead to violence. At Abertillery in Wales a crowd rushed into a grocer's shop in an attempt to secure provisions, breaking down doors and plate-glass windows in the process. According to *Grocery*, someone in the shop then produced a revolver, 'but he voluntarily handed the weapon over. When order was restored the police took charge . . . and sold a quantity of dripping and condensed milk.'[13] A month later, in March 1918, the same journal reported a near riot at Coalville in Leicestershire, when a grocer's shop was besieged by a crowd of angry women. They demanded to be supplied with jam, which was in stock in the premises. In the confusion a female assistant was assaulted by a miner's wife, and the latter was subsequently charged with the assault and with stealing a 2lb pot of jam. Fines and costs amounting to £1 4*s* 6*d* were imposed.

Elsewhere, however, price rises and other wartime disruptions brought financial disaster to some retailers. One couple, who had run a successful bakery at New Bradwell near Wolverton in Buckinghamshire for a number of years before 1914, found the increase in flour prices made their business uneconomic. 'We were losing all our money,' recalled the wife. They worked 'like slaves' but the customers owed them cash for bread and cakes. 'We came out of the shop . . . in 1916', after having lost everything.[14] In another case a credit draper and tailor from Stratford in London went bankrupt in the summer of 1917 after being in business for sixteen years. His had always been a 'hand to mouth' undertaking and when war broke out many of his customers enlisted. As a result his orders dried up and he was unable to collect the outstanding book debts. At the subsequent bankruptcy hearing his accounts showed liabilities of over £350 and assets valued at £193.[15]

The loss of staff aggravated retailers' problems. The large department stores, in particular, included many members of the Territorial Army, who were mobilised on the outbreak of war. In addition, a number of leading firms like Debenham's and Marshall & Snelgrove, as well as smaller stores like Jones & Higgins of Peckham, offered inducements to male employees to join up, or made promises that there would be a job for them on their return, at the war's end. By the spring of 1917 Jones & Higgins claimed that 193 men had left their service to join the army. 'We have now only four eligibles left,' they reported proudly, 'all married men and for the most part with families.'[16] From Debenham's and Marshall & Snelgrove jointly over 1,000 men had enlisted by December 1917, while from Harrods 3,200 members of staff joined the forces, of whom 147 lost their lives. As Maurice Corina points out in his history of the Debenham group, 'scores of London store staff won medals for gallantry'.[17]

The recruitment drive was boosted by the fact that when the war began a number of department stores saw sales sharply reduced, and they reacted by dismissing staff. Co-operative societes, too, faced similar trading difficulties in some areas, with *The Co-operative Employé* complaining that dividends should be cut rather than the wages of workers reduced or their being thrown out of work.[18] Soon the Home Office intervened to calm the situation. A meeting of London storekeepers was called at which 'it was agreed to halt the sackings and attempt to restore customer morale'.[19] However, a number of men had already enlisted, imbued with a spirit of patriotism. During the autumn of 1914 the stores were also told to dismiss all members of staff born in either Germany or Austro-Hungary.[20] In mid-1915 national appeals for the better-off to practise economy again led to a decline in the purchase of luxury goods. By July of that year Barker's of Kensington were forced to lay off staff in their household section and at Pontings, where most of the mail order business was done, there were also redundancies.[21]

In these circumstances and with increasing food shortages, many shops that had continued to have staff living in or had provided meals on the premises now decided to end the arrangement. Harrods, which had never had sleeping accommodation for assistants, offered 10s a week instead of supplying dinner and tea to employees, while John Barker's insisted on staff having all their meals out, even if they were still sleeping on the premises. Rylands & Faudel's textile warehouses in London agreed to abolish living in and to pay 20s a week to each member of staff instead of board and lodging, or 10s for board in the case of those already living out. Similar action was taken all over the country.[22]

The flow of recruits from retailing to the armed forces was such that in February 1915 one MP suggested that a quarter of the eligible males working in shops had already enlisted.[23] The enthusiastic response was confirmed by the prime minister, H.H. Asquith, during the summer of that year when he stated that 260,000 shop assistants had joined up by the spring of 1915.[24] In addition, some workers, both male and female, entered the munitions factories or other areas of wartime employment, attracted by the better pay and shorter working hours or, in the case of the men, seeing it as an alternative to military service. Emma Fray was one who made the move. She gave up a tailoring apprenticeship to take a post with the gas company in her native Southampton. She later admitted it was because of 'the money . . . I was only getting . . . six shillings a week.' In the gas company she earned 16s a week from the beginning. She and her nine fellow female recruits received a month's training and then went out repairing cookers, opening meters, soldering pipes, checking radiators and doing other tasks. Emma never returned to retailing, getting married at the end of the war to a lorry driver very much her senior, whom she had met through the gas company.[25]

The large outflow of male shop staff was accompanied by an increased recruitment of females. Official statistics suggested that in July 1914 around 55 per cent of those working in the wholesale and retail drapery, haberdashery and clothing trades were women. By October 1917 that proportion had risen to 71 per cent. A still greater change occurred among the staff in grocery and provision shops, which had always been male dominated. In July 1914, even including bakery and confectionery businesses as well as wholesale and retail groceries, only 27 per cent of the labour force was female. The number of women and girls was put at 80,000 and most of them were probably in the bakery and confectionery sectors where females had long worked. Just over three years later, in October 1917, the female proportion in these various trades had more than doubled to 56 per cent.[26] Six months after this it was estimated that over the period of the war, between July 1914 and April 1918, 101,000 extra females had entered the grocery, bakery and confectionery trades. Of these, employers considered that 92,000 had been hired to replace males.[27] That may be compared, for example, with wholesale and retail butchers, fishmongers and dairymen, who had employed 42,000 females in July 1914 and had increased that total by 27,000 during the war. In April 1918 it was suggested that out of a total female staff of around 69,000, some 30,000 were directly replacing men.[28]

Initially grocers and provision dealers were reluctant to accept inexperienced females but soon training schemes were being organised by the Institute of Certificated Grocers and the London County Council, among others.[29] However, many women learned on the job, coping as best they could. Most were successful and a contributor to the *Liverpool Courier* expressed his appreciation of their 'courtesy and good humour and business capacity . . . under very trying conditions'.[30] Even the Metropolitan Grocers' Association conceded grudgingly in the summer of 1917 that although there had been 'some disappointments and even failures', the general verdict was that the experiment had 'proved quite as successful as could be expected, remembering the suddenness of the necessary adoption'.[31]

As early as April 1915 the board of the Home and Colonial Stores had agreed to recruit female labour, anticipating a shortage of men 'in view of further calls for recruits, the approaching holiday season, and the new branches which would require staffing'.[32] By March 1917 over 2,000 of their employees were serving with the colours. At T.D. Smith's in Lancaster, too, all the fully fit adult males in the firm, including family members, signed up and were replaced by women. Some of these were given the management of branch shops with little or no training.[33]

A few grocers, however, continued to advertise in the trade press for male staff, normally specifying that they must be ineligible to fight on grounds of age or poor health. Typical of many was the appeal by Baker's Stores of Wimbledon for 'Provision Hands . . . for leading provisions in high-class stores. Above age limit or ineligible for the Forces'.[34] More realistic was the proprietor of Castle Hill Stores, Windsor, who was seeking 'a Young Lady for soliciting orders every morning. Used to cycle. Fill up time at grocer's counter.'[35]

One of the male workers' main reservations regarding this female influx was the fact that they earned less than the men. It was feared that if they took posts at lower pay, employers would not want to reinstate the men after the war, no matter what promises they may have made. To this end members of the National Association of Grocers' Assistants and the Amalgamated Union of Co-operative Employees (AUCE) were anxious to ensure that all 'substituted females' should be paid at rates higher than those usual among women staff. In the case of AUCE, parity with the men was demanded. In July 1915 it also appointed its first woman organiser to look after the interests of female members and to encourage them to participate in union affairs. But while some co-operative societies offered equal pay, others resisted and the union's annual report for 1918 admitted that although pay equality for female employees was accepted up to age 17, few societies would carry the principle through to higher ages.[36] Improved general rates of pay were nonetheless obtained to meet the rise in living costs. They were secured mainly through negotiation, although on occasion success was achieved only after a strike or the threat of a strike.[37]

The National Amalgamated Union of Shop Assistants, Warehousemen and Clerks (NAUSAW&C), by contrast, was prepared to accept gender differences in pay. This led to recriminations from its Co-operative rival that it was undermining the AUCE's equal pay strategy. 'No wonder that many committees of co-operative societies would prefer their employés to be members of such a body rather than the AUCE,' reported *The Co-operative Employé* in August 1916.[38]

Nevertheless, pay advances were secured by the National Union, too, including agreements with some of the large multiple grocery firms. But the outcome was patchy, with Lipton's, for example, accepting the union's proposed pay scales for branches from Hampshire to Cornwall and in Ireland, while Pegram's made similar concessions for staff first in Liverpool and then in the Manchester area. In some smaller towns, like Ammanford and Aberavon in Wales, all the shops, not merely the grocers, agreed to the union rates and to a 48-hour week as well.[39]

By March 1918 the AUCE was lamenting the numerous extra tasks which co-operative assistants had to perform in addition to their main duties but which fell outside the remit of those in private trade. They included dealing with 'penny bank contributions, deposits for share accounts, requests for free tickets for educational events and lectures, issuing checks on purchases . . . and a host of queries'.[40]

In the meantime the pressure on men to enlist continued relentlessly. In October 1915 a new scheme was implemented whereby every male in the relevant age group was required to 'attest', that is, to undertake to serve if and when called upon to do so. Those having good national or personal reasons could be exempted, and it was to determine the validity of these that a network of tribunals was set up in November 1915. But this half-way house to conscription failed to bring forward sufficient recruits, and in January 1916 conscription was introduced for single men. Early in May it was extended to become universal male conscription.[41] With these changes many more shop workers were caught up in the military machine, including owners of one-man businesses who had earlier been promised special exemption. Reports of the work of the tribunals indicate the variability of their decisions. In July 1916, for example, *Grocery* reported that in Rothesay, Scotland, an application for the exemption of the chief assistant in a local grocery store had been granted on the understanding that the female proprietor's 19-year-old son would join up in lieu. The youth expressed his willingness to enlist and, declared the journal complacently, 'this formed a happy and patriotic solution of the problem'.[42]

By October, however, *Grocery* was warning that the situation was likely to get far tighter. It quoted the decision of an East Ham tribunal to support the military representative's appeal against the manager of a branch shop being exempted, on the grounds that 'a woman could do the work'. This, *Grocery* declared, pointed clearly 'to the fact that the general combing out of men of military age from all forms of industry that are not directly concerned in war work, will affect the grocery trade more severely than it has been affected yet'.[43]

Sometimes a military representative's comments before the tribunals verged on the insulting. At a Norfolk Appeals Tribunal in February 1917 a 39-year-old Harleston draper was told: 'Don't you think it is a woman's job to run a draper's establishment in war-time?' The draper protested that he had to move heavy and cumbersome stock around and also deal with other business matters, but the representative responded cuttingly: 'Do you suggest that a man passed for general service should be kept at home to measure yards of lace or calico?' The tribunal evidently agreed, for it told the man he must join up, although it allowed him a period of grace up to 1 May, to enable him to find a manager.[44]

Where it proved impossible to find a substitute, either a family member or an outsider, to run a business, then it might have to be sold. This happened to Mr Wilson, a draper from Heywood, Lancashire. He was called up in the spring of 1917 and had to auction off his fixtures and fittings.[45]

In Keighley Olive Simmons, who was already an assistant in her brother's drapery store, took over the running of it when he had to enlist. A younger sister, who had been widowed in the war, helped her.[46] When the brother returned, his business was expanded and 'we . . . began to employ other people as well'.

Occasionally different solutions were found, as in Bolton, where a group of tradespeople who were not required to serve formed a panel to oversee the businesses of small shopkeepers and others while their owners were away. The panel included thirty-eight members of the local Grocers' Association.[47] Another alternative was proposed by the Lancashire Appeals Tribunal at Preston when a Chorley grocer with his own business and classed as a 'Grade 3' man was given a conditional exemption on the understanding that he gave 'assistance in other businesses if required'.[48]

On rare occasions bribery was attempted, as when the chief substitution officer in Liverpool, and John Hughes, the owner of a chain of fifty grocer's shops, were found guilty of conspiring to defeat the Military Service Acts in May 1917. Hughes was also found guilty of corruptly giving the officer £875, and the latter of accepting the money. He was sentenced to one year and nine months' imprisonment, while Hughes was given twelve months in gaol. He also had to pay £200 towards the costs of the case. Three other men involved in the scandal were imprisoned, two for nine months and the third for twelve months. It is not clear whether these were to be beneficiaries from the attempted bribery.[49]

From an early stage, however, the war had its darker side. That applied not merely to the ever-rising casualties but to the grief and anger these caused to families and friends left at home. Animosity towards Germany mounted, especially in the aftermath of the sinking of the liner *Lusitania* in the spring of 1915. It led to serious anti-German rioting and looting within Britain, directed against shops belonging to Austrian and German tradesmen. The violence seems to have begun in London on 11 March and by the following day had spread over much of the capital, with more than 150 shops attacked on the night of 12 May alone. The rioters not only smashed doors and windows and looted the furniture and contents of the shops, but they damaged the interiors as well. Staircases were hacked to pieces and walls and ceilings demolished. The police appeared powerless (or unwilling) to intervene. Not even well-established retailers were spared. Among the premises attacked were two baker's shops belonging to men of German descent who had been 'associated with public life in Poplar for a great number of years'.[50] In Kentish Town damage estimated at £20,000 was inflicted, mainly on baker's and confectioner's shops.[51] At West Ham, where attacks on German property were said to have caused £100,000 worth of damage over three days, 110 people were eventually arrested and brought to court. Most were leniently treated, with magistrates merely pointing out the folly of such conduct. One of those taking part was a young woman out to avenge the death of her brother, killed at the front. Two other women had received cards from sons who were prisoners-of-war in Germany and who complained they were being half-starved.[52]

Nor was the violence confined to London. At Newcastle upon Tyne, pork butcher's shops were attacked, and at Gateshead a young man was fined for assaulting a German butcher. Here an effort seems to have been made to punish the rioters and curb the violence, for a second man was ordered to pay £8 to cover the cost of a plate-glass window he had smashed.[53]

At Salford Robert Roberts recalled a jeering crowd gathering outside the shop and house belonging to a long-established German pork butcher. Every window was broken and then the rioters surged into the shop, tossing meat into the street. Crockery and furniture were hurled from the kitchen, while some people went upstairs and threw out furniture, ornaments and bedding. Much of this was subsequently burnt on a piece of nearby land. When the orgy of destruction had spent itself, the mob disappeared, some carrying sides of bacon and other items. The shopkeeper had lived there for twenty years and had been well liked and respected but this did not save him from ruin. 'Warned of the danger,' wrote Roberts, 'he had escaped earlier to Blackpool with his family, where, in the guise of "Belgian-refugees", they were kindly treated.'[54]

In the next days thirty more shops were similarly attacked in Salford, including some bearing Russian and Jewish names. After this, a determined effort was made to suppress the disorder, both there and elsewhere, and within a short time the lawless interlude had largely ended. It was perhaps helped by the fact that the internment of enemy aliens was set in hand throughout the country from 14 May.[55]

As the months passed concern grew at the precarious position of food supplies. In late December 1916 Lord Devonport was appointed the first Food Controller, and the Ministry of Food was set up soon after.[56] Initially, comments Arthur Marwick, Devonport had 'a fixation about what he called "flaunting"', and his early efforts were directed against shopkeepers who displayed luxury foodstuffs in their windows. Shortly after he appealed for voluntary rationing, so that each adult would restrict himself or herself to a specific amount of bread, flour, meat and sugar each week.[57] As might be expected, the plan was a failure and on 30 May 1917 Devonport resigned. His successor, Lord Rhondda, was made of sterner stuff. He speedily obtained cabinet agreement for a scheme of sugar rationing. The country was to be divided into around 2,000 districts, each with its own Food Control Committee, to which people would apply for a card entitling them to ½lb of sugar per person per week. That amount could be increased if supplies proved sufficiently plentiful.[58] In the event sugar rationing was not properly implemented until the beginning of 1918.

In the interim local rationing initiatives were taken, often amid some confusion and ill-feeling. Birmingham Co-operative Society, for example, introduced its own sugar cards in July 1917, while the appointment of the Food Control Committees encouraged certain local authorities, such as Gravesend, Pontypool and Birmingham, to draw up rationing schemes for their area. In Dewsbury a margarine ration ticket was produced, fixing the weekly allocation at 4oz per person per week. The tickets were issued through local schools, with the teachers undertaking their distribution.[59] Early in 1918 Liverpool Food Control Committee decided to ration meat on the basis of 8oz per adult per week and 4oz per child, while in Pontypridd a plan was introduced to cover butter, margarine, tea, cheese and jam.[60]

In late February 1918 the government itself imposed upon London a system of rationing for meat. It depended upon the clipping of coupons from a customer's ration card, rather than upon mere registration with a shopkeeper. Less than two months later the rationing of meat and bacon by the use of coupons was introduced on a national basis.[61] Shortly after there was rationing (by registration card, not coupons) for tea, butter and margarine.

For grocers the multiplicity of local and national schemes and the relentless issuing of orders concerning the control of prices and food allocations proved a nightmare. In February 1918 the chairman of one Food Control Committee claimed he had received 142 orders from the government,

25 of them relating to sugar alone. Little wonder one grocer remarked with resignation: 'If we read all these orders we shall soon be in an asylum; if we do not read them all we shall certainly be in gaol.'[62] That was an exaggeration but infringements of the regulations could lead to fines. In Liverpool in the summer of 1918 several traders who had sold meat and bacon without coupons faced cash penalties amounting to £49, while a Birmingham grocer who had failed to send in his fortnightly sugar returns was fined £5.[63]

Complaints were made, too, about the personnel appointed to serve on the Food Committees. In 'every little Slocum Podger', the 'local parson, squarson lawyer, bonesetter, or half-pay officer can meet . . . and lay down the law as to what shall or shall not be done. . . . The Food Committee of Lord Rhondda is an unholy Inquisition set up in every hamlet as a terror to the grocer' fumed *Grocery* in March 1918. Indeed, in May of that year at an inquest on William Henry Harris, a grocer's manager who had hanged himself, it was claimed he had recently become 'very depressed . . . in consequence of people being rude to him in the shop, and the worry attached to the new coupon business'.[64] Other grocery workers grumbled about the time it took to detach the coupons, especially in the case of large families. According to a Bristol grocer, 'experienced hands were leaving . . . because of the worry'.[65]

Nonetheless, despite the anxieties many shopkeepers who sold foodstuffs enjoyed something of a boom. From mid-1917 to the end of 1920 Robert Roberts declared that his family's small shop 'prospered as never before'. When rationing was introduced in 1918, his mother had thought this might be the end of the business: 'customers, she feared, would register at the big multiple grocers with all the advantages to be had there. Instead women once the poorest amongst us remembered her help in days past and brought in their registrations by the score. . . . Soon, for the first time in more than twenty years of married life, she opened an account at the local bank.'[66] Some of their once poverty-stricken customers had prospered, too, with both husband and wife making 'big money' in the munitions factories. 'In spite of war,' claimed Roberts, 'slum grocers managed to get hold of different and better varieties of foodstuffs of a kind sold before only in middle-class shops.'[67]

On a much larger scale the Southampton firm of Lankester & Crook, with around twelve branches dealing mainly in groceries, saw their net trading profit rise from around £3,000 per annum before the war to £5,555 in the year to April 1915 and to £7,301 in 1917 before it fell back to £5,292 in 1918. Even taking into account war-time inflation that represented an advance on their pre-1914 position.[68] Significantly by the early 1920s their situation had become much less satisfactory.

For consumers, however, rationing did not always mean that supplies would be available, especially in country districts. In Suffolk a village wheelwright and blacksmith recalled bitterly: 'Rations! That was a joke. We never saw sugar at all. We used to have golden syrup in our tea and if we couldn't get that we had black treacle.'[69] A farm worker's son from Standlake in West Oxfordshire had similar memories. Once when his father came home there was no bread in the house. 'Our baker would go round the village and deliver to the farmers and the well-offs and if he had any left you may be lucky.' His father cycled over to the next village and obtained a loaf from the baker there, but the injustice of it rankled for years after. Again, despite the compulsory sugar ration from January 1918 of ½lb per person per week, labouring households in Standlake were often unable to get supplies.[70]

Cases like this, coupled with the anxieties and pressures of the war itself, led to tension between some shopkeepers and their customers. In the spring of 1918 the *Liverpool Courier* reported that the public was 'in an ugly mood. They roll up in queues to the shops where [the] necessities are to be purchased – and, with tempers frayed by long standing in the windy street, demand to be served. . . . It is no sinecure being a grocer in these strenuous days of 1918. While the crowd is being served he has to work like a galley-slave.'[71] Later in the same year the *Watford News Letter* described the grocer as having become to 'all intents and purposes . . . a Government official. . . . [H]is work has largely resolved itself into distributing a fixed quantity of food at a fixed price, and doing a settled turnover on terms which are regulated by the Government.'[72]

For tradesmen who had prided themselves on their independence and their belief in *laissez-faire* in running their businesses, such controls seemed intolerable. It is not surprising, therefore, that shortly after the Armistice on 11 November 1918 there were demands for the dismantling of the regulatory machinery. The Defence of the Realm Act, which formed the basis of the government's policy, was condemned as 'a fearsome thing' which should be laid to rest 'once and for all, so that the honest trader may go about his daily work without being haunted by the perpetual nightmare of [its] presence'.[73] However, the continuing food shortages and transport problems ensured that rationing remained for some time. It was retained for meat until November 1919, for butter until early 1920 and for sugar until November 1920.[74]

The methods adopted to control the distribution of food were among the most controversial aspects of government intervention in retailing during the war, but they were not alone. Also significant was the compulsory regulation of shop opening hours. This came into operation from the end of October 1916 in order to conserve scarce fuel supplies. Under the scheme shops had to close at 8 p.m. on four days in the week, at 9 p.m. on Saturdays and at

1 p.m. on one further day a week.[75] The move was welcomed not only by the Early Closing Association, which had agitated for compulsory closing hours for decades, and by the shop workers, but, after some initial doubts, by the proprietors themselves. In the darkened streets late-night shopping was, in any case, unattractive. In some towns traders decided to close earlier than the regulations laid down. *The Drapers' Record* reported that the principal drapers in Paignton had opted in April 1917 to close at 6 p.m., while those at Brierley Hill decided on 7 p.m. for the summer months. At Chelmsford the drapers chose to shut at 6 p.m. on three days a week, at 1 p.m. on the Wednesday half-day, at 7 p.m. on Friday and at 8 p.m. on Saturday.[76] There were many other variations on this basic theme. However, perhaps the most significant move was when some of the leading London department stores decided to close altogether on Saturdays. Among them were Debenham's and Marshall & Snelgrove. Both had been affected by falling sales during the latter part of the war, as the well-to-do reduced their purchases of luxury goods. In addition, staffs were cut by military demands, tax burdens were increased, transport was disrupted and the supply of goods was uncertain. Some firms, including Marshall & Snelgrove, ran into financial difficulties and in 1916 it and Debenham's were linked together through Textile Securities, a trust set up largely to keep Marshall's trading during the war.[77] Against this background, early in August 1917 it was decided to introduce Saturday closing for the duration of the war. In a letter in *The Drapers' Record*, Debenham's explained that they had adopted the policy to meet the request of the Coal Controller for fuel economy during the winter months.[78] Initially the firm had intended to close from 1 October, 'but recognizing that our staff, many of whom are engaged upon war work out of business hours, have been working at a great strain for a considerable time past, we feel that the rest will be a great boon to them if introduced forthwith while the weather will enable them to enjoy healthy outdoor recreation'.[79]

Although Debenham's and Marshall & Snelgrove remained separate entities during the war, they merged formally in 1919 and in the same year Debenham's negotiated the purchase of Harvey Nichols in Knightsbridge.[80] Other amalgamations in the department store world followed in the immediate aftermath of the war, with Harrods purchasing Kendal Milne of Manchester in 1919 and John Barker & Co. taking over Derry & Toms, their neighbours in High Street, Kensington, in January 1920.[81] The merger movement then, and later, was inspired partly by a desire to cut costs and introduce centralised buying, but also by a wish to counter the threat posed by some of the chain stores, such as Marks & Spencer, which were selling clothing, too.

Initially the compulsory restrictions on shop opening hours had been introduced as a temporary measure, to last only until 30 April 1917. But the fears of the Early Closing Association that they would then lapse proved groundless. They were repeatedly renewed until 1928, when compulsory closing was established on a permanent basis. From 1921 there was a minor loosening of the original arrangement, so that the sale of fruit, table waters, sweets, chocolates and other sugar confectionery, as well as ice cream, was permitted until 9.30 p.m. on weekdays and 10 p.m. on Saturdays. For other shops the limits remained as fixed at the end of October 1916.[82]

However, while the ECA and most shop staff (both proprietors and assistants) welcomed the establishment of compulsory week-day closing hours, some were unhappy about the increase in Sunday trading. In its *Annual Report* for 1916, the ECA called this one of the 'most serious problems of the day. . . . The Sunday trading, both in streets and in shops, that takes place in various parts of the metropolis, as well as in other large cities, is a disgrace.'[83] The Home Office was criticised for allowing it to develop in this way, although it was admitted that the only law against it had been passed in 1677, during the reign of Charles II, and was primarily concerned with Sunday religious observance. The Act had been amended in 1871 so that 'no prosecutions could be brought by individuals unless they had the written agreement of local police and legal authorities to do so'.[84]

Shopkeepers had mixed views on Sunday trading. Most wanted it suppressed, to avoid having to open themselves on the Sabbath because their competitors did so. But others wanted it to continue because, in the case of small businesses, they could take advantage of the closure of larger rivals, including the multiple stores, to corner all the available trade. Attitudes in official circles were ambivalent. A number clearly felt that with the early closing of shops in the evening, Sunday trading enabled working families to stock up on supplies. The ECA was 'somewhat startled' when in 1918 the Food Control Committee at Islington issued an order instructing certain shops to open on Sunday morning, 'under the plea that customers were unable to get their supplies on Saturday night'.[85] When questioned on the subject, it was said this was a temporary measure designed to overcome 'some of the difficulties arising out of the initiation of the London and Home Counties Rationing Scheme'.[86]

The Sunday trading issue continued to cause controversy to the end of the war and beyond. As late as 1938 the ECA was demanding 'a clear recital of where and . . . what may or may not be retailed on Sundays, or after the normal week-day statutory hours'.[87] For shop assistants the erosion of their limited leisure time was a serious question, no matter from what cause it arose.

THE INTER-WAR PERIOD, 1919–39

When hostilities ended in November 1918 there was a gradual adjustment of the economy – and the labour market – to peacetime conditions. In retailing this meant that as men returned from military duties many of those who had substituted for them were dismissed, particularly the womenfolk. The number of females working in grocery and provision stores and in butcher's shops, as well as in other traditional areas of male employment, dropped sharply. Even where they were retained they were demoted, so that those who had been running shops found themselves working as cashiers or as assistants. A few did continue in a managerial role, however, among them Alice Hayes, who was in charge of one of Sainsbury's Croydon grocery stores from February 1922 to May 1928.[88] More typical was the experience of Miss Pike, who had worked in the Reading Co-operative Society's dairy during the war. In August 1919 she was given notice to leave 'on account of men returning'. A fortnight later another assistant from a branch grocery store was given two weeks' notice to depart 'in consequence of Giddings' return from Military service'.[89]

Nonetheless, in retailing as a whole there was a higher proportion of women in the labour force in 1921 than had been the case in 1914. According to the population census of that year, out of 660,465 men and women employed in retail shops in England and Wales, 53 per cent were female, and although during the 1920s the recruitment of male staff increased more rapidly than did that of females, even in 1931, out of 794,939 retail sales personnel, almost 50 per cent were women and girls.[90] They were particularly important in the textiles and clothing sector, where they comprised around 74 per cent of those at work in 1931 and in sweet shops, where they numbered 91 per cent of the total. In footwear stores, too, about two-thirds of assistants were female and even in grocery and provisions they still contributed about a quarter of the sales personnel, despite the increase in men and boys recruited. (*See* Table 1.)

TABLE 1

1931 CENSUS: OCCUPATIONS IN ENGLAND AND WALES

(a) Proportion of *females among salesmen and shop assistants* in retail trade: selected sectors:

	% who are female
Grocery and provisions	24.8
Meat	5.5
Textiles and other clothing	73.8
Boots and shoes	66.2
Greengrocery	43.7
Tobacco	72.5
Sugar confectionery (sweets)	90.7
Milk and dairy products	63.1
Ironmongery	27.2

NB Among the 794,939 male and females at work in *all sectors* of retail trade as salesmen and shop assistants, *49.6% were female.*

(b) Proportion of *females among the proprietors and managers* of retail businesses, selected sectors:

	% who are female
Grocery and provisions	23.0
Meat	6.5
Textiles and other clothing	40.9
Boots and shoes	15.2
Greengrocery	18.2
Tobacco	31.5
Sugar confectionery (sweets)	61.5
Milk and dairy products	12.9
Ironmongery	13.6

NB Among the 569,127 proprietors and managers in *all sectors* of retail trade, *26.3% were female.*

Calculated from *1931 Census: England and Wales: Occupation Tables* (London, HMSO, 1934).

But in the grocery trade there remained much prejudice against women workers. In 1921, when it was proposed to set up a Trade Board to regulate the wages of grocery staff, employers opposed the governmental initiative not only because it interfered with the way they ran their businesses but on gender grounds, too. A Hartlepool tradesman objected to the fact that rates were to be fixed by age rather than experience and ability, and although women's pay was to be substantially less than that of male colleagues he believed that girls under 21 were not worth the suggested minimum of £1 16s a week: 'Half the wage suggested would be sufficient for all under twenty or twenty-one, when you consider that you have to teach them the business and lose by their errors, breakages, clumsiness and mistakes in charging, weighing, etc.' In Chester the local Grocers' Association argued it might be impossible to afford female staff at all. A resolution was passed 'protesting against the exorbitant scale suggested for female assistants'.[91] Although the Trade Board was established in 1920, the general resistance to it and the lack of urgency displayed by the Ministry of Labour itself led to its suspension in 1925 without its suggested pay scales ever being implemented.[92] Shop work remained without any legislative regulation of assistants' wages up to the Second World War.

Even in the mid-1930s, when Linda McCullough Thew obtained a post as a 14-year-old school-leaver at Hirst Co-operative grocery store in Ashington, Northumberland, she was at first cold-shouldered by her male colleagues.[93] Relations gradually thawed, but it was made clear to her that however well she did she could not expect promotion. Hence when she took classes organised by the Co-operative Society to improve her education, one of the older men bluntly declared: 'I don't care how many exams you sit, or how many you're top of, you'll never be anything more than what you are now – a counter-hand.'[94] Nevertheless, she came to enjoy the work and her contact with the public. 'There was a fellowship at the counters even when we were at our busiest. . . .' A great deal of friendly goodwill existed between staff and customers, nearly all of whom were regulars.[95]

That goodwill manifested itself on Thursday mornings when customers who were 'on relief' because of unemployment came to the shop with their official relief notes. It was a demoralising experience, for they were restricted to the 'necessities of life', such as flour, margarine, sugar, tea corned beef and the like, all of the cheapest quality. They were allowed no luxuries. But many of the assistants were lenient. Among the most generous was a counter-hand named Jack who 'never refused to give an ounce of tobacco or a packet of Woodbines, putting these commodities down as blue mottled soap or blacking. Other goods disguised as Zebo or Brasso were tinned pineapple chunks and our cheapest mixed-fruit jam.' Cleaning products like Brasso were regarded by officialdom as 'necessities' for the conscientious housewife.[96]

However, if women's role as shop assistants increased during the inter-war years, their situation as regards shop ownership and management was less satisfactory. Even in 1931 only just over a quarter of all retail shops were owned by women, with their biggest contribution being in respect of sweet shops and drapery stores of one kind or another. (*See* Table 1.) In particular, new kinds of female-owned fashion shops increased, such as those specialising in lingerie or hosiery and knitwear. The increasing availability of branded goods helped these small retailers, since customers knew that they could obtain the same products from a nearby small outlet as they could from the large stores in the centre of town. Credit and assistance from wholesalers were easy to obtain in the early stages, and the personal service provided by such shops was attractive to customers. These little outlets were known in the trade as 'Madam shops', and often only one person would be serving. But 'the windows were usually well dressed and, more and more in this trade, display was becoming an important factor in success.'[97] A few members of the social elite also took up this kind of minor retailing as a way of earning pin-money. Poppy Baring, a close friend of Prince George, owned a dress shop named 'Poppy', while Barbara Cartland had a brief but unsuccessful career running a hat shop before she turned to writing.[98]

Alongside these, as unemployment rose during the inter-war years in the country generally, those wishing to work but unable to find anyone to employ them turned to 'running a shop', if they had sufficient savings or could obtain a bank loan. It gave a sense of independence, although it could lead to disaster for the inexperienced. Some were able to open small shops on the new housing estates which were being built on the fringes of towns, and with a fair prospect of success.[99]

In the economic depression of the early 1930s, however, even those who had been in business some years found themselves under pressure. The Southampton grocers Lankester & Crook, founded in mid-Victorian times, began to make a net trading loss in 1932–3. They decided that stringent cutbacks were necessary. This meant closing the small drapery attached to one branch store, with the dismissal of the male assistant and a transfer for the female member of staff. That was only the start. Out of twenty-nine departments within the various stores, three managers, eight male assistants, two errand boys and three female clerks lost their jobs. A further twelve managers had pay cuts, some of them substantial. The manager of Bitterne ironmongery department, for example, had his salary cut from £3 3s 3d a week to £2 10s, plus commission if he increased sales, while at Hedge End the manager of the grocery had his weekly income reduced from £3 15s to £3 10s. But the £3 10s now included the value of the house which was provided and this was put at £1 a week, so his cash earnings amounted to only £2 10s.[100] These changes brought a brief respite and by 1935 the firm was once more making a trading profit, but in 1936 it was again in the red. Bank debt also rose. However, as early as 1930, the firm had blamed its falling turnover not only on the general drop in prices but on the improved bus connections between the surrounding suburbs and villages and Southampton. This encouraged customers to shop in the centre of town.

Similar problems were encountered at a suburban branch of the Oxford department store, F. Cape & Co. In 1933 the management warned one of their senior female members of staff that because of the large decline in trade there would have to be either dismissals or reductions in salary. In her case a reduction of £20 a year in pay was suggested; for a male colleague a cut of £10 per annum was proposed and for a junior female of £5 a year. In a fourth case the girl concerned was dismissed, although she was assured that if a suitable vacancy occurred at the firm's main Oxford store, 'we shall be pleased to give you a chance. . . . We are bound to reduce staff a little at Cowley Road, as every one comes down to the City to shop these days.'[101]

Loss of employment was particularly serious for older workers, at a time when shopkeepers were seeking to reduce labour costs by recruiting large numbers of young people on low wages. Already in 1921 around one in three of all shop assistants in England and Wales was under 20.[102] A decade later more than two in five were under 21, with a further one-fifth aged between 21 and 24 inclusive. According to one estimate, in 1931 out of all male assistants aged from 45 to 54, around one in five or one in six was unemployed in the grocery, butchery and footwear trades.[103] Hence there was a note of desperation in some of the advertisements inserted by those looking for fresh employment. These included the 'Successful Manager, now disengaged', who was seeking a new post in *The Grocer* of 14 March 1931: 'Expert window-dresser and real business-getter. Life experience in all branches. Highest credentials. Distance no object.'

But if two of the major changes affecting those working behind the counter in the 1920s and 1930s were the increasing employment of women and a growing recruitment of young people, a third was the transformation in the structure of retailing itself. This included an expansion of the multiple chain stores, many of them in keen competition with one another, especially as prices began to fall from 1921 onwards. Between 1920 and 1922 the average retail price of food fell by almost a third, and of clothing and household durable goods by more than that amount over the same period.

By the early 1930s food prices were less than half their 1920 level and the fall in clothing and household durable prices was greater still.[104] For those in employment, this meant a rise in living standards and the opportunity to buy new appliances like radios, gramophones, vacuum cleaners and other electrical products which were coming on to the market. These were stocked not only by small specialist traders but by new multiple stores such as Currys, which was Britain's leading retailer of bicycles, gramophones, wirelesses and general electrical goods in the 1930s. A large proportion of its trade during the mid- to late years of that decade was conducted on hire purchase.[105]

However, the real importance of the expansion in the multiple stores was apparent in the grocery trade. They and the still buoyant co-operative movement created serious problems for many independent grocers. This is shown by the fact that in 1920 the co-operative societies were estimated to have between 18 and 20.5 per cent of total retail sales in groceries and provisions, while the multiples took between 13 and 16 per cent of the total. This left 'other retailers', mostly the independent grocers, with between 63.5 and 69 per cent of the market. By 1939 the position had been transformed. The co-operative societies had consolidated their position, particularly in the north of England, and now took between 22 per cent and 24 per cent of total trade, while the multiples had risen sharply to challenge them, with 22 to 25 per cent of total trade. That left the 'others' with little more than half the total market, at 51 to 56 per cent of sales.[106] After the Second World War their decline continued.

These larger groupings benefited from bulk buying, centralised distribution and the exertion of pressure on their shop managers and assistants to achieve greater efficiency. Indeed, as *Grocery* magazine commented in 1921, 'there is a widely-noticed disposition to carry on business with smaller staffs. In other words, as one way of reducing costs, some traders are calling for more work from fewer men.'[107] In 1921 the newly established *Home and Colonial Magazine* listed the qualifications considered necessary in a branch manager:

> Salesmanship
> Pay equal attention to all
> Be patient with new customers
> Remember customers' names
> Provide quick and cheerful service
> Parcel goods neatly
> Learn to look at things from the customer's point of view.[108]

In a later edition the magazine advised managers to make allowance for the 'faults, foibles and frailties' of their clients: 'let the customer, if he or she is so minded, score off you. Submit . . . to the mild asperity of his or her remarks, and always remember that a soft answer does really and truly turn away wrath. It is an axiom in business that "the customer is always right".'[109]

The *Home and Colonial Magazine* was launched in November 1920 with the aim of linking 'in bonds of mutual interest the thousands connected with the organisation'. In addition to the exhortations to improve efficiency, achieve good window displays and take greater care in dealing with customers, like many other in-store journals of the inter-war period, it included details of the doings of individual staff members, accounts of staff outings and articles of general interest.

But for the staff, and especially the managers, the growing competitiveness of the grocery trade meant longer hours at work. Although the shop closure legislation ensured that stores were shut at the appropriate time, there was much work carried out after hours. This included frequent stocktaking, the weighing of goods and the scrubbing of counters. According to the Select Committee on Shop Assistants, which reported in the early 1930s, that could amount to several hours of unpaid overtime each week.[110] In addition, managers of the multiple shops were often expected to eat their meals on the premises. One man said 'he took his dinner and tea behind the biscuit case, so that he could keep an eye on the shop'.[111] In smaller stores assistants sometimes ate the food they brought from home crouching behind the counter, or 'at a shelf in a corner of a dark stock-room'. Although they had a 45-minute break at midday, it was often interrupted to serve customers.

To meet these problems in 1934 a new Shops Act laid down that proper facilities were to be provided for staff taking meals on the premises. Sanitary facilities were also to be improved, along with lighting and ventilation, where these were deficient, and shopkeepers were to ensure that female assistants used the seats provided for them when they were not serving. For young workers under 18, the Act laid down that from the beginning of 1937 they were to be employed about a shop for no more than 48 hours a week, save that those between 16 and 18 might be asked to work overtime for up to a maximum of 50 hours a year.[112] No limit was placed on the working hours of those aged 18 or above, despite the efforts of trade unions and others to secure a statutory 48-hour working week for them. Only in co-operative shops was 48 hours the norm during the inter-war years.

The question of the length of the working week was made more acute by some of the changes in the legislation covering shop opening hours, notably the fact that shops selling table waters, sweets, chocolates and ice cream could from 1921 onwards stay open, if they wished, until 9.30 p.m. on weekdays and 10 p.m. on Saturdays, instead of the usual limits of 8 p.m. and

9 p.m. respectively. In addition, holiday resorts could substitute the later closing hours in respect of all shops for up to four months in the year, if the local authority agreed. The only condition was that assistants should be given additional holidays with pay, or extra wages in lieu should they cease to work at the shop before the four months had elapsed. Shops serving freshly cooked provisions or meals to be eaten off the premises could stay open later as well. Inevitably these changes led some shopkeepers to trade as long as the law allowed. The Select Committee on Shop Assistants referred particularly to the 'excessive hours' worked in the ice-cream business. It quoted the case of a young woman in an ice-cream and confectioner's shop in South Shields who worked 73 hours a week, exclusive of meals. She 'was very rarely able to leave the shop until 12 midnight, and spoke of the dark and lonely walk home when the tram service had ceased. She left because her health began to be impaired by the strain.' Similarly at a fish shop in Great Yarmouth, where the normal hours of employment were 54½ per week, during the holiday season these rose to 96. Fresh fish was sold in the morning and afternoon, there was 'a large dispatch trade in boaters . . . and fried fish was sold at night. The same assistants were employed throughout.'[113]

In other cases, even where there was no legal exemption, shopkeepers might choose to stay open beyond the official closing time, thereby risking prosecution, or they simply flouted the Sunday trading laws. In their defiance they sometimes received tacit encouragement from magistrates. In 1931 the Early Closing Association reported the comments of a Woolwich magistrate on the shop hours legislation: 'What lunatics there are in the world! . . . It makes me tired to have to administer stupid, idiotic laws of this description. It is these fatuous fools who seized upon the War to put across the people restrictions of all kinds.'[114] In Hull, where there was much Sunday trading in the 1920s and early 1930s, it was stated that over 20,000 summonses were issued annually, the 5s fines imposed by the courts clearly being no deterrent.[115]

In 1936 the Sunday Trading Restriction Act was passed requiring shops to close on the Sabbath, 'subject to a number of exceptions designed to meet the reasonable needs of the public'. The exemptions covered shops selling table waters, sweets, chocolates, ice-cream, newspapers, flowers, fruit and vegetables, as well as cooked meals and milk. Holiday resorts could also escape the restrictions for up to eighteen Sundays in the year, while in London traditional Sunday street markets were excluded from the legislation. The Act came into operation on 1 May 1937 and despite its obvious loopholes it was welcomed by the Early Closing Association as benefiting shop assistants, some of whom 'had not known what it was to enjoy a free Sunday for as long as 50 years'.[116]

Meanwhile, the multiple chain stores were expanding their outlets not only in the grocery trade, but in footwear, clothing and chemists' goods. In women's fashions firms like Marks & Spencer and C & A Modes began to challenge the traditional dominance of the old-style drapery shops and department stores. Variety stores such as Woolworths also grew, and Walter Greenhalgh, who worked for a branch of Woolworths in Manchester during the 1930s, described the daily routine of the female assistants as 'real slave work', particularly on Saturdays. They had to be down on their counters when the bell rang at 8.30 a.m. and the doors opened. The shop stayed open until 9 p.m. and at 9.15 p.m. a bell would ring and the doors would be shut. At 9.30 p.m. the bell rang again and the tills would close:

> then you waited until everybody had gone out . . . [T]he girls had to fill their counters again ready for Monday morning. In the meantime, we . . . the . . . male staff, we had to clean the floors. . . . But this meant that it was around half-past ten, eleven, twelve before you got out, depending upon how much work you'd done.[117]

Independent traders responded to the challenge of competition from the multiple stores and the co-operative societies by emphasising the superior service they offered and the high-quality assistants they employed. Smith's of Lancaster, for example, stressed their careful staff selection and the good training they offered. According to Francis Smith, who ran the business in the later 1930s, it was common for trainees, when they had completed their four-year apprenticeship, to go away 'for a year or more to a leading grocery house in another town . . . to learn other methods, broaden their outlook generally and gain valuable experience of trade. Then, if they wished to return to their own town . . . and they usually do – we take them on as assistants, promoting them according to their character and ability.' Such assistants often found their jobs becoming more specialised, so that one member of staff would spend most of his working life on the cheese counter, and another would concentrate on bacon.[118] In this way they could give expert advice to customers. Smith's also offered an extensive delivery service to their clientele, and this was improved in the 1930s by the use of motor transport. Nonetheless, as profit margins were eroded, assistants' pay was cut, so that an experienced counter-hand, who had earned £3 3s to £3 18s in 1925 was receiving only £2 18s to £3 8s a week a decade later, while in the case of a senior or charge counter-hand, the decline was from £4 8s a week in 1925 to £3 18s in the mid-1930s. For female staff, even those employed full time, pay was at an hourly rate only, so that their take-home earnings varied from week to week.[119]

But at least Smith's survived. Many independent traders went under. One assistant, who had worked for a Southampton grocer since around 1914, when he began as a 14-year-old errand boy, lost his employment in about 1934, when the grocer had to cut his staff because he 'couldn't afford' to keep them all on: 'I got a wonderful . . . reference.' This man was on the 'dole' for about three weeks and then went to work for another grocer, whose business he and his wife eventually took over. But soon after he left, the first employer went out of business: 'He was unable to keep up with the times.'[120]

Price-cutting was condemned for undermining trade and retailers who could not sell at cut prices without losing money were advised by *Grocery* to 'drop the slaughtered lines altogether'.[121] Among the price-cutters was Jack Cohen, who spent his demobilisation gratuity of £30 in 1919 on purchasing cheap groceries. He loaded these on a barrow and took a pitch in Well Street market in London. It proved a great success and within months he was 'carting his stall between two or three markets a day, drawing crowds of bargain-hunting headscarved housewives with his entertaining patter and attractive offers'.[122] In a few years he was running a network of barrows throughout the street markets of north and east London. From these, in the early 1930s he began to build up a chain of small shops, and these had reached around a hundred by 1938. The Tesco grocery business was under way. But, as Judi Bevan points out, at a time of high unemployment 'Tesco's pile-it-high, sell-it-cheap philosophy was perfect . . . Cohen loved his soubriquet "the housewife's friend".'[123] Such an approach was anathema to established grocers, who prided themselves on their high-quality service and well-displayed merchandise.

Structural changes also occurred among the department stores during these years as they responded to the challenge of the multiples, for instance in women's clothing, by amalgamating into larger groupings to take advantage of centralised buying policies and other economies of scale.[124] The stores also began to offer a wider range of customer services, with orchestras and musical trios in their restaurants and tea-rooms and daily mannequin displays to show off the latest fashions. Among the innovators was the firm of Bentall's of Kingston, one of whose early slogans was: 'Why go to the West End – when there's Bentall's of Kingston.' In the early 1930s its twice daily mannequin displays drew crowds of over 500, and its 'Bonny Baby' competition attracted over 3,000 entries. Other events included visits by sports personalities, marionette displays and fun for the children at Christmas, with an annual toy fair and an in-store circus.[125]

Such efforts to drum up business were far removed from the genteel atmosphere at Plummer Roddis, where Cicely Colyer served her apprenticeship in their Folkestone store between 1917 and 1920. She joined at the age of 14, with her family paying a premium of £25. She herself received 1s a week during the apprenticeship, and at the end of her training was offered a post at a salary of £30 per annum as a showroom assistant.[126] But she decided to take a similar position in another store for twice that amount. 'The apprenticeship was hard, but something of which I was later very proud,' she recalled more than half a century later. 'Today, I still know every kind of material, all the types of cloth, fitting, how to fold clothes, preparation of stock, and matters ranging from buying to display duties.' With this background, she became a buyer when she was about 20, visiting London and the major fashion shows to keep abreast of the latest trends. Orders were placed with the travellers who came to the shop but also by personal visits to the major wholesale houses. 'The gowns were simply stunning,' declared Cicely of her experiences as a buyer in the 1920s. 'We had to be careful not to be carried away by the splendour of the garments and the surroundings. The buyer had a budget.'[127]

To have worked in a high-class establishment like Plummer Roddis helped assistants when they wanted to move to other stores, especially during the difficult inter-war years. According to a former employee, much the same was true of Selfridges. 'I was at Selfridges', he declared, and that was always 'an open sesame to other similar jobs even in the hardest of times'.[128]

A girl who went to work in a Southampton department store in 1937 was attracted by the glamour of the job. She was apprenticed at 15 in what she called 'a beautiful shop'. 'I enjoyed selling things but because you were an apprentice you didn't do much of that . . . you spent your time in the stock room packing parcels and being shouted at by the buyer.' However, she much enjoyed a spell in the glove department: 'You had to call people Madam . . . I remember . . . these beautiful suede gloves and [the customers] sat at the counter and you smoothed the gloves on for them.' One of the highlights of her career came when at the age of 15½ she was asked to spend a week modelling clothes for young people which had been imported from the United States of America. The mannequin parade was held in the restaurant while music played. Her proud relatives came to see her parade slowly round the room. She also recalled the uniform the female staff wore. 'We had dark green dresses. They had three styles and you could choose your style and they made it for you. Some of the sales people were very glamorous.'[129]

Many department stores offered welfare facilities and benefits to staff, including discounts on purchases. Debenham's in 1921 pioneered a low-cost dental service for employees, while a school for younger staff, approved by the London County Council, was also set up. In the 1920s, too, Bentall's in

Kingston provided employees with a clinic, pensions and preferential savings schemes. 'The matron of the clinic . . . was provided with a car to visit sick members of staff, who also received food parcels and newlaid eggs from the firm.'[130] Elsewhere sports facilities were improved and although living in was much reduced, some of the stores continued to run hostels where assistants could lodge if they so desired.[131] At Maples, indeed, living in remained obligatory for apprentices during these years.

But working conditions depended very much on the attitude of individual managements and department store life had its darker side, especially at the 'popular' end of the trade. This included keeping full-time staff to a minimum and recruiting part-time workers to fill in during the busy times. In 1931 an executive of Lewis's store in Liverpool declared that if they had staffed their shops on the basis of peak demand, there would have been large numbers of assistants 'doing nothing' for part of the day. They overcame this 'by taking in temporary staff, basing the normal staff on the mean between the requirements of the very slack and the very busy period'. During the 'slack period' between 9 a.m. and 12 noon an assistant could 'take trouble and make each sale really a work of art'. But when there were people waiting it was 'a question of serving the customer as quickly as possible'.[132] On Merseyside generally, indeed, by the early 1930s there was said to be 'considerable . . . employment of part-time labour on busy days, not only in large stores but even in shops engaging only a few assistants'. One estimate put the total of shop assistants employed on this part-time basis in drapery and outfitting shops in Liverpool alone at around 1,500. One large firm engaged 100 or more extra girls every Thursday and Saturday and a smaller number on Mondays. Some were former employees of the firm who had perhaps married, but others were recruited through the Employment Exchange from sales staff in receipt of unemployment benefit. If they were satisfactory they would be sent to the same firm on one or two days a week, working from about midday to 6.30 p.m. or 8 p.m. on Saturdays. For this they received 4s 3d and two meals each day. If a girl worked for a single day only, apart from meals she received a mere 9d in extra cash because 1s was deducted from the 4s 3d as her national insurance contribution and a further 2s 6d a day was taken from her unemployment benefit of 15s a week for each day she worked. Yet to refuse would have meant the stopping of her benefit altogether. A further inducement to work was that competent girls 'always stood a chance of getting on the permanent staff'.[133]

Elsewhere, as with Cape's in Oxford, staff numbers fluctuated on a seasonal basis. The wages books show that, for example, in July 1935 ninety-one assistants were working at the firm's three stores, and the month's wages bill totalled £714 10s 4d. But as trade fell away in August, short-time working and dismissals led to just sixty assistants being at work, while the wages bill shrank to £513 13s 8d. In December, as business picked up for Christmas, the number of staff employed increased to eighty-five, with a total salary payment of £697 3s 5d.[134] The wages books also show the wide pay differentials among the staff, so that while senior male personnel were earning £50 and £37 18s 4d a month in, for example, August 1935, thirty-six of the forty-seven more junior assistants employed at the firm's main store in central Oxford obtained less than £10 a month. Of eight members of staff working at the Cowley Road branch, one earned between £10 and £15 a month, two between £5 and £10 a month, and the remaining five less than £5 a month.

In these circumstances it is not surprising that the shop workers' trade unions, outside the ranks of the co-operative societies, fared badly. In 1919 the National Amalgamated Union of Shop Assistants, Warehousemen and Clerks reached a peak membership of 125,000 and in that year, after negotiations for improved pay had failed, they backed a strike by assistants at the Army and Navy Stores in London. Within a short period the directors agreed to meet the union's representatives and a satisfactory agreement was reached, including the granting of trade union recognition.[135] Philip Hoffman, who was involved in the discussions, claimed that the strike had 'a beneficial effect upon those in retail trade all over the country'. Everywhere wage increases were reported, to match the sharp rise in prices during the war and its immediate aftermath.

However, then came a bitter dispute at the John Lewis store in Oxford Street early in 1920, as staff sought improved pay and conditions. This led to around 400 members of staff going on strike in April. Assistants from some of the other big stores, such as Harrods and the Army and Navy Stores, contributed to the strike fund. But a particular difficulty was finding lodgings for the 200 girl strikers who had lived in at the firm's hostels and now had to move out. As the strike dragged on, Lewis's refused to make any concessions and after six weeks it was called off, with large numbers of the female staff involved taking posts with the Kensington High Street stores where attitudes were less rigid.[136]

By this time conditions within the economy generally were deteriorating, as the brief postwar boom petered out. Unemployment rose, takings in the shops fell and staff wage cuts had to be accepted. By 1921, writes Hoffman, 'short time was laying a paralysing hand upon employment in retail distribution'.[137] As staff numbers were cut in many firms, especially among older, more highly paid assistants, and in the face of employer hostility to unionism, National Union membership plummeted, dropping to 65,512 in 1923 and 48,539 in 1935.[138] The union's legal department was heavily involved in trying to protect members who had been dismissed and, in the case of managers, seeking to circumvent radius agreements limiting the area where they might gain fresh employment. Among the most fraught cases, however, were those where shop assistants who had lost their jobs were threatened with the withdrawal of unemployment benefit if they refused to take other work offered to them, perhaps as a domestic servant. The union helped with their appeals to the relevant tribunals, as with one female member offered posts as a maid at 9s and 12s a week and whose benefit had been suspended because she had refused them. At the appeal it was stated that by taking such a position she would seriously prejudice her chance of getting employment again in her proper occupation of a shop assistant. She had already worked in retailing for fifteen years and in this case, as in many similar ones the union took up, the appeal succeeded.[139]

Not until the later 1930s did union membership begin to recover, reaching 80,272 in 1938. At the same time there was a slow improvement in the pay and conditions of shop staff, with successful pay negotiations entered into between union officials and representatives of some of the multiple chains and with a few of the large department stores, like Lewis's Ltd of Liverpool. The firm had branches in Manchester, Birmingham, Leeds, Leicester and Glasgow, too.[140]

Despite these developments most retail workers chose to remain outside the union movement altogether. Only in the case of co-operative stores was this not the case. In 1921 the Amalgamated Union of Co-operative Employees merged with a warehousemen's union to form the National Union of Distributive and Allied Workers (NUDAW) and from 1918 the movement renewed its campaign for there to be compulsory trade union membership in retail societies. By 1938 almost 500 societies had accepted that position.[141] Among them was the Reading Co-operative Society, which as early as August 1931 made it clear that even casual workers must join a union after they had been in the society's employ for a month.[142] Unlike in most other retail businesses, too, a 48-hour working week was widespread in co-op shops.

For most shop workers, though, be they proprietors or employees, business prospects remained uncertain even in 1939. Jean Beauchamp, writing two years earlier, had summarised the problems, at least as regards assistants, when she declared: 'perhaps the worst feature of employment in the distributive trades is its insecurity. It is becoming more and more a blind alley occupation, and the older workers live in constant fear of dismissal in favour of cheap juvenile labour. Forty-two per cent of those employed as shop assistants are under 21 years of age, and there are more insured workers aged 14 to 15 employed in the distributive trade than there are in any other eight trades or industries taken together.'[143]

Chapter 8

FROM THE SECOND WORLD WAR TO THE 'SWINGING SIXTIES'

War brought new pressures on traders' attempts to survive shortage and bomb damage. . . . [The] shops had to switch to controlled competition, regulations, rationing and even physical devastation. . . . The immediate years of peace were to see store managers and their buyers engaged in a mad scramble to find stocks of goods for people who felt an urge to spend.
Maurice Corina, *Fine Silks and Oak Counters. Debenhams 1778–1978*
(London, 1978), pp. 134 and 136.

THE IMPACT OF THE SECOND WORLD WAR

T he shortage of stock, scarcity of labour and stringent state regulation which had affected retailers during the First World War were repeated and intensified in the Second. There were even echoes of the earlier xenophobia which had led to attacks on shops owned by enemy aliens in 1915. This time the victims were Italians and the hostility they experienced in June 1940 followed the announcement by Benito Mussolini, the Italian dictator, that he was taking his country to war on the side of Germany. In cities like Liverpool and Edinburgh there were violent outbreaks which caused serious damage to property, while at Greenock all of the seventeen Italian shops were ruined. Aurelia Raffo, who owned a small general store in Liverpool, was one victim. 'My windows were going and there was a crowd outside, the police were there but there was nothing they could do. . . . The shop was smashed up, but many Italian shops were smashed.' In Newport, Cardiff and Swansea in South Wales, where there were also sizeable numbers of Italians living, the police intervened with baton charges. At one Italian shop in Swansea a crowd of around 200 gathered, windows were broken and there was some looting.[1] Mrs Viccari of Tonypandy even placed an advertisement in the *Free Press and Rhondda Leader* informing the public that as the owner of the 'Cosy Corner Cafe . . . she was a BRITISH SUBJECT' and had brothers serving in the British armed forces.[2]

However, the disturbances were never on the scale of those experienced in the First World War. This was partly because most Italian males were quickly interned – though a number were soon released – and partly because as owners of ice-cream parlours and general stores they were well integrated into the communities in which they lived.

But these matters apart, for most shopkeepers there were many other worries, as government regulation of their businesses was not only exercised at an earlier stage than in the previous conflict but proved to be more far reaching. Clothing and furniture were controlled as well as food, and the use of raw materials was closely monitored. Ration books were printed even before the outbreak of hostilities and plans were drawn up for food allocation which took account of current research into nutrition.[3] Small retailers soon complained that they were not allotted their fair share of supplies by manufacturers and wholesalers. As early as February 1940 an Essex draper claimed that while he could not obtain stockings, they were freely available at the local Woolworths. Another man added sourly that whatever the supply difficulties, there would be no shortage 'at the mammoth stores. Their grip on trade is apparently not realised by most people, but one . . . day we shall wake up to the fact that they are the real bosses of this country.'[4] About a year later an MP suggested that as many elderly people carrying on business as small shopkeepers were 'under-employed' because 'of the curtailment of supplies', 'the goods now being sold by Woolworth's, Marks & Spencer and similar stores' should be diverted to them. This would release numbers of young women 'well suited . . . for war work', and make available large open ground-floor premises for industrial purposes or storage. The President of the Board of Trade responded coldly that he did not think this would be 'in the public interest'.[5] But arguments about the supply problems of small retailers were to be articulated on many occasions during the war.[6]

When hostilities broke out on 3 September 1939 some larger shops were commandeered by the government for military or other official purposes, so that much of the Kendal Milne department store in Manchester was requisitioned for the civil service, although drapery and fashion departments still functioned on two floors, and air-raid shelters were established in the basement.[7] At Great Yarmouth another department store, Arnolds, had its basement converted into an emergency hospital while trading continued on the ground floor.[8] As early as 1939 many air-raid shelters were set up within stores for the protection of staff and customers, with basements rewalled and reinforced with steel supports. In them were stored first-aid equipment, emergency food supplies, containers of water, chemical closets, axes, torches and accumulators to supply emergency lighting.[9] Even where less ambitious arrangements were made, as at Selfridges, store basements were used as impromptu shelters.[10]

Like many other workers, Barbara Blair, who was employed at Shinners' department store in Sutton, had to do fire watching, looking out for incendiary bombs. At first this was a voluntary duty but under the 1941 Fire Prevention (Business Premises) Order it became compulsory, with agreements negotiated on pay and conditions for this extra responsibility. When air raids occurred in business hours, the Shinners' staff went down to the carpet department in the basement but, remembered Barbara, 'we were not allowed to sit and do nothing; we had knitting needles and we had to sit and knit squares!'[11]

The major chain stores like Marks & Spencer had some premises requisitioned, too, and by the outbreak of war had already arranged for over a quarter of their 20,000 staff to receive training in civil defence duties.[12] When bombing began in earnest, many of the company's shops were damaged. By 1945 over 100 of its 234 stores had suffered in some way, while 16 had been destroyed.[13] Because of government restrictions on the use of building materials, work to make good these losses was delayed until 1951 and was not completed until 1957.

Other firms had similar experiences, with seven of the Debenham group's department stores completely destroyed by enemy action between 1940 and 1942, and a further two badly damaged. Many lost part of their premises, while windows were shattered or blown in and plaster brought down, thereby damaging the stock.[14]

Cecilia Coomber described how some employees in these large shops reacted when there was an air raid. On a Saturday afternoon in 1942 the doors of the store where she worked were open for shoppers when, without warning, there was

a tip and run raid. My customers and I dropped behind a counter in a tangle of arms and legs when a bomb shook the foundations, hurling merchandise and plaster in all directions. After what seemed ages, it was all over. I looked round, no-one was hurt . . . I got to my feet and peered through a cloud of dust mingled with the . . . smell of explosive. I looked towards the open door, and heard the steady clopping of footsteps approaching along the arcade to the store entrance. The customer entered, stepped over a mound of debris, spotted me behind the haberdashery counter, and said: 'Good afternoon, may I have two yards of white baby ribbon please.'[15]

Mrs Coomber did not give her reply.

Nor was it only large businesses that were affected. In November 1940 and January 1941 air raids destroyed shops at Redcliffe Hill, Bristol. On the first occasion an incendiary landed at the back of a shop selling faggots, killing the elderly assistant. She had worked there for years and when the shopkeeper was a baby she had wheeled him about. Now he had to recover her body from the rubble. The second time a greengrocery shop was destroyed, except for two walls of a passageway. In order to continue trading, the proprietor rigged up a stall in the space between the two walls but after a time this became too dangerous and had to be demolished. By Christmas 1941 all the small shops in that area had become little more than bare skeletons.[16]

Where possible, those who were bombed out moved to new premises, although for some this proved impossible and they simply went out of business. Sometimes staff arrived for work only to find they must clear up a bomb-damaged shop before trading could continue. If conditions were too bad, they would go away until new arrangements could be made or they had to look for a fresh job.

These physical hardships and hazards apart, retailers also had to cope with additional tax burdens, including purchase tax, introduced in October 1940, and an excess profits tax, designed to prevent businesses from cashing in on the war-time shortages. For those in the grocery trade it was necessary to come to terms with the new rationing scheme, which was introduced early in January 1940. Initially it covered bacon, ham, butter and sugar, with the weekly allowance per person set at 4oz for bacon, ham and butter and 12oz for sugar.[17] Soon, however, the bacon and butter rations were increased to 8oz and over the next eighteen months other goods began to be included, such as cheese, preserves, eggs and tea. Butcher's meat was rationed, too, and there was a constant tinkering with the quantities provided, to take account of fluctuating supplies. Thus on 11 June 1941 *The Times* reported that the monthly ration of jam, marmalade, syrup or treacle was to be reduced to a maximum of ½lb per person. Anyone who had already exceeded that amount in June would have it deducted from their July allocation. Three days later the same newspaper noted that the basic domestic cheese ration of 1oz per person per week was to be raised to 2oz from 30 June, while on the same date the 8oz fat ration was to include only 2oz of butter, with the rest made up by margarine and cooking fat. Prior to that date the butter allowance had been 4oz[18] Against this background in January 1942 a shopkeeper, tongue in cheek, submitted a rhyme to the trade journal *The Grocer*, to help assistants make sure they had included all the basic items in a person's weekly ration:[19]

Sugar and tea, butter and cheese,
Margarine, fat and bacon,
Preserves and egg (for this they beg),
Make up the customer's ration.

To keep track of the changes and ensure that the exact weight was supplied and the correct price charged proved a constant worry for retailers. One grocer complained that with a 4oz ration for butter, which had a controlled price of 1s 7d a pound, they would need 'a good supply of farthings, and, with a family of five or seven to be served . . . we shall need to be careful to avoid mistakes'.[20] A Birmingham shopkeeper grumbled that of the thirty cash tills in use in his business 'none . . . registered farthings'.[21]

To add to the burden, the coupons for rationed goods had to be cut out from the individual books. On a national basis this led to what one manager called 'a 270,000,000 coupons Blitzkrieg'.[22] A Southampton grocery assistant recalled taking coupons home to count them – a tedious task for which he received no extra pay:

We used to count the butter coupons and the tea coupons with a pin cuz they were so small . . . I 'ad a box on the counter, which I made, cut little slots in it, and marked tea, sugar, whatever . . . put the coupon in it an' we 'ad to count through 'em so that we 'ad enough sugar next time they came round [with deliveries].[23]

Sometimes the children of the family helped, as with the Lancaster grocers T.D. Smith. Although the firm had a large office staff, young Ian Smith recalled his father bringing home boxes of coupons, with as many as 5,000 or 6,000 to be counted in a single evening. According to Ian, his mother stuck rigidly to her rations as a matter of principle, 'never having an egg or ounce of butter' more than the family was entitled to. However, his father occasionally brought an extra pound of butter or sugar, perhaps to be used to bake cakes for friends or for a special occasion.[24]

In January 1941 the government acknowledged the time-consuming nature of this coupon-cutting exercise and allowed the coupons to be cancelled by a stamp or indelible pencil.[25] But the respite was brief, for with the coming of a new rationing scheme for other commodities later in the year the process of coupon-cutting and counting was resumed. Kathleen Wilson, who worked at one of the International Tea Company's shops in Brighton, recalled helping the manageress to count them on Saturday afternoons. 'This was about one of the only times we could sit down.'[26]

Small specialist food retailers suffered as a result of rationing since most consumers chose to register with dealers who carried a full range of groceries and provisions, in the hope they would be able to buy from them some of the non-rationed goods in short supply. The co-operative stores proved particularly popular, with about a quarter of all registered persons going to them for basic rations. Many found the co-op dividend an added attraction, for with controlled uniform prices in both private and co-operative shops, the gain to the customer of the dividend on purchases was clearly evident.[27] Some specialists survived by extending their range, but often the small size of their shops, the restricted supplies and their lack of pre-war contracts with suppliers drove them out of business. Government regulations contributed to this. According to James Jefferys, in 1940 there were 170,000 small-scale retailers with registered customers for the sale of sugar. A year later the Ministry of Food introduced a minimum registration rule requiring them to have at least twenty-five registered customers, and some could not meet that target. By the end of 1941 the number of small retailers with customers registered for sugar had fallen to 133,000. As Jefferys comments, some disappeared as a result of bombing or staff shortage, but a number of small dealers in groceries before the Second World War must have had a very limited turnover indeed.[28]

The difficulties associated with food rationing were compounded by a fall in the number of experienced shop workers, since retail distribution was not a reserved occupation. It employed large numbers of young people, who were particularly likely to be moved to war production or military service through scheduled conscription. By June 1943 J.R. Leslie MP, a former general secretary of the Shop Assistants' Union, could claim that the sector had 'contributed more men to the Armed Forces than any other occupation' in the country.[29] Hence out of just under 10,000 male staff employed by the three main companies of the Allied Suppliers Group – a group which included Home and Colonial, Maypole Dairy, Lipton's, Meadow Dairy and Pearks – only 1,585 were left in 1944. Nor were female staff exempt, since 2,000 of them had left the group to join the services.[30]

Some of those joining up were volunteers, perhaps having been, as in the case of staff at Debenham's and Marks & Spencer, members of the Territorial Army before the war. Marks & Spencer encouraged staff to join the Territorials by releasing them for training on full pay, in addition to their annual holidays. By May 1940, out of 2,000 male employees, 550 were already in the armed forces and at the end of the war that figure had risen to 1,500. Of the female staff around 800 joined the armed forces or another war service, and others carried out voluntary duties after working hours.[31]

Many co-operative societies and private firms, including Marks & Spencer, also paid extra allowances to employees on war service, to bring their military pay up to something like their normal civilian wages.

When the war started, reserved status was promised to shop managers and buyers above a certain age (30 in the case of food shops and 35 for other retail establishments). But with war demands intensifying, these concessions were largely withdrawn. Already by the autumn of 1941 the reserved age of food shop managers had been raised to 35 years, and managers in non-food trades had entirely lost their special status.[32]

On a national basis the compulsory registration of females aged 19 to 40 began in March 1941. By 1943 that had been extended to those aged 19 to 50. Women and girls selected from the register were allocated to jobs to which, if they refused to go, they could be 'directed' by law. In November 1941 the *Distributive Trades Journal* complained that all women aged 20 to 25 inclusive working in non-food shops were being sent to other employment. Conscription of single women aged 20 to 21 began in January 1942, and mainly involved entry into the ATS or munitions production, where labour shortages were most acute. By 1943 conscription had been extended to single girls aged from 19 to 24. From February 1942 females aged 20 to 30 (with certain exemptions) could be recruited only through employment exchanges, the intention being to ensure they took work deemed essential to the war effort. In January 1943 this was extended to those aged up to 40, and at that time females could be directed into part-time as well as full-time posts.[33]

The effect of this was that while male former grocery workers could find themselves sent to shipyards, girls from milliners' shops might be dispatched to factories making tanks or munitions. Recognition was, however, given to the need to maintain an adequate food distribution network, so that experienced women grocery workers like Kathleen Wilson were allowed to stay at their posts. Nonetheless, when Kathleen turned 18 she had to become a part-time member of the Fire Service, the Civil Defence or the Red Cross. She opted for the latter and in October 1944 received her St John Ambulance Association certificate for 'First Aid to the Injured'.[34]

Many firms recruited married women, since these were exempted from conscription, and those businesses that had once applied a marriage bar found themselves having to abandon it. They did not always do so with good grace. According to the general manager of Beattie's department store in Wolverhampton, once an assistant married her efficiency declined sharply and she lost interest in the job.[35] At Reading Co-operative Society in December 1939 the Management Committee decided that female members of staff who married must still resign, as had been the custom, so that their contract of service could be terminated. But they might then continue to be employed 'on a temporary basis at the discretion of the officials'.[36]

By the end of the war, as staffing grew ever tighter, the hiring of married women became a necessity, some of them working as part-timers only. This was true of the Debenham group. A large number had never served in a shop before but nevertheless proved valuable employees. They 'handled with great skill and fairness the queues that wound round department stores as some stock of nylon stockings, dress fabrics, sheets, towels or culinary ware became available'.[37]

In a very minor way experiments were also made with self-service trading, notably by the London Co-operative Society to ease its staffing problems. The concept had been pioneered before the First World War in the United States but both there and in Canada it had been much expanded in the 1920s. In 1923 the British multiple grocer David Greig also converted one of his London branches to self-service, but it proved unpopular with customers. Partly this was because there were too few ready-packaged, branded goods available – a vital prerequisite for a successful self-service store. Greig quickly reverted to the traditional counter service. A measure of self-selection was also adopted by the variety chain stores, like Woolworths, and by bargain basements in department stores, but these had several pay-points rather than a single checkout, and they retained an element of counter service. However, faced with the labour problems of the Second World War, Harold Wicker of the London Co-operative Society took up the idea in 1942 and created a small, self-service section at one of the society's stores at Romford in Essex. Mrs Marion Hurrell became the first self-service grocery assistant, and within six weeks the unit proved a modest success, serving over 1,000 customers.[38] Other London Co-operative shops followed suit, for example at Barkingside in 1944, but the initiative was hampered by the impossibility of using it for rationed goods and by war-time restrictions preventing the installation of the fittings needed for a proper self-service conversion. Not until the second half of the 1940s did the self-service revolution really begin.[39]

As in the First World War a number of women took over as manageresses and buyers, normally on the understanding that they would have to make way for the men they were replacing when these returned at the end of hostilities. Despite the setting-up of national wage-negotiating machinery through the establishment of Joint Industrial Councils (the first of them in December 1940 for the grocery trade, and with others following for drapery, retail meat, furnishing and other sectors over the next few months), gender pay differences remained. A similar situation applied to the co-operative stores, which had their own negotiating arrangements. Although it was theoretically possible for women to obtain male pay rates if they could show they were carrying out 'the full range' of duties which the men they were replacing had previously performed, this was difficult to demonstrate under war conditions. So while male branch shop managers in London with a weekly trade of under £60 were to be paid a minimum weekly rate of £3 10s in the grocery and provisions trade, their female counterparts obtained only £2 18s a week; for a weekly trade of £200, the respective sums were £4 10s and £3 18s.[40] Similar gender differences applied to the official war bonuses granted to take account of the higher cost of living. In all, nine war bonuses were paid between 1939 and 1945, with male assistants aged 21 and over receiving an extra £1 4s 6d a week as a result, while their female counterparts secured £1 3s 6d. Only for those under 18 was bonus equality established, with an extra 13s a week awarded by the end of the war.[41]

Demands for equal pay formed part of the official policy of both the National Shop Assistants' Union and the co-operative-based National Union of Distributive and Allied Workers, with a male delegate to a conference of the former union claiming that if a woman did '99 per cent of the man's work she was . . . paid the women's rate. He believed women could do just as much as men in practically every sphere. . . . Women are our comrades, and we must fight to the last to get them the same wages as were paid to the men whose jobs they have taken.'[42] Despite this, in most cases the pay differentials persisted, reinforced by the fact that the women were usually taking responsibility on a temporary basis only, until the men returned. This undermined their bargaining position, while leaving some of them feeling their contribution was not properly recognised.[43]

Among those demoted at the end of the war was Molly Mitchell, the popular and efficient manageress of the International branch shop in Brighton where Kathleen Wilson worked. Eighteen months after peace was declared she was replaced by a male manager, a humourless character who did little to win the goodwill of his staff, unlike Molly. She now became under-manager, a position leading to tensions and one she did not enjoy.[44] Kathleen herself was more fortunate. Although she was in charge of the provisions side of the shop, none of the men who had done her job before the war wanted to return to it, and 'since it appeared that I was very efficient, I was allowed to continue in my position'. That included training apprentices, one of whom became her husband. He came as a mature trainee to learn the trade.[45]

Shopkeepers also sought to cover war-time staff shortages by recruiting older men as managers or retaining staff who had reached retirement age. In September 1939 Reading Co-operative Society decided that the butchery manager at their Basingstoke Road branch was to be asked to carry on, even though he was over 65 years of age, 'in view of the present situation'.[46] Similarly, in January 1940 *The Grocer* included an appeal for a 'Manager, over military age, smart and energetic, fully experienced all departments, good-class family trade, used to buying, control large staff and turnover'.[47] Sometimes a managerial substitute had to be found because the proprietor himself was required to join up. In December 1941 an advertisement in *The Drapers' Record* called for a 'Manager, over military age, Drapery, Ladies' and Gent's Outfitting, Furnishing, Country market town. Owner liable for call up'.[48] Occasionally, to add to the attractiveness of a post at a time of heavy bombing, advertisers of vacancies in rural shops would mention that the business was located in a 'safety-zone' or in a 'safe area in provinces'.[49]

The problems caused by inexperienced staff were most severe in the grocery and provisions trade. If the wrong weight was given for rationed goods or an incorrect price charged at a time when prices were controlled, shopkeepers could be prosecuted, as in the First World War. Food inspectors went round to ensure the regulations were being properly observed. Hence early in 1940 a grocer from Hansford, Stoke-on-Trent, was fined £1 for selling packets of butter which were of short weight, and a further £1 for a similar offence in respect of packets of dried currants. In his defence the man explained that he had entrusted the weighing to 'inexperienced assistants he had had to engage because his regular staff had left owing to the war'. The prosecution, however, treated the matter seriously, declaring the public had a right to receive their full rations and to get value for money. 'Where shopkeepers are found to have supplied rationed food short of weight we shall ask for heavy penalties.'[50]

If rationed goods were supplied without coupons to registered customers, or were sold to those who were not registered at the shop, prosecution could also follow. In February 1940 the manager of a Tesco branch store at Greenford Market was accused of supplying ½lb of butter without a ration coupon. When asked to explain, he said that as it was near the end of the week and some customers had not taken up their rations he thought it would be in order to sell the butter to someone else, since it was 'a perishable article'. The court disagreed and a fine of £10 and costs of £5 5s were imposed on the firm.[51]

Some breaches of the rationing order were more blatant. At Pontardawe in South Wales in February 1942 the Home and Colonial Stores were fined £100 on each of four summonses for selling butter, margarine, cooking fat and sugar in excess of the proper quantity, and a further 10s on each of thirty-four counts for supplying goods to other than registered customers. They were also ordered to pay £75 towards the cost of the prosecution, a total of £492. The branch manager was fined £10 on each of two summonses for aiding and abetting the excess sales, and 5s per case on thirty-four summonses for his role in supplying rationed goods to unregistered customers. This made an aggregate penalty of £28 10s.[52]

Such 'under the counter' transactions led the Ministry of Food to issue an advertisement in June 1941 calling on consumers to observe the rationing system with scrupulous fairness:

> You've met the friend who tells you in a whisper that she got a couple of chops from the butcher without coupons. It isn't clever. No more clever than looting. . . . Tell your friends that if they try to beat the ration, they are trying to beat the Nation.[53]

Accusations of black marketeering were also made, with MPs pressing the government for stiffer penalties to be imposed on those found guilty. By the end of December 1941 the Ministry of Food had instituted almost 40,000 prosecutions for infringements of the food control regulations. However, the parliamentary secretary to the ministry claimed that most were 'minor offences, some due to the inexperience and shortness of staff. It would be most unfair to the traders of this country to assume that all the prosecutions we have to undertake refer to the black market.' Under current regulations, anyone convicted could face a maximum term of two years' imprisonment or a fine of up to three times the price that an article might fetch, or both imprisonment and a fine.[54]

Some traders were fined for selling adulterated goods, such as egg substitute which consisted mainly of self-raising flour and bicarbonate of soda, with only a tiny amount of dried egg included. In another case a Preston grocer was convicted of selling pressed beef which was in fact largely horseflesh. The man said he had been in business for thirty-six years and this was the first complaint he had received. He blamed an assistant for inadvertently removing the notice which stated the meat contained horseflesh, and accused the salesman who had supplied it of stating that the product had only 20 per cent horseflesh in it, rather than the high proportion it in fact contained. The case ended with the man being fined £5 for selling horseflesh to a purchaser who had not asked for it, £3 for selling pressed beef which was in practice mostly horseflesh and £2 for failing to display a notice in a conspicuous position informing customers that horseflesh was on sale.[55]

Difficulties also arose in respect of articles like canned food and dried fruit, which were in short supply but initially were not rationed. Linda McCullough Thew recalled that at the co-operative grocery store in Ashington,

Northumberland, where she worked, all choice disappeared: 'customers had to take what was available, rather than what they wanted. Tinned stuff that had hitherto lain unwanted now sold like hot cakes. In the end, customers took what they were given. . . . As far as we could, we gave out "extras" on a rota basis – Weekly One one time, Weekly Two the next, and so on.'[56]

In these circumstances ill-feeling could arise between shop workers and customers, with the latter suspecting the former of keeping 'off the ration' goods for their friends or for disposal at an enhanced price on the black market. In June 1941 *The Distributive Trades Journal* complained that despite the publicity provided by the government to explain to the public 'just why they cannot get all they want, there are women who seem to think that the people in the shops are deliberately withholding their stocks. . . . They accuse the assistant of being unfair and storm out of the shop.'[57]

In July 1943, however, a contributor to the *Journal* criticised the power of assistants to prevent a shopper 'getting anything above her bare rations'. It was 'the little petty things' that most irritated and embittered the housewife:

> when she sees the girl from the pharmacy go into the multiple grocers next door with a handful of shampoo powders that she solemnly swore to the housewife only this morning that she hadn't seen for months, and comes back with some chocolate biscuits and a bottle of coffee, also which the grocery assistant swore was not in stock. . . . The butcher, the fishmonger, the confectioner, the grocer, the greengrocer, the draper, etc., all these people, the housewife complains, [are] exercising their power as relentlessly as the totalitarian powers we are fighting against.

The comments called forth a storm of protest and denial from shop workers. But a minority did admit that there were a few 'black sheep' among them, who should be denounced to the manager if they were detected.[58]

Many retailers and their staff, for their part, looked askance at housewives who registered at more than one shop, perhaps by dividing their rations between different retailers, or registering individual family members at different shops. The aim was to enable them to get goods in short supply from more than one source. Kathleen Wilson and her colleagues at the International stores in Brighton labelled such purchasers 'scroungers': 'They were out for all they could get. Taking the best of everything in short supply from every shop they were registered at. It did not always work well for them because we had a system of our own on how to allocate these little extras to everyone fairly.'[59] *The Distributive Trades Journal* shared her sentiments. 'Shop workers are not blind,' it declared angrily. 'They know that there are women who will visit all

the shops in the neighbourhood in order to get all the goods they require. . . .
So to meet this situation shop workers have tried to ration their supplies. This
gives them one perpetual headache.'[60] Frequently the customer would attempt
to blackmail the assistants 'by threatening to register elsewhere'.

Against this background in December 1941 the Ministry of Food introduced
a system of rationing for what were classed as non-essential foodstuffs, such as
canned fruit, meat and fish. Under this each person was allocated a number of
coupons to be 'spent' on the regulated goods according to the number of
points put on them. Thus by placing a high points value on something in short
supply, the authorities could make it less attractive to potential purchasers. But
that could create difficulties for the shopkeeper. In Tynemouth the president of
the local Grocers' Association complained that although his customers wanted
to buy tinned salmon, they refused to sacrifice twenty-four precious points for
what proved to be third-grade fish. Similar problems applied in regard to tinned
pilchards and herrings, where the points value was also too high.[61] Later, as
tempers shortened and frustrations built up, quarrels broke out between
assistants and customers, with the latter accusing staff of 'stealing' coupons
by detaching more than they ought for a particular item. In one case a woman
was fined for assaulting a shop manageress who had allegedly cut out more
'points' than had been spent.[62] In other instances customers changed their
retailers on the grounds that 'I will do better for short supply stuff if I register
with so-and-so.'

Nor did rationing prevent the problem of queues, since allocations
depended on the quantity of goods available, at a time when enemy action
was disrupting overseas trade and home produce was affected by seasonal
factors and the weather. Bread, cakes and greengrocery, except for oranges,
remained 'off the ration' for the duration of the war, as did rabbits and, from
time to time, meat offal. When supplies of these were known to be in stock,
word got round and the shop concerned was soon surrounded by hopeful
customers. *The Distributive Trades Journal* warned shopkeepers to exercise
common sense if they wished to avoid long queues. It quoted the case of one
manager who had displayed a notice saying that tomatoes would be on sale at
1.30 p.m. 'Naturally a queue formed.'[63]

Even in small communities these pressures applied. Hazel Wheeler
remembered her father's difficulties in the grocery business he owned on
the outskirts of Huddersfield. The situation was aggravated by the fact that
her mother took little interest in the shop and allowed customers to help
themselves to rationed goods if neither her husband nor the female
assistant were on hand. That might mean that at the end of the week there
was not enough to supply the registered customers. 'No wonder Dad's

angina became worse with the strain of trying to accommodate everybody,'
wrote Hazel years later. She also described the changed retailing ethos
compared to the pre-war period:

> everything was more or less under cover in war-time, including bars of
> soap. Whereas in peace-time shopkeepers displayed their wares as
> prominently and attractively as possible, enticement and sales being the
> keynote, during the war years most things were hidden away beneath the
> counters. Except for non-rationed goods, most shelves remained barren,
> while those of us living on the shop premises felt [ourselves] to be in a
> continuous state of siege. When delivery vans drew up outside the door
> dozens of pairs of avaricious eyes strained to see what was arriving.
> Curtains were drawn to one side, and anxious faces peered out. We could
> almost feel those unseen figures waiting to pounce as soon as the van drew
> away, sometimes even before the driver had time to clamber back into his
> cab. . . . Because everyone was assured of the basic necessities, such as
> food, it was the non-essentials such as cigarettes and chocolate that caused
> near riots. How Central Stores was assailed when word went round that
> 't' cigs' had been.[64]

However, Hazel's father did have his favourites, with a few cigarettes kept
back for 'What Ho!', a rough and ready character who lived in a caravan and
did odd jobs, supplemented by poaching. 'What Ho!' would bring a rabbit to
boost the family's meat ration and be rewarded with cigarettes in exchange.[65]

Some retailers continued in business by turning to repair work to
supplement meagre sales of new goods. That applied to ironmongers,
hardware dealers and wireless retailers. There was a thriving trade in the sale
and repair of second-hand bicycles, too. The same was true of the jewellery
trade, with repairs to watches and clocks a significant aspect of business.[66]

At first only foodstuffs were rationed, but early in June 1941 clothing, too,
was covered. Each person was allocated sixty-six coupons to be used on
articles of clothes and footwear, according to their respective points
allocation. Thus a man's suit required twenty-six points. In general, articles
were classed according to the yarn or fabric they contained, but from
September 1941 new 'Utility' clothes were introduced. These were intended
as a means of providing goods of reasonable quality at controlled prices, and
free from purchase tax. They also required fewer points than corresponding
non-Utility items. So while a Utility nightdress required five points, a non-
Utility one, as well as being more expensive, needed six coupons. For a divided
woollen skirt, the respective amounts were four coupons and six coupons.[67]

Some of the major retailers reacted to this situation by advising potential customers through their advertisements to buy high-quality goods, since they would last longer than cheap articles and would thus conserve coupons. 'Spend your coupons wisely where results will be lasting,' recommended Burberrys Ltd, while Harrods stated firmly: 'Shopping with COUPONS. It pays you BEST to buy the BEST. Get it at Harrods.' Similar claims were made by Debenham & Freebody, Marshall & Snelgrove and a number of others.[68] A 'remodelling' service, whereby old clothes could be remade to conform to the latest fashion, was offered by leading department stores like Marshall & Snelgrove: 'Much can be done with old fur coats, and no coupons are needed if the lining can be utilized.'[69]

To prevent the illicit sale of clothing coupons, they had to be detached from ration books by the retailer. It was illegal to accept (or to offer) loose coupons and failure to observe this led to the prosecution of ten West End firms in late September 1941. They included D.H. Evans & Co. of Oxford Street. The firm defended itself by claiming that assistants had been told to obey the regulations but then had been 'made the object of cajolery, threat, abuse and often ridicule' by customers proffering the coupons and claiming that other shops were prepared to take them.[70]

The clothing coupon allocation was cut to forty-eight during 1942–3 and in the final year of the war fell for a time to an annual rate of thirty-six coupons.[71] This made it very difficult to buy new clothes and encouraged the growth of a black market, with customers prepared to pay higher prices for articles obtained without coupons. In November 1941 *The Drapers' Record* reported the sale of dress fabrics without coupons in Romford market and angrily called on Board of Trade officials to end it, as 'other local traders', who were obeying the regulations, were 'suffering'.[72]

In practice the rationing of clothes and footwear continued until March 1949, while Utility goods, with their distinctive symbol, were also made for some years after the war. Indeed, in 1949 the maximum retail prices of these were reduced by cutting the profit margins of wholesalers and retailers – something which shopkeepers much resented.[73]

During the war furniture, too, was in short supply, and a simple Utility range was introduced for this as well. Even prestigious firms like Maples had to conform to the Utility range for the limited amount of furniture they made during these years.[74]

The life of shop staff was also affected by changes in their working hours. Although the officially permitted closing times remained 9 p.m. on the late night and 8 p.m. on most days of the week, and with a weekly half-holiday, as established in the 1920s, these were reduced throughout the war during the winter months to conserve fuel. From the beginning of November to March each year the maximum opening time was 7 p.m. on the late night and 6 p.m. on other days, with the half-day remaining as before.[75] Certain categories of shops, such as newsagents, tobacconists and confectioners, were allowed to stay open later, and a limited amount of discretion was permitted to local authorities to fix a slightly later general closing time if they deemed it necessary. Initially the new restrictions were greeted with hostility by some retailers. That included men's outfitters, who claimed it would be impossible for their customers to come in after work to be measured and fitted for suits, as was their practice, if a 7 p.m. closure was imposed on the late night. On 9 November 1939 the proprietors of the Fifty Shillings Tailors wrote to the town clerk of York, for example, asking for closing times to be relaxed in the city. They pointed out that some local authorities had extended opening hours to 7 p.m. on week-days and 8 p.m. on Saturdays, 'which we do not consider unreasonable under the present conditions'. The manager of Montague Burton's men's outfitters in Ousegate, York, wrote in a similar vein, but the city authorities refused to make any concessions.[76]

In the event the bombing and the blackout discouraged late shopping anyway, and even when restrictions were lifted in March of each year, few firms reverted to the 8 p.m. and 9 p.m. regime. Shop assistants, through their trade unions, demanded that the de facto earlier closure be legally recognised, but no changes were made to the official position. Even when a new Shops Act was introduced in 1950 it still laid down an 8 p.m. limit, with 9 p.m. for the late night.[77] Unofficially many shops shut a good deal earlier than this after the war. A survey conducted in 1955 by the Union of Shop, Distributive and Allied Workers revealed that the closing hours which prevailed throughout the country ranged between 5 p.m. and 6 p.m. In grocery just 3 per cent of firms surveyed closed later than 6 p.m., while in drapery, only 1.5 per cent did so. The principal exceptions were newsagents, confectioners and the tobacco trade, with 21 per cent of newsagents and around 30 per cent of those selling confectionery and tobacco products open after 6 p.m.[78] A major gain for shop workers arising from the war years, therefore, was a shorter working week – a trend which was maintained for several decades after 1945. By the beginning of the 1970s a large number of shop assistants were on a standard working week of forty hours.[79]

Meanwhile, the ending of hostilities in 1945 was greeted with joy and relief by those employed in shops, as it was by other sectors of society. Kathleen Wilson, at one of the International group's shops in Brighton, recalled the celebrations on Victory in Europe Day (8 May 1945): 'A weight had been lifted from everyone's shoulders. I begged Molly Mitchell's permission to decorate our provisions window out with red, white and blue crepe paper. . . . Street parties sprang up everywhere.'[80] Similar rejoicing followed the victory over Japan in August of that year. But then came a sense of anti-climax: 'nothing major changed. Life went on as usual . . . I continued to train the apprentices, although now we often had two lads at the same time.'[81]

Although the reinstatement of those who had been involved in war work or in the armed services meant redundancy or demotion for many of those who had substituted for them, in reality a large number of men were reluctant to return 'behind the counter'. They preferred to take better-paid jobs in commerce, transport or industry. Retailing became increasingly dominated by women and girls, many of them very young. According to the 1951 population census, females comprised just over 66 per cent of all shop assistants, with over a quarter of them under the age of 20. A decade later just over 75 per cent of shop assistants were women and girls, of whom more than half were married. In the grocery and provisions trade alone – once very much a male preserve – females numbered about 66 per cent of those employed in 1951, and in confectionery, tobacco and newspaper vending they formed nearly 90 per cent of those at work. In the variety chain stores, where girls had always been important, they were just over 98 per cent of those at work in 1951; more than a third of them were under 20.[82]

However, this female dominance did not extend to shop ownership or to managerial employment. In 1951 28.7 per cent of proprietors and managers were female, according to the census, and that figure had risen only slightly to 30.2 per cent in 1961. Even in the confectionery, tobacco and newsagents sector, where small shops were common, just 36.6 per cent of managers and owners were women in 1951, while in grocery and provisions it was 28 per cent.[83] The old difficulties of restricted access to capital, a lack of managerial training and perhaps family commitments restricted female involvement in the upper ranks of retailing, as they had always done. There had been progress compared to the early years of the century, but it was limited.

The postwar labour force was highly mobile, too. Some workers moved on quickly to jobs outside retail distribution. Others left to get married or to start and bring up a family. There was a high proportion of part-time married women, too. Indeed, in confectionery, tobacconists' and newsagency businesses, out of 297,762 persons at work in the whole country in 1966, 183,883 were part-timers.[84] Although no other retail sector had such a heavy preponderance of part-time staff, according to Sir William Richardson, 25 per cent of all shop employees were part-timers by the early 1970s. Among the women alone, the figure was 33 per cent. The 'in-and-out' nature of the occupation was illustrated by information collected by the Union of

Shop, Distributive and Allied Workers for the year to October 1971. This involved 1,600 firms and revealed that of around 200,000 sales staff recruited during that period, only 110,000 remained with their original employers at the year's end. There was also a 7 per cent loss of managers during the year.[85]

It is to the changes and developments in postwar retailing that we must now turn.

YEARS OF TRANSITION: 1945 TO THE 1960s

When the period began shopkeepers and their staff were still grappling with the effects of rationing, government controls and the difficult economic circumstances which followed the ending of the war. By the 1960s British society had embarked on a consumer revolution, with the growth of self-service supermarkets, the widespread sale of domestic consumer durables, such as television sets, washing machines and refrigerators, and an upsurge in trendy boutiques for the fashion conscious. The number of department stores had also increased and some, like Harrods and Maples, opened new provincial outlets in the hope of widening their market appeal. In the late 1940s, for example, Harrods acquired businesses in Sheffield, Liverpool, Torquay and Newton Abbot. The John Walsh store in Sheffield was purchased in 1946, and the management subsequently commented on its poor administration at the time of acquisition and the problems experienced in getting stock. 'Goods were obtained and no questions asked as to where they came from.'[86]

Overall, the total of department stores climbed from 360 in 1950 to 533 in 1957. Part of the rise was, of course, accounted for by the rebuilding of bombed premises.[87] Other stores changing hands included the acquisition by Lewis's of Liverpool of the prestigious Selfridges store in London in 1951, and the absorbing by Bentall's of Kingston of two firms in Worthing and Ealing respectively in the immediate postwar period.[88]

During the late 1940s retailing, especially the grocery and provisions sector, was still affected by war-time restrictions. The economic difficulties and general shortages caused food rationing to be more stringent at times after 1945 than it had been in the war itself, with bread rationed between July 1946 and mid-1948 and potatoes between November 1947 and the spring of 1948.[89] Neither had been rationed during the war. In practice, food rationing did not end finally until 1954, with butter, margarine, cooking fat and cheese de-rationed in May of that year and meat in June. It was perhaps indicative of the constant official adjustments to the amounts allocated and the alterations in price controls that as late as 1950 some advertisements for grocery shop managers included the proviso that the successful candidate must have a 'full knowledge of . . . Ministry of Food regulations'.[90] The continued use of the points system for many items also gave rise to complaints. As *The Grocer* commented sourly in January 1950, it had 'outlived its usefulness, if only because some of the commodities still named in it are nowhere obtainable. It is . . . a common saying in grocers' shops that there is nothing on which Points can be spent.'[91] Perhaps to meet these criticisms points rationing was ended in May of that year.

As well as coping with the various restrictions, shopkeepers had to overcome the difficulty of working with young and inexperienced assistants. In 1951 over 20 per cent of all staff in grocery and provisions stores were under 20, and if females only were considered, that total climbed to 25 per cent.[92] Yet prosecutions could still take place if the rules were infringed, possibly by cancelling coupons for basic rations before the due date or charging more than the controlled price for an article. At Bradford-on-Avon in Wiltshire, for example, the local co-operative society was fined £3 on each of sixteen counts, after pleading guilty to overcharging a customer for bacon, and a further £2 for selling bacon at less than the weight it purported to be. In evidence the Ministry of Food inspector claimed that on sixteen occasions over the previous twelve months the society had charged 2s 8d a pound for bacon whose maximum price should have been 2s 3d. In defence the society's secretary blamed the errors on 'a mistake by one of the assistants'.[93]

Not until the second half of the 1950s did the sale of food revert to something like normality, at a time when new retailing trends were emerging. Even in village shops refrigerators were being installed for the sale of such diverse products as fish, fruit, meat, poultry, vegetables, butter and cream. More packaged and branded goods were available, often promoted by manufacturers' advertisements. Their popularity could pressurise retailers into stocking them, even if their profit margins were not particularly attractive. The canning industry, too, improved the quality and range of the goods offered. The advent of mass-produced foodstuffs, which was to be carried much further with the expansion of self-service shopping, inevitably deskilled those working in the grocery and provisions trade, at a time when, paradoxically, some of the trade's leaders were calling for more training to be provided so as to raise the occupation's status and improve the calibre of the staff.[94]

A major complaint about shop assistants after the war was their 'independence' and lack of commitment either to their employer or their customers.[95] The war and the 'take it or leave it' attitude it had induced were blamed for the deterioration. Even in prestigious stores like Selfridges the firm's staff magazine referred to the 'frayed nerves' which were a product of the war years and added plaintively: 'if courtesy were practised a little more, life for all of us would be very much more pleasant'.[96] Over the following months the magazine published suggestions to improve the standard of service. Among them was the reminder that 'A CUSTOMER' was 'the most important person in this Store. . . . A CUSTOMER is not an interruption of our work − he is the purpose of it. We are not doing him a favour by serving him, he is doing us a favour by giving us the opportunity to do so.'[97] At sales times a 'friendly rivalry' was also to be encouraged between departments so as to see which could achieve the best results.[98]

The Drapers' Record also lamented 'haughty' assistants who did little to promote either sales or customer goodwill. In the 1940s working-class customers entering the prestigious Brown's department store in Chester grumbled that 'the assistants, unless you are well-dressed, treat you like dirt'.[99]

Among the new breed of 'independent' store saleswomen was Miss T., a 24-year-old who had been in the Land Army during the war. In the late 1940s she was living in lodgings. When interviewed at that time by Seebohm Rowntree and G.R. Lavers, she made clear her dislike of life 'as a shop girl' and complained that 'her superior [was] always rebuking her for laziness'. But she compensated for her discontent at work by her leisure activities. These included 'an active sexual life'. As she frankly admitted she did not see 'harm in it. I always have one steady lover and it doesn't hurt him if I have an occasional fellow besides.' She smoked heavily and drank a good deal, too.[100] Another assistant interviewed by Rowntree and Lavers was Miss A., who claimed to be 21 but who, they thought, was probably about 28. She escaped from the drudgery of shop life by going to the cinema three or four times a week and indulging in romantic fantasies as a consequence. She, too, was described as 'sexually promiscuous'.[101]

Alongside their alleged lack of interest in their work, many retail assistants had difficult relations with customers, and they particularly disliked being reproved for mistakes in front of clients.[102] Some resented the 'customer is always right' philosophy, as with a young temporary salesman employed by Selfridges in the summer of 1957; he expressed his frustrations in verse:

> Modom may be outrageous,
> Modom may be quite tight,
> Modom may be demented but
> Modom is always right.[103]

A further cause of ill-feeling was management's expectation that staff would carry out unpaid ancillary duties. One co-op grocery employee noted bitterly that in his shop the assistants were expected to combine their retailing role with the handling of members' share contributions and withdrawals, as well as dealing with funeral furnishing orders, requests for coal or payments into a mutuality club:

> They take in laundry bundles and boot and shoe repairs. Additional to selling the goods one would expect them to sell, they retail cakes, bread, drugs, hardware, fruit and vegetables and, just before Good Friday, small quantities of fish. 'And now, to cap it all,' said the disgruntled grocer . . . 'we are being asked to sell tomato plants and bedding plants during the spring.'[104]

Even in the mid-1960s full-time employment in co-operative shops remained male-dominated, unlike the position in retailing generally, and in the postwar period the men were lukewarm about equal pay when this was mooted by the leaders of the Union of Shop, Distributive and Allied Workers (USDAW). One contributor to its newspaper, *The New Dawn*, summarised the attitude of many of the sceptics when he wrote in June 1952: 'it is going to be terribly difficult to convince co-operative society officials that all women shop-workers match up with men in the quality of their work. In many societies three women assistants are employed as against two countermen formerly.'[105]

Dislike of ancillary duties was, however, not confined to co-operative employees. Department store and drapery staff, too, resented having to carry out such tasks as dusting, marking up merchandise, checking stock and the like, alongside their principal activities. One woman said angrily: 'I am not really a shop assistant here at all, but something of everything, a Jack of all trades; we have to do the fetching and carrying, and all odd jobs.' In another store a saleswoman was being 'sent to Coventry' because, it was said, she refused to do her share of the extra duties. In departments where some but not all assistants received commission, there was a tendency to load ancillary tasks on those being paid on time rates. This might mean that senior assistants avoided the 'extras', including those of an administrative nature. The same was true of part-timers and that could lead to tensions and ill-feeling within a department.[106]

Even the payment of commission caused jealousy where senior staff, as was customary, had priority in serving customers and thus took the largest share of the cash available. This helped to contribute to that 'absence of any feeling of "solidarity" with colleagues' which was commented on by Joan Woodward in her study of department store life at the end of the 1950s.[107]

Ella Bland, who began working for the high-class shoe firm Lilley & Skinner in London in the early 1950s, recalled that as a junior her commission was 3*d* in the £1. As she drily commented: 'this was not riches even on a busy day. However, a "spiff", that is, an extra commission of say 1*s*, 2*s* 6*d* or even 5*s* if one could sell an older or less popular model, was quite a consideration with basic wages at £3 a week.' She also recalled the hard work involved in selling shoes, with 'a lot of to-ing and fro-ing to the stockroom'. Maintaining the stock was 'quite a job', too. 'It often happened that twenty boxes of new stock would arrive to be fitted in where there was apparently no space and this meant a great deal of shifting about and up and down ladders.'[108]

Nonetheless, despite criticisms of the less compliant attitude of shop assistants in the postwar years compared to the situation before 1939, there is little doubt that in the first two postwar decades many sales staff still had to observe stringent discipline. Large numbers had to wear a uniform and in the case of dress shops and department stores that usually consisted of unrelieved black. Laura Claughton, who was employed at Bourne & Hollingsworth between 1948 and 1956, recalled that on one occasion an assistant arrived on the shop floor wearing black shoes with touches of white on them.

> Mr Peters, who was the floor walker, came in the department and said . . . 'What's this with the shoes?' So the . . . girl said: 'Mr Peters, I'm so sorry, but I only have one pair of black shoes, and they are being mended, so today I have to come in these.' 'She can't stay on the floor with those on. Put her in the stock room for the day.' And she had to go in the stock room. . . . [At] Bourne & Hollingsworth you had to rehearse how you were going to approach a customer. . . . You had to go to a session, and the person who was training you would put you right.[109]

Despite the existence of legislation covering the provision of chairs for female assistants dating back to the late nineteenth century, none of the girls at Bourne & Hollingsworth was allowed to sit down when on the shop floor. 'I suppose it gave a feeling of inefficiency, if you were sitting down.'[110]

By the late 1950s, however, women sales staff in many stores began to resent wearing a uniform. It became a status issue, especially where buyers and senior personnel were allowed to wear what they liked.[111] When Ella Bland moved to Lillywhites, selling sports clothes, her uniform comprised a light grey skirt and white shirt. But she remembered her stint there with little affection. It was 'an old-fashioned firm and I think even in the late 1950s it was considered quite a privilege to be allowed to work there'. Staff facilities were poor, despite the shop's elite reputation.[112] This contrast between the lavish furnishings and fittings in the parts of the shop the customers saw and the often shabby and austere facilities for those behind the scenes in packaging departments, staff quarters and stock rooms was common both before and after the Second World War.

Those seeking promotion in high-class department stores often transferred from one to another within a select grouping, or, as with the Harrods group, they might move from one constituent business to another. Thus in 1949 when Miss Haggis was appointed buyer for the suit department at Selfridges it was noted she had begun her retailing career at Bourne & Hollingsworth, where she had become a buyer in the coat department. She then moved to Peter Robinson, again as a buyer of coats, and from there went to Selfridges.[113] Similarly Mr Levinson, appointed buyer of the ladies' shoe department at Selfridges in July 1951, commenced his career at Harrods and, after war service, returned there briefly before going to Bourne & Hollingsworth. From there he went to Selfridges.[114]

Among younger women customers, however, there was a growing desire to break away from the staid fashions and conventional retailing atmosphere of their mother's generation – a longing for fashion to be fun. It was to cater for them that from the mid-1950s a multiplicity of specialist boutiques emerged. Mary Quant pioneered this trend, designing the clothes she sold and adopting an informal retailing style that appealed to the well-to-do *avant garde* women and girls who patronised her Chelsea shop, Bazaar. She ran this from 1955 with her partner and future husband Alexander Plunket Greene. One of her first assistants was a beautiful debutante named Susie Leggatt, who took the job because she thought 'it might be rather jolly to work for a couple of weeks' but who then stayed on. Susie had style and knew how to show off the Quant clothes to best advantage. When Mary opened her second Bazaar shop in Knightsbridge in 1961, Susie Leggatt took it over and had six, sometimes eight, girls working for her, 'mostly debs and ex-debs like herself. All these girls wore high black leather boots, black stockings and black leather coats. . . . The girls really put "the look" across', wrote Mary, years later.[115] Quant clothes also began to be sold by some of the prestigious department stores. In 1963 Harrods' staff magazine praised the 'foresight and courage' of one of Kendal Milne's buyers for bringing 'Mary Quant Ginger Group clothes' to Manchester. The town 'was taken by storm and the young fell for these exciting co-ordinates in a big way'.[116]

By the late 1960s boutiques were found in most provincial towns, and a rash of other innovators emerged. Among them was Biba, described by Arthur Marwick as 'that cathedral of innovatory sixties fashion and consumer enjoyment'.[117]

Even old-established drapery firms took note of the new mood, and especially of the emergence of a 'teenage' fashion market, and modified their selling policies accordingly. In March 1960 the 'Teen and Twenty' fashion parade organised by Cavendish House of Cheltenham proved so popular that the firm began planning almost immediately how to accommodate all those who might wish to attend its autumn show. At Thomas White of Aldershot the teenage department was staffed entirely by teenagers 'to make customers feel at home'. According to *The Drapers' Record*, the young assistants were allowed to wear 'their gayest clothes, in contrast to the black dresses of other sales assistants'.[118] The Drapers' Chamber of Trade reacted to the current trend by advising retailers concerned about staff recruitment to have 'a bright, contemporary look about [their] shops', if they wished to attract the assistants they needed. 'Young people', it declared, 'are very much influenced by the surroundings in which they are expected to work, and this is one of the most important single aspects of . . . staff recruitment.'[119]

While these changes were under way in drapery and department stores, still more sweeping reforms were occurring in the sale of groceries and provisions. Following the establishment of Wages Councils from 1945, giving a guaranteed minimum wage to the sales staff they covered, as well as specifying holiday entitlements, labour costs in retailing began to rise. It must be emphasised that compared to most other occupations, shop work remained relatively poorly paid and the gender wage gap persisted, with even senior female members of staff earning much less than their male counterparts. For example, an investigation by the Prices and Incomes Board in 1966 of earnings in retail drapery revealed that while average weekly earnings for males in the managerial sector amounted to £22 17s a week (ironing out the important regional variations), for their female counterparts, the total was £15 9s 6d. For sales assistants, the respective figures were £15 16s 1d and £9 14s 9d. Significantly, too, almost 40 per cent of the adult male full-time workers surveyed were in managerial grades, compared to around 16 per cent of the adult female full-timers.[120] Nevertheless, the general rise in wage costs, which themselves amounted to perhaps two-thirds of retailers' total expenses, led to initiatives to improve staff efficiency and cut their numbers where possible. In grocery and provisions, self-service began to be seen as a solution, based on American and Canadian models. The co-operative movement had, as we have seen, introduced a few self-service stores during the war, but expansion was hampered by continued rationing and other restrictions, and by an inability to acquire the equipment needed for a successful conversion of stores from counter service to self-service. As late as 1947 there were only ten self-service shops in the country, although by

1950 this had risen to almost 500, of which over 90 per cent belonged to co-operative societies.[121]

But some multiple grocery firms started to get involved, too. Both Jack Cohen of Tesco and Alan Sainsbury of the Sainsbury stores visited the United States in the late 1940s and were impressed by what they saw. Tesco opened a small self-service unit at St Albans in 1947, with its young manager Redford Fisher promised 3d in the pound commission, in addition to his basic salary, on all sales over £300 a week. Rationed goods were supplied from a small counter where the coupons of registered customers were collected, but the money was paid at the turnstile check-outs. Cohen thought that self-service would not only reduce labour costs but would help to eliminate the queues which still plagued most grocery shops. The St Albans experiment was a modest success and, helped by a team of lads, Fisher kept it running for nearly a year, before it was decided to revert to counter service.[122] However, the switch was only temporary. In the autumn of 1949 St Albans resumed its self-service operations, aided by improved fixtures and fittings. At the end of 1950 the firm had twenty self-service units open and a year later that figure had risen to fifty-seven, almost half of all Tesco branches.[123] The group's first supermarket, opened at Maldon, Essex, in 1956 on an old cinema site, sold groceries, provisions, fresh meat, fruit and vegetables. Three years later its new supermarket at Hatfield, Hertfordshire, also offered a selection of drapery goods, including shirts, towels and tablecloths.[124] Over the following decade branches increased rapidly, so that by the end of the 1960s the firm had around 800 outlets, including more than 200 shops acquired by its takeover of the Victor Value chain in 1968.[125]

But many Tesco shops were small and uncomfortable for the staff, even when they became self-service. Ian MacLaurin, who joined the firm as its first graduate trainee in 1959, later described a large number as 'a disgrace – tiny and hugely busy but with no heating and no staff facilities apart from a loo out the back and a kettle somewhere'.[126] He also commented on Cohen's idiosyncratic management style. This led to what MacLaurin labelled 'buncing', whereby managers were free to adjust prices to cover 'shrinkages' arising from shoplifting, losses caused by spoilt stock and other factors. It was accepted they could add a halfpenny on any item under a shilling; a penny on anything between one shilling and two, 'and whatever they could raise at anything above that'. However, managers used this for their own benefit, partly to compensate for their poor pay, on the principle of 'One for him, and two for me'. According to MacLaurin, some were so successful that 'one maestro of buncing called his purpose-built villa on the south coast "Costa Plenty" – not least, as far as Tesco's returns were concerned'.[127]

Tesco managers were not the only senior members of staff suspected of dubious trade practices. A report in the *Co-operative Review* of June 1959 claimed that retail buyers in the butchery departments of co-op stores were given so-called 'luck money' by wholesalers anxious to induce orders to be placed with their firm. It was suggested a similar system of 'bribery' existed in the co-operative greengrocery trade, too, and to a lesser extent in respect of groceries.[128]

Meanwhile, Alan Sainsbury had converted his firm's large Croydon store to self-service in 1950. By that date the worst rigours of rationing were coming to an end, and there was a wider range of non-rationed foods from which to choose. 'The friendly white-coated counter staff were replaced by checkout girls,' comments Judi Bevan, although some counter staff remained and there were assistants patrolling the aisles to help shoppers make their selections.[129] At this date it was still argued that although self-service allowed staffing economies, it had not extinguished the art of salesmanship, since the way merchandise was displayed and promoted and the advisory role of the remaining assistants gave them an opportunity to stimulate sales.[130]

Not all customers welcomed the change. One woman threw a wire shopping basket back at Alan Sainsbury when he handed it to her at the Croydon store entrance.[131] But these teething problems were overcome and in 1952 Sainsbury's opened their first purpose-built self-service store in Eastbourne. Another followed in Southampton in 1954.

In 1947 there had been ten self-service shops in Britain; by 1960 that figure had risen to 6,000, and the trend was upwards thereafter.[132] In 1966, according to the Census of Distribution, there were 20,254 self-service outlets in Britain, almost all of them selling groceries and provisions, and with the co-operative movement now contributing well under a third of the total.[133] At this date there were 193,903 employees in self-service grocery shops, compared to 352,500 workers in other kinds of grocery outlets. Of those 193,903, 106,154 worked for one or other of the multiple chains, compared to 43,480 engaged in the various co-op self-service shops, and 44,269 working for independent grocers. However, this latter figure was small when compared with the 272,595 people employed in traditional independent grocery stores.[134]

Among the multiple chains that played a leading role in the self-service revolution was the Weston group headed by the Canadian entrepreneur Garfield Weston, with his Fine Fare stores. Canadian staff were apparently brought over to instruct their British counterparts in the art of self-service selling.[135] But many older 'multiples', such as Home and Colonial, the Maypole Dairy, and Lipton's (all part of the Allied Suppliers group), were slow to adopt the new selling methods. Partly this was because they ran a multiplicity of small shops that were unsuitable for conversion to self-service and sold a limited range of products. Partly it was a result of inertia and a reluctance on the part of some managers to change their ways.[136] Reforms did nevertheless take place within the Allied Suppliers group as competition intensified, and the 4,000 branch shops open in the 1950s had dwindled to under 3,000 by 1965, as smaller, less-well-placed stores were shut and self-service units began to be set up. By 1965 there were 1,100 of these in the group, or about a third of all its stores.[137]

These developments inevitably affected the staff. One of those involved was Mrs R. Bryant, who had managed the Maypole Dairy's Aston Cross shop for almost seventeen years before it closed. She was kept on as a relief manageress at a lower rate of pay for about eighteen months but with a promise that she would get another shop in the near future. This occurred when she was sent to a counter-service outlet at nearby Kingstanding on the full manageress's rate of pay. She only held the post for two months, however, before this shop, too, was shut. She was subsequently offered a post at a new supermarket in the district but at lower pay. This she refused and with the backing of her trade union, USDAW, in 1967 she eventually obtained £286 13s under the Redundancy Payments Act.[138]

Research carried out in the mid-1960s revealed a high turnover among supermarket staff, amounting in some cases to an annual rate of around 100 per cent. It was highest among females aged between 15 and 24, who had worked for the company concerned for less than a year, performing shelf-filling and general shop duties. Although replacements were usually easy to find and at little cost in terms of advertising and training, this was only part of the story. Rapid staff turnover led to low morale among those remaining, as well as disrupting the organisation of work because of the recurrent changes in the team, with the rest of the staff under pressure to carry out additional work. On occasion, relatively highly paid employees had to be deployed on lower-grade jobs to cover gaps in the team.[139]

Inevitably, the self-service revolution had serious implications for independent traders, although many small shopkeepers proved surprisingly resilient. According to the 1961 Census of Distribution, out of a total of 508,529 retail establishments, 49.8 per cent of them were shops in which not more than two persons were engaged, and 76.8 per cent had not more than four persons engaged, including working proprietors and managers.[140] Indeed, it has recently been suggested that as late as 1980–1 small independent stores still accounted for more than 30 per cent of total British retail trade.[141]

Some small shopkeepers remained in business by offering a specialist service, like the sale of antiques, books, cameras or high-quality fashion goods, or they found a niche market catering for local needs. There were also many small-scale convenience stores selling sweets, a few items of grocery, tobacco products, newspapers and the like. Others again extended the range of products they offered, so that grocers stocked common patent medicines, greengrocery and a limited range of drapery, while greengrocers retailed 'paraffin and tinned fruit and tinned beer and cigarettes'.[142] Many responded to demand in their own locality by diversifying their activities, as Frank Danning and his wife did in the Wadebridge area of Cornwall. In 1950 they took over a village shop, which included a post office, a grocery store and the sale of fish and chips on three evenings a week. 'We had a couple of tables in our sitting room for those who wanted to eat their fish and chips on the spot,' recalled Frank. He also took on an early shift as a postman. Later they acquired a mobile shop, which he worked with the aid of a girl school-leaver. Subsequently he and his wife built a greenhouse and were soon selling plants, as well as garden produce, including tomatoes, cucumbers and lettuce. These were retailed both through the shop and in the van. The Dannings continued to run their business for twenty years until, as Frank admitted, 'I had a feeling of a change coming . . . I think that the supermarket finished off the small trader.' He decided to establish a garden centre, and that expanded and prospered, latterly under the direction of his youngest son.[143]

Some tradesmen took a less innovative path by seeking to increase their business through an evasion of shop closure hours, opening late into the evening and on Sundays. Others adopted self-service selling, while in many towns by the end of the 1960s late-night trading on one day a week had become accepted as the norm.[144] A number of 'independent' grocers also joined buying groups to secure the benefits of bulk purchasing. These groups included Spar, Londis and the Wavy Line Grocers' Association, which claimed to have been created to keep 'private business in private hands'.[145]

Nonetheless many small traders succumbed to the price-cutting and the fierce competition of the major multiples. Between 1957 and 1966 alone the number of independent retail establishments of all kinds (not merely those in the grocery trade) in Britain fell from 489,355 to 403,876, while the total of those working in them dropped by around 160,000 (from 1.8 million at the earlier date to 1.64 million at the later).[146]

The Lancaster grocer T.D. Smith was among those affected by the new thrusting commercialism. When rationing ended in the mid-1950s the firm resumed its traditional trading methods, based on the twin principles of 'Quality and Reliability' and with a high standard of service to customers.

But as trade became more competitive, with the end of war-time price controls and the erosion of old-style resale price maintenance on the part of suppliers, this became increasingly difficult to sustain. Pay rates rose, too, so that an experienced counter-hand, paid £3 to £3 15s a week in 1945, was earning £7 a decade later; for a senior or charge counter-hand the £4 8s of 1945 had been converted to £10 in 1955. Even for apprentices the meagre 10s a week paid by Smith's in 1945 had risen to a more acceptable £2 1s 10d a week ten years later.[147] As late as 1958 the firm still employed over eighty staff, including some part-timers, at its main shop in Lancaster and at three branch stores. But as the pace of change quickened, profit margins were squeezed. Between April 1959 and October 1960 the firm's three branch shops were shut and in late September 1960 Francis Brian Smith himself announced he was going to retire owing to failing health. With no family member to succeed him, the firm's premises in central Lancaster were sold to a firm of hosiery and outfitting specialists. For Smith himself, supermarkets were anathema – a contradiction of all he believed in. Unfortunately, growing numbers of his customers were more concerned with competitive pricing than with personal service, and with turnover declining from over £3,000 a week in 1957 to under £2,400 three years later, he withdrew from the business.[148]

Among the factors adding to the pressures on independent traders like Smith was the ending of resale price maintenance. Under this, manufacturers had been able to specify the price at which their products were to be sold and, as with war-time controlled prices, that meant smaller traders were selling at the same price as ardent price-cutters like Jack Cohen of Tesco. However, during the 1950s, under pressure from Cohen and those who shared his philosophy, many of the retail price restrictions in the grocery trade came to an end. The final death knell came in 1964 with the passage of the Resale Prices Act. One MP, who had herself kept a small shop and who opposed the Act's passage, predicted it would lead to 'a period of intense agony' for small retailers. Although some manufacturers sought to register their products for exemption from this abolition of price control, they were opposed by Cohen in the courts.[149] By 1967 resale price maintenance and the restrictions that went with it were virtually dead, as price-cutting and other forms of competitive trading by the major multiples became the order of the day.

These developments meant that independent retailers experienced the full force of competition from the multiple chains and major retailers not only in food and provisions but in other sectors as well, including clothing, furniture and electrical appliances. In a mass-production age the small man could not benefit by offering a superior after-sales or repair service, in the way that had once been the case, since there was less call for this than had been the case during the war and its immediate aftermath. Nevertheless numerous small shops and independent stores did survive, and even in 1966 over 57 per cent of electrical appliances, 60 per cent of furniture and bedding and 68 per cent of radio and television sets, record-players and the like were being sold by 'independents'. The multiples supplied between 27 and 35 per cent of sales in these sectors in 1966.[150]

Small shops were more likely to survive in market towns, in villages, on new housing estates and in close-knit communities in cities. They often acted as social centres, where shoppers met to make purchases and exchange gossip, much as they might have done a century earlier. In Bethnal Green, where there was one shop for every fourteen households even in the mid-1950s, they offered 'the same small face-to-face groups [of neighbours] . . . continual opportunities to meet'.[151]

Up to the 1960s self-service had not penetrated much beyond the grocery and provisions trade, but there was a growth of semi self-service, for example in women's clothing and footwear. This was based on 'the principle of pricing and arranging goods in such a way that the customers [could] help themselves and save the time and wages of shop assistants. Some multiple shoe-shops, for instance, [expected] women customers to select a style and price that [suited] them, from a big display, and only approach the sales staff for a fitting in a particular [size].'[152] In certain multiple clothes stores, like C & A Modes, customers selected the articles they wanted from racks and then perhaps tried them on in a fitting-room before either returning them to the stands from which they had been taken or carrying them to the counter for wrapping and payment.[153]

Throughout these postwar years the shopworkers' trade union movement sought to respond to the changing situation by introducing its own reforms. In 1947, after more than half a century of uneasy coexistence, the Shop Assistants' Union merged with the predominantly co-operative store membership of the National Union of Distributive and Allied Workers to form a new Union of Shop, Distributive and Allied Workers (USDAW).[154] At the time of the merger the new union adopted as its slogan a demand for 'a £5 per week minimum wage for a five day week of forty hours' for all shopworkers and sought to achieve a membership of one million (not all of them in retail distribution) within five years. Although by the early 1970s most members had secured a forty-hour working week and, through the adoption of staff rotas, a number of those working in the larger firms had achieved a five-day working week, the membership target was never achieved.[155]

USDAW began life with 343,137 members and in the first years the level of support fluctuated. Part of the problem was the 'in-and-out' nature of much of shop work, and a surprising lack of awareness among many assistants of its existence. Thus Kathleen Wilson, working for a very demanding new manager at the International stores in Brighton, recalled ruefully: 'Employees of today would never have tolerated the conditions under which we worked, but then, we never knew anything different. We had no union to fight our cause.'[156]

USDAW was particularly concerned at the way in which even when recruitment rose, a high proportion of new members quickly deserted it. During the 1960s the problem was aggravated by the large-scale reorganisation and consequent redundancies in co-operative stores, since these had always been trade union strongholds. Indeed, in 1955 some 564 of the retail societies would only employ trade union labour. During 1963, therefore, the union conducted an investigation into some of its lapsed membership. There were 354,701 members at the end of the year, during which 101,199 new supporters had been enrolled but 102,536 members had lapsed. A survey of 7,273 of the latter revealed that 29.2 per cent had given up employment altogether, 55.8 per cent had taken a post in a trade outside the scope of USDAW, and the rest had left because of dissatisfaction with the union or because they were employed in a shop where there was no collector of union dues, or for some other reason. The report concluded gloomily: 'The striking fact is that 85 per cent of these lapses were unavoidable.'[157]

Nevertheless there were other reasons for USDAW's disappointing recruitment record. As in the 1890s, so in the 1950s and 1960s status and social aspirations remained important. One union activist, George Greenwood, commented drily that there were large numbers of shop workers who thought trade union membership was 'quite beyond the pale'. That applied not merely in small 'select' shops but in large emporia as well.[158]

A second factor was the large number of shops where an average of only three or four people, including the proprietor or manager, were employed. In such circumstances it was difficult to create any sense of solidarity among such small groups or even to arrange for the collection of union dues. Furthermore, many of these assistants were 'directly susceptible to anti-trade union pressures' by their employers.[159]

A final influence was the creation of national pay bargaining machinery through the establishment of Wages Councils and Joint Industrial Councils, which were of particular importance after 1945. Many workers did not see why they should spend hard-earned cash contributing to USDAW when official machinery to improve working conditions already existed. It thus became one of the union's aims to secure better pay and conditions than the statutory minimum, by entering into negotiations with the multiple firms and with some of the major department stores. There were modest successes, as, for example, in 1963 when an agreement for a five-day working week was reached in respect of the multiple grocery trade in England and Wales, following two years of negotiations. About 100 firms were involved, with thousands of shops, ranging from supermarkets to small counter-service branches. A year later a five-day forty-hour working week was agreed for those employed in retail co-operative shops.[160] Yet, despite these efforts, even in the late 1970s shop workers still occupied a low ranking in the national league table of earnings.[161]

CONCLUSION

The two decades after 1945, then, were in many ways years of transition in retail distribution, witnessing as they did the emergence of new wage machinery for the workers and new forms of retailing for proprietors, including the growth of self-service supermarkets on the one hand and of small specialist fashion boutiques on the other. During the two and a half centuries covered by this book, life for those employed 'behind the counter' had changed radically. In the eighteenth century most shopkeepers and their assistants were male, and many young people who embarked on a period of training for their particular trade would have anticipated running their own business in later life – even if not all achieved that ambition. During the nineteenth century, with the emergence of multiple chains and of department stores, that aspiration became increasingly difficult to attain for all but the most able, the most determined, or those fortunate enough to have access to capital provided by family and friends. In the Victorian era, too, women began to enter the world of retailing in increasing numbers, although the main upsurge in female participation took place during the two world wars and their aftermath. Finally, even the expression 'behind the counter' was becoming outmoded by the end of the 1960s, as self-service shopping and turnstile checkouts replaced personal service in increasing numbers of the larger retail outlets. At the end of the twentieth century this decline in counter service was reinforced by the growth of mail order business and, in the early twenty-first century by the increase in online shopping. New roles were emerging for shop staff as shelf fillers, checkout cashiers and packers of goods ordered by mail, telephone and online. In these circumstances relations with customers, except in the smallest or most specialised shops, became increasingly impersonal, even if much stress was placed by supermarket managements on the need to be 'pleasant' to those passing through the stores.

Joanna Blythman, who worked briefly on a supermarket checkout in the early years of the twenty-first century, provided a sobering assessment of what retail employment might become in the future (although with customers undertaking the scanning of their own shopping in some supermarkets, even checkout cashiers could become an endangered species). Blythman found her shop-floor colleagues were 'kind, welcoming and supportive' and:

> Snatched five-minute chats with fellow workers at break times were treats that lit up the day, as was the banter with the more amiable customers. But this wasn't enough to compensate for the tedious monotony of the checkout, nor the stressful and tiring nature of the work environment . . . I began to appreciate why more often than not checkout staff look jaded. There was no daylight or fresh air. I sat under strip lights. The air-conditioning and heating fans clicked on and off all the time. . . . After several hours at a time, any urge to be cheery or pleasant was overtaken by an all-pervasive, mind-numbing blankness. . . . Even if you wanted to try to be pleasant with people, after only so long it was impossible to keep it up.[162]

By Saturday, 'at the end of a killer ten-hour shift (eight and a half hours with an hour for lunch and two fifteen-minute tea breaks)', Joanna felt 'virtually brain dead and physically exhausted'. This was at one of the 'better' firms, which offered various benefits to staff who remained with the company. These included an employee share scheme, a 10 per cent staff discount, a pension, career breaks, parental leave and more besides. But Joanna understood why many members of staff did not stop long enough to gain those perquisites and why the firm's annual staff turnover rate 'was running at 29 per cent'.[163] She herself had taken the job as an experiment, to find out what life was like at a busy checkout. Once that had been accomplished, she hastily departed.

As for the traditional 'corner shop' run by an owner, perhaps with the aid of family members or a part-time assistant, its days are seemingly numbered, if a report in *The Times* in January 2006 is to be believed. The forecast is that such small enterprises will have succumbed to supermarket competition within ten years. Time alone will show whether the experts' gloomy prediction is correct.[164]

NOTES

NA = National Archives, Kew
PP = Parliamentary Papers
TUC = Trades Union Congress Library at London Metropolitan University

INTRODUCTION

1. Nancy Cox, '"Beggary of the Nation": moral, economic and political attitudes to the retail sector in the early modern period', in John Benson and Laura Ugolini (eds), *A Nation of Shopkeepers. Five Centuries of British Retailing* (London, 2003), p. 37.
2. R. Campbell, *The London Tradesman* (London, 1747), p. 147.
3. Daniel Defoe, *The Complete English Tradesman* (Gloucester, 1987 edn), p. 38. First published in 1726.
4. Peter Earle, *The World of Defoe* (London, 1976), p. 238.
5. Neil McKendrick, John Brewer and J.H. Plumb, *The Birth of a Consumer Society* (London, 1983 edn), p. 30.
6. John Benson and Laura Ugolini, 'Introduction. Historians and the Nation of Shopkeepers', in Benson and Ugolini (eds), *Five Centuries*, p. 6.
7. Hugh Barty-King, *Maples. Fine Furnishers* (London, 1992), pp. 24–6, 66–7 and 85.
8. Quoted in Barty-King, *Maples*, p. 66.
9. Nancy Cox, *The Complete Tradesman. A Study of Retailing, 1550–1820* (Aldershot, 2000), p. 77.
10. Reminiscences of James Treloar at Qualidata, University of Essex, C.707/412/1–2.
11. Reminiscences of J. Wolfendale, who was born at Bolton in 1889. At Qualidata, University of Essex, C.707/151/1–3.
12. Andrew Alexander, Gareth Shaw and Deborah Hodson, 'Regional Variations in the Development of Multiple Retailing in England, 1890–1939', in Benson and Ugolini (eds), *Five Centuries*, pp. 127–8.
13. James B. Jefferys, *Retail Trading in Britain 1850–1950* (Cambridge, 1954), p. 73.
14. Journal of Marmaduke Strother for 1784–5 at the British Library, Egerton MSS 2479, f. 79. Entry for 11 February 1785.

15. Journal of Marmaduke Strother, f. 121, entry for 5 July 1785, and *York Courant*, 10 May 1785, advertisement inserted by Roger Beckett announcing that he had recently taken over a woollen draper's shop in York.

16. William Paine, *Shop Slavery and Emancipation* (London, 1912), pp. 47–8.

17. Paine, *Shop Slavery*, p. 51. Another estimate suggests that 31 per cent of shop assistants were women in 1911. Benson and Ugolini, 'Introduction', in Benson and Ugolini (eds), *Five Centuries*, p. 7.

18. Lee Holcombe, *Victorian Ladies at Work. Middle-Class Working Women in England and Wales 1850–1914* (Newton Abbot, 1973), pp. 105–7.

19. W.F. Fish, *The Autobiography of a Counter-Jumper* (London n.d. [1929]), p. 28.

20. Paine, *Shop Slavery*, p. 12.

21. *Board of Trade: Report on the Census of Distribution and other Services, 1966* (London, 1970), p. 2/110. *Board of Trade Journal*, 4 September 1959, 'Report on Self-Service Trading'.

22. Earle, *The World of Defoe*, p. 168.

23. Roy Porter, *English Society in the Eighteenth Century* (London, 1991 edn), pp. 366–7, and Hoh-Cheung and Lorna H. Mui, *Shops and Shopkeeping in Eighteenth-Century England* (Kingston, Montreal and London, 1989), p. 147.

24. Porter, *English Society*, p. 361.

25. Mui, *Shops and Shopkeeping*, p. 13.

26. Mui, *Shops and Shopkeeping*, p. 13, quoting P.J. Corfield.

27. Cox, *The Complete Tradesman*, p. 206.

28. Mui, *Shops and Shopkeeping*, p. 12. T.S. Willan, *An Eighteenth-Century Shopkeeper. Abraham Dent of Kirkby Stephen* (Manchester, 1970), pp. 41–2.

29. Mui, *Shops and Shopkeeping*, p. 21. Willan, *An Eighteenth-Century Shopkeeper* p. 6.

30. Order Book of Walthal Fenton, clothier and draper, at the British Library, Add. MSS 36,666, ff. 32 and 43.

31. Order Book of Walthal Fenton, letter dated 7 September 1774. It was accompanied by thirty small pieces of woollen cloth of various colours and qualities, and these still survive. Michael J. Winstanley, *The Shopkeeper's World 1830–1914* (Manchester, 1983), p. 3.

32. Roy Porter, 'The Wonderful Extent and Variety of London', in Sheila O'Connell (ed.), *London 1753* (London, 2003), p. 9.

33. Roy Porter, *London, A Social History* (London, 2000), p. 164.

34. Quoted in Porter, *London*, p. 173.

35. Quoted in Porter, *London*, p. 174.

36. Trevor Fawcett, 'Eighteenth-Century Shops and the Luxury Trade', in *Bath History*, vol. III (1990), pp. 49 and 54.

37. Trevor Fawcett, *Bath Commercialis'd. Shops, Trades and Market at the 18th-Century Spa* (Bath, 2002), pp. 53–4.

38. Bailey's *British Directory for 1784* (London, 1784), sections on Bath, pp. 336–41, and York, pp. 740–5.

39. Earle, *The World of Defoe*, p. 324.

40. *Bath Chronicle*, 3 April 1800.

41. Claire Walsh, 'The newness of the department store: a view from the eighteenth century', in Geoffrey Crossick and Serge Jauman (eds), *Cathedrals of Consumption. The European Department Store 1850–1939* (Aldershot, 1999), pp. 47–9.

42. Defoe, *The Complete English Tradesman*, p. 180.

43. Cox, *The Complete Tradesman*, pp. 77–80.

44. Cox, *The Complete Tradesman*, p. 81. Mui, *Shops and Shopkeeping*, p. 211. On occasion Wood allowed bills to be settled through barter, as when the wife and daughter of William Birch, a shoemaker, made hay to pay off their debt to him.

45. Fawcett, 'Eighteenth-Century Shops', p. 56.

46. Peter Earle, *The Making of the English Middle Class. Business, Society and Family Life in London, 1660–1730* (London, 1989), p. 116.

47. McKendrick, Brewer and Plumb, *The Birth of a Consumer Society*, p. 91.

48. Account Book of Mary Medhurst and Thomas North at Hampshire Record Office, 96M82/P225.

49. David Vaisey (ed.), *The Diary of Thomas Turner 1754–1765* (Oxford, 2000 edn), p. 149, entry for 22 May 1758.

50. Cox, *The Complete Tradesman*, p. 160.

51. Dorothy Davis, *A History of Shopping* (London, 1966), pp. 184–5. Ian Mitchell, 'Pitt's Shop Tax in the history of retailing', in *The Local Historian*, vol. 14, no. 6 (May 1981), p. 348. It has been estimated that even in the seventeenth century shopkeepers in 822 cities, towns and villages in England and Wales issued trade tokens; these included 330 non-market towns.

52. Vaisey (ed.), *The Diary of Thomas Turner*, p. 112, entry for 26 September 1757, for example: 'In the afternoon I rode out a-money-catching, but got none.'

53. J.D. Marshall (ed.), *The Autobiography of William Stout of Lancaster 1665–1752* (Manchester, 1967), pp. 25 and 148–50.

54. Maureen Weinstock, *More Dorset Studies* (Dorchester, n.d. [*c.* 1962]), pp. 89–90.

55. John Oldfield, *Printers, Booksellers and Libraries in Hampshire, 1750–1800* (Hampshire Papers No. 3, Hampshire County Council, 1993), pp. 8–9, quoting from the *Hampshire Chronicle*, 29 September 1783 and 13 December 1784.

56. Oldfield, *Printers, Booksellers and Libraries*, p. 8.

57. Weinstock, *More Dorset Studies*, pp. 85, 86 and 89.

58. Mui, *Shops and Shopkeeping*, pp. 119 and 130.

59. *London Chronicle*, 12–14 October 1762.

60. Terry Friedman, *Engrav'd Cards of Tradesmen in the County of York* (Leeds Art Galleries, 1976), no. 44 (not paginated).

61. Marshall (ed.), *The Autobiography of William Stout*, p. 143, entry for 1703.

62. Cox, *The Complete Tradesman*, p. 194.

63. Campbell, *The London Tradesman*, p. 188.

64. *Ipswich Journal*, 8 October 1785, advertisement by Thos Burrage of Ipswich of 'cheap linen-drapery'.

65. *Reminiscences of an Old Draper* (London, 1876), pp. 31–9.

66. Mary Thale (ed.), *The Autobiography of Francis Place* (Cambridge, 1972), pp. 211–16.

67. Thale (ed.), *The Autobiography of Francis Place*, p. 226.

CHAPTER 1

1. David Alexander, *Retailing in England during the Industrial Revolution* (London, 1970), p. 78.

2. Dorothy Davis, *A History of Shopping* (London, 1966), p. 264.

3. Accounts of Joseph Hepworth of York, travelling draper, in Debtors' Accounts in York City Archives, 203a.

4. Nancy Cox, *The Complete Tradesman. A Study of Retailing 1550–1820* (Aldershot, 2000), pp. 194–5.

5. K.L. McCutcheon, *Yorkshire Fairs and Markets to the End of the Eighteenth Century* (Leeds, The Thoresby Society, vol. 39, for 1939, 1940), pp. 148 and 174.

6. Cox, *The Complete Tradesman*, p. 195.

7. David Vaisey (ed.), *The Diary of Thomas Turner 1754–1765* (Oxford, 2000 edn), pp. 111, 183, 190, 206 and 207, entries for 19 September 1757, 14 May 1759, 20 October 1758, 16 and 30 June 1760, for example.

8. Kathryn A. Morrison, *English Shops and Shopping* (New Haven and London, 2003), p. 18.

9. Quoted in Pamela Horn, *Life and Labour in Rural England 1760–1850* (Basingstoke, 1987), pp. 4–6.

10. Morrison, *English Shops*, p. 19. Horn, *Life and Labour*, p. 6.

11. Vaisey (ed.), *The Diary of Thomas Turner*, p. 215, entry for 27 December 1760.

12. J.D. Marshall (ed.), *The Autobiography of William Stout of Lancaster 1665–1752* (Manchester, 1967), pp. 24, 90, 151 and 162.

13. *Royal Commission on Market Rights and Tolls*, PP1888, vol. LIV, Report on Canterbury, p. 147, Qu. 7036–7.

14. *Royal Commission on Market Rights*, 1888, p. 147, Qu. 7035.

15. James Schmiechen and Kenneth Carls, *The British Market Hall. A Social and Architectural History* (New Haven and London, 1999), p. 21.

16. *Final Report of the Royal Commission on Market Rights and Tolls*, PP1890–1, vol. XXXVII, p. 85.

17. Schmiechen and Carls, *The British Market Hall*, p. 21.

18. Schmiechen and Carls, *The British Market Hall*, pp. 14–15.

19. Roger Scola, *Feeding the Victorian City. The Food Supply of Manchester, 1770–1870* (Manchester, 1992), p. 179. Michael J. Winstanley, *The Shopkeeper's World 1830–1914* (Manchester, 1983), p. 5.

20. Pamela Horn (ed.), *Life in a Country Town: Reading and Mary Russell Mitford (1787–1855)* (Sutton Courtenay, Abingdon, 1984), p. 31.

21. Charles Kightly, *Country Voices. Life and Lore in Farm and Village* (London, 1984), p. 105.

22. Trevor Fawcett, *Bath Commercialis'd. Shops, Trades and Market at the 18th Century Spa* (Bath, 2002), p. 72.

23. Fawcett, *Bath Commercialis'd*, pp. 71–2.

24. *Bath Journal*, 19 March 1753.

25. *Bath Chronicle*, 21 June 1787.

26. Scola, *Feeding the Victorian City*, pp. 150–1 and 158.

27. Scola, *Feeding the Victorian City*, p. 159.

28. Scola, *Feeding the Victorian City*, p. 167.

29. *Second Report of the Royal Commission on the Employment of Children, Young Persons and Women in Agriculture*, PP1868–9, vol. XIII, Report by J. Henry Tremenheere on Cumberland and Westmorland, p. 143.

30. Marshall (ed.), *The Autobiography of William Stout*, pp. 79–80.

31. *Final Report of the Royal Commission on Market Rights*, pp. 86–7.

32. *Royal Commission on Market Rights*, 1888, pp. 124–5, Qu. 6534–6 and 6554–6.

33. *Royal Commission on Market Rights and Tolls*, PP1888, vol. LV, pp. 419–20, Qu. 6402–4.

34. *Final Report of the Royal Commission on Market Rights*, p. 60. *Royal Commission on Market Rights*, 1888, p. 398, Qu. 15,068–15,070 and 15,081. This shopkeeper also sold 'a little groceries and crockery ware and stays, and needles, and note paper' as well as meat.

35. Janet Blackman, 'The Food Supply of an Industrial Town. A Study of Sheffield's Public Markets 1780–1900', in *Business History*, vol. IV, no. 2 (June 1963), p. 96.

36. Myra Marsh, 'Shopping in Denton in the early years of the Twentieth Century', in Alice Lock (ed.), *Looking Back at Denton* (Stalybridge, 1985), p. 75.

37. Susan D. Pennybacker, *A Vision for London 1889–1914: Labour, everyday life and the LCC experiment* (London, 1995), p. 173. Roy Porter, *London. A Social History* (London, 2000 edn), p. 171.

38. Pennybacker, *A Vision for London*, p. 180.

39. Doris Schwartz, *'The Kid from Strut'. A Memoir* (London, 2003), pp. 5–6.

40. Walter Southgate, *That's the Way it Was. A Working Class Autobiography 1890–1950* (Oxted, 1982), pp. 47–8.

41. Southgate, *That's the Way it Was*, pp. 83–4.

42. Henry Mayhew, *London Labour and the London Poor*, vol. I (London, 1861), p. 199.

43. Deborah Hodson, '"The Municipal Store": Adaptation and Development in the Retail Markets of Nineteenth-Century Urban Lancashire', in Nicholas Alexander and Gary Akehurst (eds), *The Emergence of Modern Retailing 1750–1950* (London and Portland, Oregon, 1999), p. 100. Davis, *A History of Shopping*, p. 253.

44. K. Grady, 'Profit, Property Interests and Public Spirit: The Provision of Markets and Commercial Amenities in Leeds, 1822–29', in *The Thoresby Society*

Publications, vol. LIV (Part 3), 1976, pp. 165–8. A fourth market hall, the Free Market, was financed around the same time out of the rates (p. 171). Davis, *A History of Shopping*, p. 253.

45. *Royal Commission on Market Rights and Tolls*, PP1890–1, vol. XXXVIII. Evidence before Mr C.M. Chapman, p. 490.

46. Schmiechen and Carls, *The British Market Hall*, p. 175.

47. Hodson, '"The Municipal Store"', p. 105. Schmiechen and Carls, *The British Market Hall*, pp. 173–4.

48. Schmiechen and Carls, *The British Market Hall*, p. 176.

49. Schmiechen and Carls, *The British Market Hall*, p. 177.

50. Schmiechen and Carls, *The British Market Hall*, p. 165.

51. *Royal Commission on Market Rights and Tolls*, Evidence before Mr C.M. Chapman, p. 486, Qu. 14,379.

52. *Royal Commission on Market Rights*, 1888, p. 219, Qu. 9146 and 9157.

53. Goronwy Rees, *St Michael. A History of Marks & Spencer* (London, 1969), pp. 4, 6–9.

54. Hodson, '"The Municipal Store"', pp. 106–7.

55. Hodson, '"The Municipal Store"', pp. 106–7.

56. *Final Report of the Royal Commission on Market Rights*, pp. 18 and 21.

57. Winstanley, *The Shopkeeper's World*, p. 6.

58. Reminiscences of Miss Ada Carlile, b. 1899, in Qualidata, University of Essex, C.707/416/1–2.

59. *Inter-Departmental Committee on Child Employment*, PP1902, vol. XXV, pp. 15 and 371. Evidence of the headmaster of the Chaucer Board School for Boys, Southwark.

60. Pamela Horn, 'Aspects of Child Employment, 1890–1914: Continuity and Change', in *Children at Risk*, ed. V. Alan McClelland, *Aspects of Education* (Journal of the Institute of Education, University of Hull, no. 50, 1994), p. 135. David Rubinstein, *School Attendance in London, 1870–1904: A Social History* (University of Hull Publications: Occasional Papers in Economic and Social History no. 1, 1969), pp. 73–4.

61. Schmiechen and Carls, *The British Market Hall*, p. 165.

62. Schmiechen and Carls, *The British Market Hall*, p. 186.

63. Hoh-Cheung and Lorna H. Mui, *Shops and Shopkeeping in Eighteenth-Century England* (Kingston, Montreal and London, 1989), p. 79.

64. Sheila O'Connell (ed.), *London 1753* (London, 2003), p. 79.

65. Quoted in E. Robinson, 'Eighteenth-Century Commerce and Fashion: Matthew Boulton's Marketing Techniques', in *Economic History Review*, 2nd Series, vol. 16, no. 1 (1963), p. 59. Matthew Boulton to R. Chippendall, 9 August 1794.

66. John Benson, *The Penny Capitalists. A Study of Nineteenth-Century Working-Class Entrepreneurs* (Dublin, 1983), p. 99.

67. M.F. Davies, *Life in an English Village* (London, 1909), p. 114.

68. Peter Earle, *A City Full of People. Men and Women of London 1650–1750* (London, 1994), p. 146.

69. Mayhew, *London Labour*, vol. I, p. 88.

70. Mayhew, *London Labour*, vol. I, p. 91.

71. Mayhew, *London Labour*, vol. I, p. 7.

72. Alexander, *Retailing in England*, pp. 80–1.

73. Harold Hardy, 'Costers and Street Sellers', in Charles Booth, *Life and Labour of the People in London*, vol. 3 (London, 1903), p. 260.

74. *Royal Commission on Market Rights*, 1888, p. 277, Qu. 11,053, comment by Mr Shorto, managing clerk to the Town Clerk of Exeter.

75. Benson, *The Penny Capitalists*, p. 36.

76. Inventory of Jacob Gipson, Chapman, Late Deceased, 8 February 1702/3, at Hampshire Record Office, 21M65/D3/503.

77. Davis, *A History of Shopping*, pp. 243–4.

78. *Reminiscences of an Old Draper* (London, 1876), pp. 146–8.

79. Rees, *St Michael*, pp. 3–6.

80. Robert Owen, *The Life of Robert Owen Written by Himself*, vol. I (London, 1857), p. 12.

81. Owen, *The Life of Robert Owen*, p. 12.

82. John Beresford (ed.), James Woodforde, *The Diary of a Country Parson 1758–1802* (Oxford, 1978 edn), pp. 183, 244, 454, 512 and 601.

83. Deirdre Le Faye (ed.), *Jane Austen's Letters*, 3rd edn (Oxford, 1995), p. 22. Jane Austen to her sister Cassandra, 25 November 1798.

84. Winstanley, *The Shopkeeper's World*, pp. 200–1.

85. Benson, *The Penny Capitalists*, p. 103.

86. *1851 Census of Population: Occupations*, PP1852–3, vol. LXXXVIII, Parts 1 and 2. Whereas Lancashire had 5,707 male and female hawkers and pedlars in 1851, Norfolk had 482, Lincolnshire 507 and even remote Northumberland recorded only 623.

87. Mayhew, *London Labour*, vol. II, pp. 1 and 2.

88. Mayhew, *London Labour*, vol. I, p. 149 and vol. II, pp. 1–2. The weekly profit of these humbler vendors was put as low as 3s 6d, compared to the 10s or even 15s a week cleared through the year by more expert or more energetic traders.

89. Davis, *A History of Shopping*, p. 241.

90. Minutes of the Court of Common Council of the Corporation of London at the Corporation of London Record Office, COL/CC/01/01/67, f. 254, 14 June 1785.

91. *Journals of the House of Commons*, vol. XL, 27 June 1785, p. 1107.

92. Davis, *A History of Shopping*, p. 241. 8 & 9 William 3, c. 25, 1697. An Act on Hawkers and Pedlars. The legislation was made permanent under Queen Anne.

93. *Ipswich Journal*, 14 May 1785.

94. *Journals of the House of Commons*, vol. XL, 18 May 1785, p. 1001.

95. *Journals of the House of Commons*, vol. XL, 27 and 30 May 1785, pp. 1026 and 1030–1.

96. *Hansard's Parliamentary History*, vol. XXV (London), 13 June 1785, col. 886.

97. 25 Geo. III c. 78. *An Act for Additional Duties on Hawkers, Pedlars and Petty Chapmen*, 1785. Davis, *A History of Shopping*, pp. 245–6.

98. *Journals of the House of Commons*, vol. XL, 27 June 1785, p. 1107.

99. *Ipswich Journal*, 5 November 1785.

100. 29 Geo. III c. 26.

101. 35 Geo. III c. 91. The Act repealed that part of the 1789 legislation which had restrained pedlars and hawkers from 'selling Goods, Wares, or Merchandize, within a certain Distance from any City or Market Town'.

102. 34 & 35 Vict. c. 96 and 44 & 45 Vict. c. 45. The latter legislation made it no longer necessary to apply for an extra endorsement for another police district. *An Act for Granting Certificates to Pedlars*, 1871, had provided that the applicant must be of good character, above 17 years of age, in order to carry on the trade of a pedlar.

103. 51 & 52 Vict. c. 33. *An Act to Consolidate Excise Licences for Hawkers*, 1888.

104. Pamela Horn, *Pleasures and Pastimes in Victorian Britain* (Stroud, 1999), p. 132.

105. *Royal Commission on Market Rights*, 1888, p. 288, Qu. 11,299.

106. *Royal Commission on Market Rights*, 1888, p. 312, Report by Arthur J. Ashton, Assistant Commissioner.

107. *Final Report of the Royal Commission on Market Rights*, p. 61.

108. Gerry R. Rubin, 'From Packmen, Tallymen and "Perambulating Scotchmen" to Credit Drapers' Associations, *c.* 1840–1914', in *Business History*, vol. 28, no. 2 (1986), pp. 207–9.

109. Lady Bell, *At the Works. A Study of a Manufacturing Town (Middlesbrough)* (Newton Abbot, 1969 edn), pp. 70–1 and 81–3. The book was first published in 1907. Margot C. Finn, *The Character of Credit. Personal Debt in English Culture, 1740–1914* (Cambridge, 2003), p. 283.

110. Finn, *The Character of Credit*, pp. 283 and 308.

111. Rubin, 'From Packmen, Tallymen', p. 212.

112. Quoted in Finn, *The Character of Credit*, p. 284.

113. Alice Foley, *A Bolton Childhood* (Manchester, 1973), p. 17.

114. Pamela Horn, *The Victorian Town Child* (Stroud, 1999 edn), pp. 120–2 and Lionel Rose, *The Erosion of Childhood* (London, 1991), pp. 72–8.

115. Reminiscences of Jack Brenner (b. 1900), in Qualidata, University of Essex, C/707/391/1–3.

116. Kightly, *Country Voices*, p. 112.

117. *Royal Commission on Labour*, The Agricultural Labourer, PP 1893–4, vol. XXXV, Mr Chapman's Report on districts in Buckinghamshire, Berkshire, Cambridgeshire, Cornwall, Devon, Oxfordshire, Shropshire, &c., p. 45.

118. Peter Mathias, *Retailing Revolution. A History of Multiple Retailing in the Food Trades based upon the Allied Suppliers Group of Companies* (London, 1967), pp. 82–4. By 1914 Broughs had thirteen branches outside Newcastle itself.

CHAPTER 2

1. S.I. Mitchell, 'Retailing in Eighteenth- and Early Nineteenth-Century Cheshire', in *Transactions of the Historic Society of Lancashire and Cheshire for*

1980, vol. 130 (Liverpool, 1981), p. 45. Andrew Hann, 'Retail change and the urban renaissance: recasting the shopping hierarchy', in *Economic History Society Annual Conference: Abstracts of Academic Papers* (Leicester, 2005), p. 202, and lecture by Andrew Hann at the University of Leicester, 9 April 2005.

2. Ian Mitchell, 'Pitt's Shop Tax in the history of retailing', in *The Local Historian*, vol. 14, no. 6 (May 1981), p. 349.

3. Tax returns for Suffolk for the years ending 5 April 1788 and 1789 at the NA, E.182.969, Part 2.

4. Probate documents at the NA, PROB.24/47, 1707, f. 332, Walter Collett, witness to the Will of John Murray.

5. T.S. Willan, *The Inland Trade* (Manchester, 1976), pp. 98–9, mentions a number of seventeenth-century shopkeepers with farming interests, but considered that overall 'back-yard farming' was of 'no great significance'. An Account of the Goods, Chattels and Credits of Samuel Brown, late of Alton, Hampshire, 1742, at Hampshire Record Office, 171M86/1.

6. Janice Crowther and Peter A. Crowther (eds), *The Diary of Robert Sharp of South Cave. Life in a Yorkshire Village 1812–1837* (Oxford, 1997), pp. 186–7 and 220. The Sharps decided to close the shop in the spring of 1833 (p. 410).

7. Pamela Horn, *The Victorian Country Child* (Stroud, 1990 edn), p. 71.

8. Michael J. Winstanley, *The Shopkeeper's World 1830–1914* (Manchester, 1983), p. 201.

9. William Lovett, *The Life and Struggles of William Lovett* (2 vols), vol. 1 (London, 1920 edn), pp. 40–1.

10. John Benson, *The Penny Capitalists. A Study of Nineteenth-Century Working-Class Entrepreneurs* (Dublin, 1983), p. 114.

11. Alice Foley, *A Bolton Childhood* (Manchester, 1973), p. 19.

12. Bankruptcy MSS of Joseph Gibbs, B.3/2095 at the NA; depositions on 10 December 1834 of Charlotte Hill and Alice Allured.

13. Peter Earle, *The Making of the English Middle Class. Business, Society and Family Life in London, 1660–1730* (London, 1989), p. 161.

14. Helena Wojtczak, *Women in Victorian Sussex: Their Status, Occupations, and Dealings with the Law 1830–1870* (Hastings, 2003), pp. 52–3.

15. Wojtczak, *Women in Victorian Sussex*, p. 52.

16. Earle, *The Making of the English Middle Class*, p. 109.

17. Joan Lane, *Apprenticeship in England 1600–1914* (London, 1996), p. 125. For girls wishing to become mantua-makers in Wiltshire during the period 1710–60 a premium of £10 to £12 was commonly paid, and they usually served for five years or less (p. 121).

18. David Vaisey (ed.), *The Diary of Thomas Turner 1754–1765* (Oxford, 2000 edn), pp. 2–3 and 215–16, entries for 9 April 1754 and 1 January 1761.

19. R. Campbell, *The London Tradesman* (London, 1747), pp. 188 and 189.

20. Campbell, *The London Tradesman*, pp. 195–6, 215 and 283.

21. Roger Scola, *Feeding the Victorian City. The Food Supply of Manchester, 1770–1870* (Manchester, 1992), p. 212.

22. Scola, *Feeding the Victorian City*, p. 207.

23. Scola, *Feeding the Victorian City*, pp. 218–19.

24. H.D. Willcock (ed.), *Browns and Chester. Portrait of a Shop 1780–1946* (London, 1947), pp. 23–4 and 35–6.

25. Hugh Barty-King, *Maples. Fine Furnishers* (London, 1992), pp. 1–4 and 7–8.

26. *York Courant*, 2 August 1785.

27. Robert Owen, *The Life of Robert Owen Written by Himself*, vol. I (London, 1857), p. 12.

28. *Reminiscences of an Old Draper* (London, 1876), pp. 5–6.

29. *Reminiscences of an Old Draper*, pp. 7, 18 and 24–5.

30. *Reminiscences of an Old Draper*, pp. 7, 9 and 15–16.

31. *Reminiscences of an Old Draper*, p. 58.

32. Vincent Brome, *H.G. Wells. A Biography* (London, 1951), pp. 30–1.

33. H.G. Wells, *Experiment in Autobiography* (New York, 1934 edn), pp. 116–17 and 121–3. Brome, *H.G. Wells*, p. 32.

34. Booth MSS, at the British Library of Political and Economic Science, London School of Economics, B.133, f. 6. Janet Blackman, 'The Development of the Retail Grocery Trade in the Nineteenth Century', in *Business History*, vol. IX, no. 2 (July 1967), p. 115.

35. Booth MSS B.133, ff. 19–20, interview with Mr Panet, 4 July 1895.

36. Booth MSS B.114, f. 62, interview with James H. Wilson of Crouch End, 8 July 1895.

37. F. Cape & Co. MSS at Oxfordshire Record Office, B/7/PL2/1, Indenture dated 1 April 1895.

38. Alison Adburgham, *Shops and Shopping 1800–1914* (London, 1989 edn), p. 150.

39. Owen, *The Life of Robert Owen*, pp. 18–19.

40. Owen, *The Life of Robert Owen*, pp. 20 and 22.

41. Journal of Marmaduke Strother at the British Library, Egerton MSS 2479, f. 79, entry for 10 February 1785.

42. Vaisey (ed.), *The Diary of Thomas Turner*, p. 16, entry for 1 November 1755: 'My brother Moses came over and dined with us and . . . kept shop while my wife and I went to Lewes.' About a month earlier Moses and Thomas had gone to Lewes to meet 'the Manchesterman', a packman from the north of England, selling mainly cotton goods (p. 15).

43. Joyce Donald (ed.), *The Letters of Thomas Hayton, Vicar of Long Crendon, Buckinghamshire 1821–1887* (Buckinghamshire Record Society, vol. 20, 1979), p. x.

44. Quoted in Margot C. Finn, *The Character of Credit. Personal Debt in English Culture, 1740–1914* (Cambridge, 2003), p. 303.

45. Bankruptcy MSS for Joseph Gibbs at N.A., B3/2095.

46. York Corporation House Book B.44 at York City Archives, ff. 386–8 and 399. Return from York to William Pitt, 1797, with details of estimated annual income and expenditure and assessed taxes of leading citizens in Chatham MSS PRO.30/8/281 in NA. Hereafter cited as Return to William Pitt, 1797.

47. York Corporation House Book, ff. 389–90 and 395. Register of the Freemen of the City of York at York City Archives. Return of Licensed Tea Dealers in the City of York in 1784, PRO.30/8/293 at NA.

48. York Corporation House Book, f. 397.

49. Trevor Fawcett, 'Wedgwood's Bath Showrooms', in *Pickpocketing the Rich* (Holburne Museum of Art, Bath, catalogue, 2002), p. 104. Neil McKendrick, John Brewer and J.H. Plumb, *The Birth of a Consumer Society. The Commercialization of Eighteenth-century England* (London, 1983 edn), pp. 118 and 120–1.

50. Quoted in Fawcett, 'Wedgwood's Bath Showrooms', p. 107.

51. McKendrick, Brewer and Plumb, *The Birth of a Consumer Society*, p. 121.

52. Stanley Chapman, 'The "Revolution" in the Manufacture of Ready-made Clothing 1840–60', in *London Journal*, vol. 29, no. 1 (2004), pp. 44–5 and 51–2.

53. Katrina Honeyman, 'Tailor-Made: Mass Production, High Street Retailing and the Leeds Menswear Multiples, 1918 to 1939', in *Northern History*, vol. XXXVII (December 2000), p. 298. Gareth Shaw, 'The European Scene: Britain and Germany', in John Benson and Gareth Shaw (eds), *The Evolution of Retail Systems c. 1800–1914* (Leicester, 1992), p. 30.

54. *Royal Commission on the Truck System*, vol. I, *Report*, PP1871, vol. XXVI, pp. v–vii and xi. David Alexander, *Retailing in England during the Industrial Revolution* (London, 1970), p. 23.

55. *Royal Commission on the Truck System, Minutes of Evidence: Summary*, p. 34.

56. *Royal Commission on the Truck System, Minutes of Evidence*, p. 35, Qu. 19,314.

57. *Report of the Commissioner to Inquire into the Operation of the Truck Act in the Mining Districts, 5 & 6 Vict. c.99*, PP1852, vol. XXI, pp. 8–9 and 12.

58. *Report of the Commissioner to Inquire into the Operation of the Truck Act*, p. 22.

59. *Royal Commission on the Truck System: Minutes of Evidence, Summary*, p. 34, evidence of W. Pratt, one of the shop managers.

60. *Royal Commission on the Truck System: Minutes of Evidence, Summary*, p. 37, evidence of T. Parry, who had worked at the Blaenavon Company's shop.

61. Booth MSS B.115, f. 92, interview with Mr Wright in Harringay.

62. Charles Booth, *Life and Labour of the People in London*, 2nd Series, *Industry*, vol. 3 (London, 1903), pp. 251–5.

63. Earle, *The Making of the English Middle Class*, pp. 106–8.

64. Alexander, *Retailing in England*, pp. 206–7.

65. Alexander, *Retailing in England*, p. 207.

66. Alexander, *Retailing in England*, pp. 208–10.

67. Robert Roberts, *A Ragged Schooling. Growing Up in the Classic Slum* (Manchester, 1976), p. 2.

68. J.D. Marshall (ed.), *The Autobiography of William Stout of Lancaster 1665–1752* (Manchester, 1967), p. 89.

69. Marshall (ed.), *The Autobiography of William Stout*, pp. 200–1.

70. Daniel Defoe, *The Complete English Tradesman* (Gloucester, 1987 edn), p. 15. Bankruptcy MSS of Joseph Gibbs, B.3/2095, at NA.

71. Bankruptcy MSS of Joseph Gibbs, B.3/2095.

72. Bankruptcy MSS of Joseph Gibbs, B.3/2095.

73. *The Times*, 10 July 1882.

74. Beverley Lemire, *Dress, Culture and Commerce. The English Clothing Trade before the Factory, 1660–1800* (Basingstoke, 1997), pp. 86–7.

75. Colin Hughes, *Lime, Lemon & Sarsaparilla. The Italian Community in South Wales 1881–1945* (Bridgend, 2003 edn), pp. 36–7 and 43.

76. Hoh-Cheung and Lorna H. Mui, *Shops and Shopkeeping in Eighteenth-Century England* (Kingston, Montreal and London, 1989), p. 27.

77. James Lackington, *Life of J. Lackington, Bookseller* (London, privately printed, n.d. [*c.* 1791]), pp. 136–7, 141–2, 212–13 and 265.

78. Henry Curwen, *A History of Booksellers. The Old and the New* (London, n.d.), p. 74.

79. Curwen, *A History of Booksellers*, pp. 74–5. Kathryn A. Morris, *English Shops and Shopping* (New Haven and London, 2003), p. 38.

80. Defoe, *The Complete English Tradesman*, pp. 46 and 48.

81. Booth MSS B.115, f. 93.

82. Finn, *The Character of Credit*, p. 301.

83. James Budgett & Son Credit Ledgers and References, MS 20,364, ff. 426 and 431 at the Guildhall Library Record Office, London.

84. James Budgett & Son Credit Ledgers and References, MS 20,364, f. 528.

85. See 1881 Census for Buckingham at the Family Records Centre, RG.11/1485.

86. James Budgett & Son Credit Ledgers and References, MS 20,365, f. 246.

87. James Budgett & Son Credit Ledgers and References, MS 20,365, f. 117 and memorandum from Davy Crowe, grocer and tea dealer, 10 May 1904.

88. Scola, *Feeding the Victorian City*, p. 225.

89. Winstanley, *The Shopkeeper's World*, p. 55.

90. Vaisey (ed.), *The Diary of Thomas Turner*, p. 169.

91. Robert Roberts, *The Classic Slum. Salford Life in the First Quarter of the Century* (Manchester, 1971), p. 61. Roberts, *A Ragged Schooling*, pp. 17–18.

92. Roberts, *The Classic Slum*, p. 175 and Roberts, *A Ragged Schooling*, p. 142.

93. Roberts, *A Ragged Schooling*, p. 142.

94. Roberts, *The Classic Slum*, p. 61.

95. Mui, *Shops and Shopkeepers*, p. 212.

96. Vaisey (ed.), *The Diary of Thomas Turner*, pp. 10–11, entry for 23 July 1755.

97. E.W. Martin, *The Shearers and the Shorn. A Study of Life in a Devon Community* (London, 1965), pp. 91–2.

98. Martin, *The Shearers and the Shorn*, p. 95.

99. Christopher P. Hosgood, 'The "Pigmies of Commerce" and the Working-Class Community: Small Shopkeepers in England, 1870–1914', in *Journal of Social History*, vol. 22, no. 3 (Spring 1989), pp. 442–3.
100. Hosgood, 'The "Pigmies of Commerce"', p. 443.
101. Roberts, *The Classic Slum*, p. 61.
102. *Western Mail*, 20 November 1913.
103. Mitchell, 'Retailing in Eighteenth- and Early Nineteenth-Century Cheshire', p. 57. 25 Geo. III c.30. *An Act for Duties on Shops in Great Britain, 1785.*
104. *Population Census of 1801: England and Wales* (London, 1802). An Account of the Number of Shops Shewing their Rents in the Towns and Parishes of Suffolk, PRO.30/8/281, ff. 145–6, at the NA. Shop tax revenue for Suffolk for the year ending 5 April 1788, E.182.969, Part 2, at the NA.
105. Mitchell, 'Pitt's Shop Tax', p. 349.
106. *Reading Mercury*, 12 July 1785. *Gentleman's Magazine*, vol. LV, Part II (July 1785), p. 564.
107. *Ipswich Journal*, 18 June 1785 and *Bath Chronicle*, 16 June 1785.
108. Minutes of the Court of Common Council of the Corporation of London at the Corporation of London Record Office, COL/CC/01/01/69, ff. 48–9 and 75, entries for 1 February and 24 April 1788.
109. *Journals of the House of Commons*, vol. XLI, 31 January 1786, f. 155.
110. *Gentleman's Magazine*, vol. LV, Part II (July 1785), p. 564.
111. 26 Geo. III c.9. *An Act for Duties on Shops in Great Britain, 1786. Gentleman's Magazine*, vol. LVII, Part I (February 1787), p. 144.
112. *Gentleman's Magazine*, vol. LVII, Part I (February 1787), p. 144.
113. Mui, *Shops and Shopkeepers*, p. 85.
114. Stephen Dowell, *A History of Taxation and Taxes in England*, vol. 2 (London, 1965 edn), p. 193.
115. See Chatham MSS at NA PRO.30/8/281, ff. 18 and 20. Returns of Householders &c.
116. Mui, *Shops and Shopkeepers*, pp. 119–20.
117. *Royal Commission on Market Rights and Tolls*, PP1888, vol. LV, p. 118, Qu. 2304.
118. Winstanley, *The Shopkeeper's World*, p. 46.
119. Roberts, *The Classic Slum*, p. 85. Hosgood, 'The "Pigmies of Commerce"', p. 440. Charles Booth declared that the poor went to the shop 'as an ordinary housewife to her canisters'.
120. Foley, *A Bolton Childhood*, p. 19.
121. Roberts, *The Classic Slum*, pp. 27 and 103–4.
122. Hosgood, 'The "Pigmies of Commerce"', pp. 441 and 448.
123. Hosgood, 'The "Pigmies of Commerce"', p. 453.
124. Hosgood, 'The "Pigmies of Commerce"', p. 445.
125. Thea Vigne and Alun Howkins, 'The Small Shopkeeper in Industrial and Market Towns', in Geoffrey Crossick (ed.), *The Lower Middle Classes in Britain* (London, 1977), p. 205.

126. *Report from the Select Committee on Co-operative Stores*, PP1878–9, vol. IX, Evidence of Henry Cushen, grocer, p. 117, Qu. 2243–2245.
127. Quoted in Winstanley, *The Shopkeeper's World*, p. 54.
128. Quoted in Winstanley, *The Shopkeeper's World*, p. 54.
129. Vigne and Howkins, 'The Small Shopkeeper', pp. 206–7.

CHAPTER 3

1. James B. Jefferys, *Retail Trading in Britain 1850–1950* (Cambridge, 1954), p. 73. Martin Purvis, 'Co-operative retailing in Britain', in John Benson and Gareth Shaw (eds), *The Evolution of Retail Systems c. 1800–1914* (Leicester, 1992), p. 107.
2. Martin Purvis, *Nineteenth Century Co-operative Retailing in England and Wales. A Geographical Approach* (Oxford D.Phil. Thesis, 1987), p. 30. Purvis, 'Co-operative retailing', p. 109. W. Hamish Fraser, *The Coming of the Mass Market, 1850–1914* (London and Basingstoke, 1981), p. 121.
3. Fraser, *The Coming of the Mass Market*, p. 121.
4. Christopher P. Hosgood, 'The "Pigmies of Commerce" and the Working-Class Community: Small Shopkeepers in England, 1870–1914', in *Journal of Social History*, vol. 22, no. 3 (Spring 1989), p. 445.
5. Purvis, *Nineteenth Century Co-operative Retailing*, p. 324.
6. Martin Purvis, 'Stocking the Store: Co-operative Retailers in North-East England and Systems of Wholesale Supply, *c.* 1860–77', in Nicholas Alexander and Gary Akehurst (eds), *The Emergence of Modern Retailing, 1750–1950* (London and Portland, Oregon, 1999), p. 55.
7. Purvis, *Nineteenth Century Co-operative Retailing*, p. 60.
8. Purvis, 'Co-operative retailing', p. 108.
9. Purvis, *Nineteenth Century Co-operative Retailing*, p. 37.
10. William Lovett, *Life and Struggles of William Lovett*, vol. 1 (London, 1920 edn), pp. 41–2.
11. Lovett, *Life and Struggles*, p. 44.
12. Purvis, *Nineteenth Century Co-operative Retailing*, p. 54. Lovett, Life and Struggles, pp. 43 and 89.
13. Arnold Bonner, *British Co-operation* (Manchester, 1961), p. 42.
14. Bonner, *British Co-operation*, pp. 44–9 and 515–16.
15. Bonner, *British Co-operation*, pp. 50–1 and 512.
16. Bonner, *British Co-operation*, pp. 482–3 and 508–9.
17. Bonner, *British Co-operation*, p. 516.
18. Purvis, *Nineteenth Century Co-operative Retailing*, p. 180.
19. *Reports of the Chief Registrar of Friendly Societies for the Year ending 31 December 1913*, Part B, Distributive Trading Societies, PP1914, vol. LXXVI, p. 88.
20. *Reports of the Chief Registrar for 1913*, p. 56.
21. Purvis, *Nineteenth Century Co-operative Retailing*, p. 245.

22. Purvis, 'Co-operative retailing', p. 108.
23. Purvis, *Nineteenth Century Co-operative Retailing*, pp. 413 and 446.
24. Purvis, 'Stocking the Store', p. 57.
25. *Report from the Select Committee on Co-operative Stores: Minutes of Evidence, PP1878–9*, vol. IX, p. 238, Qu. 6,242.
26. Purvis, *Nineteenth Century Co-operative Retailing*, p. 389.
27. Quoted in Purvis, *Nineteenth Century Co-operative Retailing*, p. 369.
28. Kathryn A. Morrison, *English Shops and Shopping* (New Haven and London, 2003), pp. 146–7.
29. Morrison, *English Shops*, p. 148.
30. Morrison, *English Shops*, p. 150.
31. W. Henry Brown, *A Century of Liverpool Co-operation* (Liverpool, n.d. [c. 1930]), p. 48. Liverpool's first co-operative efforts had been made at the end of the 1820s, with seven or eight societies in operation by the summer of 1830. All faded away by the early 1830s. Brown, *A Century of Liverpool Co-operation*, pp. 16–30.
32. Brown, *A Century of Liverpool Co-operation*, p. 50.
33. Brown, *A Century of Liverpool Co-operation*, pp. 51–8.
34. Brown, *A Century of Liverpool Co-operation*, pp. 59–60 and 73–4.
35. Brown, *A Century of Liverpool Co-operation*, pp. 75–8.
36. Purvis, *Nineteenth Century Co-operative Retailing*, pp. 218 and 228.
37. *The Co-operative Employé*, October 1908.
38. Sir William Richardson, *A Union of Many Trades. The History of USDAW* (Manchester, n.d. [c. 1979]), p. 19.
39. Testimonial from F. Austen Williams to Mr Rose, President of Reading Co-operative Society, 14 October 1893, D/EX 1497/1/29/4 at Berkshire Record Office. This testimonial covered both of the candidates mentioned.
40. Richardson, *A Union of Many Trades*, p. 19.
41. *The Co-operative News*, 'The Man Behind the Counter', 25 March 1911.
42. Purvis, 'Stocking the Store', p. 60.
43. *Reading Co-operative Society*, pamphlet, n.d. D/EX/1497/16/1, p. 9, at Berkshire Record Office.
44. Management Committee Minutes of Reading Co-operative Society, D/EX/1497/1/4, entry for 30 November 1887, at Berkshire Record Office.
45. T.C. Barker and J.R. Harris, *A Merseyside Town in the Industrial Revolution. St Helens 1750–1900* (London, 1993 edn), p. 479.
46. Barker and Harris, *A Merseyside Town*, p. 479. See also p. 456.
47. Barker and Harris, *A Merseyside Town*, p. 479.
48. Michael J. Winstanley, *The Shopkeeper's World 1830–1914* (Manchester, 1983), pp. 83–8. *The Times*, 18 August 1902.
49. Winstanley, *The Shopkeeper's World*, p. 88.
50. Winstanley, *The Shopkeeper's World*, pp. 88–9.
51. Purvis, 'Stocking the Store', p. 61.
52. Fraser, *The Coming of the Mass Market*, p. 123.

53. Myra Marsh, 'Shopping in Denton in the early years of the Twentieth Century', in Alice Lock (ed.), *Looking Back at Denton* (Stalybridge, 1985), p. 81.

54. Marsh, 'Shopping in Denton', p. 80.

55. *Amalgamated Union of Co-operative Employés Coming of Age Souvenir 1891–1912* (Manchester, Annual Delegate Meeting, 1912), Edward E. Dale, 'A Pioneer's Reminiscences', p. 30, at the TUC Library, London Metropolitan University.

56. *Management Committee Minutes of Reading Co-operative Society*, D/EX/1497/1/4 entries for 25 December 1885 and 16 July 1886.

57. *The Co-operative Employé*, September 1908, discussing 'The Commission System'.

58. *The Co-operative Employé*, 'The Commission System'.

59. Purvis, 'Stocking the Store', p. 65.

60. Purvis, *Nineteenth Century Co-operative Retailing*, p. 447.

61. *The Co-operative Employé*, July, August, September, November and December 1908.

62. *The Co-operative Employé*, November and December 1908.

63. *The Co-operative Employé*, December 1908.

64. *Reading Co-operative Society Management Committee Minutes* D/EX/1497/1/14, entry for 7 October 1909.

65. Commission at Reading was discontinued finally in May 1887.

66. *The Co-operative Employé*, July 1909.

67. *The Co-operative Employé*, September 1909.

68. *The Co-operative Employé*, November 1909. In October 1909 the journal had commented bitterly that the Stafford management committee had 'adopted an attitude which has long since been discarded by the ordinary capitalist employer of labour'.

69. Richardson, *A Union of Many Trades*, pp. 8–9.

70. See also *The Co-operative Employé*, March 1909, when it was reported that the Ashton-under-Lyne Society had added a day to the annual holiday of employees, making seven working days in all. They had also decided to close their shops at 9 p.m. instead of 9.30 p.m. on Friday nights.

71. Qualidata, University of Essex, C.707/54/1–3, interview with Frank Benson in 1969.

72. H.J. Twigg, *An Outline History of Co-operative Education* (Manchester, 1924), pp. 24, 28 and 31, at the Co-operative College, Manchester.

73. Qualidata, University of Essex, C.707/151/1–3, interview with Mr J. Wolfendale.

74. Reading Co-operative Society Management Committee Minutes, D/EX/1497/1/4, entries for 15 January 1886 and 9 September 1886, and Reading Co-operative Society Management Committee Minutes, D/EX/1497/1/6, entries for 5 and 19 March 1891.

75. Reading Co-operative Society Management Committee Minutes, entries for 1 January and 5 February 1891.

76. Reading Co-operative Society Management Committee Minutes, entries for 5 May and 25 November 1886.

77. Reading Co-operative Society Management Committee Minutes, D/EX/1497/1/4, entries for 6 April, 6 July, 12 October and 19 October 1887.

78. *The Shop Assistant*, November 1897, 'Co-operative Shops and their Employees'.

79. *The Co-operative Employé*, July 1908, article by Joseph Hallsworth, 'The Co-operative Movement and the Trade Union Organisation of its Employés'.

80. Qualidata, University of Essex, C.707/170/1–2. Mr Snowden was born in 1892 and interviewed in 1970.

81. Linda McCullough Thew, *The Pit Village and the Store. The Portrait of a Mining Past* (London, 1985), p. 138.

82. Thew, *The Pit Village*, pp. 125 and 144.

83. Julia Hood and B.S. Yamey, 'The Middle-Class Co-operative Retailing Societies in London, 1864–1900', in Oxford Economic Papers, New Series, vol. 9, no. 3 (October 1957), pp. 310–11.

84. *Report of the Select Committee on Co-operative Stores*, Evidence of James Lawson, p. 277, Qu. 6109, 6112–13 and 6115. Hood and Yamey, 'The Middle-Class Co-operative Retailing Societies', pp. 311–12.

85. *Report of the Select Committee on Co-operative Stores*, p. 282, Qu. 6238, 6241, 6252, p. 286, Qu 6343 and p. 297, Qu. 6624–5. Hood and Yamey, 'The Middle-Class Co-operative Retailing Societies', pp. 312–13.

86. Hood and Yamey, 'The Middle-Class Co-operative Retailing Societies', pp. 313–14.

87. *Report of the Select Committee on Co-operative Stores*, p. 244, Qu. 5321.

88. *Report of the Select Committee on Co-operative Stores*, p. 127, Qu. 2457 and p. 128, Qu. 2462.

89. *Report of the Select Committee on Co-operative Stores*, p. 131, Qu. 2556.

90. Hood and Yamey, 'The Middle Class Co-operative Retailing Societies', pp. 321–2.

91. Purvis, 'Co-operative retailing', pp. 107 and 126.

92. Winstanley, *The Shopkeeper's World*, p. 37.

93. Morrison, *English Shops and Shopping*, p. 201. Ruth Martin, W.H. Smith (Hove, 1983), section 16 (not paginated).

94. Morrison, *English Shops and Shopping*, p. 201.

95. Fraser, *The Coming of the Mass Market*, p. 118.

96. Jane Mace (ed.), *'Call yourself a draper?' Memories of life in the trade* (London, 1993), p. 32.

97. Dorothy Davis, *A History of Shopping* (London, 1966), pp. 282 and 284.

98. Winstanley, *The Shopkeeper's World*, p. 39.

99. *The Times*, 18 August 1902, article on 'The Passing of the Grocer'.

100. Michael French, 'Commercials, careers, and culture: travelling salesmen in Britain, 1890s–1930s', in *Economic History Review*, vol. LVIII, no. 2 (May 2005), p. 367.

101. Jefferys, Retail Trading in Britain, p. 52. Will Paine, Shop Slavery and Emancipation (London, 1912), p. 48.

102. Goronwy Rees, *St Michael. A History of Marks & Spencer* (London, 1969), pp. 14, 15 and 89–90. By 1914 the firm had 133 shops and only 10 market hall

stalls; 56 of the shops were in London, where the company had consolidated its position by acquiring the Arcadia Bazaar Company and the London Penny Bazaar Company. Morrison, *English Shops and Shopping*, p. 230. Winstanley, *The Shopkeeper's World*, p. 39.

103. Olive Howarth (ed.), *Textile Voices. Mill Life This Century* (Bradford Libraries and Information Service, n.d.), p. 35. John K. Winkler, *Five and Ten. The Fabulous Life of F.W. Woolworth* (London, 1941), pp. 151–9. Gareth Shaw, Andrew Alexander, John Benson and John Jones, 'Structural and Spatial Trends in British Retailing: The Importance of Firm-Level Studies', in Nicholas Alexander and Gary Akehurst (eds), *The Emergence of Modern Retailing 1750–1850* (London and Portland, Oregon, 1999), pp. 86–7.

104. Fraser, *The Coming of the Mass Market*, p. 118.

105. Sir Thomas J. Lipton Bt, *Leaves from the Lipton Logs* (London, n.d. [1932]), pp. 39, 65, 79–80, 83, 95–6.

106. Lipton, *Leaves from the Lipton Logs*, pp. 88 and 110.

107. Peter Mathias, *Retailing Revolution. A History of Multiple Retailing in the Food Trade based upon the Allied Suppliers Group of Companies* (London, 1967) p. 47.

108. Lipton, *Leaves from the Lipton Logs*, pp. 91–3.

109. Lipton, *Leaves from the Lipton Logs*, p. 99.

110. Lipton, *Leaves from the Lipton Logs*, pp. 100 and 123. Mathias, *Retailing Revolution*, pp. 101–3.

111. Quoted in Fraser, *The Coming of the Mass Market*, p. 110.

112. Mathias, *Retailing Revolution*, p. 98. The first London shop opened in April 1888 in Bayswater.

113. Lipton, *Leaves from the Lipton Logs*, p. 114.

114. Lipton, *Leaves from the Lipton Logs*, pp. 112–13.

115. Lipton, *Leaves from the Lipton Logs*, p. 163.

116. Mathias, *Retailing Revolution*, p. 107.

117. Davis, *A History of Shopping*, p. 283.

118. Quoted in Davis, *A History of Shopping*, p. 282.

119. Jefferys, *Retail Trading in Britain*, p. 146.

120. Jefferys, *Retail Trading in Britain*, p. 146.

121. Mathias, *Retailing Revolution*, p. 49.

122. P.C. Hoffman, *They Also Serve. The Story of the Shop Worker* (London, 1949), p. 89.

123. Judi Bevan, *Trolley Wars. The Battle of the Supermarkets* (London, 2005), pp. 26–7.

124. Bevan, *Trolley Wars*, pp. 32–5.

125. Mathias, *Retailing Revolution*, pp. 101, 128, 171 and 238. Paine, *Shop Slavery*, p. 48.

126. Jefferys, *Retail Trading in Britain*, p. 72.

127. Mathias, *Retailing Revolution*, p. 123.

128. Mathias, *Retailing Revolution*, p. 123.

129. Qualidata, University of Essex, C.707/116/1–2.

130. Hoffman, *They Also Serve*, p. 89.

131. Lee Holcombe, *Victorian Ladies at Work. Middle-Class Working Women in England and Wales 1850–1914* (Newton Abbot, 1973), p. 116.

132. *Twenty-third Annual Report of the National Amalgamated Union of Shop Assistants, Warehousemen and Clerks for 1913*, p. 5, at TUC Library.

133. See *Twenty-fourth Annual Report of NAUSAW&C for 1914*, p. 8.

134. *Minutes of Evidence before the Select Committee on Shop Assistants*, PP1930–1, vol. IX, p. 316, Qu. 3969, evidence of Mr 'B'.

135. Hoffman, *They Also Serve*, p. 89.

136. Hoffman, *They Also Serve*, p. 90.

137. Mathias, *Retailing Revolution*, p. 143.

138. Booth MSS B.133, note of interview with Mr C.C., 4 July 1895, ff. 14–15.

139. *Minutes of Evidence before Select Committee on Shop Assistants*, p. 304, Qu. 3620. The worker could apply for a job again when he had recovered. (Qu. 3623).

140. Christopher Hosgood, 'A "Brave and Daring Folk"? Shopkeepers and Trade Associational Life in Victorian and Edwardian England', in *Journal of Social History*, vol. 26, no. 2 (1992), p. 307, note 79.

141. Gareth Shaw, 'The evolution and impact of large-scale retailing in Britain', in John Benson and Gareth Shaw (eds), *The Evolution of Retail Systems c. 1800–1914* (Leicester, 1992), p. 162.

142. Hosgood, 'A "Brave and Daring Folk"?' pp. 293–4.

143. Hosgood, 'A "Brave and Daring Folk"?' pp. 297–8. W.G. Copsey, *The Modern Grocer and Provision Dealer* (London, 1951 edn), vol. 3, pp. 302–3.

144. Winstanley, *The Shopkeeper's World*, pp. 124–5, 127 and 136.

145. Michael Winstanley (ed.), *A Traditional Grocer. T.D. Smith's of Lancaster 1858–1981* (Lancaster, Centre for North-West Regional Studies, University of Lancaster, Occasional Papers no. 21, 1991), p. 18.

146. Stanley Chapman, *Jesse Boot of Boots the Chemists. A study in business history* (London, 1974), pp. 37–9.

147. Chapman, *Jesse Boot*, pp. 40 and 57.

148. Chapman, *Jesse Boot*, pp. 56–60.

149. Chapman, *Jesse Boot*, pp. 77 and 90.

150. Chapman, *Jesse Boot*, p. 160.

151. Chapman, *Jesse Boot*, pp. 161–3.

152. Chapman, *Jesse Boot*, pp. 105, 108 and 114.

153. Fraser, *The Coming of the Mass Market*, p. 120.

CHAPTER 4

1. Hoh-Cheung and Lorna H. Mui, *Shops and Shopkeeping in Eighteenth-Century England* (Kingston, Montreal and London, 1989), pp. 238–9.

2. Account book of William Baker of Banbury, tailor and outfitter, in the Bodleian Library, Oxford, MS Top.Oxon.*c*.453. Baker seems to have taken out a patent for the waterproofing of leggings.

3. Michael Moss and Alison Turton, *A Legend of Retailing. House of Fraser* (London, 1989), p. 293. Alison Adburgham, *Shops and Shopping 1800–1914* (London, 1989 edn), p. 51. Bath Trade Cards at Bath Local History Library 242b, W. Tuckwell, linen draper, 1831.

4. David Alexander, *Retailing in England during the Industrial Revolution* (London, 1970), p. 130.

5. Michael J. Winstanley, *The Shopkeeper's World 1830–1914* (Manchester, 1983), pp. 202, 205 and 209. Hazel Wheeler, *Half a Pound of Tuppenny Rice. Life in a Yorkshire Village Shop* (Stroud, 1993), pp. 3 and 9.

6. *The Drapers' Journal*, 27 May 1880.

7. Charles Booth, *Life and Labour of the People in London: Second Series: Industry*, vol. 3 (London, 1903), pp. 68–9.

8. In Bath Trade Cards collection at Bath Local History Library, 242b.

9. Booth MSS B.114, evidence of Thomas Oakman, f. 65, at the British Library of Economic and Political Science, London School of Economics.

10. Booth MSS B.114, f. 66.

11. Booth MSS B.114, f. 67.

12. *Reminiscences of an Old Draper* (London, 1876), p. 54.

13. *Reminiscences of an Old Draper*, p. 54.

14. Alexander, *Retailing in England*, p. 140.

15. Adburgham, *Shops and Shopping*, pp. 145–6.

16. Maurice Corina, *Fine Silks and Oak Counters. Debenhams 1778–1978* (London, 1978), p. 45.

17. Winstanley, *The Shopkeeper's World*, p. 59.

18. York Trade Cards at York City Archives, 1847, Messrs Bland and Halley at 6 High Ousegate, York.

19. Angela and John Airey, *The Bainbridges of Newcastle. A Family History* (Newcastle upon Tyne, privately published, 1979), pp. 39, 45, 46 and 47.

20. Lee Holcombe, *Victorian Ladies at Work. Middle-Class Women in England and Wales 1850–1914* (Newton Abbot, 1973), p. 103.

21. Calculated from the 1851, 1871 and 1911 Population Census Reports, PP1852–3, vol. LXXXVIII, Part I for 1851; 1873, vol. LXXI, Part I for 1871; 1913, vol. LXXVIII for 1911.

22. Population Census Report for England and Wales for 1911, p. ciii. The General Report (p. cii) noted that between 1901 and 1911 there had been an increase of 23.6 per cent of females employed in the drapery sector, but a decline among males of 1.3 per cent. Some of the rise in the females was attributed to 'the inclusion of a larger proportion than formerly of relatives assisting in the business'.

23. Booth MSS B.114, f. 53, and A.20, f. 71.

24. M. Jeune [Lady Jeune], 'The Ethics of Shopping', in *The Fortnightly Review*, vol. 63 (January 1895), p. 126.

25. Bill Lancaster, *The Department Store. A Social History* (London and New York, 1995), p. 130. M. Jeune, 'The Ethics of Shopping', pp. 123–4.

26. Jeune, 'The Ethics of Shopping', p. 124.

27. Adburgham, *Shops and Shopping*, pp. vii–viii.

28. M. Jeune, 'The Ethics of Shopping', p. 124.

29. Richard S. Lambert, *The Universal Provider. A Study of William Whiteley and the Rise of the London Department Store* (London, 1938), p. 25.

30. Will Anderson, *The Counter Exposed* (London, 1896), p. 10. This polemical pamphlet is in the Bodleian Library, Oxford, 23216.e.22.

31. Moss and Turton, *A Legend of Retailing*, p. 84.

32. *The Drapers' Journal*, 27 May and 17 June 1880.

33. Mary Agnes Hamilton, *Margaret Bondfield* (London, 1924), pp. 43–4. *Reminiscences of an Old Draper*, p. 59.

34. Cutting from the *Weekly Dispatch*, 24 May 1914 in Tuckwell MSS 106a/23 at the TUC Library.

35. Quoted in Hamilton, *Margaret Bondfield*, p. 47.

36. Hamilton, *Margaret Bondfield*, pp. 47–8.

37. Hamilton, *Margaret Bondfield*, p. 48.

38. The Rt Hon. Margaret Bondfield, *A Life's Work* (London, n.d. [*c.* 1948]), p. 62.

39. P.C. Hoffman, *They Also Serve. The Story of the Shop Worker* (London, 1949), p. 28.

40. Hoffman, *They Also Serve*, p. 27.

41. Holcombe, *Victorian Ladies at Work*, p. 110.

42. *The Select Committee on Shop Hours Regulation Bill*, PP1886, vol. XII, Appendix 7, p. 272, statement by Mr S. Strange, 8 May 1886.

43. *Seats for Shop Assistants Act, 1899*, 62 & 63 Vict., c.21.

44. *Report from the Select Committee on Shop Assistants*, PP1929–30, vol. VII, Evidence of Dr Ethel Bentham, 25 July 1930, p. 186, Qu. 2447.

45. For details of Alfred Cosford see 1881 Census for Moreton Pinkney, Northamptonshire, R.G.11.1533 and for Oxford in 1901, when he was living in at Cape's Cowley Road premises, R.G.13.1379, at the Family Records Centre. Salary Receipt Book for 1911–18 B/7/F2/1 at Oxfordshire Record Office, entries for Cosford, and B/7/X/8 Buyers' Wages and Commission, also with the Cape MSS at Oxfordshire Record Office. In 1901 he was shown as 'outfitter's assistant' and was aged 24.

46. Booth MSS B.114, f. 57, evidence of Richard Lane, draper's assistant at Messrs T. Allin & Co., Lambeth Walk. Booth, *Life and Labour*, p. 72.

47. Calculated from Register of Employees at Liberty 1883–94 at Westminster Record Office, Acc/1932/49. The departments involved (C, D, E, G and H) had a total staff at work in 1889 of sixty, according to a list of staff members at Liberty in that year, Acc/788/151 at Westminster Record Office. For details of the firm's development see, for example, Stephen Calloway (ed.), *The House of Liberty. Masters of Style and Decoration* (London, 1992).

48. William Judd, 'A Few Early Recollections', in *The 'Liberty' Lamp*, March 1925, p. 4, at Westminster Record Office. This was a house magazine. *The 'Liberty' Lamp*, May 1925, noted that in that year sixty-seven staff members had been

with the firm thirty years or more. Calloway estimates the staff at that time numbered 'a thousand or more', compared to the 255 listed in 1889. Calloway (ed.), *The House of Liberty*, p. 30 and Acc/788/151 for the 1889 list.

49. Airey, *The Bainbridges of Newcastle*, pp. 47–8.

50. Hoffman, *They Also Serve*, p. 23.

51. Norman Hancock, *An Innocent Grows Up* (London, 1947), p. 124. Booth, *Life and Labour*, p. 79. Booth suggested that 'after thirty-five years of age, an assistant has not much chance of obtaining a new situation'. Cutting from the *Weekly Dispatch*, 26 April 1914, article by James Sherliker, in Tuckwell MSS 103/41.

52. Cutting from *Modern Society*, 16 April 1910 in Tuckwell MSS 107/12.

53. Quoted in Hoffman, *They Also Serve*, p. x.

54. Aubrey Niel Morgan, *David Morgan 1833–1919. The Life and Times of a Master Draper in South Wales* (Newport, Gwent, 1977), pp. 65 and 124.

55. Morgan, *David Morgan*, pp. 126–7.

56. Booth MSS B.114, f. 60, and Rules on page opposite f. 60.

57. Anderson, *The Counter Exposed*, p. 81, quoting from *Today*, 7 December 1895.

58. Bondfield, *A Life's Work*, p. 63.

59. Quoted in Erika D. Rappaport, '"The Halls of Temptation": Gender, Politics, and the Construction of the Department Store in Late Victorian London', in *Journal of British Studies*, vol. 35, no. 1 (January 1966), p. 76.

60. Richard Foster, F. *Cape & Co. of St Ebbes Street, Oxford. From Draper's Shop to Department Store* (Oxford, n.d.) at Oxfordshire Centre for Local Studies, Oxford, OXFO.658.8. The booklet is not paginated.

61. H.D. Willcock (ed.), *Browns and Chester. Portrait of a Shop 1780–1946* (London, 1947), pp. 113, 207 and 212. Booth MSS A.20, f. 17, interview with Mr Turner, 10 September 1895. According to Turner, 'a frock coat' was 'compulsory for all' male assistants in some businesses. If clothing was 'worn or shabby you will be told of it'.

62. Quoted in Christopher P. Hosgood, '"Mercantile Monasteries": Shops, Shop Assistants, and Shop Life in Late Victorian and Edwardian Britain', in *Journal of British Studies*, vol. 38, no. 3 (July 1999), pp. 328 and 330.

63. Bankruptcy proceedings involving Thomas Broad, draper, in the National Archives, B.3.560. Alexander, *Retailing in England*, pp. 193 and 197.

64. Hancock, *An Innocent Grows Up*, pp. 1, 21, 62, 73.

65. Hancock, *An Innocent Grows Up*, pp. 80–1.

66. Claire Walsh, 'A Social Meaning and Social Space in the Shopping Galleries of Early Modern London', in John Benson and Laura Ugolini (eds), *A Nation of Shopkeepers. Five Centuries of British Retailing* (London and New York, 2003), pp. 52–6 and 59. The smallest of the galleries, located in Westminster Hall, had just sixty-nine shops.

67. Walsh, 'Social Meaning and Social Space', p. 77.

68. Walsh, 'Social Meaning and Social Space', p. 68.

69. Adburgham, *Shops and Shopping*, p. 18.

70. Revd J. Nightingale, *The Bazaar, Its Origin, Nature and Objects Explained*, 2nd edn (London, 1816), p. 5, and Adburgham, *Shops and Shopping*, p. 23.
71. Nightingale, *The Bazaar*, pp. 6 and 26–7.
72. Nightingale, *The Bazaar*, pp. 7–10.
73. Quoted in Rappaport, '"The Halls of Temptation"', p. 69.
74. Nightingale, *The Bazaar*, pp. 7–8.
75. Nightingale, *The Bazaar*, p. 12.
76. Charles Knight, *Knight's Cyclopaedia of London* (London, 1851), p. 762.
77. Adburgham, *Shops and Shopping*, p. 18, quoting from the *World of Fashion*.
78. Kathryn A. Morrison, *English Shops and Shopping* (New Haven and London, 2003), pp. 95–6 and 99.
79. Moss and Turton, *A Legend of Retailing*, pp. 337–8 and 342. *Jolly & Son Ltd, Bath* (n.d.) catalogue at Bath Record Office. In 1831 an advertisement in the *Bath Chronicle* for the Bath Emporium noted that the bazaar department was to include a 'Splendid Selection of Foreign China, Italian Alabaster urns, vases, and figures', and 'almost all the multifarious Articles usually kept in Bazaars'.
80. Adburgham, *Shops and Shopping*, p. 19.
81. Adburgham, *Shops and Shopping*, p. 20.
82. Adburgham, *Shops and Shopping*, p. 21.
83. *Kendals: One Hundred and Fifty Years 1836–1986* (1986), pamphlet in Manchester Local History Library, Q.658.871.Ke.4 (not paginated).
84. Moss and Turton, *A Legend of Retailing*, pp. 343–4.
85. Moss and Turton, *A Legend of Retailing*, p. 344.
86. Morrison, *English Shops and Shopping*, p. 99.
87. Asa Briggs, *Friends of the People. The Centenary History of Lewis's* (London, 1956), p. 118.
88. John Stobart, 'The spread of department stores in provincial England *c.* 1872–1932', a paper presented on 9 April 2005 to the Economic History Society Annual Conference at Leicester University. James B. Jefferys, *Retail Trading in Britain 1850–1950* (Cambridge, 1954), p. 327.
89. Gareth Shaw, 'The evolution and impact of large-scale retailing in Britain', in John Benson and Gareth Shaw (eds), *The Evolution of Retail Systems c. 1800–1914* (Leicester, 1992), p. 143.
90. Jefferys, *Retail Trading*, pp. 28, 59, 78 and 327.
91. Tim Dale, *Harrods. A Palace in Knightsbridge* (London, 1995), p. 47. Alison Adburgham, Introduction to *Victorian Shopping. Harrods Catalogue, 1895* (New York, 1972), not paginated, and contents of the catalogue.
92. Brent Shannon, 'Refashioning Men: Fashion, Masculinity, and the Cultivation of the Male Consumer in Britain, 1860–1914', in *Victorian Studies*, vol. 46, no. 4 (Summer 2004), pp. 608–9.
93. Corina, *Fine Silks and Oak Counters*, p. 184, and John Stobart, 'The spread of department stores'.
94. Jefferys, *Retail Trading*, pp. 325, 328 and 329.

95. Michael B. Miller, *The Bon Marché. Bourgeois Culture and the Department Store, 1869–1920* (London, 1981), pp. 30–1, 39 and 43.

96. Briggs, *Friends of the People*, pp. 36–7. Geoffrey Crossick and Serge Jaumain, 'The world of the department store: distribution, culture and social change', in Geoffrey Crossick and Serge Jaumain (eds), *Cathedrals of Consumption. The European Department Store 1850–1939* (Aldershot, 1999), p. 14.

97. Corina, *Fine Silks and Oak Counters*, p. 71.

98. Shaw, 'The evolution and impact of large-scale retailing', p. 149.

99. Shaw, 'The evolution and impact of large-scale retailing', p. 150.

100. *Victorian Shopping. Harrods Catalogue, 1895*. Crossick and Jaumain, 'The world of the department store', p. 8. Lancaster, *The Department Store*, p. 43.

101. Lambert, *The Universal Provider*, pp. 62, 66, 69 and 70.

102. Lambert, *The Universal Provider*, pp. 72, 85–6 and 163–214. Rappaport, '"The Halls of Temptation"', pp. 58–9.

103. Jefferys, *Retail Trading*, p. 330.

104. Lancaster, *The Department Store*, pp. 25 and 128.

105. Miller, *The Bon Marché*, p. 98.

106. Crossick and Jaumain, 'The world of the department store', p. 18.

107. Crossick and Jaumain, 'The world of the department store', pp. 16–17.

108. Crossick and Jaumain, 'The world of the department store', p. 17.

109. Lancaster, *The Department Store*, pp. 138, 139 and 141. Edward Cadbury, M. Cecile Matheson and George Shann, *Women's Work and Wages* (London, 1906), p. 117.

110. David Wyn Davies, *Owen Owen. Victorian Draper* (Aberystwyth, n.d. [?1984]), pp. 21–2 and 130. *Dictionary of National Biography* (Oxford, 2004 edn), entry for Owen Owen.

111. Lancaster, *The Department Store*, p. 128.

112. Gordon Honeycombe, *Selfridges. Seventy-Five Years. The Story of the Store 1909–1984* (London, 1984), p. 181.

113. Honeycombe, *Selfridges*, pp. 182 and 186. *The Drapery Times*, 13 March 1909.

114. Lancaster, *The Department Store*, p. 138. Dale, *Harrods*, p. 86.

115. Honeycombe, *Selfridges*, pp. 165 and 181. *The Drapers' Record*, 20 March 1909.

116. Crossick and Jaumain, 'The world of the department store', pp. 17–18.

117. Qualidata, University of Essex, C.707/271/1, John Searby, b. Dealby, Lincolnshire, in 1888.

118. Howard Williams to Margaret Gladstone, 13 October 1896, in Macdonald 1 MSS, f. 12 at the British Library of Political and Economic Science, London School of Economics. Crossick and Jaumain, 'The world of the department store', pp. 117–18.

119. Booth MSS B.114, ff. 29–33. Some 500 of the staff were provided with board and lodging, and the rest were married and lived outside the store.

120. Lambert, *The Universal Provider*, pp. 154–6. *Leader*, 12 June 1895, recounting a case in which Frederick Smith, a shop assistant formerly employed by Whiteley,

claimed £6 7s 4d for a month's wages and damages in lieu of a month's notice. The court awarded him a month's wages only.

121. Dale, *Harrods*, p. 86.
122. Booth MSS B.114, ff. 24, 34 and 42, and Booth MSS A.20, f. 70. At the 1891 Census of Population, eleven female shop assistants and eleven males slept above the Jones Bros shop, together with three porters and eleven domestic servants. R.G.12.178, f. 74, at the Family Records Centre.
123. Lancaster, *The Department Store*, p. 128. *Report of the Departmental Committee on the Truck Acts*, Report by Miss L.A.E. Deane, one of HM Lady Inspectors of Factories, PP1908, vol. LIX, p. 355.
124. Hosgood, '"Mercantile Monasteries"', p. 326.
125. *Report of the Departmental Committee on the Truck Acts*, Evidence of, pp. 71–2. See also evidence of Miss Margarita Oliver, p. 315, Qu. 18,376–7.
126. Davies, *Owen Owen*, pp. 31 and 94. *Dictionary of National Biography*, entry for Owen Owen.
127. *Report of the Departmental Committee on the Truck Acts*, Evidence of Ernest Debenham, p. 192, Qu. 14,920 and General Report, p. 73.
128. *Report of the Departmental Committee on the Truck Acts*, General Report, p. 74.
129. *The Times*, 6, 7 and 22 November 1912. Hoffman, *They Also Serve*, pp. 60–3.
130. Miller, *The Bon Marché*, p. 194.
131. *Report of the Departmental Committee on the Truck Acts*, Evidence of William Alexander Sergeant, p. 199, Qu. 15,148.
132. *Report of the Departmental Committee on the Truck Acts*, Evidence of William Alexander Sergeant, p. 202, Qu. 15,210 and 15,213.
133. *An Act to Amend the Truck Acts, 1896*, 59 & 60 Vict., c.44.
134. Macdonald 1 MSS, f. 14.
135. A. Parry to Margaret Gladstone, 10 September 1896 in Macdonald 1 MSS, f. 3.
136. Rules of W. Whiteley's Establishment in HO.45/9802/B5581 at the National Archives.
137. G. Lushington to Henry Matthews, Home Secretary, 9 April 1889, in HO.45/9802/B5581. On this date, 30 March 1889, three other assistants incurred fines of 6d, e.g. for a 'Mistake in Check Sheet' and for 'Linen undercharged'.
138. Rules of W. Whiteley's Establishment, Rule 15.
139. Rules for Kendal Milne, 1 January 1883, quoted in J.M. Thomas, *Shopping 1721–1900*. History at Source (London, n.d.). The book is not paginated.
140. *Royal Commission on Labour*, Report on the Employment of Women in Provincial Shops, PP1893–4, vol. XXXVII, pp. 88–9.
141. Hoffman, *They Also Serve*, pp. 39–40.
142. Macdonald 1 MSS, f. 14.
143. Macdonald 1 MSS, ff. 14–21.
144. Holcombe, *Victorian Ladies at Work*, p. 114.
145. Lancaster, *The Department Store*, p. 125.

146. Macdonald 1 MSS ff. 26–7.
147. Calculated from the 1901 census of population return for David Morgan's shop, The Hayes, Cardiff, R.G.13.4981, at Cardiff Local History Library.
148. *Western Mail*, 24 November 1913. Hoffman, *They Also Serve*, p. 59.
149. Morgan, *David Morgan*, pp. 175–6.
150. Shaw, 'The evolution and impact of large-scale retailing', p. 153.
151. Jefferys, *Retail Trade*, p. 345.
152. Lancaster, *The Department Store*, p. 145.
153. Lancaster, *The Department Store*, pp. 36–7.

CHAPTER 5

1. Beverley Lemire, 'The Theft of Clothes and Popular Consumerism in Early Modern England', in *Journal of Social History*, vol. 24, no. 2 (1990), p. 265.
2. J.M. Beattie, *Policing and Punishment in London 1660–1750. Urban Crime and the Limits of Terror* (Oxford, 2002 edn), pp. 328–30.
3. Beattie, *Policing and Punishment*, p. 329.
4. Beattie, *Policing and Punishment*, pp. 329–30.
5. Beattie, *Policing and Punishment*, pp. 331 and 334.
6. Peter Linebaugh, *The London Hanged. Crime and Civil Society in the Eighteenth Century*, 2nd edn (London and New York, 2003), p. 253, and Beattie, *Policing and Punishment*, pp. 354 and 357.
7. *Old Bailey Sessions Papers 1749–50* (London, 1750), 26 February 1749/50, at the Guildhall Library, London.
8. *Old Bailey Sessions Papers 1749–50*, 25–30 April 1750.
9. Richard S. Lambert, *The Universal Provider. A Study of William Whiteley and the Rise of the London Department Store* (London, 1938), p. 126.
10. Lambert, *The Universal Provider*, pp. 126–7.
11. *The Drapery Times*, 17 April 1909.
12. *The Drapery Times*, 12 June 1909.
13. Michael Moss and Alison Turton, *A Legend of Retailing. House of Fraser* (London, 1989), p. 106.
14. *The Drapery Times*, 5 September 1908 and 24 July 1909.
15. John Birch Thomas, *Shop Boy* (London, 1985 edn), p. 72.
16. Bill Lancaster, *The Department Store. A Social History* (London and New York, 1995), p. 185.
17. *The Drapery Times*, 5 June 1909.
18. Lancaster, *The Department Store*, pp. 185–6.
19. Jaeger MSS 1327/36, rough notes by Lewis R.S. Tomalin on setting up his business, at Westminster Record Office.
20. *The Drapery Times*, 5 June 1909.
21. *The Drapers' Journal*, 17 June 1880.
22. *The Drapery Times*, 6 March 1909.

23. Lambert, *The Universal Provider*, pp. 155–6.

24. Lambert, *The Universal Provider*, p. 156.

25. Correspondence of F. Cape & Co. Ltd in 1933 in B7/X/8, ff. 46, 47, 48, 50, 51, 52, 53 and entries for the relevant employees in Salary Book F/7F2/4 at Oxfordshire Record Office.

26. Reading Co-operative Society Management Committee Minutes D/EX/1497/1/22, entries for 13 and 20 January 1938 and 12 October 1939. Reading Co-operative Society Finance Sub-Committee Minute Book, D/EX/1497/5/1, entry for 9 October 1939, both at Berkshire Record Office.

27. Reading Co-operative Society Management Committee Minutes, entry for 4 November 1937 and Reading Co-operative Society Finance Sub-Committee Minute Book, entry for 15 November 1937.

28. Margot C. Finn, *The Character of Credit. Personal Debt in English Culture 1740–1914* (Cambridge, 2003), pp. 289–90.

29. Finn, *The Character of Credit*, p. 292.

30. Finn, *The Character of Credit*, pp. 292–4.

31. *The Drapery Times*, 15 May 1909.

32. Alannah Tomkins, 'Pawnbroking and the survival strategies of the urban poor in 1770s York', in Steven King and Alannah Tomkins (eds), *The Poor in England 1700–1850. An economy of makeshifts* (Manchester, 2003), p. 168.

33. Quoted in J.J. Tobias, *Crime and Industrial Society in the 19th Century* (London, 1967), pp. 108–9 and 168.

34. Melanie Tebbutt, *Making Ends Meet. Pawnbroking and Working-Class Credit* (London, 1984 edn), p. 96.

35. Tomkins, 'Pawnbroking and the survival strategies', pp. 171–2.

36. John Burnett, *Plenty and Want* (Harmondsworth, 1968 edn), p. 103. Michael J. Winstanley, *The Shopkeeper's World 1830–1914* (Manchester, 1983), p. 64.

37. Burnett, *Plenty and Want*, p. 103.

38. Wilfred B. Whitaker, *Victorian and Edwardian Shopworkers. The Struggle to Obtain Better Conditions and a Half-Holiday* (Newton Abbot, 1973), p. 16.

39. *First Report of the Select Committee on Adulterations of Food, Drinks, and Drugs*, PP1855, vol. VIII, Evidence of A.H. Hassall, p. 30, Qu. 186.

40. *Report of the Select Committee on Adulterations*, Evidence of A. Normandy, p. 54, Qu. 537–8.

41. *Report of the Select Committee on Adulterations*, Evidence of A. Normandy, p. 54, Qu. 542, and p. 73, Qu. 777.

42. *Report of the Select Committee on Adulterations*, Evidence of A. Normandy, p. 73, Qu. 777.

43. Arnold Bonner, *British Co-operation* (Manchester, 1961), p. 68.

44. Burnett, *Plenty and Want*, pp. 256–8.

45. Burnett, *Plenty and Want*, p. 259. Winstanley, *The Shopkeeper's World*, p. 63. The formation of the Society of Analysts in 1874 helped to improve enforcement levels.

46. *Report of the Select Committee on Adulteration of Food Act, 1872*, PP1874, vol. VI, Evidence of Thomas Potter Davy, p. 99, Qu. 1827–30.

47. *Report of the Select Committee on Adulteration of Food*, p. 105, Qu. 2005, and p. 107, Qu. 2062–3.

48. Winstanley, *The Shopkeeper's World*, pp. 63–4.

49. *General Report of the Select Committee on Adulteration of Food*, p. viii.

50. Letter from Mr Leonard Chamberlain of Beer, Devon, to the author, 13 May 2005.

51. Robert Roberts, *The Classic Slum. Salford Life in the first quarter of the century* (Manchester, 1971), p. 81.

52. Margaret Llewelyn Davies (ed.), *Life As We Have Known It* (London, 1977 edn), pp. 20–2.

53. Llewelyn Davies (ed.), *Life As We Have Known It*, p. 21.

54. *Annual Report of the Chief Officer of the Public Control Department, 1896–97*, p. 8 in PC/GEN/2/18 at the London Metropolitan Archives. The Weights and Measures Acts of 1878 and 1889 required shopkeepers to possess accurate equipment when selling goods by weight or volume and to make it available for inspection when required to do so by the relevant local authority official. Winstanley, *The Shopkeeper's World*, p. 64.

55. Correspondence on 29 April, 5 May and 6 June 1898 from greengrocers and fruiterers in New Charlton and replies by J.W. Hildreth, Inspector, to the Chief Officer, Public Control Department, in LCC/MIN/9671 at the London Metropolitan Archives.

56. *Annual Reports of the Chief Officer of the Public Control Department, for 1893–94 and 1900–1901* in PC/GEN/2/18 at the London Metropolitan Archives.

57. Roberts, *The Classic Slum*, p. 81.

58. Reminiscences at Southampton Heritage Centre, C0038.

59. *The Drapery Times*, 13 February 1909.

60. *The Drapery Times*, 6 February 1909.

61. Reminiscences at Southampton Heritage Centre C0005.

62. Gordon Honeycombe, *Selfridges. Seventy-Five Years. The Story of the Store 1909–1974* (London, 1984), p. 191.

63. Marjorie Gardiner, *The Other Side of the Counter. The Life of a Shop Girl 1925–1945* (Brighton, Queenspark book no. 17, n.d.), pp. 9, 11, 14 and 17.

64. Cuttings in Tuckwell MSS 106/6 and 106/33 at TUC Library.

65. P.C. Hoffman, *They Also Serve. The Story of the Shop Worker* (London, 1949), p. 4.

66. Robert Roberts, *A Ragged Schooling. Growing up in the Classic Slum* (Manchester, 1976), pp. 8 and 10.

67. Reminiscences at Southampton Heritage Centre, C0038.

68. *Annual Report of the Early Closing Association for 1891*, p. 11, at the British Library, 8276.bbb.44. All the *Annual Reports* of the ECA are at this location. Lee Holcombe, *Victorian Ladies at Work. Middle-Class Working Women in England and Wales 1850–1914* (Newton Abbot, 1973), p. 109.

69. Holcombe, *Victorian Ladies at Work*, p. 109.

70. *The Drapery Times*, 6 March 1909.

71. *Annual Report of the Early Closing Association for 1886*, p. 48.

72. Whitaker, *Victorian and Edwardian Shop Workers*, p. 38.

73. *Annual Report of the Early Closing Association for 1883*, speech by the Rt Hon. W.E. Forster MP, at the Association's annual meeting, p. 8.

74. Whitaker, *Victorian and Edwardian Shop Workers*, p. 51.

75. Whitaker, *Victorian and Edwardian Shop Workers*, pp. 38–9. Hoffman, *They Also Serve*, p. 4.

76. Whitaker, *Victorian and Edwardian Shop Workers*, p. 41.

77. *Annual Report of the Early Closing Association for 1853*, speech by Lord John Manners, p. 12.

78. *Report of the Sixth Annual Meeting of the Metropolitan Early Closing Association, 1848*, p. 7, at the British Library, 8276.bbb.44.

79. *Annual Report of the Early Closing Association for 1883*, p. 17. The same *Report* (p. 14) noted that in the City Road, London, not only had many visits been made but 'boardmen have been employed to perambulate the streets with the society's large pictorial bill, "Never Shop after Five on Thursdays".' Again, the efforts met with limited success only.

80. Whitaker, *Victorian and Edwardian Shop Workers*, p. 66.

81. Whitaker, *Victorian and Edwardian Shop Workers*, pp. 98–9.

82. *Annual Report of the Early Closing Association and Traders' Parliamentary Alliance for 1903*, p. 9.

83. Whitaker, *Victorian and Edwardian Shop Workers*, p. 8.

84. Whitaker, *Victorian and Edwardian Shop Workers*, p. 21.

85. *Hansard*, 3rd Series, vol. 325, col. 1172.

86. *Hansard*, 3rd Series, vol. 325, cols 1132 and 1166.

87. Horace G. Hutchinson, *Life of Sir John Lubbock. Lord Avebury* (2 vols), vol. 1 (London, 1914), p. 266.

88. *Shop Hours Regulation Act*, 49 & 50 Vict. c.55.

89. *Return Relating to the Shop Hours Act for England and Wales*, PP1896, vol. LXXVI.

90. *Report of the Public Control Committee for consideration on 17 June*, 1898, p. 5, LCC/MIN/9671 at the London Metropolitan Archives.

91. *Annual Report of the Early Closing Association for 1891*, p. 14.

92. *Annual Report of the Early Closing Association for 1892*, p. 6.

93. Geoffrey Crossick, 'Shopkeepers and the state in Britain, 1870–1914', in Geoffrey Crossick and Heinz-Gerhard Haupt (eds), *Shopkeepers and Master Artisans in Nineteenth Century Europe* (London, 1986 edn), pp. 252–3. Whitaker, *Victorian and Edwardian Shop Workers*, p. 77.

94. Crossick, 'Shopkeepers and the state', pp. 254–5.

95. Crossick, 'Shopkeepers and the state', p. 255.

96. *Hansard*, 4th Series, vol. 173, col. 969.

97. Whitaker, *Victorian and Edwardian Shop Workers*, p. 159.

98. See letter from a Mr G. Norman of Felixstowe to the Home Office, August 1913, in HO.45/1100/23760. He had worked for much of the four-month period without a half-holiday but had then been dismissed. He asked the Home Office for guidance; officials suggested he contact the local authority for help, in National Archives. *Annual Report of the National Amalgamated Union of Shop Assistants, Warehousemen and Clerks for 1914* (NAUSAW&C), pp. 14–15 at the TUC Library covers similar cases.

99. Whitaker, *Victorian and Edwardian Shop Workers*, pp. 166–7.

100. Manifesto and Rules of the United Shop Assistants' Union, established October 1889, HD.6661.Z7 at the TUC Library.

101. Booth MSS A.20, ff. 13–14, in the British Library of Political and Economic Science, London School of Economics.

102. Christopher P. Hosgood, '"Mercantile Monasteries": Shops, Shop Assistants and Shop Life in Late Victorian and Edwardian Britain', in *Journal of British Studies*, vol. 38, no. 3 (July 1999), p. 347.

103. Hoffman, *They Also Serve*, p. 2. Seventeen delegates attended from Manchester, Liverpool, London, Sunderland, Leeds, Hull, Birmingham, Bolton, Oldham, Ashton and South Wales.

104. Rules of the NAUSAW&C in the National Archives, FS.26/79. In regard to the female members' marriage portion, that was payable if the member had been in full membership for at least two years and had received no out-of-employment or sick benefit during her membership.

105. Hosgood, '"Mercantile Monasteries"', p. 350.

106. Hoffman, *They Also Serve*, p. 75.

107. Hoffman, *They Also Serve*, p. 5.

108. Margaret Bondfield, *A Life's Work* (London, n.d. [c. 1948]), p. 29.

109. Michael Winstanley (ed.), *A Traditional Grocer. T.D. Smith's of Lancaster 1858–1981* (Lancaster, Occasional Papers no. 21, Centre for North-West Regional Studies, University of Lancaster, 1991), p. 35.

110. Hosgood, '"Mercantile Monasteries"', p. 347.

111. *Annual Report and Balance Sheet for 1923 of NAUSAW&C*, p. 2; membership figures for 1893–1923 in HD.6661.Z7 at the TUC Library.

112. *Annual Report and Balance Sheet for 1923*, p. 2. Membership fell back in 1914, with the onset of war, to 81,250, before climbing again in 1915.

113. Sir William Richardson, *A Union of Many Trades. The History of USDAW* (Manchester, n.d. [c. 1979]), p. 31.

114. Richardson, *A Union of Many Trades*, p. 39.

115. Richardson, *A Union of Many Trades*, p. 42.

116. *The Co-operative Employé*, September 1908.

117. Holcombe, *Victorian Ladies at Work*, p. 121.

118. Hoffman, *They Also Serve*, p. 79.

119. Joseph Hallsworth and Rhys J. Davies, *The Working Life of Shop Assistants* (Manchester, 1910), p. 134.

120. Hoffman, *They Also Serve*, pp. 82–91.
121. Holcombe, *Victorian Ladies at Work*, p. 114.
122. Hoffman, *They Also Serve*, pp. 48–9.
123. Hoffman, *They Also Serve*, pp. 53–5.
124. *Annual Report of the NAUSAW&C for 1913*, pp. 8–9.
125. *Edwin Jones Blotter* (1933), p. 31 at Southampton Archives, D/Z 634/2.
126. Holcombe, *Victorian Ladies at Work*, p. 120.
127. Richardson, *A Union of Many Trades*, p. 53.
128. Richardson, *A Union of Many Trades*, p. 319.
129. Richardson, *A Union of Many Trades*, p. 53.

CHAPTER 6

1. S.I. Mitchell, 'Retailing in Eighteenth- and Early Nineteenth-Century Cheshire', in *Transactions of the Historic Society of Lancashire and Cheshire for the Year 1980*, vol. 130 (Liverpool, 1981), p. 49.
2. Qualidata, University of Essex, C.707/54/1–3.
3. P.C. Hoffman, *They Also Serve. The Story of the Shop Worker* (London, 1949), p. vi.
4. Thea Vigne and Alun Howkins, 'The Small Shopkeeper in Industrial and Market Towns', in Geoffrey Crossick (ed.), *The Lower Middle Class in Britain* (London, 1977), pp. 196 and 202.
5. Michael J. Winstanley, *The Shopkeeper's World 1830–1914* (Manchester, 1983), p. 214.
6. Quoted in Geoffrey Crossick and Heinz-Gerhard Haupt, *The Petite Bourgeoisie in Europe 1780–1914. Enterprise, Family and Independence* (London and New York, 1995), p. 92.
7. Peter Mathias, *Retailing Revolution* (London, 1967), p. 152.
8. *Saturday Half-Holidays* (pamphlet issued by the Early Closing Association) (London, 1856), p. 17, at the British Library, 8276.bbb.44.
9. Quoted in Hoffman, *They Also Serve*, pp. 18–19 and photograph between pp. 22 and 23.
10. Hoffman, *They Also Serve*, pp. 24 and 30.
11. Michael Winstanley (ed.), *A Traditional Grocer. T.D. Smith's of Lancaster 1858–1981* (Lancaster, Centre for North-West Regional Studies, Occasional Papers no. 21, 1991), pp. 42–3.
12. Vigne and Howkins, 'The Small Shopkeeper', p. 203.
13. Bill Lancaster, *The Department Store. A Social History* (London and New York, 1995), p. 111.
14. Lancaster, *The Department Store*, p. 111.
15. David Wyn Davies, *Owen Owen. Victorian Draper* (Aberystwyth, n.d. [?1984]), pp. 45 and 69.
16. Visitors' Book of Miss Eliza Anne Ridding at Southampton Archives, D/PM Box 40/32, entries for February and May 1830.

17. Visitors' Book of Miss Eliza Anne Ridding, entries for February and May 1830. There was also an elderly former servant lodging at the house.

18. Wilfred B. Whitaker, *Victorian and Edwardian Shop Workers* (Newton Abbot, 1973), pp. 42–3.

19. John Birch Thomas, *Shop Boy* (London, 1983), pp. 136–9. He was working as an assistant in a toy shop at this time.

20. David Vaisey (ed.), *The Diary of Thomas Turner 1754–1765* (Oxford, 2000 edn), pp. xxvii and xxxvi.

21. Vaisey (ed.), *The Diary of Thomas Turner*, pp. 40, 64, 66, 99 and 109.

22. Vaisey (ed.), *The Diary of Thomas Turner*, pp. 97 and 131.

23. Vaisey (ed.), *The Diary of Thomas Turner*, p. 347.

24. Journal of Marmaduke Strother, 1784–5, at the British Library, Egerton MSS 2479, entry for 16 August 1784, f. 8.

25. Journal of Marmaduke Strother, entry for 16 and 17 March 1785, ff. 96–7.

26. Journal of Marmaduke Strother, entries for 25 October 1784 and 21 February 1785, ff. 46 and 89. On 17 July 1785 he decided to end the journal as 'it is not Proper for a Tradesman to keep a Journal without he has enough of Time & a plentifull fortune'. Strother clearly felt he had neither.

27. The Rt Hon. Margaret Bondfield, *A Life's Work* (London, n.d. [*c.* 1948]), pp. 28–9.

28. W.F. Fish, *The Autobiography of a Counter-Jumper* (London, n.d. [1929]), pp. 30–1.

29. Fish, *The Autobiography of a Counter-Jumper*, pp. 47 and 68.

30. Fish, *The Autobiography of a Counter-Jumper*, p. 72.

31. T. Spencer Jones, *The Moral Side of Living-In* (London, 1907), p. 5, at the TUC Library, HD6661.Z7.

32. Hoffman, *They Also Serve*, pp. 60–1.

33. *The Drapery Times*, 20 February 1909. *The Drapers' Record*, 27 March 1909. The *Record* admitted that 'love of fine clothes, luxury or pleasure' had been 'the ruin of many girls, shop assistants, as well as clerks or domestic servants, but it denied this was due to 'starvation wages' in the drapery trade.

34. *The Drapery Times*, 30 January 1909.

35. Alison Adburgham, *Shopping in Style. London from the Restoration to Edwardian Elegance* (London, 1979), p. 7.

36. Quoted in Spencer Jones, *The Moral Side of Living-In*, p. 3.

37. Quoted in Spencer Jones, *The Moral Side of Living-In*, p. 3.

38. Richard S. Lambert, *The Universal Provider. A Study of William Whiteley and the Rise of the London Department Store* (London, 1938), p. 149.

39. Alec Waugh, *The Lipton Story. A Centennial Biography* (London, 1951), pp. 60, 61 and 67.

40. Alison Settle, *A Family of Shops. Marshall & Snelgrove* (London, n.d. [*c.* 1950]), pp. 27–8.

41. Minutes of the Management Committee of Reading Co-operative Society, entry for 30 July 1885, D/EX/1497/1/4, at Berkshire Record Office.

42. *The Co-operative Employé*, August 1908.
43. Pamela Horn, *Pleasures and Pastimes in Victorian Britain* (Stroud, 1999), pp. 158–9.
44. Lambert, *The Universal Provider*, pp. 150–1.
45. Frank Danning in correspondence with the author, May 2005. Angela and John Airey, *The Bainbridges of Newcastle. A Family History 1679–1976* (Newcastle upon Tyne, 1979), p. 115.
46. *The Drapery Times*, 27 February 1909.
47. Davies, *Owen Owen*, p. 32.
48. *The 'Liberty' Lamp*, May, recollections of Miss Jessie Flood, at Westminster Record Office. Airey, *The Bainbridges of Newcastle*, p. 115.
49. Booth MSS B.133, f. 9, interview on 1 July 1895.
50. Elizabeth Roberts, *A Woman's Place. An Oral History of Working-Class Women 1890–1940* (Oxford, 1985 edn), pp. 62–4.
51. Whitaker, *Victorian and Edwardian Shop Workers*, p. 68.
52. *The Drapery Times*, 15 May 1909.
53. Settle, *A Family of Shops*, p. 27.
54. *The Drapery Times*, 20 February 1909.
55. *The Drapery Times*, 13 and 20 February 1909.
56. *The Drapery Times*, 6 March 1909.
57. *The Drapery Times*, 20 March 1909.
58. *The Drapery Times*, 27 February 1909.
59. Quoted in Mitchell, 'Retailing', pp. 47–8.
60. Mitchell, 'Retailing', p. 48.
61. Mitchell, 'Retailing', p. 48.
62. Airey, *The Bainbridges of Newcastle*, pp. 62 and 131.
63. Davies, *Owen Owen*, pp. 59, 95, 130.
64. Davies, *Owen Owen*, p. 131.
65. Marghanita Laski, 'Domestic Life', in Simon Nowell-Smith (ed.), *Edwardian England, 1901–1914* (London, 1964), p. 186.
66. Laski, 'Domestic Life', p. 186. Hugh Barty-King, *Maples. Fine Furnishers* (London, 1992), pp. 24–6 and 46.
67. Entry for Sir John Barker in the *Dictionary of National Biography*.
68. T.J. Nossiter, 'Shopkeeper Radicalism in the 19th Century', in T.J. Nossiter, A.H. Hanson, Stein Rokkan (eds), *Imagination and Precision in the Social Sciences* (London, 1972), pp. 408–9.
69. Vaisey (ed.), *The Diary of Thomas Turner*, p. xxii.
70. Vaisey (ed.), *The Diary of Thomas Turner*, p. 101. Turner described it as 'the merriest funeral that ever I served, for I can safely say there was no crying'.
71. *1832 Reform Act*, 2 Wm. IV c.45.
72. Nossiter, 'Shopkeeper Radicalism', pp. 412–13.
73. J.R. Vincent, *Pollbooks. How Victorians Voted* (Cambridge, 1967), p. 45.
74. Nossiter, 'Shopkeeper Radicalism', pp. 410–11.

75. Nossiter, 'Shopkeeper Radicalism', p. 411.

76. L.P. Jacks, *The Confessions of an Octogenarian* (London, 1942), p. 36.

77. Jacks, *The Confessions of an Octogenarian*, pp. 34–6 and 50.

78. Winstanley, *The Shopkeeper's World*, p. 21.

79. Winstanley, *The Shopkeeper's World*, p. 23.

80. Barrie Trinder, *Victorian Banbury* (Banbury Historical Society, vol. 19, 1982), p. 29.

81. Mark Rutherford, *Autobiography and Deliverance* (Leicester, 1969 edn), p. 103. Rutherford's real name was William Hale White.

82. Vigne and Howkins, 'The Small Shopkeeper', p. 202.

83. Vigne and Howkins, 'The Small Shopkeeper', p. 202.

84. Crossick and Haupt, *The Petite Bourgeoisie in Europe*, p. 194.

85. Pamela Horn (ed.), *Agricultural Trade Unionism in Oxfordshire 1872–81* (Oxford, Oxfordshire Record Society, vol. XLVIII, 1974), pp. 13, 41 and 45.

86. Vincent, *Pollbooks*, pp. 11 and 14–16.

87. Vincent, *Pollbooks*, p. 15.

88. Winstanley, *The Shopkeeper's World*, pp. 100–3.

89. Winstanley, *The Shopkeeper's World*, p. 19.

90. Asa Briggs, *Victorian Cities* (Harmondsworth, 1968 edn), p. 108.

91. Briggs, *Victorian Cities*, pp. 108–9 and 235.

92. Briggs, *Victorian Cities*, pp. 235 and 259.

93. Lady Bell, *At the Works. A Study of a Manufacturing Town (Middlesbrough)* (Newton Abbot, 1969, reprint), pp. 8–9. The book was first published in 1907.

94. John Wyn Pritchard, '"Fit and Proper Persons" – Councillors of Denbigh, Their Status and Position, 1835–94', in *Welsh Historical Review*, vol. 17 (1994), p. 191.

95. Julie Light '" . . . mere seekers of fame"?: personalities, power and politics in the small town: Pontypool and Bridgend, *c.* 1860–95', in *Urban History*, vol. 32, part 1 (May 2005), pp. 92–9.

96. Winstanley, *The Shopkeeper's World*, p. 27.

97. Winstanley, *The Shopkeeper's World*, p. 101.

98. Richard Foster, *F. Cape & Co. of St Ebbes Street, Oxford. From Draper's Shop to Department Store* (Oxford pamphlet, n.d.) in Centre for Oxfordshire Studies, Oxford, OXFO.658.8. It is not paginated.

99. Lancaster, *The Department Store*, p. 32.

100. Lancaster, *The Department Store*, pp. 34–6.

101. Chris Hosgood, 'A "Brave and Daring Folk"? Shopkeepers and Trade Associational Life in Victorian and Edwardian England', in *Journal of Social History*, vol. 26, no. 2 (1992), p. 287.

102. Winstanley (ed.), *A Traditional Grocer*, pp. 43–4.

103. Hosgood, 'A "Brave and Daring Folk"?', p. 286.

104. Winstanley (ed.), *A Traditional Grocer*, pp. 44–5.

105. *The Drapery Times*, 6 March 1909.

106. Hosgood, 'A "Brave and Daring Folk"?', pp. 293–4.

107. *Grocery*, March 1918, commented on the increase in membership of the trade associations.

108. Crossick and Haupt, *The Petite Bourgeoisie in Europe*, p. 155.

109. Hosgood, 'A "Brave and Daring Folk"?', p. 299.

110. *The Drapery Times*, 20 February and 27 March 1909.

111. See entry for Sir John Barker in the *Dictionary of National Biography*.

112. Barty-King, *Maples*, pp. 27, 33–4, 47 and 66.

113. Michael Stenton and Stephen Lees (eds), *Who's Who of British Members of Parliament*, vol. III, *1919–45* (Sussex, 1979), p. 321.

114. Stenton and Lees (eds), *Who's Who of British Members of Parliament*, vol. III, and entry for Margaret Bondfield in the *Dictionary of National Biography*.

115. Stenton and Lees (eds), *Who's Who of British Members of Parliament*, vol. III.

116. Barty-King, *Maples*, pp. 26–7.

117. Lambert, *The Universal Provider*, pp. 244–67 and entry for William Whiteley in the *Dictionary of National Biography*.

CHAPTER 7

1. Robert Roberts, *The Classic Slum. Salford life in the first quarter of the century* (Manchester, 1971), p. 149.

2. *The British Economy Key Statistics 1900–1970* (London, 1970), p. 12. Arthur Marwick, *The Deluge. British Society and the First World War* (London, 1965), p. 195. Peter Mathias, *Retailing Revolution* (London, 1967), p. 222.

3. *Grocery*, May 1916.

4. *Grocery*, January 1918.

5. *Grocery*, October 1918.

6. Quoted in *Grocery*, March 1918.

7. Quoted in Pamela Horn, *Rural Life in England in the First World War* (Dublin, 1984), pp. 190–1.

8. *Grocery*, July 1918.

9. Mathias, *Retailing Revolution*, p. 219.

10. *Grocery*, October 1918.

11. *Grocery*, March and May 1918.

12. *Grocery*, January 1918. For a case involving the excessive use of water in bacon see *Grocery*, February 1918.

13. *Grocery*, February 1918.

14. Reminiscences of Ada Crofts, born 1889, 6655 at the Imperial War Museum Sound Archives. Crofts was her surname from a second marriage.

15. *The Drapers' Record*, 25 August 1917.

16. *The Drapers' Record*, 14 April 1917.

17. Maurice Corina, *Fine Silks and Oak Counters. Debenhams 1778–1978* (London, 1978), pp. 77 and 79. Tim Dale, *Harrods. A Palace in Knightsbridge* (London, 1995), p. 99.

18. *The Co-operative Employé*, October 1914. Michael Moss and Alison Turton, *A Legend of Retailing. House of Fraser* (London, 1989), p. 107.

19. Moss and Turton, *A Legend of Retailing*, p. 107.

20. Moss and Turton, *A Legend of Retailing*, p. 107.

21. Moss and Turton, *A Legend of Retailing*, p. 112.

22. P.C. Hoffman, *They Also Serve. The Story of the Shop Worker* (London, 1949), pp. 64–5.

23. *Hansard*, 5th Series, vol. 69 (2–18 February 1915), 9 February 1915, col. 480, comment by Tyson Wilson.

24. Sir William Richardson, *A Union of Many Trades. The History of USDAW* (Manchester, n.d. [*c.* 1979]), p. 69.

25. Reminiscences of Emma Fray, born in the late 1890s, 9385/2/1–2 at the Imperial War Museum Sound Archives.

26. Based on a 'Report on the Increased Employment of Women during the War', in Beveridge/Reconstruction/2/99 MSS at the British Library of Political and Economic Science at the London School of Economics.

27. *Report of the Board of Trade on the Increased Employment of Women during the War in the United Kingdom up to April 1918*, PP1918, vol. XIV, p. 15, Table X.

28. *Report of the Board of Trade up to April 1918*, p. 15, Table X.

29. *Grocery*, March 1916, reporting the annual meeting of the Institute of Certificated Grocers.

30. Quoted in *Grocery*, March 1918.

31. *Grocery*, July 1917.

32. Mathias, *Retailing Revolution*, pp. 143–5.

33. Michael Winstanley (ed.), *A Traditional Grocer. T.D. Smith's of Lancaster 1858–1981* (Lancaster, Centre for North-West Regional Studies, Occasional Papers no. 21, 1991), pp. 32–3.

34. *The Grocer*, 4 March 1916.

35. *The Grocer*, 4 March 1916.

36. Richardson, *A Union of Many Trades*, pp. 70–1.

37. Richardson, *A Union of Many Trades*, p. 71. *The Co-operative Employé*, January and February 1916, reporting disputes at Oldham, Castleford and Carlisle.

38. *The Co-operative Employé*, August 1916.

39. Hoffman, *They Also Serve*, p. 98.

40. *The AUCE Journal*, March 1918, in an article on 'The Shop-worker'.

41. Marwick, *The Deluge*, pp. 77–9.

42. *Grocery*, July 1916.

43. *Grocery*, October 1916.

44. *The Drapers' Record*, 24 February 1917.

45. *The Drapers' Record*, 7 April 1917.

46. Reminiscences of Olive Simmons, born 1890, in Qualidata, University of Essex, C.707/335/1–2.

47. *Grocery*, September 1916.

48. *Grocery*, April 1918.

49. *Grocery*, May 1917.

50. *The Times*, 11 and 13 March 1915. *Annual Register for 1915* (London, 1916), 'Chronicle', p. 13.

51. *The Times*, 13 May 1915.

52. *The Times*, 14 and 15 May 1915.

53. *The Times*, 13 May 1915.

54. Roberts, *The Classic Slum*, pp. 155–6.

55. *Annual Register for 1915*, 'Chronicle', p. 13.

56. Marwick, *The Deluge*, p. 191. Edith H. Whetham, *The Agrarian History of England and Wales*, vol. VIII, *1914–1939* (Cambridge, 1978), p. 90.

57. Marwick, *The Deluge*, pp. 191 and 193.

58. Marwick, *The Deluge*, pp. 193–4.

59. *Grocery*, January 1918, and Marwick, *The Deluge*, p. 194.

60. *Grocery*, February 1918. According to the journal, Pontypridd had put 'into operation the first food distribution scheme in Wales'.

61. Marwick, *The Deluge*, p. 195. Horn, *Rural Life*, p. 191.

62. *Grocery*, February 1918.

63. *Grocery*, June 1918.

64. *Grocery*, May 1918.

65. *Grocery*, September 1918.

66. Roberts, *The Classic Slum*, pp. 174–5.

67. Roberts, *The Classic Slum*, p. 160.

68. Annual Reports and Accounts of Lankester & Crook Ltd at Southampton Archives, D/LC/4. See also letter from Ogden, Palmer & Langton, Chartered Accountants, 15 August 1911, to S.B. Crook, Esq., noting that over the previous five years there had been 'a net average annual Profit available for dividend of £2,745'.

69. Horn, *Rural Life*, p. 190.

70. Horn, *Rural Life*, p. 191.

71. Quoted in *Grocery*, March 1918.

72. Quoted in *Grocery*, September 1918.

73. *Grocery*, November 1918.

74. Horn, *Rural Life*, p. 192.

75. Details included in, for example, *Annual Report of the Early Closing Association for 1916*, p. 8, at the British Library, 8276.bbb.44.

76. *The Drapers' Record*, 7 and 14 April 1917.

77. Bill Lancaster, *The Department Store. A Social History* (London & New York, 1995), p. 90. Corina, *Fine Silks and Oak Counters*, p. 77. Alison Settle, *A Family of Shops. Marshall & Snelgrove* (London, n.d. [*c.* 1950]), p. 34. *The Drapers' Record*, 4 August, letter from Debenham & Co.

78. *The Drapers' Record*, 4 August 1917, letter from Debenham & Co.

79. *The Drapers' Record*, 4 August 1917.

80. Corina, *Fine Silks and Oak Counters*, p. 84.

81. Moss and Turton, *A Legend of Retailing*, p. 117. Lancaster, *The Department Store*, p. 90.

82. See *Shops (Early Closing) Act (1920) Amendment Act, 1921*, 11 & 12 Geo. 5, c.60. Also *Shops (Hours of Closing) Act, 1928*, 18 & 19 Geo. 5, c.33.

83. *Annual Report of the Early Closing Association for 1916*, p. 7.

84. Michael J. Winstanley, *The Shopkeeper's World 1830–1914* (Manchester, 1983), p. 57. *An Act for the better Observation of the Lord's Day, commonly called Sunday, 1677*. If the act had been put into operation during the war, its penalties would have been severe since it provided that 'every Person so offending, shall forfeit the same Goods . . . exposed to Sale'.

85. *Annual Report of the Early Closing Association for 1918*, p. 6.

86. *Annual Report of the Early Closing Association for 1918*, p. 6.

87. *Annual Report of the Early Closing Association for 1938*, p. 6.

88. Judi Bevan, *Trolley Wars. The Battle of the Supermarkets* (London, 2005), p. 37.

89. Management Committee Minutes of Reading Co-operative Society for 1919 D/EX/1497/1/17, entries for 21 August and 4 September 1919, at Berkshire Record Office.

90. Calculated from *Population Census for 1921: Occupations* (London, 1924) and *Population Census for 1931: Occupations* (London, 1934).

91. *Grocery*, January 1921.

92. Sir Hubert Llewellyn Smith (ed.), *The New Survey of London Life and Labour*, vol. V. *London Industries*, II (London, 1933), p. 174.

93. Linda McCullough Thew, *The Pit Village and the Store. The Portrait of a Mining Past* (London, 1985), p. 145.

94. Thew, *The Pit Village*, p. 169.

95. Thew, *The Pit Village*, p. 153.

96. Thew, *The Pit Village*, pp. 209–10.

97. James B. Jefferys, *Retail Trading in Britain 1850–1950* (Cambridge, 1954).

98. Pamela Horn, *Women in the 1920s* (Stroud, 1995), p. 33.

99. Hermann Levy, *The Shops of Britain. A Study of Retail Distribution* (London, 1948), pp. 6 and 10.

100. Lankester & Crook Ltd, Reports and Accounts: Summary of Branch Profit and Expenses as at October 1933, in D/LC 4/38/1 at Southampton Archives.

101. F. Cape & Co., Oxford: Buyers' Wages and Commission, B7/X/8, letter to Miss Griffin from Russell Lewis, 28 March 1933, f. 43. Correspondence in this book clearly covered more junior staff as well as the buyers.

102. Calculated from the *Population Census for 1921*.

103. T.W. Cynog-Jones, *The Regulation of Wages in the Retail Trades 1936–1945* (London, n.d. [c. 1945]), pp. 9–10.

104. *British Economy Key Statistics*, p. 12.

105. Peter Scott, 'The Twilight World of Interwar British Hire Purchase', in *Past and Present*, no. 177 (November 2002), p. 212. In 1938 the Hire Purchase Act

introduced various safeguards, including the need to provide details in writing of the price of the article concerned and the amount and date of instalments. Levy, *The Shops of Britain*, p. 114.

106. Jefferys, *Retail Trading in Britain*, p. 163.
107. *Grocery*, June 1921.
108. *The Home and Colonial Magazine*, vol. 1, no. 6 (April 1921), at the British Library, PP5793.bae.
109. *The Home and Colonial Magazine*, vol. VIII, no. 3 (July–September, 1928).
110. *Report from the Select Committee on Shop Assistants*, PP1930–1, vol. IX, p. 37.
111. *Report from the Select Committee on Shop Assistants*, p. 70.
112. *Shops Act, 1934*, 24 & 25 Geo. 5, c.42.
113. *Report from the Select Committee on Shop Assistants*, pp. 33 and 35. *Shops (Early Closing Act) Amendment Act, 1921*, 11 & 12 Geo. 5, c.60, and *Shops (Hours of Closing) Act, 1928*, 18 & 19 Geo. 5, c.33.
114. *Annual Report of the Early Closing Association for 1931*. Similar complaints were made in the *Annual Report of the Early Closing Association for 1923*.
115. *Annual Report of the Early Closing Association for 1928*, including an extract from the *Yorkshire Post* of 3 January 1929. *Annual Report of the Early Closing Association for 1929*, for comments on the 'evil of Sunday Trading'.
116. *Annual Report of the Early Closing Association for 1938*. Nonetheless it condemned the exemptions granted, particularly to Sunday markets, which it called 'a National disgrace'.
117. Reminiscences of Walter Greenhalgh at the Imperial War Museum Sound Archives, 11187/9/2. Mr Greenhalgh was born on 9 January 1914.
118. Winstanley (ed.), *A Traditional Grocer*, pp. 33–4.
119. Winstanley (ed.), *A Traditional Grocer*, p. 35.
120. Reminiscences of a male grocery worker at Southampton Heritage Centre, C.0009. He was born in about 1900.
121. *Grocery*, March and April 1921.
122. Bevan, *Trolley Wars*, p. 52.
123. Bevan, *Trolley Wars*, p. 56.
124. Corina, *Fine Silks and Oak Counters*, pp. 97 and 114–18, and Jefferys, *Retail Trading*, p. 345.
125. Lancaster, *The Department Store*, pp. 96–8.
126. Corina, *Fine Silks and Oak Counters*, p. 80.
127. Corina, *Fine Silks and Oak Counters*, pp. 81–3.
128. Gordon Honeycombe, *Selfridges. Seventy-Five Years. The Story of the Store 1909–1984* (London, 1984), pp. 188–9.
129. Reminiscences of a female assistant at Southampton Heritage Centre, C.0129. She was born on 6 December 1922.
130. Lancaster, *The Department Store*, p. 145. Geese and turkeys were given each Christmas to senior staff at Bentall's as well. Corina, *Fine Silks and Oak Counters*, p. 85.
131. Llewellyn Smith (ed.), *The New Survey*, pp. 153 and 155.

132. *The Drapers' Record*, 16 May 1931.

133. D. Caradog Jones (ed.), *The Social Survey of Merseyside*, vol. 2 (Liverpool 1934), pp. 212–13.

134. F. Cape & Co. Wages Book for 1935–8, B7/F2/7, at Oxfordshire Record Office. At the smallest shop, in Walton Street, Oxford, five employees were at work in August 1935. One earned £5 per month.

135. Hoffman, *They Also Serve*, pp. 173–9. For NAUSAW&C membership figures see *Thirty-third Annual Report and Balance Sheet for 1923*, in the TUC Library.

136. Hoffman, *They Also Serve*, pp. 180–94.

137. Hoffman, *They Also Serve*, pp. 211–12.

138. See *Report and Balance Sheet for 1923* of NAUSAW&C, and G. Maurice Hann, *The Progress, Activities and Achievements of Your Trade Union*, report dated November 1937, HD.6661.Z7, in the TUC Library.

139. *Annual Report and Accounts* of the union for 1923 and 1929.

140. Hoffman, *They Also Serve*, pp. 232–44.

141. Richardson, *A Union of Many Trades*, pp. 76–7, 83, 87, 100 and 116.

142. Reading Co-operative Society Management Committee Minutes, D/EX/1497/1/20, entry for 20 August 1931, at Berkshire Record Office.

143. Jean Beauchamp, *Women Who Work* (London, 1937), p. 46.

CHAPTER 8

1. *South Wales Echo and Express*, 11 June 1940; *Western Mail*, 11 and 12 June 1940, Paul di Felice, 'Manchester's Little Italy at War, 1940–1945: "Enemy Aliens or Reluctant Foe?"', in *Northern History*, vol. 39 (March 2002), pp. 116–17. *The Times*, 11 June 1940.

2. Colin Hughes, *Lime, Lemon and Sarsaparilla. The Italian Community in South Wales 1881–1945* (Bridgend, 2003 edn), pp. 75 and 93–5.

3. John Burnett, *Plenty and Want. A Social History of Diet in England from 1815 to the Present Day* (Harmondsworth, 1968 edn), p. 323.

4. *The Drapers' Record*, 3 and 10 February 1940.

5. *Hansard*, 5th Series, vol. 370, 18 March 1941, cols 14–15.

6. On 11 February 1942 one MP complained that small greengrocers were having difficulty in obtaining supplies even of plentiful vegetables. *Hansard*, 5th Series, vol. 377, 11 February 1942, col. 1528. James B. Jefferys, *Retail Trading in Britain 1850–1950* (Cambridge, 1954), pp. 174–5.

7. Michael Moss and Alison Turton, *A Legend of Retailing. House of Fraser* (London, 1989), p. 345.

8. Maurice Corina, *Fine Silks and Oak Counters. Debenhams 1778–1978* (London 1978), p. 187.

9. Corina, *Fine Silks and Oak Counters*, p. 127.

10. Gordon Honeycombe, *Selfridges. Seventy-Five Years. The Story of the Store 1909–1984* (London, 1984), p. 200.

11. Jane Mace (ed.), *'Call yourself a Draper?' Memories of life in the trade* (London, 1993), p. 25. Sir William Richardson, *A Union of Many Trades. The History of USDAW* (Manchester, n.d. [*c.* 1979]), p. 155.

12. Goronwy Rees, *St Michael. A History of Marks & Spencer* (London, 1969), pp. 130 and 136. Judi Bevan, *The Rise and Fall of Marks & Spencer* (London, 2002 edn), p. 40.

13. Bevan, *The Rise and Fall of Marks & Spencer*, pp. 40–1.

14. Corina, *Fine Silks and Oak Counters*, p. 127.

15. Corina, *Fine Silks and Oak Counters*, p. 132.

16. Reminiscences of shopkeepers from Redcliffe Hill, Bristol, in the Imperial War Museum Sound Archives, 18322.

17. *Annual Register for 1940* (London, 1941), p. 3.

18. *The Times*, 14 June 1941.

19. *The Grocer*, 31 January 1942.

20. *The Grocer*, 6 January 1940.

21. *The Grocer*, 6 January 1940, reporting on a Birmingham Grocers' Association meeting.

22. *The Distributive Trades Journal*, September 1940.

23. Reminiscences of a male grocery worker from Southampton at Southampton Heritage Centre, C.0009.

24. Michael Winstanley (ed.), *A Traditional Grocer. T.D. Smith's of Lancaster 1858–1981* (Lancaster, Centre for North-West Regional Studies, University of Lancaster, Occasional Paper no. 21, 1991), p. 31.

25. *The Distributive Trades Journal*, January 1941.

26. Kathleen Wilson, *International Service* (Brighton, 2002), pp. 40–1.

27. Arthur Bonner, *British Co-operative* (Manchester, 1961), p. 225. Nichole Robertson, 'The British Co-operative Movement as a consumer pressure group, 1914–45', in *Economic History Society Annual Conference: Abstracts of Academic Papers* (Leicester, 8–10 April 2005), p. 60.

28. Jefferys, *Retail Trading*, pp. 174–5. Hermann Levy, *The Shops of Britain. A Study of Retail Distribution* (London, 1948), pp. 70–1. In a sample of 263 small shopkeepers on Merseyside at the beginning of the 1930s, it was shown that almost 30 per cent of them made only £1 10s a week or less. H.J.H. Parker, 'The Independent Worker and the Small Family Business. A Study of their Importance on Merseyside', in *Journal of the Royal Statistical Society*, vol. 95, Part III (1932), pp. 540–1.

29. *The Distributive Trades Journal*, June 1943, quoting a debate in the House of Commons.

30. Peter Mathias, *Retailing Revolution. A History of Multiple Retailing in the Food Trades based upon the Allied Suppliers Group of Companies* (London, 1967), p. 357.

31. Rees, *St Michael*, p. 137. Before the war the company had employed around 20,000 men and women; by mid-1944 that figure had fallen to 11,500, and even in 1946 had risen to only 13,600.

32. *The Distributive Trades Journal*, March and July 1940 and November 1941.

33. Pamela Horn, *Life Below Stairs in the 20th Century* (Stroud, 2003 edn), p. 327.

34. Wilson, *International Service*, pp. 58 and 60.

35. *The Drapers' Record*, 13 January 1940.

36. Reading Co-operative Society Management Committee Minutes, entry for 21 December 1939, D/EX/1497/1/22 at Berkshire Record Office.

37. Corina, *Fine Silks and Oak Counters*, p. 134.

38. Maurice Corina, *Pile it High, Sell it Cheap. The Authorised Biography of Sir John Cohen, Founder of Tesco* (London, 1971), p. 113. Kathryn A. Morrison, *English Shops and Shopping* (New Haven and London, 2003), pp. 275 and 323.

39. Morrison, *English Shops*, pp. 275–6.

40. *The Distributive Trades Journal*, July 1941. P.C. Hoffman, *They Also Serve. The Story of the Shop Worker* (London, 1949), p. 246. Sir William Richardson, *A Union of Many Trades. The History of USDAW* (Manchester, n.d. [c. 1979]), pp. 149–50. *Report of the Ministry of Labour and National Service for 1939–46*, PP1946–7, vol. XII, pp. 276 and 375.

41. Richardson, *A Union of Many Trades*, p. 147.

42. *The Distributive Trades Journal*, May 1942. Richardson, *A Union of Many Trades*, p. 149.

43. *The Distributive Trades Journal*, May 1942.

44. Wilson, *International Service*, pp. 80 and 89.

45. Wilson, *International Service*, pp. 80 and 89.

46. Reading Co-operative Society Management Committee Minutes, entry for 7 September 1939.

47. *The Grocer*, 6 January 1940.

48. *The Drapers' Record*, 13 December 1941.

49. *The Drapers' Record*, 8 November 1941. *The Grocer*, 6 January 1940.

50. *The Grocer*, 13 January 1940.

51. *The Grocer*, 24 February 1940.

52. *The Grocer*, 14 February 1942.

53. *The Times*, 18 June 1941.

54. *Hansard*, 5th Series, vol. 377, 8 January 1942, cols 47–8; 11 February 1942, cols 1526–7; and 19 February 1942, col. 1902.

55. *The Grocer*, 31 January 1942.

56. Linda McCullough Thew, *The Pit Villagers and the Store. The Portrait of a Mining Past* (London, 1985), p. 224.

57. *The Distributive Trades Journal*, June 1941. In the February 1941 issue it was noted that 'awkward' customers marched into a shop and expected to be served immediately. They stormed and shouted if no assistant was free to attend to them, and 'consider the assistant personally responsible if the required article is not in stock'.

58. *The Distributive Trades Journal*, July 1943 and August 1943.

59. Wilson, *International Service*, p. 38.

60. *The Distributive Trades Journal*, April 1941. The *Journal* dubbed such purchasers 'food grabbers'.

61. *The Grocer*, 20 December 1941.

62. *The Distributive Trades Journal*, September 1943.

63. *The Distributive Trades Journal*, August 1941.

64. Hazel Wheeler, *Half a Pound of Tuppenny Rice. Life in a Yorkshire Village Shop* (Stroud, 1993), pp. 130–1.

65. Wheeler, *Half a Pound of Tuppenny Rice*, pp. 132–4.

66. Levy, *The Shops of Britain*, p. 215. J.D. Hughes and S. Pollard, 'Gross Margins in Retail Distribution', in *Oxford Economic Papers*, New Series, vol. 9, no. 1 (February 1957), p. 77.

67. *The Drapers' Record*, 20 December 1941. *Annual Register for 1941* (London, 1942), p. 48. Corina, *Fine Silks and Oak Counters*, pp. 132–3. Moss and Turton, *A Legend of Retailing*, p. 162.

68. *The Times*, 9 June 1941.

69. *The Times*, 16 June 1941. Similarly Debenham & Freebody offered 'a competent service of renovations and remodelling which will make old dresses look fresh and stylish'.

70. *The Drapers' Record*, 4 October 1941. However, one Welsh woman remembered sheets of clothing coupons being bought off men who were perhaps going into the forces. 'They'd sell children's clothing coupons for a pound.' Phil Carradice, *Coming Home. Wales After the War* (Llandysul, 2005), p. 106.

71. Rees, *St Michael*, p. 131.

72. *The Drapers' Record*, 29 November 1941.

73. *Annual Register for 1949* (London, 1950), pp. 17 and 461.

74. Hugh Barty-King, *Maples. Fine Furnishers. A Household Name for 150 Years* (London, 1992), p. 125. The firm's Tottenham Court Road premises were almost totally destroyed by bombing in April 1941.

75. Defence Regulation 60A.B. (1939) and for subsequent years during the war. Copies of these regulations are, for example, in Acc.1778/1 at York City Archives. *The Distributive Trades Journal*, November 1939.

76. Letter from P.G. Bishop, an inspector for the Fifty Shilling Tailors to the town clerk of York, 9 November 1939 in Acc.1778/1 at York City Archives, and letter from W. Lucas, manager of Montague Burton Ltd, to the Chairman of the Watch Committee, York, 10 November 1939, also in Acc.1778/1.

77. Richardson, *A Union of Many Trades*, pp. 223–5.

78. Richardson, *A Union of Many Trades*, pp. 226–7.

79. Richardson, *A Union of Many Trades*, p. 231.

80. Wilson, *International Service*, p. 72.

81. Wilson, *International Service*, p. 73.

82. Calculated from the *1951 Census of Population: Occupations: England and Wales* (London, HMSO, 1956).

83. Calculated from the *1951 Census of Population: Occupations* and the *1961 Census of Population: Occupations: England and Wales* (London, 1965).

84. *Board of Trade: Report on the Census of Distribution and Other Services, 1966* (London, 1970), p. 1/35.

85. Richardson, *A Union of Many Trades*, p. 231.

86. *Harrodian Gazette*, August 1963, article on John Walsh store in Sheffield. This Harrods journal was first produced in 1913. At British Library, P.P.8002.pk.

87. Bill Lancaster, *The Department Store. A Social History* (London and New York, 1995), pp. 195–7.

88. Rowan Bentall, *My Store of Memories* (London, 1974), pp. 236 and 248.

89. Richardson, *A Union of Many Trades*, p. 187, and *Annual Register for 1948* (London, 1949), p. 449.

90. *The Grocer*, 14 January 1950, for example. *Decontrol of Food and Marketing of Agricultural Produce*, PP1953–4, vol. XXVI, p. 3.

91. *The Grocer*, 28 January 1950.

92. Calculated from the *1951 Census: Occupations*.

93. *The Grocer*, 4 March 1950.

94. *The Grocer*, 28 January 1950. See also *The Drapers' Record*, 29 April 1950, welcoming the establishment of a National Certificate scheme for retail distribution. See also W.G. Copsey (ed.), *The Modern Grocer and Provision Dealer*, vol. III (London, 1951 edn), p. 302, giving details of the examinations of the Institute of Certificated Grocers.

95. *The Grocer*, 28 January 1950.

96. *The Key*, August 1949. Copies of this journal are in the British Library, P.P.5793.blc.

97. *The Key*, July 1952 and Summer 1954, on the back cover in each case.

98. *The Key*, July 1952.

99. Lancaster, *The Department Store*, p. 196. *The Drapers' Record*, 19 March 1960. One discontented shopper reported that his wife had been told by a Birmingham shop assistant that although they had 'a nice selection' of merchandise, 'I am afraid they are too expensive for you'.

100. B. Seebohm Rowntree and G.R. Lavers, *English Life and Leisure. A Social Study* (London, 1951), p. 15.

101. Rowntree and Lavers, *English Life and Leisure*, p. 76.

102. Joan Woodward, *The Saleswoman* (London, 1960), p. 75.

103. *The Key*, August 1957.

104. *The New Dawn*, 12 April 1952. See also similar comments in *The New Dawn*, 16 May 1959, with a manager complaining of the 'work and worry' of these '"sideline" duties'.

105. *The New Dawn*, 7 June 1952.

106. Woodward, *The Saleswoman*, pp. 43–4 and 51.

107. Woodward, *The Saleswoman*, p. 74. *The Drapers' Record*, 5 March 1960.

108. Ella Bland, 'Behind the Counter', in *Costume*, no. 17 (1983), p. 112.

109. Mace (ed.), *'Call yourself a draper?'*, pp. 39 and 42.

110. Mace (ed.), *'Call yourself a draper?'*, p. 38.

111. Woodward, *The Saleswoman*, p. 43.

112. Bland, 'Behind the Counter', p. 116.

113. *The Key*, June 1949. *Harrodian Gazette*, July 1963, for inter-store moves.

114. *The Key*, August 1951.

115. Mary Quant, *Quant by Quant* (Bath, 1966), pp. 35, 41–4, 94–5 and 97–9.

116. *Harrodian Gazette*, October 1963. Kendal Milne was part of the Harrods Group.

117. Arthur Marwick, *The Sixties. Cultural Revolution in Britain, France, Italy and the United States, c. 1958–c. 1974* (Oxford, 1998 edn), pp. 56, 66 and 751.

118. *The Drapers' Record*, 12 and 26 March 1960. Harrods also developed its own 'Clothes for Teens' section in the 1960s. *Harrodian Gazette*, October 1963.

119. *The Drapers' Record*, 12 March 1960.

120. *The New Dawn*, April 1967, and *National Board for Prices and Incomes Report No. 27. Pay of Workers in the Retail Drapery, Outfitting and Footwear* (London, 1967), pp. 12–13. Pay levels varied regionally, so that weekly earnings for shop managers in London averaged £24 17s 8d for males and £19 17s 5d for females; in the best provincial districts they were £22 12s 5d and £14 11s respectively. Similar differences applied to the assistants.

121. *Board of Trade Journal*, 4 September 1959, 'Report on Self-Service Trading'.

122. Corina, *Pile it High, Sell it Cheap*, pp. 119–20.

123. Corina, *Pile it High, Sell it Cheap*, pp. 129–30.

124. *The New Dawn*, 31 October 1959.

125. Judi Bevan, *Trolley Wars. The Battle of the Supermarkets* (London, 2005), p. 46. Ian MacLaurin, *Tiger by the Tail. A Life in Business from Tesco to Test Cricket* (London, 2000 edn), p. 39.

126. Bevan, *Trolley Wars*, p. 57.

127. MacLaurin, *Tiger by the Tail*, p. 16.

128. *The New Dawn*, 27 June 1959.

129. Bevan, *Trolley Wars*, p. 41.

130. *Retail Salesmanship and C.W.S. Production* (Manchester, 1957), not paginated; in the archives of the Co-operative College, Manchester. Copsey (ed.), *The Modern Grocer*, vol. II, p. 49.

131. Bevan, *Trolley Wars*, p. 41.

132. Corina, *Pile it High, Sell it Cheap*, p. 145.

133. *Board of Trade: Report on the Census of Distribution, 1966*, pp. 2/110 and 2/112.

134. *Board of Trade: Report on the Census of Distribution, 1966*, p. 2/113. Of the 193,903 self-service employees in grocery shops, 65,311 were part time.

135. Lecture at the Economic History Society Annual Conference, 9 April 2005, on 'Knowledge and the transfer of the supermarket from North America to Britain 1950–70' by Andrew Alexander and Gareth Shaw.

136. Mathias, *Retailing Revolution*, pp. 395–6.

137. Mathias, *Retailing Revolution*, pp. 395–6.

138. *The New Dawn*, August 1967.

139. 'Staffing in Supermarkets', in *The New Dawn*, April 1967.

140. *The Grocer*, 5 March 1966. *Board of Trade: Report on the Census of Distribution and Other Services, 1961*, Part I (London, 1963), p. 1/48.

141. John Benson and Laura Ugolini, *A Nation of Shopkeepers. Five Centuries of British Retailing* (London and New York, 2003), p. 5.

142. Dorothy Davis, *A History of Shopping* (London, 1966), p. 286.

143. Frank Danning in correspondence with the author, May 2005.

144. Survey on 'Shop Trading Hours', in *The New Dawn*, April 1958. In 1953 33.2 per cent of towns had a late night for grocery traders and 27.5 per cent for drapery stores. In 1968 the respective percentages were 59.7 and 46.5.

145. *The Grocer*, 2 and 9 April 1960, for example. Davis, *A History of Shopping*, pp. 297–8.

146. *Board of Trade: Report on the Census of Distribution, 1966*, p. 1/29.

147. Winstanley (ed.), *A Traditional Grocer*, pp. 31 and 35.

148. Winstanley (ed.), *A Traditional Grocer*, pp. 46–7.

149. Bevan, *Trolley Wars*, p. 48. Corina, *Pile it High, Sell it Cheap*, pp. 6–10 and 31–5. *Hansard*, 5th Series, vol. 69, 10 March 1964, col. 310.

150. *Board of Trade: Report on the Census of Distribution, 1966*, p. 1/100.

151. Michael Young and Peter Willmott, *Family and Kinship in East London* (London, 1957), p. 127.

152. Davis, *A History of Shopping*, p. 297. *Board of Trade: Report on the Census of Distribution, 1966*, p. 2/110.

153. Davis, *A History of Shopping*, p. 297.

154. Richardson, *A Union of Many Trades*, pp. 166–72.

155. Richardson, *A Union of Many Trades*, pp. 201, 231, 242–4.

156. Wilson, *International Service*, p. 86. Richardson, *A Union of Many Trades*, p. 202.

157. Richardson, *A Union of Many Trades*, pp. 252 and 255.

158. *The New Dawn*, 16 May 1959.

159. *The New Dawn*, 16 May 1959, quoting from a review of USDAW by the Labour Correspondent of *The Times*.

160. Richardson, *A Union of Many Trades*, pp. 203, 205–9 and 243–4.

161. Richardson, *A Union of Many Trades*, p. 194.

162. Joanna Blythman, *Shopped. The Shocking Power of the Supermarkets* (London, 2004), pp. 127–9. For an examination of aspects of the mail order business see Richard Coopey and Dilwyn Porter, 'Agency Mail Order in Britain *c.* 1900–2000: Spare-time Agents and their Customers', in Benson and Ugolini (eds), *A Nation of Shopkeepers*, pp. 226–48.

163. Blythman, *Shopped*, p. 129.

164. *The Times*, 2 January 2006.

BIBLIOGRAPHY

NB Only *printed sources* are given here. All manuscripts and oral history material used
has been detailed in the Notes.

PP = Parliamentary Papers
HMSO = Her Majesty's Stationery Office.

OFFICIAL PAPERS

Adulteration of Food Act, 1872, Select Committee on, PP1874, vol. VI.

Adulterations of Food, Drinks, and Drugs, Select Committee on, PP1855, vol. VIII.

*Board of Trade, Report of, on the Increased Employment of Women During the War in the
United Kingdom up to April 1918*, PP1918, vol. XIV.

Board of Trade, Reports on the Census of Distribution and other Services: for 1961, Part 1
(London, HMSO, 1963); for 1966 (London, HMSO, 1970).

Child Employment, Inter-Departmental Committee on, PP1902, vol. XXV.

Co-operative Stores, Report of the Select Committee on, PP1878–9, vol. IX.

*Friendly Societies, Reports of the Chief Registrar of, for the Year ending 31 December
1913*, PP1914, vol. LXXVI.

Labour and National Service, Ministry of, Report for 1939–46, PP1946–7, vol. XII.

Labour, Royal Commission on: The Agricultural Labourer, PP1893–4, vol. XXXV; *The
Employment of Women in Provincial Shops*, PP1893–4, vol. XXXVII.

Market Rights and Tolls, Royal Commission on, PP1888, vol. LIV; 1888, vol. LV;
1890–1, vol. XXXVII; 1890–1, vol. XXXVIII.

*National Board for Prices and Incomes Report no. 27. Pay of Workers in Retail Drapery,
Outfitting and Footwear* (London, HMSO, 1967).

Population Census of 1801: England and Wales (London, 1802).

Population, Censuses of: Occupations: for 1851, PP1852–3, vol. LXXXVIII, Parts 1 and 2:
for 1871, PP1873, vol. LXXI, Part 1; *for 1911*, PP1913, vol. LXXVIII; *for 1921*
(London, HMSO, 1924); *for 1931* (London, HMSO, 1934); *for 1951* (London, HMSO,
1956); *for 1961* (London, HMSO, 1965).

Shop Assistants, Select Committee on, PP1929–30, vol. VII; 1930–1, vol. IX.

Shop Hours Regulation Bill, Select Committee on, PP1886, vol. XII.

Truck Acts, Report of the Departmental Committee on the, PP1908, vol. LIX.

Truck Act in the Mining Districts, Report of the Commissioner to Inquire into the Operation of, PP1852, vol. XXI.
Truck System, Royal Commission on the, PP1871, vol. XXVI.

Hansard's Parliamentary History
Hansard
Journals of the House of Commons

NEWSPAPERS AND JOURNALS

Annual Register
AUCE Journal, The
Bath Chronicle
Co-operative Employé, The
Co-operative News
Distributive Trades Journal, The
Drapers' Journal, The
Drapers' Record, The
Drapery Times, The
Gentleman's Magazine
Grocer, The
Grocery

Harrodian Gazette
Home and Colonial Magazine, The
Ipswich Journal
Key, The
'Liberty' Lamp, The
New Dawn, The
Reading Mercury
Shop Assistant, The
South Wales Echo and Express
Times, The
Western Mail
York Courant

BOOKS AND ARTICLES

Adburgham, Alison, 'Introduction', *Victorian Shopping. Harrods Catalogue, 1895* (New York, 1972).

——, *Shopping in Style. London from the Restoration to Edwardian Elegance* (London, 1979).

Adburgham, Alison, *Shops and Shopping 1800–1914* (London, 1989 edn).

Airey, Angela and John, *The Bainbridges of Newcastle. A Family History* (Newcastle upon Tyne, 1979).

Alexander, David, *Retailing in England during the Industrial Revolution* (London, 1970).

Alexander, Nicholas and Akehurst, Gary (eds), *The Emergence of Modern Retailing 1750–1950* (London and Portland, Oregon, 1999).

Anderson, Will, *The Counter Exposed* (London, 1896).

Barker, T.C. and Harris, J.R., *A Merseyside Town in the Industrial Revolution. St Helens 1750–1900* (London, 1993 edn).

Barty-King, Hugh, *Maples. Fine Furnishers* (London, 1992).

Beattie, J.M. *Policing and Punishment in London 1660–1750. Urban Crime and the Limits of Terror* (Oxford, 2002 edn).

Beauchamp, Jean, *Women Who Work* (London, 1937).

Bell, Lady, *At the Works. A Study of a Manufacturing Town (Middlesbrough)* (Newton Abbot, 1969 edn).

Benson, John, *The Penny Capitalists. A Study of Nineteenth-Century Working-Class Entrepreneurs* (Dublin, 1983).

—— and Shaw, Gareth (eds), *The Evolution of Retail Systems c. 1800–1914* (Leicester, 1992).

—— and Ugolini, Laura (eds), *A Nation of Shopkeepers. Five Centuries of British Retailing* (London, 2003).

Bentall, Rowan, *My Store of Memories* (London, 1974).

Bevan, Judi, *The Rise and Fall of Marks & Spencer* (London, 2002 edn).

——, *Trolley Wars. The Battle of the Supermarkets* (London, 2005).

Blackman, Janet, 'The Food Supply of an Industrial Town. A Study of Sheffield's Public Markets 1780–1900', in *Business History*, vol. IV, no. 2 (June 1963).

——, 'The Development of the Retail Grocery Trade in the Nineteenth Century', in *Business History*, vol. IX, no. 2 (July 1967).

Bland, Ella, 'Behind the Counter', in *Costume*, no. 17 (1983).

Blythman, Joanna, *Shopped. The Shocking Power of the Supermarkets* (London, 2004).

Bondfield, The Rt Hon. Margaret, *A Life's Work* (London, n.d. [*c.* 1948]).

Bonner, Arnold, *British Co-operation* (Manchester, 1961).

Booth, Charles (ed.), *Life and Labour of the People in London*, 2nd Series, *Industry*, vol. 3 (London, 1903).

Briggs, Asa, *Friends of the People. The Centenary History of Lewis's* (London, 1956).

——, *Victorian Cities* (Harmondsworth, 1968 edn).

Brome, Vincent, *H.G. Wells. A Biography* (London, 1951).

Brown, W. Henry, *A Century of Liverpool Co-operation* (Liverpool, n.d. [*c.* 1930]).

Burnett, John, *Plenty and Want. A Social History of Diet in England from 1815 to the Present Day* (Harmondsworth, 1968 edn).

Cadbury, Edward, Matheson, M. Cecile and Shann, George, *Women's Work and Wages* (London, 1906).

Calloway, Stephen (ed.), *The House of Liberty. Masters of Style and Decoration* (London, 1992).

Campbell, R., *The London Tradesman* (London, 1747).

Caradog-Jones, D. (ed.), *The Social Survey of Merseyside*, vol. 2 (Liverpool, 1934).

Chapman, Stanley, *Jesse Boot of Boots the Chemists. A study of business history* (London, 1974).

——, 'The "Revolution" in the Manufacture of Ready-made Clothing 1840–60', in *London Journal*, vol. 29, no. 1 (2004).

Copsey, W.G. (ed.), *The Modern Grocer and Provision Dealer* (London, 1951 edn).

Corina, Maurice, *Pile it High, Sell it Cheap. The Authorised Biography of Sir John Cohen, Founder of Tesco* (London, 1971).

——, *Fine Silks and Oak Counters. Debenhams 1778–1978* (London, 1978).

Cox, Nancy, *The Complete Tradesman. A Study of Retailing, 1550–1820* (Aldershot, 2000).

Crossick, Geoffrey (ed.), *The Lower Middle Class in Britain* (London, 1977).

Crossick, Geoffrey and Haupt, Heinz-Gerhard (eds), *Shopkeepers and Master Artisans in Nineteenth-Century Europe* (London, 1986 edn).

——, *The Petite Bourgeoisie in Europe 1780–1914. Enterprise, Family and Independence* (London and New York, 1995).

Crossick, Geoffrey and Jauman, Serge (eds), *Cathedrals of Consumption. The European Department Store 1850–1939* (Aldershot, 1999).

Crowther, Janice and Peter A. (eds), *The Diary of Robert Sharp of South Cave. Life in a Yorkshire Village 1812–1837* (Oxford, 1997).

Curwen, Henry, *A History of Booksellers. The Old and the New* (London, n.d.).

Cynog-Jones, T.W., *The Regulation of Wages in the Retail Trades 1936–1945* (London, n.d. [*c.* 1945]).

Dale, Tim, *Harrods. A Palace in Knightsbridge* (London, 1995).

Davies, David Wyn, *Owen Owen. Victorian Draper* (Aberystwyth, n.d. [*c.* 1984]).

Davies, M.F., *Life in an English Village* (London, 1909).

Davies, Margaret Llewelyn (ed.), *Life As We Have Known It* (London, 1977 edn).

Davis, Dorothy, *A History of Shopping* (London, 1966).

Defoe, Daniel, *The Complete English Tradesman* (Gloucester, 1987 edn).

Dictionary of National Biography (Oxford, 2004 edn).

Dowell, Stephen, *A History of Taxation and Taxes in England*, vol. 2 (London, 1965 edn).

Earle, Peter, *The World of Defoe* (London, 1976).

——, *The Making of the English Middle Class. Business, Society and Family Life in London, 1660–1730* (London, 1989).

——, *A City of People. Men and Women of London 1650–1750* (London, 1994).

Early Closing Association, Annual Reports of (at British Library).

Fawcett, Trevor, 'Eighteenth-Century Shops and the Luxury Trade', in *Bath History*, vol. III (1990).

——, *Bath Commercialis'd. Shops, Trades and Market at the 18th-Century Spa* (Bath, 2002).

——, 'Wedgwood's Bath Showrooms', in *Pickpocketing the Rich* (Holburne Museum of Art, Bath, Catalogue, 2002).

Felice, Paul di, 'Manchester's Little Italy at War, 1940–1945. "Enemy Aliens or Reluctant Foe?"', in *Northern History*, vol. 39 (March 2002).

Finn, Margot C., *The Character of Credit. Personal Debt in English Culture, 1740–1914* (Cambridge, 2003).

Fish, W.F., *The Autobiography of a Counter-Jumper* (London, n.d. [1929]).

Foley, Alice, *A Bolton Childhood* (Manchester, 1973).

Foster, Richard, *F. Cape & Co. of St Ebbes Street, Oxford. From Draper's Shop to Department Store* (Oxford, n.d.).

Fraser, W. Hamish, *The Coming of the Mass Market, 1850–1914* (London and Basingstoke, 1981).

French, Michael, 'Commercials, careers and culture: travelling salesmen in Britain, 1890s–1930s', in *Economic History Review*, vol. LVIII, no. 2 (May 2005).

Friedman, Terry, *Engrav'd Cards of Tradesmen in the County of York* (Leeds Art Galleries, 1976).

Gardiner, Marjorie, *The Other Side of the Counter. The Life of a Shop Girl 1925–1945* (Brighton, n.d.).

Grady, K., 'Profit, Property Interests and Public Spirit: The Provision of Markets and Commercial Amenities in Leeds, 1822–29', in *The Thoresby Society Publications*, vol. LIV, Part 3 (1976).

Hallsworth, Joseph and Davies, Rhys J., *The Working Life of Shop Assistants* (Manchester, 1910).

Hamilton, Mary Agnes, *Margaret Bondfield* (London, 1924).

Hancock, Norman, *An Innocent Grows Up* (London, 1947).

Hoffman, P.C. *They Also Serve. The Story of the Shop Worker* (London, 1949).

Holcombe, Lee, *Victorian Ladies at Work. Middle-Class Working Women in England and Wales 1850–1914* (Newton Abbot, 1973).

Honeycombe, Gordon, *Selfridges. Seventy-Five Years. The Story of the Store 1909–1984* (London, 1984).

Honeyman, Katrina, 'Tailor-Made: Mass Productions, High Street Retailing and the Leeds Menswear Multiples, 1918 to 1939', in *Northern History*, vol. XXXVII (December 2000).

Hood, Julia and Yamey, B.S., 'The Middle-Class Co-operative Retailing Societies in London, 1864–1900', in *Oxford Economic Papers*, New Series, vol. 9, no. 3 (October 1957).

Horn, Pamela, *Rural Life in England in the First World War* (Dublin, 1984).

——, *The Victorian Country Child* (Stroud, 1990 edn).

——, *Women in the 1920s* (Stroud, 1995).

——, *Pleasures and Pastimes in Victorian Britain* (Stroud, 1999).

——, *The Victorian Town Child* (Stroud, 1999 edn).

——, *Life Below Stairs in the 20th Century* (Stroud, 2003 edn).

Hosgood, Christopher P., 'The "Pigmies of Commerce" and the Working-Class Community: Small Shopkeepers in England, 1870–1914', in *Journal of Social History*, vol. 22, no. 3 (Spring 1989).

——, 'A "Brave and Daring Folk"? Shopkeepers and Trade Associational Life in Victorian and Edwardian England', in *Journal of Social History*, vol. 26, no. 2 (1992).

——, '"Mercantile Monasteries": Shops, Shop Assistants, and Shop Life in Late-Victorian and Edwardian Britain', in *Journal of British Studies*, vol. 38, no. 3 (July 1999).

Hughes, Colin, *Lime, Lemon & Sarsaparilla. The Italian Community in South Wales 1881–1945* (Bridgend, 2003 edn).

Hughes, J.D. and Pollard, S., 'Gross Margins in Retail Distribution', in *Oxford Economic Papers*, New Series, vol. 9, no. 1 (February 1957).

Jacks, L.P., *The Confessions of an Octogenarian* (London, 1942).

Jefferys, James B., *Retail Trading in Britain 1850–1950* (Cambridge, 1954).

Jeune, M. [Lady Jeune], 'The Ethics of Shopping', in *The Fortnightly Review*, vol. 63 (January 1895).

Jones, T. Spencer, *The Moral Side of Living-In* (London, 1907).

Kightly, Charles, *Country Voices. Life and Lore in Farm and Village* (London, 1984).

King, Steven and Tomkins, Alannah (eds), *The Poor in England 1700–1850. An economy of makeshifts* (Manchester, 2003).

Lackington, James, *Life of J. Lackington, Bookseller* (London, n.d. [*c.* 1791]).

Lambert, Richard S., *The Universal Provider. A Study of William Whiteley and the Rise of the London Department Store* (London, 1938).

Lancaster, Bill, *The Department Store. A Social History* (London and New York, 1995).

Lane, Joan, *Apprenticeship in England 1600–1914* (London, 1996).

Leek, Sybil, *A Shop in the High Street* (London, 1962).

Lemire, Beverley, 'The Theft of Clothes and Popular Consumerism in Early Modern England', in *Journal of Social History*, vol. 24, no. 2 (1990).

——, *Dress, Culture and Commerce. The English Clothing Trade before the Factory, 1660–1800* (Basingstoke, 1997).

Levy, Hermann, *The Shops of Britain. A Study of Retail Distribution* (London, 1948).

Light, Julie, '". . . mere seekers of fame"?: personalities, power and politics in the small town: Pontypool and Bridgend, *c.* 1860–95', in *Urban History*, vol. 32, Part 1 (May 2005).

Linebaugh, Peter, *The London Hanged. Crime and Civil Society in the Eighteenth Century*, 2nd edn (London and New York, 2003).

Lipton, Sir Thomas J., Bt, *Leaves from the Lipton Logs* (London, n.d. [*c.* 1932]).

Lock, Alice (ed.), *Looking Back at Denton* (Stalybridge, 1985).

Lovett, William, *The Life and Struggles of William Lovett* (London, 1920 edn).

McCutcheon, K.L., *Yorkshire Fairs and Markets to the end of the Eighteenth Century* (Leeds, Thoresby Society, vol. 39, 1940).

Mace, Jane (ed.), *'Call yourself a draper?' Memories of life in the trade* (London, 1993).

McKendrick, Neil, Brewer, John and Plumb, J.H., *The Birth of a Consumer Society* (London, 1983 edn).

MacLaurin, Ian, *Tiger by the Tail. A Life in Business from Tesco to Test Cricket* (London, 2000 edn).

Marshall, J.D. (ed.), *The Autobiography of William Stout of Lancaster 1665–1752* (Manchester, 1967).

Martin, E.W., *The Shearers and the Shorn. A Study of Life in a Devon Community* (London, 1965).

Marwick, Arthur, *The Deluge. British Society and the First World War* (London, 1965).

——, *The Sixties. Cultural Revolution in Britain, France, Italy and the United States, c. 1958–c. 1974* (Oxford, 1998 edn).

Mathias, Peter, *Retailing Revolution. A History of Multiple Retailing in the Food Trades Based upon the Allied Suppliers Group of Companies* (London, 1967).

Mayhew, Henry, *London Labour and the London Poor*, 4 vols (London, 1861).

Miller, Michael B., *The Bon Marché. Bourgeois Culture and the Department Store 1869–1920* (London, 1981).

Mitchell, Ian, 'Pitt's Shop Tax in the history of retailing', in *The Local Historian*, vol. 14, no. 6 (May 1981).

Mitchell, S.I., 'Retailing in Eighteenth- and Early Nineteenth-Century Cheshire', in *Transactions of the Historic Society of Lancashire and Cheshire for 1980*, vol. 130 (1981).

Morgan, Aubrey Niel, *David Morgan 1833–1919. The Life and Times of a Master Draper in South Wales* (Newport, 1977).

Morrison, Kathryn, A., *English Shops and Shopping* (New Haven and London, 2003).

Moss, Michael and Turton, Alison, *A Legend of Retailing. House of Fraser* (London, 1989).

Mui, Hoh-Cheung and Lorna H., *Shops and Shopkeeping in Eighteenth-Century England* (Kingston, Montreal and London, 1989).

National Amalgamated Union of Shop Assistants, Warehousemen and Clerks, Annual Reports of (At Trades Union Congress Library, London Metropolitan University).

Nightingale, Revd J., *The Bazaar, Its Origin, Nature and Objects Explained*, 2nd edn (London, 1816).

Nossiter, T.J., Hanson, A.H., Rokkan, Stein (eds), *Imagination and Precision in the Social Sciences* (London, 1972).

Nowell-Smith, Simon (ed.), *Edwardian England, 1901–1914* (London, 1964).

O'Connell, Sheila (ed.), *London 1753* (London, 2003).

Oldfield, John, *Printers, Booksellers and Libraries in Hampshire 1750–1800* (Hampshire Papers no. 3, Hampshire County Council, 1993).

Owen, Robert, *The Life of Robert Owen Written by Himself* (London, 1857).

Paine, William, *Shop Slavery and Emancipation* (London, 1912).

Parker, H.J.H., 'The Independent Worker and the Small Family Business. A Study of their Importance on Merseyside', in *Journal of the Royal Statistical Society*, vol. 95, Part III (1932).

Pennybacker, Susan D., *A Vision for London 1889–1914: Labour, everyday life and the LCC experiment* (London, 1995).

Porter, Roy, *English Society in the Eighteenth Century* (London, 1991 edn).

——, *London. A Social History* (London, 2000).

Pritchard, John Wyn, '"Fit and Proper Persons" – Councillors of Denbigh, Their Status and Position, 1835–94', in *Welsh Historical Review*, vol. 17 (1994).

Quant, Mary, *Quant by Quant* (Bath, 1966).

Rappaport, Erika D., '"The Halls of Temptation": Gender, Politics and the Construction of the Department Store in Late Victorian London', in *Journal of British Studies*, vol. 35, no. 1 (January 1996).

Rees, Goronwy, *St Michael. A History of Marks & Spencer* (London, 1969).

Reminiscences of an Old Draper (London, 1876).

Richardson, Sir William, *A Union of Many Trades. The History of USDAW* (Manchester, n.d. [*c.* 1979]).

Roberts, Elizabeth, *A Woman's Place. An Oral History of Working-Class Women 1890–1940* (Oxford, 1985 edn).

Roberts, Robert, *The Classic Slum. Salford Life in the First Quarter of the Century* (Manchester, 1971).

——, *A Ragged Schooling. Growing Up in the Classic Slum* (Manchester, 1976).

Robinson, E., 'Eighteenth-Century Commerce and Fashion: Matthew Boulton's Marketing Techniques', in *Economic History Review*, 2nd Series, vol. 16, no. 1 (1963).

Rose, Lionel, *The Erosion of Childhood* (London, 1991).

Rowntree, B. Seebohm and Lavers, G.R., *English Life and Leisure. A Social Study* (London, 1951).

Rubin, Gerry R., 'From Packmen, Tallymen and "Perambulating Scotchmen" to Credit Drapers' Associations *c.* 1840–1914', in *Business History*, vol. 28, no. 2 (1986).

Rutherford, Mark, *Autobiography and Deliverance* (Leicester, 1969 edn).

Schmiechen, James and Carls, Kenneth, *The British Market Hall. A Social and Architectural History* (New Haven and London, 1999).

Schwartz, Doris, *'The Kid from Strut'. A Memoir* (London, 2003).

Scola, Roger, *Feeding the Victorian City. The Food Supply of Manchester, 1770–1870* (Manchester, 1992).

Scott, Peter, 'The Twilight World of Interwar British Hire Purchase', in *Past and Present*, no. 177 (November 2002).

Settle, Alison, *A Family of Shops. Marshall & Snelgrove* (London, n.d. [*c.* 1950]).

Shannon, Brent, 'Refashioning Men: Fashion, Masculinity and the Cultivation of the Male Consumer in Britain, 1860–1914', in *Victorian Studies*, vol. 46, no. 4 (Summer 2004).

Smith, Sir Hubert Llewellyn (ed.), *The New Survey of London Life and Labour,* vol. V. *London Industries*, II (London, 1933).

Southgate, Walter, *That's the Way it Was. A Working Class Autobiography 1890–1950* (Oxted, 1982).

Stenton, Michael and Lees, Stephen (eds), *Who's Who of British Members of Parliament*, vol. III, 1919–45 (Sussex, 1979).

Tebbutt, Melanie, *Making Ends Meet. Pawnbrokers and Working-Class Credit* (London, 1984 edn).

Thale, Mary (ed.), *The Autobiography of Francis Place* (Cambridge, 1972).

Thew, Linda McCullough, *The Pit Village and the Store. The Portrait of a Mining Past* (London, 1985).

Thomas, John Birch, *Shop Boy* (London, 1985 edn).

Tobias, J.J., *Crime and Industrial Society in the 19th Century* (London, 1967).

Trinder, Barrie, *Victorian Banbury (Banbury Historical Society*, vol. 19, 1982).

Twigg, H.J., *An Outline History of Co-operative Education* (Manchester, 1924).

Vaisey, David (ed.), *The Diary of Thomas Turner 1754–1765* (Oxford, 2000 edn).

Vincent, J.R., Pollbooks. *How Victorians Voted* (Cambridge, 1967).

Waugh, Alec, *The Lipton Story, A Centennial Biography* (London, 1951).

Weinstock, Maureen, *More Dorset Studies* (Dorchester, n.d. [c. 1962]).

Wells, H.G. *Experiment in Autobiography* (New York, 1934 edn).

Wheeler, Hazel, *Half a Pound of Tuppenny Rice. Life in a Yorkshire Village Shop* (Stroud, 1993).

Whitaker, Wilfred B., *Victorian and Edwardian Shop Workers. The Struggle to obtain Better Conditions and a Half-Holiday* (Newton Abbot, 1973).

Willan, T.S., *An Eighteenth-Century Shopkeeper. Abraham Dent of Kirkby Stephen* (Manchester, 1970).

——, *The Inland Trade* (Manchester, 1976).

Willcock, H.D. (ed.), *Browns and Chester. Portrait of a Shop 1780–1946* (London, 1947).

Wilson, Kathleen, *International Service* (Brighton, 2002).

Winkler, John K., *Five and Ten. The Fabulous Life of F.W. Woolworth* (London, 1941).

Winstanley, Michael J., *The Shopkeeper's World 1830–1914* (Manchester, 1983).

Winstanley, Michael (ed.), *A Traditional Grocer. T.D. Smith's of Lancaster 1858–1981* (Lancaster, Centre for North-West Regional Studies, University of Lancaster, Occasional Papers no. 21, 1991).

Wojtczak, Helena, *Women in Victorian Sussex: Their Status, Occupations, and Dealings with the Law 1830–1870* (Hastings, 2003).

Woodforde, James, *The Diary of a Country Parson 1758–1802*, ed. John Beresford (Oxford, 1978 edn).

Woodward, Joan, *The Saleswoman* (London, 1960).

Young, Michael and Willmott, Peter, *Family and Kinship in East London* (London, 1957).

THESIS

Purvis, Martin, 'Nineteenth Century Co-operative Retailing in England and Wales. A Geographical Approach' (Oxford D.Phil. thesis, 1987).

INDEX